Mapping Foreign Correspondence in Europe

I0878330

The book studies the current trends of foreign correspondence in Europe. The European Union's expansion has had abundant effects on news coverage, and some of the European capitals have become home to the biggest international press corps in the world. So who are these "professional strangers" stationed in Europe, and how do they try to make their stories, which are clearly important in today's interconnected world, interesting for viewers and readers?

This book represents the first pan-European study of foreign correspondents and their reporting. It includes chapters from 27 countries, and it aims to study them and the direction, flow, and pattern of their coverage, as well as answer questions regarding the impact of new technologies on the quantity, frequency, and speed of their coverage. Do more sophisticated communications tools yield better international news coverage of Europe? Or does the audience's increasing apathy and the downsizing of the foreign bureaus offset these advances? And how do the seemingly unstoppable media trends of convergence, commercialization, concentration, and globalization affect the way Europe and individual European countries are reported?

Georgios Terzis, PhD, is an Associate Professor and a Senior Associate Researcher at Vrije Universiteit Brussel (Vesalius College & Institute for European Studies), and a Senior Expert at the Global Governance Institute. His research focuses on media and security governance, European media governance, and the development of pan-European media. He is the Founding Chair of the Journalism Studies Section of the European Communication Research and Education Association. He worked as Brussels correspondent for Greek Media and as a course leader for the European Journalism Centre, training journalists from 25 countries on EU affairs.

Routledge Studies in European Communication Research and Education

Edited by Nico Carpentier, Vrije Universiteit Brussel, Belgium and Charles University, Czech Republic, François Heinderyckx, Université Libre de Bruxelles, Belgium and Claudia Alvares, Lusofona University, Portugal

Series Advisory Board: Denis McQuail, Robert Picard and Jan Servaes

ECREA

http://www.ecrea.eu

Published in association with the European Communication Research and Education Association (ECREA), books in the series make a major contribution to the theory, research, practice, and/or policy literature. They are European in scope and represent a diversity of perspectives. Book proposals are refereed.

1 **Audience Transformations**
Shifting Audience Positions in Late Modernity
Edited by Nico Carpentier, Kim Christian Schrøder and Lawrie Hallett

2 **Audience Research Methodologies**
Between Innovation and Consolidation
Edited by Geoffroy Patriarche, Helena Bilandzic, Jakob Linaa Jensen and Jelena Jurišić

3 **Multiplayer**
The Social Aspects of Digital Gaming
Edited by Thorsten Quandt and Sonja Kröger

4 **Mapping Foreign Correspondence in Europe**
Edited by Georgios Terzis

5 **Revitalising Audience Research**
Innovations in European Audience Research
Edited by Frauke Zeller, Cristina Ponte and Brian O'Neill

Mapping Foreign Correspondence in Europe

Edited by Georgios Terzis

Routledge
Taylor & Francis Group
New York London

First published 2015
by Routledge
711 Third Avenue, New York, NY 10017

and by Routledge
2 Park Square, Milton Park, Abingdon, Oxon OX14 4RN

First issued in paperback 2017

Routledge is an imprint of the Taylor & Francis Group, an informa business

© 2015 Taylor & Francis

The right of the editor to be identified as the author of the editorial material, and of the authors for their individual chapters, has been asserted in accordance with sections 77 and 78 of the Copyright, Designs and Patents Act 1988.

All rights reserved. No part of this book may be reprinted or reproduced or utilised in any form or by any electronic, mechanical, or other means, now known or hereafter invented, including photocopying and recording, or in any information storage or retrieval system, without permission in writing from the publishers.

Trademark Notice: Product or corporate names may be trademarks or registered trademarks, and are used only for identification and explanation without intent to infringe.

Library of Congress Cataloging-in-Publication Data
Mapping foreign correspondence in Europe / edited by Georgios Terzis.
pages cm. — (Routledge studies in European communication research and education)
Includes bibliographical references and index.
1. Foreign news. 2. Foreign correspondents—Europe. 3. Europe—Press coverage. 4. Europe—Foreign public opinion. I. Terzis, Georgios, editor.
PN4784.F6M25 2014
070.4′332—dc23
2014021902

ISBN 13: 978-1-138-09774-2 (pbk)
ISBN 13: 978-0-415-71900-1 (hbk)

Typeset in Sabon
by Apex CoVantage, LLC

To Dimitri Terzi for holding the book and Anthoula Xanthopoulou for holding the light

Contents

Editor's Preface

Two out of the four directors of the schools of journalism where I studied were ex-members of intelligence and foreign services and they were not hiding it. Ten out of my ten colleagues in Brussels who covered the story of Greece adopting the euro and I knew that the country was 'cooking the books' but we were all hiding this in our reports. We were also all hiding our stage fright in front of the cameras when we asked questions at NATO press conferences that were broadcast live worldwide by CNN and others during the Kosovo war.

In the past 25 years that I have studied, practised, and taught foreign correspondence, some of my classmates, colleagues, and students went on to cover the wars in Bosnia and Libya and 'collected' several physical and psychological injuries; others went undercover wearing burkas to cover the situation of women in Iran; one went into hiding for many years after receiving death threats because of his reporting of the terrorist attack in Japan's subway in 1995 and in 2014 won a Pulitzer Prize, while others became speech writers for high calibre politicians or even ambassadors themselves.

These are some of the 'flashy' aspects of foreign correspondents' lives that make it into the numerous movies that involve foreign correspondent (FC) characters. Foreign correspondence is also a major attraction for students who decide to launch into a career in journalism, in spite of the fact that very few will ever practise it. But despite its 'celebrity' professional status, FC academic research is one that attracts little attention. This book, in a small way, is trying to plug this gap.

For more than 150 years, world news leadership has been exercised by Europe and the United States, but Europe has been the world news leader at least since 1990 (Tunstall, 2011). Despite its leadership, most of the research on foreign correspondents has been on those based in the United States (Hess, 1996, 2006; Gross & Kopper, 2011), while research in the way that Europe and individual European countries are covered by foreign correspondents, with some notable exceptions, is almost non-existent (Morrison & Tumber, 1985; Hannerz, 2004; Mazzoleni & Splendore, 2007; AIM FP 6 project, 2006–2007).

Franks (2005, p. 1) explains how 'globalisation, the interdependent nature of modern society and the precarious state of international relations post 9/11' necessitates that everyone should be interested in foreign news coverage. So, who are these 'professional strangers' stationed in Europe, the world news leader, and how do they try to make their stories that are clearly important in today's interconnected world interesting for audiences?

This book is the first of its kind. It involves the mapping of foreign correspondents and their reporting in 27 European countries with a common survey questionnaire[1] completed by nearly 1,000 foreign correspondents of the approximately 2,500 contacted, and hundreds of interviews with FCs based in all these countries.[2] It aims to study FCs and the direction, flow, and pattern of their coverage, as well as the impact of new technologies on the quantity, frequency, and speed of their coverage.[3]

Throughout the book, analysis of the political, economic, and social importance of foreign reporting in each country is given. Europe has witnessed a silent revolution in the last 20 years as the EU has extended its powers and members to become the world's biggest economic power, trade bloc, and aid donor. The effects of this on news coverage and media presence in Europe are abundant. As journalists follow power and money, the European capitals became home to some of the biggest international press corps in the world.

The analysis then turns to the current make-up of the European foreign press corps: their numbers, backgrounds, the pressures they are under, and their national obsessions. It analyses different factors affecting their coverage, resources devoted to European foreign bureaus, the tensions between parachuted correspondents and old-timers, and public versus commercial media. This is followed by a detailed breakdown of the key international media players and media sectors.

Analysis continues by looking at the different news sources of foreign correspondents, and where they overlap, complement, and contradict each other. The different national institutions and embassies as well as other smaller 'official sources' are analysed together with a number of unofficial ones, such as think tanks, NGOs, and lobbies.

Throughout the volume, the main challenges of communicating from a European country or the EU headquarters in Brussels are candidly discussed through interviews with FCs. Which are the dominant news frames and why is 'Europe' such a hard sell? We look at the problems that are intrinsic – such as the lack of a European public sphere, the physical and political 'distance', and others that are related to media routines and practices, such as pack reporting, disciplinary structures and other institutional influences, power structures, and professional conventions. As the reader will find, the current state of foreign correspondence varies across these 27 states.

The conclusion studies the current trends of foreign correspondence in Europe. Do more and more sophisticated communications tools help to get better international news coverage from Europe? Or does the audiences' increasing apathy and the downsizing of the foreign bureaus offset these advances? And how do the seemingly unstoppable media trends of convergence, commercialisation, concentration, and globalisation affect the way Europe and individual European countries are reported?

Georgios Terzis
Brussels, May 2014

NOTES

1. See the Appendix for a copy of the questionnaire.
2. Due to logistical limitations, three countries did not conduct the survey but interviewed FCs based on the same groups of questions.
3. The authors of each chapter decided independently whether to use the names of the FCs interviewed or to make them anonymous.

REFERENCES

AIM (2006-2007). Adequate Information Management in Europe Studies, Sixth EU Framework Programme – Priority 7. [Online] Available from: www.aim-project.net.

FRANKS, S. (2005). Lacking a clear narrative: Foreign News Reporting after the Cold War. *The Political Quarterly*. 76 (1), pp. 91–101.

GROSS, P. & KOPPER, G. (2011). *Understanding Foreign Correspondence*. New York: Peter Lang.

HANNERZ, U. (2004). *Foreign News: Exploring the World of Foreign Correspondents*. Chicago: The University of Chicago Press.

HESS, S. (1996). *International News & Foreign Correspondents*. Washington: Brookings Institution Press.

———. (2006) *Through Their Eyes: Foreign Correspondents in the United States*. Washington: Brookings Institution Press.

MAZZOLENI, G. & SPLENDORE, S. (2007). Italian Foreign Correspondents: Fashioning Representation of France. In Palmer, M. and Aubert, A. (eds). *L'Actualite Internationale Vue Depuis La France*. Paris: Universite Sorbonne Nouvelle.

MORRISON D. E. & TUMBER, H. (1985). The foreign correspondent: date-line London. *Media Culture and Society*. 7(4), pp. 445–70.

TUNSTALL, J. (2011). Europe as World News Leader. In Trappel, J., Meier, W., D'Haenens, L., Steemers, J. & Thomass, B. (eds). *Media in Europe Today*. Bristol: Intellect.

Acknowledgements

I would like to thank the ECREA book series editorial team, especially François Heinderyckx for his attentive comments, and the 51 authors of the 31 chapters of this book for all their efforts, trust, and patience. I would also like to express my gratitude to my research assistant Marina Lynch for her uncompromising dedication and copious work throughout the review process, and my subeditor Kulbir Natt for his excellent work.

Prologue: Foreign Correspondence 50 Years Later

Some 50 years ago I had been so greatly puzzled by two problems in connection with foreign news that I decided to do some research on reporting in Cuba, Cyprus and Congo. The research was first published in January 1963.[1]

The first problem was empirical: how do events become national or international news? Of the enormities of events happening around the world—from any point of observation by professional journalists, foreign correspondents, or not—how come some are elevated to the level of news? What is news anyhow?

The second problem was more normative: why is there a predilection for negative news? Why, but then also why not? You are driving on a road, and there is a flash on the radio: 'there is a boulder blocking the road around the next sharp turn" matters more than "the road ahead is curvy but smooth.' The positive and the negative, the good and the bad, are not symmetric attributes.

I had done some journalism myself for the Norwegian Broadcasting Corporation—in the US South, Cuba, India, Africa—but as reporting, stories, narratives, not as events carved out from their space-time context. As a social scientist, I wanted to see events, news or not, as conditioned, not determined, by the context. Interviews with Fidel Castro and the Dalai Lama were inserted in contexts, including sounds. And I had met many journalists who could not care less about contexts and seemed to have no doubts about what was news.

Four factors seem to be decisive for events to become news:

- the more the event concerns elite states,
- the more the event concerns elite people,
- the more the event is due to personal action,
- the more negative the event is in its consequences, the more likely it will become a news item.

A trivial consequence is the addition hypothesis: the more of the four factors that the event satisfies, the more likely it is to become news.

And then a less trivial consequence is the compensation hypothesis: a high level on some factors may compensate for a low level on others.

The perfect event according to the addition hypothesis is indeed the assassination of US President John F. Kennedy. The veracity of the reporting is another matter; the hypothesis is about the event.

How about the death of Mandela, an elite person but not in an elite country? Death is negative, but it was not due to action, as opposed to impersonal 'structure', 'culture,' 'process' (including of the body). Death and elite add up to a +2 as an event, but it was not an action (suicide would have been), and the country was not elite. So the event had to be magnified as relevant for all of Africa and for the whole world, and it was Mandela alone, with little or nothing about the indispensable Tutu and de Klerk. This distortion went on for weeks. In other words, events have to be helped a little to become top news; unassisted, they may not make it.

Negate the first two of the four 'less trivial' factors, and we get the vast masses of humanity living in what used to be called 'Third World' countries. How can they ever make news? By something super negative, like a major earthquake, typhoon, tsunami, or human-made, like military coups with much killing and major wars. Whereas the opposite, elite people in elite countries, can make news even when something positive happens, like the birth of a prince(ss). As a result, a systemic bias in the reporting about centre and periphery countries occurs that reinforces the structure and makes the world unprepared for something like BRICS.

The structure of foreign news construction matters greatly. But how do we explain how it came about that way?

The first two factors are simple: first, social class, both in the global structures and second, social class in the domestic structures, of top significance in the country often seen as the creator of journalism, foreign and at home.

For the third factor, the focus is on personal action, maybe the subject-predicate-object (SPO) structure of a correctly formulated Indo-European sentence. A corpse by the wayside is an important event, but unlikely to become news with only P and O; no "who done it," no S. News is also syntax driven, not just event driven.

For the fourth factor, negativism, maybe the place to look is at the classical Aristotelian theory of drama? News should be dramatic, that is, already in the idea of something new, not olds, not there at the last edition of read-listen-view media. A discontinuity. But drama, we are told, comes in two varieties, tragedy and comedy; a drama either has a tragic ending or is entertaining. In news, the two can come together in the notion of "infotainment" because the information is usually negative. A third category seems to be needed, maybe not only in media but also in literature: muddling through with ups and downs but with something acceptable in the end. Transcending, going beyond.

News should vary with language structures and narratives that break the (false) tragedy–comedy dichotomy. In Japanese, less so in Chinese, a

PO sentence is complete, the subject is dispensable. "A shot killed him" or "There is an opinion" does not call for who fired, who holds that opinion. Structure, culture, and process come more easily.

And positive news comes more easily. *China Daily* today reports projects to improve housing conditions for the underprivileged, that the economy will be smooth and stable in 2014, that high-speed trains are on the fast track with 12,000 kilometres—more than half of the world—and more yin/yang news. *Periphery India* also figures with train news: 'at least 26 killed in train fire'. And the *New York Times*?

Politics and economics, domestic and global: all negative. But arts, sports, fashion in the United States, they all get positive coverage.

All of this may correspond to facts or not, but the point is what events were reported. 'Propaganda', many would say about the Chinese reporting, truthfully or not; 'they are hiding the shadowy sides'. Maybe.

But maybe an overload of negativism is also propaganda, and in that case for what? To watch out, do not take anything for granted; the road looks smooth, but is a boulder waiting for you?

But most negative news is about factors beyond ordinary people's control, whereas positive news may affect them positively. The former may instil pessimism, the latter optimism.

Violence is reported, often unnecessarily detailed. But there is little or no reporting about underlying conflicts, let alone about solutions, leading to feelings of apathy that nothing can be done. Solution reporting could lead to optimism and learning; it is as if violence is untouchable, to be protected, like war, as a state prerogative. Propaganda for state-ism of the worst kind. But such is the collective subconscious of Western media journalism that it is not easily changed except, maybe, by practicing the opposite, not substituting Pollyanna for Cassandra news, but a mix of the positive and negative, the good and bad, yin/yang, throwing in important olds with the news.

In this very impressive study, a world record in the study of foreign correspondence in 27 European countries, some significant trends emerge. They are not about the collective subconscious, the deep culture of foreign news just explored, but about crucial factors affecting that culture. We may talk about reporting deep structure.

As a point of departure: what kind of ideal reporting structure would we like to have, not necessarily visible to the naked eye, nor planned but present as an empirical fact? What would we like to know?

What happens around the world, relevant to them and to us, in countries high and low, to people high and low, due to action, process, and permanence, adding the good-positive to the bad-negative. Degree of relevance is what matters, not those four criteria.

For that we do not need foreign correspondents. We need a page or so in our paper, some time on radio-TV reporting the headlines around the world, giving us an image of what matters to them and, as importantly, of similarities and differences in the choices. Media referring to themselves as a global paper-radio-TV should be sensitive to their strong Anglo-American accent in their choices and spend some space and time reporting from the horse's own mouth, listening to local voices—*Al Jazeera* is very good at that.

Foreign correspondents are needed around the world for what is relevant to us, which is not necessarily what is most relevant to them. They have to be of our own kind, loaded with our perspectives on the world. Taken alone, as the only source of information about the world, 'relevant to us' becomes national egocentrism with us at the centre of the world. Added to 'relevant to them', we may get a more global perspective.

How does this image stand up to today's reality? The study carried out in this book gives much information and many dimensions. General tendency: the decline of foreign correspondence, but the picture is mixed.

There is a move toward freelancing, which may inject some fresh perspectives but may also be lacking in professionalism. The Chinese correspondents increase in numbers, doing their 'relevant-for-us' job. Foreign correspondents remain influenced by their own journalistic culture. To the extent that means the deep culture referred to, much weeding is needed and more so with Western media agencies taking over. However, adding *Tass* and *Xinhua* to *AP-UPI-Reuters-AFP* reporting about Afghanistan and Iraq already makes for a richer perspective. And the competition among foreign correspondents and agencies may also do some good, like reporting beyond sound bites.

Then comes renewed time pressures, lack of financial resources, and the impact of the Internet as the new medium that is used by foreign correspondents as well as by their audiences, not only to be informed but also to create their own medium though social media, all squeezing out classical foreign correspondents. I still remember with nostalgia excellent correspondents for Norwegian media, not youngsters but experienced journalists spending a lot of time living abroad.

London seems still to be the foreign correspondents press hub above all others, probably stimulating homogeneity built around that deep culture. London may soon be outcompeted by some place in the East, just as so much else in the West is outcompeted but not necessarily for the better unless they do that weeding. Two hubs together might make sense.

Today foreign correspondents must cover regions, not only states, and all fields: economics, finance, politics, military, culture, social. Too much for one person, possibly a death blow to an old institution.

What comes in its place? Probably a combination of freelancers and civic journalists on the Internet; reporting from anywhere about anything, while 'experts' would be more than happy to pontificate. The perspectives will vary, but they will be increasingly global and holistic, more 'relevant to all of us'," less framed as us vs. them.

There may even be space for solutions! The future will tell.

Johan Galtung
Alfaz, December 2013

NOTE

1. See Galtung, J. (1980). The Structure of Foreign News, Peace and World Structure. *Essays in Peace Research*. 4. Copenhagen: Ejlers, pp. 118–151, fn 690–693 [Online]. Available from: www.transcend.org/tup.

Introduction

Foreign Correspondents in Perspective

Stylianos Papathanassopoulos and Iliana Giannouli

The foreign news is covered in various ways (Hess, 1996; Wu & Hamilton, 2004), but what distinguishes foreign correspondents from their colleagues is that they, to an extent, feel more independent compared to their colleagues. According to the results of a survey conducted by Yu and Luter, correspondents themselves suggested an average of 80 per cent of the stories they produced. Only about 20 per cent of the stories were suggested or requested by the home offices (1964, p. 6). In the past years, the foreign correspondents' autonomy has been significantly shortened, especially for those who work for TV networks. Recent studies have indicated that producers, not correspondents, determine 'what is news' (Foote, 2005). In other words, if the correspondents fail to absorb the 'organizational culture' of the media they work for, they face the risk of not seeing their stories published or, even worse, of losing their jobs.

The decision on what is worthwhile sharing with audiences depends, according to Naveh, on the following items: ideology as the basic orientation of the news editor, 'surpriseness' of the event, and importance of the event—which from the international perspective means that the event should involve the powerful global elite in terms of countries and leaders (2002, p. 7). In addition, events that are violent or that can be defined as negative will get better coverage. Moreover, an event must be relevant to the nation whose media cover it, and it must be accessible to coverage. Finally, reporters prefer an event that is familiar in terms of previous news patterns.

Additionally, foreign correspondents have to adapt global information into the local framework in a way that renders faraway events comprehensible, appealing, and relevant to domestic audiences, a process known as news 'domestication' (Clausen, 2003, pp. 14–15). According to Clausen, the production of international news may be characterized by a tension between the particularistic and the common (2003, p. 42). On the one hand, efforts were made to make international news a window on the world; on the other hand, efforts were made to 'domesticate' international information for national audiences. Thus, we see a dialectical process in which universal communication features are used in local meaning creation.

Concerning the presentation of news, most studies have shown that there is a distinction among correspondents, depending on whether they work for international news agencies or smaller national media. In general, it could be said that the correspondents of news agencies share a more neutral 'perspective', whereas journalists representing national media offer more opinionated stories as well as background reporting and in-depth analysis for their articles (Van Dijk, 1988, pp. 120–122). The latter doesn't seem to be a priority for agencies, which have been blamed for producing short and superficial news.[1] Most correspondents admit that the lack of 'depth' reporting is attributed to a variety of factors, mainly to the rush to meet deadlines. Correspondents can run into problems trying to fit events that transpire within one place to deadlines designed for somewhere else (Hess, 2005). Some correspondents are separated from their editors and audience by several time zones, making their working day very long, inasmuch as the latter is ordered by two clocks: the one at home and the one on the news beat (Hannerz, 2004, p. 211).

Routinely, FCs have an early contact with their editors from the foreign news desk at home, and they inform them about the topic agenda. Together they decide which stories should be covered. Technological changes and especially the advent of the Internet have made it easier for correspondents to communicate with their foreign desks but have also increased the editors' control of correspondents' work because they know what to expect from them. Archetti (2013) noted that the Internet and social media have rendered news production a highly collaborative process across all its development stages, where foreign correspondents constantly exchange information with a wide range of actors.

According to Wu and Hamilton's survey on the impact of the Internet on the work of US foreign correspondents, the majority of correspondents admit that the Internet made it easier to get background information, although many correspondents reported that the Internet helped them get sources and monitor competitors' coverage (2004, p. 526). The survey also indicated that the Internet creates additional pressures; several correspondents noted that due to the Internet, they have to file stories more often and that they need to update their stories more frequently. Furthermore, it should be mentioned that, despite the increasing fear of the appearance of more 'borrowed news' in the Internet era, foreign correspondents—far from being rushed into 'churnalism'—make efforts to produce exclusive content with unique insights (Archetti, 2012, p. 851).

Real-time broadcasting seems to cause additional pressures to correspondents because the 'obsession' with speed of news coverage increases the possibility of error. Moreover, real-time broadcasting pushes journalists to rush to judgment, even when it is not clear what is going on. Finally, television technology distances the TV correspondent from what is happening inasmuch as live broadcasting ties reporters to the technology instead of to the story (Hess, 1996, pp. 64–65). Many TV correspondents recall the days when they had the opportunity to spend time in the region they covered, familiarizing themselves with the local background, culture, and history. The new demands of television as a medium leave no time for background or context (Ibrahim, 2003, p. 90). Wire services correspondents also face challenges to maintain speed and to keep up with technology in order to remain competitive.

Despite the time pressure on the work of foreign correspondents attributed to the technology, a correspondent has to face additional challenges associated with the different social, political, and cultural spaces in which foreign reporters have to work.

Foreign correspondents have to speak the language of the country they cover in order to be able to catch the 'pulse' of the local society. When correspondents don't speak the local language, they have to make use of 'fixers.' According to the first comprehensive study of fixers, held by Jerry Palmer and Victoria Fontan, the purposes for which fixers are used are the following: to interpret the interviews and translate the local media; to arrange interviews; and to provide background briefings about the identities of potential interviewees, situations, or social groups, as well as security assessments (2007, p. 10). Another problem associated with the practice of journalism in a foreign country is the access to a network of local contacts. Many studies have indicated that foreign correspondents share common experiences of discrimination based on the relative size and importance of the news organization they work for (Lecheler, 2008). However, Cozma (2010) noted that the standards for excellence in journalism generally have changed; editors put a higher value on using a wide variety of sources, rather than on just gaining access to officials.

That's why many correspondents heavily rely on the domestic media as important news sources. Already identified in 1984 by Ghorpade's survey on the sources used by Washington's foreign correspondents, media sources—including newspapers, magazines, and news agencies—were rated among the most regularly used sources. Thirty years later, the conclusions of this volume fully support his findings.

Furthermore, foreign correspondents use the international news agencies as information sources. Moreover, these powerful news organizations, mostly because of their organizational structure, are the first ones to distribute the news around the world and thus determine the international news agenda. However, it should be emphasized that this 'intermedia' agenda-setting function largely affects the perception of correspondents about what happens around them or, more accurately, of the event that should focus their attention (Ginneken, 1998, pp. 133–135). To sum up, as Archetti (2012) puts it, newsgathering routines of foreign correspondents are strongly shaped by the opportunities and constraints of the 'information environment' they operate in.

Correspondents' relationship with their colleagues has been researched by anthropologist Ulf Hannerz, among others. Hannerz notes that their relations are significantly determined by the security situation of the country or the region they are posted in. In addition, reporters working for radio or print media work better together (2004, pp. 155–160). In contrast, those working in the press tend to be more 'happy' when TV crews are not around. Generally, correspondents get informed about one another's work and often exchange information.

Foreign correspondents are among the first important cultural framers of events. Reportage that is sensitive to the social, cultural, and political characteristics demands a depth of historical and social knowledge, which must be acquired by a correspondent. This means that correspondents have to rise above their own nationalistic considerations and show an image of the world free from stereotypes and prejudices (Masterton, 2009). In their study, Starck and Villanuena (1992) conducted in-depth interviews with six foreign correspondents with the aim of examining 'how they felt culture figured in their work'. Their interviews revealed that a 'lack of cultural preparation' and a 'lack of cultural sensitivity' were common problems cited by correspondents. In addition, several correspondents criticized journalism education for not including cultural sensitivity training in the curriculum.

Due to cost reductions, the growing competition from international news agencies, and new media outlets, the profession of foreign correspondent is in crisis (Utley, 1997). Correspondents no longer have hegemony over foreign news. The position correspondents held in the organization is changing, and the correspondents' role must be redefined. In other words, as Hamilton and Jenner suggest, foreign news coverage has the potential to survive (2004b). New forms of foreign affairs coverage emerge from more diverse and cost-effective sources; bloggers, parachute journalists, or local or national journalists often replace the 'traditional' foreign correspondents. As the authors conclude, we are witnessing the evolution, rather than the extinction, of foreign correspondents.

However, as Peter Goodman (2013), editor at *The Huffington Post*, pointed out: 'despite the obvious and abundant promises of the web, and despite the inarguable fact that the digital future is now irretrievably the present, foreign news is at a crisis point'; there is no substitute for professional foreign correspondents who go back again and again, 'having conversations that go on longer than needed merely to grab a handy quote to jam in a story.'

In this 'golden age' of news, global audiences can access foreign news at a click of a button. But before we decide whether foreign correspondents are redundant, we should bear in mind that foreign news is one of the fields in news reporting that needs the most contextualization, analysis, explanation, and clarification. That is the value added by a foreign correspondent. Steven Livingston and Gregory Asmolov make a crucial point when they ask: 'Do we understand Iranian politics any more clearly because of seeing Neda's last moments on YouTube, or tracking post-election violence on a GIS application? . . . Without direction from a trusted interpreter of events on the ground, someone very much like a traditional foreign correspondent, will anyone know to look? Will anyone care?' (2010, p. 756).

Foreign correspondents are still the only secure answer to the understanding of foreign affairs because 'through their eyes' we can hope to shape a more comprehensive image of the 'global village' that is today smaller and yet more complex than ever before.

NOTE

1. See Camaj, L. (2010, p. 649).

REFERENCES

ARCHETTI, C. (2011). Reporting the Nation: Understanding the Role of Foreign Correspondents in 21st Century Public Diplomacy. Paper presented for the International Studies Association (ISA) Annual Convention. Montreal, 16–19 March 2011.

———. (2012). Which Future for Foreign Correspondence? London Foreign Correspondents in the Age of Global Media. *Journalism Studies.* 13 (5–6), pp. 847–856.

———. (2013). Journalism in the Age of Global Media: The Evolving Practices of Foreign Correspondents in London. *Journalism: Theory, Practice and Criticism.* 14 (3), pp. 419–436.

BOYD-BARRETT, O. (1982). Western News Agencies and the 'Media Imperialism' Debate: What Kind of Data-base? *Journal of International Affairs.* 35 (2), pp. 247–260.

BOYD- BARETT, O., & Rantanen, T. (1998), *The Globalization of News.* London: Sage.

CAMPBELL, V. (2004). *Information Age Journalism: Journalism in an International Context.* London: Arnold.

CAMAJ, L. (2008). Media Framing through Stages of a Political Discourse: International News Agencies' Coverage of Kosovo's Status Negotiations. *International Communication Gazette.* 72 (7), pp. 635–653.

———. (2010). Media Framing through Stages of a Political Discourse: International News Agencies' Coverage of Kosovo's Status Negotiations. *International Communication Gazette.* 72 (7), p. 649.

CLAUSEN, L. (2003). *Global News Production.* Copenhagen: Copenhagen Business School Press.

———. (2004). Localizing the Global: 'Domestication' Processes in International News Production. *Media, Culture and Society.* 26 (1), pp. 25–44.

COLE, J., & HAMILTON, J.M. (2008). The History of a Surviving Species: Defining Eras in the Evolution of Foreign Correspondents. *Journalism Studies.* 9 (5), pp. 798–812.

COZMA, R. (2010). From Murrow to Mediocrity? *Journalism Studies.* 11 (5), pp. 667–682.

FOOTE, J.S. (2005). The Changing Role of TV Network News Correspondents. In TUNSTALL, J. (ed.), *Media Occupations and Professions: A Reader.* New York: Oxford University Press, pp. 158–160.

GHORPADE, S. (1984). Sources and Access: How Foreign Correspondents Rate Washington, D.C. *Journal of Communication.* 34 (1), pp. 32–40.

GINNEKEN, J. (1998). *Understanding Global News: A Critical Introduction.* London: Sage.

GOODMAN, S.P. (2013). Foreign News at a Crisis Point. *The Huffington Post* [Online]. Available from http://huff.to/1lNzQKj.

HACHTEN, W.A., & Scotton, J.F. (2007). *The World News Prism: Global Information in a Satellite Age.* Malden, MA: Blackwell.

HAMILTON, J.M. (2009). In the Foothills of Change: Foreign Coverage Seems Doomed, but It's Only Just Begun. *Columbia Journalism Review.* 47 (6), pp. 51–54.

———. (2010). Reporting from Faraway Places: Who Does It and How? *Nieman Reports*. 6 (3), pp. 4–5.

———. (2004b). Foreign Correspondence: Evolution, Not Extinction. *Nieman Reports*. 58 (3), pp. 98–100.

HAMILTON, J. M., & PERLMUTTER, D.D. (2007). *From Pigeons to News Portals: Foreign Reporting and the Challenge of New Technology*. Baton Rouge: Louisiana State University Press.

———. (2004). *Foreign News: Exploring the World of Foreign Correspondents*. Chicago: University of Chicago Press.

HESS S. (1996). *International News and Foreign Correspondents*. Washington, DC: Brookings Institution Press.

———. (2005). *Through Their Eyes: Foreign Correspondents in the United States*. Washington, DC: Brookings Institution Press, pp. 69–76.

IBRAHIM, D. (2003). Individual Perceptions of International Correspondents in the Middle East. An Obstacle to Fair News. *International Communication Gazette*. 65 (1), pp. 87–101.

KELLER, B. (2013). It's the Golden Age of News. *New York Times* [Online]. Available from http://nyti.ms/QOGh65.

LECHELER, S. (2008). EU Membership and the Press: An Analysis of the Brussels Correspondents from the New Member States. *Journalism*. 9 (4), pp. 443–464.

LIVINGSTON, S., & ASMOLOV, G. (2010). Networks and the Future of Foreign Affairs Reporting. *Journalism Studies*. 11 (5), pp. 745–760.

LUBMAN, S. (2000). China and the Foreign Press. *Nieman Reports*. 53–54 (4/1), pp. 204–207.

MASTERTON, M. (2009). A Class of Cultures for Foreign Correspondents. *Pacific Journalism Review*. 15 (1), pp. 19–30.

NAVEH, C. (2002). The Role of the Media in Foreign Policy Decision-Making: A Theoretical Framework. *Conflict and Communication Online*. 1 (2), pp. 1–14.

PALMER, J., & FONTAN, V. (2007). Our Ears and Our Eyes: Journalists and Fixers in Iraq. *Journalism Theory Practice and Criticism*. 8 (1), pp. 5–24.

PAPATHANASSOPOULOS, S. (2011). The Greek Crisis and the European Media. Presented at the International Conference: Soothsayers of Doom? Covering the Global Financial Crisis in Comparative and Historical Perspective, organized by the City University London, the Institute of Contemporary History, King's College, London and the British Academy, London, 12–13 December 2011.

REYNOLDS J. (2010). Correspondents: They Come in Different Shapes and Sizes. *Nieman Reports*. 64 (3), pp. 8–11.

SAMBROOK R. (2010). Are Foreign Correspondents Redundant? The Changing Face of International News. Oxford: Reuters Institute for the Study of Journalism.

STARCK, K., & Villanueva, E. (1992). Cultural Framing: Foreign Correspondents and Their Work. *Education Resources Information Center, pp*. 1–41.

TUNSTALL, J. (2005). *Media Occupations and Professions: A Reader*. New York: Oxford University Press.

UTLEY, G. (1997). The Shrinking of Foreign News: From Broadcast to Narrowcast. *Foreign Affairs*. 76 (2), pp. 2–10.

VAN DIJK, T. A. (1988). News Analysis: Case Studies of International and National News in the Press. Hillsdale, NJ: Lawrence Erlbaum.

WU, H.D., & Hamilton, J.M. (2004). U.S. Foreign Correspondents: Changes and Continuity at the Turn of the Century. *International Communication Gazette*. 66 (6), pp. 517–532.

YU, F., & LUTER, J. (1964). The Foreign Correspondent and His Work. *Columbia Journalism Review*. 3 (1), pp. 5–12.

1 Foreign Correspondents in Austria

Vienna: a Central and Eastern Europe-base in Transition

Roman Hummel, Johanna Dorer, Sarah A. Ganter, Gerit Götzenbrucker and Dimitri Prandner

INTRODUCTION

In the second half of the 19th century, an elaborate press landscape gradually developed throughout Europe, moving away from the hitherto usual practice of 'statement journalism'. Together with the rise of the mass press, the interest in credible information about events beyond a country's borders marked the beginning of international journalism and at the same time the formation of a specific group of correspondents who reported for their medium from the power centres of the world.

Up until the end of the Austro-Hungarian monarchy in the autumn of 1918, Vienna was counted alongside London and Paris, St. Petersburg and Berlin as one of the most important cities in Europe and was therefore home to a particularly large number of foreign correspondents who reported on the tensions between nationalization and internationalization (Geppert, 2010). During those approximately 60 years, the expanding newspaper market in Europe was doubly focused on Vienna: it was necessary to convey the events and decisions from the centre of the Habsburg monarchy, unadulterated and as quickly as possible, not only to other European countries, but also to the capitals of the kingdoms, lands, and territories of Cisleithania (the northern and western parts of Austria-Hungary), as well as to Budapest in Hungary. Even if this latter level required no foreign correspondents in the narrow sense (Rumpler & Urbanitsch, 2006), two separate but overlapping circles of correspondents active in Vienna can still be assumed here.

Even in the politically and economically insignificant First Republic (1918–1938), the number of foreign correspondents, and increasingly female foreign correspondents, remained about the same. The great American journalist Dorothy Thompson, among others, began her career in the early 1920s as a foreign reporter in Vienna (cf. Kurth, 1990).

This interest in Vienna had several reasons: for one, Vienna had long been a city with a low cost of living; for another, it was regarded as a base for centralized reporting on Eastern Europe, the Balkans, and the Communist countries. Thus, the Communist International ('Comintern') established its base in Vienna from 1919 to 1927 because Eastern European members of the press already were active there (McLoughlin, Leidinger, & Moritz, 2009, p. 124). The extent to which the activities of the foreign correspondents of those years transitioned smoothly into work for intelligence services was vividly described by George Gedye (1947) in his radical espousal of a social democratic Vienna. Even in the years of the Nazi regime (1938–1945), Vienna remained a major media city: here foreign correspondents could hope to get a clearer view of the Nazi power structure than they could from the control centre of Berlin; at the same time, the regime itself could emphasize their own medial and political activities on Southeast Europe, such as Ronneberger's bureau (Heinelt, 2004).

Even after 1945, Vienna remained the focus of the international press. First the emphasis was on the democratic aspirations of the newly recreated Austria (Koppensteiner, 1975–1976; Kober, 2005), but soon the journalistic and intelligence influence of the Allies on the Austrian press after 1945 and the location of Vienna/Eastern Austria for propaganda efforts in the early Cold War, such as Radio Free Europe, rose to great international importance (Beer, 2000; Pirker, 2012, p. 457). With the rapid division of Europe into two power blocs, Vienna was once again a central base of operations for foreign correspondents from the end of the 1940s. From the communist seizure of power in Czechoslovakia until the fall of the Iron Curtain in 1989, Vienna not only offered many international correspondents a secure base but also represented a place to collect special, sensitive information. This was particularly true during the Hungarian Uprising in 1956 and the Prague Spring in 1968. Vienna was the 'hub of the East', from where the correspondents could often be 'sent on the march' when needed to Prague, Budapest, Bucharest, or the Balkans (Schreiberhuber, 2010, p. 76). The still relevant concept of 'Balkan' or 'Central Europe correspondent' has long been synonymous with a base camp in Vienna.

At the beginning of the 1970s, 300 foreign correspondents were still operating from Vienna. As the first representative study from Alfred Lugert (1974) points out, they worked for 565 different media from 45 countries. However the survey also proves, on the one hand, that nearly a third of the correspondents dealt solely with processes in countries of the Eastern Bloc. On the other hand, the majority of the correspondents claimed that their employers were interested not in Austrian policies but only in the activities of international organizations located in Vienna (Lugert, 1974). These included OPEC and numerous agencies of the United Nations.

The end of the Cold War, however, combined with the trends toward concentration in journalism and the need for austerity measures, particularly in the print sector, have led to a marked reduction in the number of foreign correspondents. Since then, journalists as well as major news agencies, have moved directly to Prague or Budapest, while the Viennese office occasionally still remains as the coordinating point for Eastern Europe, as the example of *Agence France Press* (*AFP*) shows. Since 1945 the *Verband der Auslandskorrespondenten* (Association of Foreign Correspondents), which was renamed to *Verband der Auslandspresse* (Foreign Press Association) in 1958, has acted as the coordination and contact point for international journalists working in Vienna (Dimitrakoudis, 2012).

WHO: WHO ARE AUSTRIA'S FOREIGN CORRESPONDENTS AND FOR WHOM DO THEY WORK?

Recruiting of Participants

Today, no complete list of foreign correspondents in Austria exists. As a consequence of Austria's EU membership, foreign correspondents are required to seek accreditation only if they are non-EU citizens. This accreditation is carried out by the Federal Chancellery (Bundeskanzleramt), subject to the requirements that the candidate can provide proof of employment in the respective medium, a valid press card, evidence of past journalistic work (newspaper articles, press photos/videos, etc.) and that the candidate has already gone through the necessary steps to request a residence permit.[1] Thankfully, we could send out invitations for the survey via this list of foreign accredited journalists, though in this case, due to privacy laws, we were not allowed direct insight into the address database. Because of this, the exact coverage rate that was realized with these invitations remains unknown.

Further information could be generated with the help of the two journalistic trade organizations in Austria, which foreign correspondents may choose to join. The first one is the Foreign Press Association (*Verband der Auslandspresse*),[2] which, in addition to accepting foreign correspondents, also embraces press attachés, diplomats, and spokespersons from various international organizations. The second is the Concordia[3] press club, which has its own foreign press division and, according to its own website, accepts writers and journalists who have published at least one commercially available book. As we concluded in our research, the lax membership policy enforced by both of these organizations frequently results in people who are at best only peripherally associated with journalism becoming members, not least because of the increased prestige that a press card entails.

From the address databases of these two organizations, a total of 164 potential foreign correspondents were identified and invited to participate in completing the questionnaire. Further research on this group via web and social media revealed that only 106 individuals could reliably be identified as foreign correspondents. Among those who were rejected are diplomats, those only peripherally associated with journalism (e.g. artists, scientists, translators), as well as journalists working for foreign language publications published in Austria (e.g., in English, Japanese, or Turkish, with tourists or expats as the target group) or journalists no longer working in Austria because they moved to another country.

Using this sample of 106 'real foreign correspondents', it became possible to get what is most likely an accurate insight into the Austrian foreign correspondent population: 57 per cent are male, 43 per cent are female. The media they work for are spread across 31 countries—most frequently, Germany (26 respondents), followed by Spain and Japan (7 each), France, United States, Russia, and Finland (6 each), UK (4), and China (3). In other words, most foreign correspondents reporting from Austria work for European media (35 total), though Asian ones have a surprisingly large share of representation. Africa is represented by two regions, the Americans only via the United States, and Australian/Oceanian media representation is missing entirely. Twenty-seven correspondents work for press agencies, 37 for print media, and 22 for broadcasting media. The principal medium of employment remains unclear for about 20 of the correspondents.

Questionnaire Analysis

A total of 56 individuals responded to the online survey that was developed in coordination with our German and Swiss colleagues; however, after data cleaning, only 23 cases were suitable for evaluation,[4] which poses a rather low sample size. Consequently, the only choice was to adhere purely to an approach based on frequency-to-data evaluation.

Who Are the Foreign Correspondents?

As in the population, our sample leans slightly toward the male side (10:7; 6 declined to answer). The majority are over 40 years old (11, with only one individual under 30; 6 declined to answer) and live in Austria, the host country, with their spouses. The nationality of respondents is spread out over a wide range of countries: 13 out of the 23 respondents hail from various EU member countries, with an additional two from other European countries, two from the Middle East, as well as four Americans and one Australian. The correspondents have a high level of formal education: most have a university degree, almost exclusively in the social sciences (most frequently communication science or journalism).

Six individuals specified English to be their mother tongue; five indicated German. Other responses were Arabic, Bosnian/Serbo-Croatian, French, Finnish, Dutch, Polish, Romanian, Russian, Spanish, Turkish, and Hungarian. All respondents claim to understand German well; in fact, the overwhelming majority claim to speak it at least fluently. Most (15) also indicated German as being the dominant language when working or doing research. Two respondents claim to use English, and six responded with other languages (presumably as a result of doing research in other countries). Most (10 of 13) respondents chose to answer the questionnaire in German.

Professionalism

Eighteen of the 23 respondents claimed journalism to be their primary profession. The remaining five correspondents invested between 10 and 30 per cent of their total working time in journalistic activities. The correspondents are predominantly veterans in their field: they have spent a significant amount of time in journalism (median, 17 years), as well as in foreign correspondence (median, 11 years). The opportunity for foreign correspondence usually presents itself only after a certain amount of journalistic experience; the mean here is six years, although seven individuals responded that they had been foreign correspondents for as long as they had been journalists. Most (17) claimed to be members of a journalistic association in Austria. (Nine mentioned the Concordia press club, and 8 mentioned the Foreign Press Association, whose membership database was mined for potential respondents.)

For the most part, these correspondents work for only one media establishment (10); seven respondents claim to work for two. Those who work for five or more establishments (3) are also full-time freelance journalists. Only 15 of the 23 respondents answered questions regarding their salary. Six respondents earn a net monthly income of €1,000–€4,000, four claim to earn more than €4,000, and five claim to earn less than €1,000, the latter group consisting exclusively of part-time journalists. Less than half of the respondents have permanent employment (10), 12 are freelancers, and one is a self-proclaimed part-time journalist.

Most respondents work for a press agency (11), seven work for print/online media, and four are in public sector broadcasting; only one claimed to work for private sector TV. Not a single respondent claimed to work for private sector radio. Surprisingly, the Internet is not very strongly represented as a journalistic medium: 14 out of the 23 respondents do not publish in online media, four have their own Website, four have blogs, and one individual uses Twitter journalistically—in addition to YouTube, Facebook, and Google+—but this particular respondent was a part-time foreign correspondent who claims to be a full-time online editor.

At this stage, we must preempt the stereotype of the cosmopolitan, globe-trotting foreign press correspondent: on average, the foreign correspondents represented in our sample have been active in Austria for quite some time (median, 11 years). Only eight claimed to have foreign correspondent experience beyond Austria, which in four cases meant Germany and Switzerland, in three cases Eastern (or Southeastern) Europe, and in one case Venezuela. It is no surprise, then, that in most cases the reported reasons for choosing Austria were predominantly of a personal nature (multiple answers were allowed): 'personal interest' and 'specific knowledge of the country' (11 responses each), 'personal ties to Austria' (10 responses), 'language proficiency' (9). After these answers were concrete offers by media establishments in Austria (8 responses), and only one respondent claimed to be in Austria more or less by coincidence—'there was a job opening'.

The foreign correspondents in our sample seem to be well integrated into and appreciated by Austrian society. Three-quarters received at least one invitation in the past year to write articles for Austrian publications or to hold public lectures; in four cases, more than 10 such invitations were received.

WHAT, WHEN, AND WHERE: WHAT MAKES IT INTO THE FOREIGN CORRESPONDENT'S REPORTING AGENDA?

The media houses that our sample of foreign correspondents writes for are primarily in EU countries (11 cases, 5 of which were Germany), followed by the United States. Additional responses were Bosnia, China, Russia, and Syria (1 each). In most cases, respondents (17 total) described the reach of their medium as international; seven described theirs as national. Only in one case was the correspondent's publication described as regional/local (in this case, a Swiss publication).

Thematically, art and culture fulfil the Austrian cliché of being the primary font of journalistic reporting for foreign correspondents (17 responses), followed by politics (16) and the economy (15). About half of the correspondents (12) also cover societal topics, and one respondent seems to be an expert on health. When asked about reports they were currently working on, the landscape shifts slightly toward politics (8 mentions), followed by art and culture (5), UN, economy, and society (3 each).

All respondents considered Austria to be within their scope of reporting, with almost half (10) claiming their scope to be restricted exclusively to Austria. The scope of the other respondents extends in most cases to countries bordering Austria. Two respondents report from 12 to 14 countries, respectively: in addition to neighbouring countries, these correspondents also cover the entire Balkans region, as well as Ukraine and Turkey.

Eleven respondents claimed to write only one to two articles a week; five respondents claim to write between three and five articles. On the other hand, two respondents write around ten stories a week, and an additional four write between 10 and 20 stories. The more prolific correspondents are exclusively full-time journalists. Although most of them (15 of 21) are not interested in what percentage of their work gets published, five reported that a proportion of 50–80 per cent of their researched work makes it all the way to publication. Only one respondent claimed a success rate of only 10 per cent; closer inspection revealed this to be a correspondent for a US media house reporting primarily about the United Nations.

Exclusive stories do not seem to be an issue of particular importance. (In the range between '1–unimportant' and '5–very important', the median of responses is 3.) Similarly, reports about Austria for foreign audiences seem to be of average importance (with a mean of 3.35). Nonetheless, according to our sample, the level of interest for Austrian affairs in international media (and with international audiences) has increased over time. (Only two out of 19 respondents claimed it to have decreased.)

The primary source for the stories of foreign press correspondents seem to be media within the host country (13 responses), followed by lobbies (12) and 'other official sources' (11). Experts and scientists are not quite as important (8 responses), while information gleaned from 'regular citizens' via social media or blogs is inspiration for only a quarter of the respondents' reporting. Surprisingly, politicians, regardless of whether for the government or for the opposition, are at the bottom of the spectrum of importance for foreign correspondents. This may be explained by the fact that fewer than half of the respondents chose 'politics' as a regularly occurring topic in their reporting. Access to information is universally characterized by the respondents as simple and easy.

Perceived Problems

It is precisely the accessibility of information that the respondents ascribe most influence to in their reporting, along with their own personal social network (10 mentions each). Work colleagues, news editors, and time constraints follow as influential factors in reporting (9 mentions).

This rift in importance (strong influence/some influence vs. little to no influence) is visualized in Figure 1.1, which shows that the respondents having an influence on reporting universally perceive factors with negative values. Other factors included in the questionnaire (journalism laws, politicians, lobbies, and special interest groups, both of the host country and the home country) were almost universally regarded as negligible.

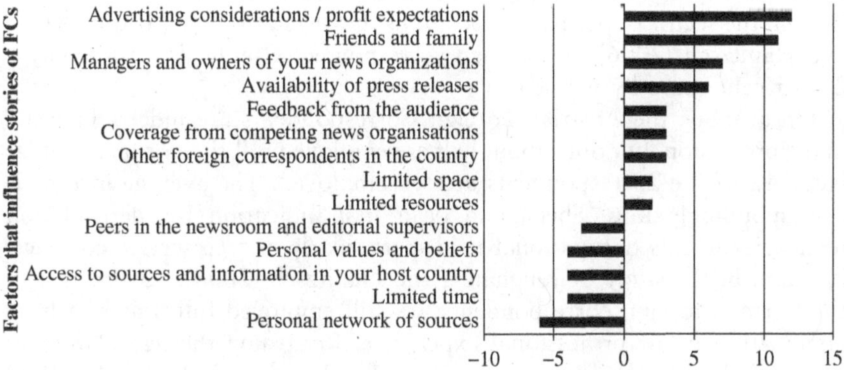

Figure 1.1 Influencing factors to FCs' news agenda in Austria: Difference between 'item has influence' and 'item now has influence'.

Respondents generally were not worried about job stability: most believe it is unlikely that their current job positions could be downsized or that interest in foreign news could decline in the near future. On the other hand, most claim that the pressure under which they work has increased and that certain resources, such as travel budgets, have decreased. There seems to be a consensus, however, that the number of foreign correspondents in the respondents' respective institutions has not decreased, that there has been a significant replacement of correspondents with so-called 'parachute journalists', and that foreign correspondents in general seem to be as thriving as ever. In spite of this, according to our respondents, the job of being a foreign correspondent has, in recent years generally, taken a turn for the worse—obviously due to the aforementioned worsened working conditions.

CONCLUSION: DISCUSSION OF FINDINGS

With a return rate of 22 per cent, the online survey seems to be only to a limited extent an appropriate tool for collecting data on the occupational situation of foreign correspondents in Austria, because the questions deal in many cases with complex issues and contexts, such as for instance personal influence networks and networked practices. For comparison, the study of Junghanns and Hanitzsch (2006) reported a response rate of 35 per cent, on a population of 502 German foreign correspondents. However, this is also due to the fact that this study refers to German foreign correspondents abroad who are mainly involved institutionally and not to those in the host country.

With regard to the sociodemographic data from previous or other studies, the gender distribution of the foreign correspondents has changed significantly; 43 per cent of the population surveyed in Austria are female, in contrast to the study of Lugert (1974), showing a female share of 14 per cent. In the sector of permanent positions, however, the study of Junghanns and Hanitzsch (2006) on German correspondents showed in turn only a 22 per cent share by women.

On average, the Austrian Foreign Correspondents are indeed 11 years in the profession, but only about half are employed full-time or on a regular basis; 12 of the 23 respondents are self-employed. The average income is correspondingly low. This could be a first indication for deregulation tendencies in this occupational field, particularly as free service contracts increase. In the study of Junghanns and Hanitzsch (2006), 93 per cent of the German foreign correspondents are still employed full-time and have about 20 years of professional experience. Regarding the age of foreign correspondents, both Lugert (1974) and Junghanns and Hanitzsch (2006) point to about 40 years as an average.

With regard to professional education and training, the foreign correspondents in Austria fall within the average of studies that mention higher vocational education and years of experience. In Austria, the whole professional myth of the 'cosmopolitans' was dismantled, particularly because most of our sample had been living a long time in Austria and reported mostly personal reason for this (interest, country, personal relationships).

Regarding the selection of topics and the process of finding a topic, foreign correspondents follow the 'tradition' of the self-referentiality of the media, which refers to the two-way interactions with the media, particularly the media of the host country, during the construction of topics as a transnational factor (Brüggemann, 2012, p. 90) and as an important point of reference. This was also the outcome of a long-term study about US foreign correspondents in Paris (Merle, 2013, p. 166). Already in 1974, the study of Lugert mentioned that 94 per cent of foreign correspondents in the country use Austrian daily newspapers as source of information. Other influential networks in Austria are currently lobbies and other official national sources, similarly to the 'National Authorities and public figures' in the Merle (2013) study or to the 'prominent politician' in the Brüggemann study 2012 (p. 90). In her study on foreign correspondents in the global era, Renneberg (2009) concludes that the agendas of German foreign correspondents, even in public broadcasting programmes, are strongly influenced by agency reports and are increasingly shaped by stiff competition. Whereby an overall intensifying trend toward soft and colourful themes was identified (Rennenberg, 2009, p. 262), this was also confirmed in Austria, with a preference for cultural and social issues. It should be underlined that, in general, many of the foreign correspondents working in Austria report not with a national focus but a regional one. The EU enlargement gives additional relevance to this regionalization of the foreign correspondents' work, and it seems that this triggers, to a certain degree, the decentralization of professional networks in the region, inasmuch as Austria has been traditionally a hub to gather and access information about Eastern European countries. This is a role that lost its importance after the political changes in this region, since 1990.

Regarding their professional future, foreign correspondents in Austria surprisingly have a relatively positive attitude, and they neglect signs of changes in the occupation relating to increasing economic constraints. For example, although they admitted that the pressure grew, travel budgets have been reduced and, in the case of German public television channels, a future structural expansion of the correspondent network is unlikely (Renneberg, 2009). US correspondents in Paris, however, see their influence diminishing and rather fear that the Internet will turn into the most important source of information (Merle, 2013, p. 167). This assessment is shared by Renneberg in Austria (2009), who interprets the increasing use of multiple sources of information by the recipients as a consequence of the 'light' foreign journalism that is increasingly unable to satisfy the growing demand for a wide range of information. A focus on 'soft issues of coverage' certainly becomes obvious in the statements of the respondents.

From the end of the Cold War, Austria has evolved from being a hub of international political reporting, to being a city of secondary importance where cultural stories have gained prominence. Thus, both comparisons with the foreign reporting before 1989 (Lugert, 1974), as well as with current international 'hot spots' are possible only to a limited extent.

NOTES

1. See http://bit.ly/1eCDMhP.
2. See http://bit.ly/1m9uM6k.
3. See http://bit.ly/1eVveh1. We thank Dr. Astrid Zimmermann for her cooperation.
4. Sixteen people answering the questionnaire had to be excluded because they did not comply with the criteria for being foreign correspondents (e.g., working mainly for Austrian media or even mostly not as journalists). Further, 23 respondents had left Austria before the survey. Their answers were therefore not integrated in the results.

REFERENCES

BEER, S. (2000). Rund um den 'Dritten Mann': Amerikanische Geheimdienste in Österreich 1945–1955 [About the 'Third Man': American Intelligence Agencies in Austria 1945–1955]. In SCHMIDL, E.A. (ed.), *Österreich im frühen Kalten Krieg. 1945–1958. Spione, Partisanen, Kriegspläne* [Austria during the Early Cold War, 1945–1958: Spies, Partisans, War Plans]. Vienna/Cologne/Weimar: Böhlau, pp. 73–99.

BRÜGGEMANN, M. (2012). Transnationale Kulturen des Journalismus. Praktiken journalistischer Themenfindung im Vergleich [Transitional Cultures of Journalism. A Comparison of Journalistic Topic Selection Practices]. *Medien & Kommunikationswissenschaft*. 60 (2), pp. 76–92.

DIMITRAKOUDIS, D. (2012). *Verband/Geschichte* [Association/History] [Online]. Available from http://bit.ly/1pcClLY.

GEDYE, G. E. R. (1947). *Die Bastionen fielen. Wie der Faschismus Wien und Prag überrannte* [The Bastions Fell: How Fascism Overran Vienna and Prague]. Vienna: Danubia.

GEPPERT, D. (2010). Zwischen Nationalisierung und Internationalisierung. Europäische Auslandsberichterstattung um 1900 [Between Nationalization and Internationalization: European Foreign Reporting around 1900]. In DANIEL, U., and SCHILDT, A. (eds.), *Massenmedien im Europa des 20. Jahrhunderts* [Mass Media in 20th Century Europe], Cologne/Weimar/Vienna, Böhlau, pp. 203–228.

HEINELT, P. (2004). Portrait eines Schreibtischtäters. Franz Ronneberger (1913–1999) [Portrait of a Deskbound Criminal: Franz Ronneberger (1913–1999)]. In DUCHKOWITSCH, W., HAUSJELL, F., & SEMRAD, B. (eds.), *Die Spirale des Schweigens. Zum Umgang mit der nationalsozialistischen Zeitungswissenschaft* [The Coil of Silence: Approaches to National Socialist Journalism]. Münster: LIT, pp. 193–218.

JUNGHANNS, K., & HANITSCH, T. (2006). Deutsche Auslandskorrespondenten im Profil [German Foreign Correspondents in Profile]. *Medien & Kommunikationswissenschaft*, 55 (3). pp. 412–429.

KOBER, K. (2005). Österreich in den US-Amerikanischen Medien zwischen 1945 und 1955. Ein (Neben-)Schauplatz des Kalten Krieges [Austria in the US Media between 1945 and 1955. A (Side) Theater of the Cold War]. *Medienimpulse*. 50, pp. 40–44.

KOPPENSTEINER, J. (1975–1976). Das Bild Österreichs in amerikanischen Nachrichtenmagazinen [The Image of Austria in American News Magazines]. *Zeitgeschichte*. 3 (5), pp. 129–139.

KURTH, P. (1990). *All American Cassandra. The Life of Dorothy Thompson*. Boston: Little Brown.

LUGERT, A. C. (1974). *Auslandskorrespondenten im internationalen Kommunikationssystem* [Foreign Correspondents and the International Communication System]. München: Pullach bei.

MC LOUGHIN, B., LEIDINGER, H., and MORITZ, V. (2009). *Kommunismus in Österreich. 1918–1938* [Communism in Austria, 1918–1938]. Innsbruck/Vienna/Bozen: Studien-Verlag.

MERLE, P. (2013). City of Lights? The Waning Elitism of US Correspondents in Paris between 1998 and 2010. *International Communication Gazette*. March (75), pp. 153–173.

PIRKER, P. (2012). *Subversion deutscher Herrschaft. Der britische Kriegsgeheimdienst SOE und Österreich. Eine transnationale Analyse der subversiven britischen Politik im (Exil-) Widerstand und Partisanenkampf gegen die NS-Herrschaft in Zentraleuropa* [Subversion of German Rule. The British Wartime SOE Intelligence Service and Austria. A Transnational Analysis of Subversive British Policies in the (Exile) Resistance and Guerrilla Warfare against the Nazi Regime in Central Europe]. Göttingen: V&R unipress.

RENNEBERG, V. (2009). *Auslandskorrespondenten im globalen Zeitalter. Herausforderungen der modernen TV Auslandberichterstattung* [Foreign Correspondents in the Global Age. Challenges of Modern TV Reporting]. Wiesbaden: VS.

RUMPLER, H. & URBANISTCH, P. (eds.). (2006). *Die Habsburgermonarchie 1848–1918. Band VIII: Politische Öffentlichkeit und Zivilgesellschaft. 2. Teilband: Die Presse als Faktor der politischen Mobilisierung* [The Habsburg Monarchy 1848–1918, Vol. VIII: Public Policy and Civil Society. 2nd Part: The Press as a Factor in Political Mobilization]. Vienna: Verlag der Österreichische Akademie der Wissenschaften.

SCHREIBERHUBER, H. (2010) Der Osten ist 'rosa', aber immer noch 'in' [The East is 'Pink', but still 'In']. *Der Österreichische Journalist*. 8+9, pp. 76–77.

2 Foreign Correspondents in Belgium

Brussels Correspondents' Struggle to Make the Important Interesting

Georgios Terzis and Gareth Harding

INTRODUCTION

Journalists follow power and money. Brussels has both. Along with Washington, D.C., it is the other capital of global power. It is the headquarters of the European Union—the world's biggest economic power, aid donor, and trading bloc with a budget of over €140 billion a year. It is also the seat of NATO, the most powerful military club on the planet. However, this chapter will focus on coverage of the EU, rather than NATO or Belgium, inasmuch as this is the primary focus of the vast majority of Brussels-based correspondents.

The EU is growing—in both size and powers. Just two decades ago, it had 12 members; now it has 28, with another half a dozen Balkan states set to join in the future. It has also gained extraordinary new powers. At the start of the 1990s, the EU was still little more than a glorified free trade club. Since then it has amassed many of the competencies associated with nation states—a central bank, common currency and interest rates for Eurozone members, greater leverage over all members' economic policies, and the goal of forging a common foreign and security policy (McCormick, 2013).

As the Union's powers and members have grown, so has the size of the Brussels press corps. In 1976, when the then European Economic Community had nine members and few tangible powers, only 259 journalists were accredited to the European institutions (Raeymaeckers, Cosijn, & Deprez, 2007). By 1987, after the entry of Greece, Portugal, and Spain and the signing of the Single European Act—the first major treaty change since the foundation of the club three decades earlier—there were 480 accredited journalists.

Another leap forward occurred in the early 1990s with the signing of the Maastricht Treaty—which ushered in the single currency and made the EU a global actor. In 1991, the year in which the landmark treaty was signed, 520 journalists were accredited to the European institution. By 1995, this figure had increased to 783 (Raeymaeckers, Cosijn & Deprez, 2007).

The EU press corps witnessed further growth in the late 1990s and early 21st century as a dozen mainly former communist countries negotiated membership. By the time 10 of these states joined on May 1, 2004, 929 journalists were accredited to the EU. Since then, despite the addition of three more members—Bulgaria and Romania in 2007 and Croatia in 2013—and notwithstanding the EU's increase of powers with the Lisbon Treaty, there has been only a small rise in the number of accredited journalists. The enlargement process may have slowed down and plans to create a United States of Europe shelved, but the economic crisis that has gripped the EU—and in particular the Eurozone—since 2009 has proved a boon to journalists who once struggled to convince editors that Brussels mattered.

Indeed, recent figures show that contrary to many press reports of an 'incredible shrinking EU press corps' (Rennie, 2010; Castle, 2010), the number of accredited journalists in Brussels has gone up slightly since the start of the crisis—from 962 in April 2009 to 1,022 in September 2013, based on European Commission figures. By contrast, 1,550 foreign journalists were accredited in Washington, D.C., in 2010 (Castle, 2010) and 'over 1,700' in the United Kingdom, according to the Foreign Press Association and the data provided in Chapter 27, on the UK, in this volume.

There are several reasons for the levelling off in correspondent numbers. Firstly, newsrooms across Europe—where most of the Brussels-based correspondents come from—have been shedding staff since the mid-1990s due to the economic crisis, the falling revenue streams, and the costs of maintaining expensive bureaus abroad that stretch cash-strapped media organizations. Secondly, the number of foreign correspondents is declining because the time devoted to international news by traditional media drops (Moore, 2010). Thirdly, many of the journalists from Central and Eastern

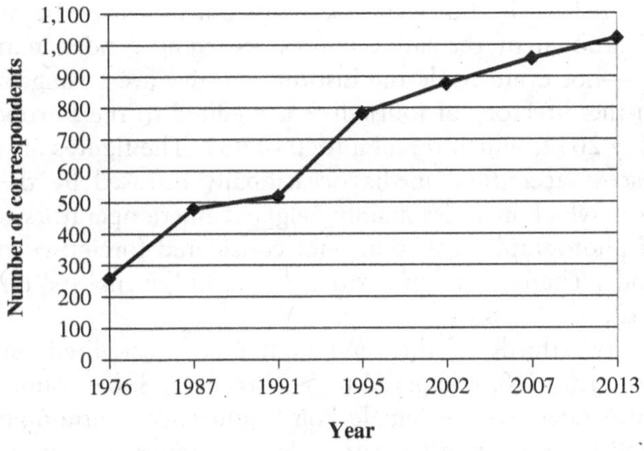

Figure 2.1 Evolution of the Brussels press corps.

Europe who came to Brussels to cover their countries' accession to the EU went home after those states joined.

Numbers are not the only thing to have changed over the last two decades. In the beginning of the 1990s, French was the only language allowed in the pressroom, and most European Commission documents were written in the language of Molière. Now English is the EU's lingua franca with over 90 per cent of documents drafted in that language. Frédéric Bouchard, Brussels Bureau Chief of the pan-European TV station *Euronews*, describes the Brussels journalistic scene as an 'English-dominated news bubble.'

WHO ARE THE FOREIGN CORRESPONDENTS IN BRUSSELS?

This section provides demographic information on the foreign correspondents (FCs) in Brussels, including their experience, education, languages they speak, and the organizations they work for. Much of the data come from the official directory of journalists accredited to the European institutions in 2012. It also comes from interviews with 15 journalists and a survey of Brussels-based correspondents conducted by the authors in November and December 2013. In total, we mailed our survey to over 300 journalists and received replies from 35. Our respondents came from Northern and Southern, Eastern and Western Europe, from EU member states, from future member states, and from non-European countries. They worked as employees and freelancers for TV and radio stations, news agencies, and newspapers, online outfits and newsletters. Roughly two-thirds were male and one-third female. We believe this to be a diverse, if somewhat small, sample.

According to the latest figures in September 2013, 1,022 journalists were accredited to the European Commission. However, because there is yet no breakdown of the latest figures regarding gender, nationality, or media type—not even inside the institutions—we are basing our research on data in the directory of journalists accredited to the European institutions in May 2012, which reveal a total of 952. The figures are lower than another list of accredited media occasionally diffused by the European Commission, which includes mainly Belgian camera operators, sound engineers, and photographers who are not considered foreign correspondents for this study. There were approximately 1,230 'journalists' on this list in March 2012.

Roughly two-thirds of the total number of accredited journalists in Brussels are men (610, compared to 342 women). Some countries do well in terms of gender parity—female Polish journalists outnumber males by 10 to 3, and there is almost parity in Spain. However, in most countries, reporting the EU is a very male pastime. All 11 Turkish correspondents are male, and only 20 journalists in Brussels are female, compared to 56 male. There are more than twice as many male as female correspondents from France and the United Kingdom. 'It's a boy's club,' says one senior female journalist, pointing to the fact that the European Commissioner for Economic Affairs, Olli Rehn, held background briefings in the Commission's sauna, where clothes were very much optional, until 2012. Only male journalists attended.

Despite the large total size of the Brussels press corps, being a correspondent in the city can be a 'lonely' job because the number of reporters per media outlet is very small. Out of the 952 accredited journalists in May 2012—we excluded the 33 freelancers whose media was not specified—358 worked alone, 72 worked for media organizations with one other journalist, 27 with two other journalists, and 10 with 3 others. Fourteen media outlets had a bureau with five to nine people (including the German broadcaster ZDF, the *Financial Times* [*FT*], and *Parliament Magazine*), and 10 had 10–14 correspondents (including *Deutsche Presse Agency*, *Deutsche Welle*, *Bloomberg*, *Agence Europe*, *Euronews*, *European Voice*, French wire AFP, and the regulatory affairs newsletter *MLex*). Only five news organizations had more than 15 journalists—German TV station ARD (24), Chinese news agency *Xinhua* (23), Brussels-based EU newsletter *Europolitics* (*Europolitique*) (20), *Thomson Reuters* (17), and the BBC (15).

In May, the 2,012 accredited journalists represented media with headquarters in 67 different countries. By comparison, in 1983, 43 countries were represented (Raeymaeckers, Cosijn, & Deprez, 2007). The largest contingents worked for German media (113, or 12.1 per cent of the total) and

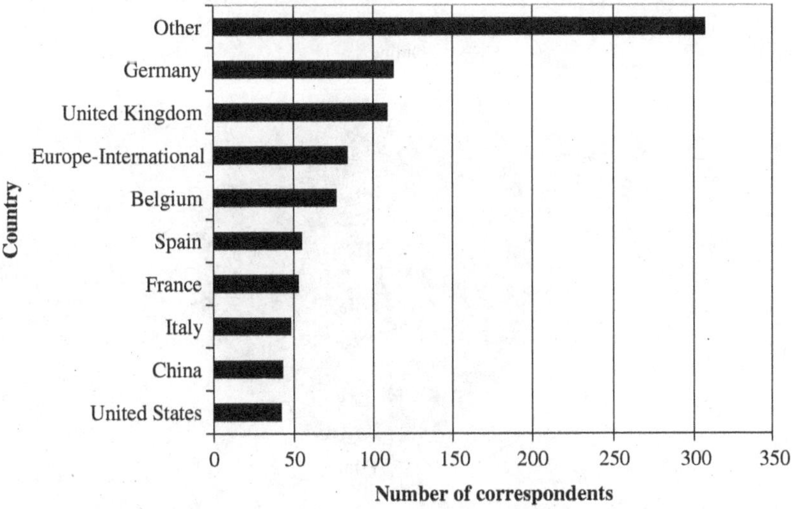

Figure 2.2 Country of origin of the media organizations represented in Brussels.

UK media (109, or 10.7 per cent of the total), followed by Belgian media (77), Spanish (55), French (53), Italian (48), and US media (42). Together, journalists from these seven countries make up over half the Brussels press corps. There were also 85 accredited journalists working for 'European-International' media, mainly for EU specialist outlets such as *European Voice* and *Agence Europe*.

Compared to 2004, the number of journalists working for German media has dropped from 131 to 113, Italian media from 65 to 48, and Dutch from 37 to 25. However, there has been a spectacular rise in the number of Chinese journalists—43 in 2012 compared to 17 in 2004—largely due to the *Xinhua* news agency's having its European hub in Brussels. There has also been a slight rise in the number of journalists working for UK media—109 from 97 in 2004. However, this figure is not due to a renewed passion for reporting the EU by British press but to the fact that pan-European and international media outlets like *EurActiv*, *MLex*, and *Parliament Magazine* have their company headquarters in the UK.

In terms of the breakdown per media type, since 2004 there has been a modest shift away from print journalists and toward online media, news agencies, and audiovisual (radio and TV). Ten years ago, almost half the accredited journalists in Brussels worked in print. In May 2012, just over 40 per cent did. The fall in print journalists numbers has been compensated for by rises in journalists working for news agencies (up from 22.4 per cent to 25.6 per cent), online only (from 2.4 per cent to 5.3 per cent), and television (26.3 per cent to 28.8 per cent).

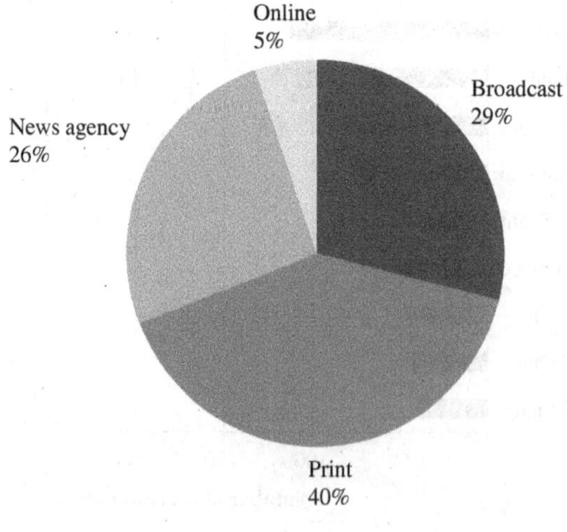

Figure 2.3 Breakdown by media type in Brussels (freelance journalists not included).

Brussels is seen as a major posting for international correspondents. Therefore it attracts experienced journalists, not rookies. In our survey, the average number of years worked as a journalist was 17.5, including 11 as a foreign correspondent. The correspondents we surveyed were also highly educated. Twenty-six of the 35 who replied to our questionnaire had a master's degree or higher, with just over half having studied journalism or communications in university. Twenty-nine of the 35 said they spoke at least one other language in addition to French and English. Asked what primary working language they used when conducting interviews and doing research in Brussels, all but five of the correspondents surveyed said 'English.'

WHAT MAKES IT ONTO THE REPORTING AGENDA?

There is a popular belief that Brussels-based correspondents struggle to convince their editors of the importance of the EU. In an episode of the Danish TV series *Borgen*, fictional editor-in-chief Michael Laugesen fumes to his journalists, 'No one wants to read about the EU. It's too complicated and unsexy.' However, our survey showed that most journalists had no problems getting their work broadcast or printed. Asked whether it was difficult to get stories about the EU into the media they worked for, 15 said 'not at all,' seven 'not much' and only two 'to a great extent.' Of the 7.5 stories pitched, on average, by our respondents every week, 91 per cent were published or broadcast. Only eight agreed that their audience cared less about international news than in the past.

Thematic polarization was noted by Nosty in 1997 and is still seen today. A report by the Association of European Journalists and Fundesco found that stories on the economy were nine times more common than those on society and culture. This trend continues today, with most of the 'Brussels' or EU affairs news reported abroad revolving around economics.

Asked what types of stories they mostly cover in our survey, all but two of the journalists said 'politics', and all but four mentioned 'economics'. This is unsurprising due to the fact that the EU was originally created as an economic project and today many countries share a common currency. Since the crisis began, journalists have had to pay even more attention to financial, economic, and monetary issues, which—given the gravity of the problems facing the Eurozone—has helped propel their stories on to the front pages. Asked whether it had become easier to get stories published since the start of the Eurozone crisis, 23 of the 35 journalists who answered our survey said 'to a large extent' or 'to a great extent'.

'Why do you go into journalism?' asks *Financial Times* (*FT*) Bureau Chief Peter Spiegel. 'To cover a big, globally important story. And that's here with this crisis. I spent seven years covering two wars and now I'm covering a story that is even more important than the wars are, because no one is covering Iraq and Afghanistan any more.'

Spiegel says that with the financial crisis he is now 'pushing on an open door' to get articles on the EU in his paper—although the *FT* does specialize in stories about international finance. He notes that when the UK budget was announced in March 2013, the top six stories on the *FT*'s website were about the Cyprus banking crisis and the seventh was about the British budget. 'There is no more core story to the *FT* than the euro crisis', he says—an opinion shared by other correspondents interviewed by the authors.

WHEN DOES SOMETHING BECOME NEWS FOR A BRUSSELS FOREIGN CORRESPONDENT?

EU news is 'hardly visible during routine periods and modestly visible during key events' (de Vreese, 2005, p. 116). Such news triggers include summits, elections, and one-off events like the introduction of the euro or the accession of a new member state like Croatia in July 2013. For Brussels-based journalists, this means that some periods of the year are busier than others. Much of the rhythm is dictated by the calendar of the country holding the rotating presidency of the EU. The six-month period starts slowly, picks up around the middle with the first summit, and then reaches a peak at the end of the presidency with the second meeting of EU leaders. In December 2002, at the end of the Danish presidency of the EU, 2,500 journalists were accredited to a summit in Copenhagen (Raeymaeckers, Cosijn, & Deprez, 2007). The numbers have fallen since 2002—when European Councils started to take place only in Brussels—although the frequency of summits has increased because EU leaders have held emergency meetings to deal with the Eurozone crisis. According to figures from the Council of the EU, between 1,211 and 1,788 journalists attended the nine summits that took place between October 2011 and December 2013.

The European Parliament agenda also influences the pace of journalists' work. Many Brussels-based correspondents head to Strasbourg every month to attend the monthly plenary session of the legislative body. However, live-streaming of parliament meetings on *EuroparlTV*—the assembly's own web TV station—and on the EU broadcasting arm *Europe by Satellite* means that fewer and fewer reporters make the trek to Alsace.

The slow and often repetitive legislative cycle is both an advantage and disadvantage for EU reporters. On the plus side, if a journalist 'misses' a story once, he or she will have plenty of other opportunities to report it as it churns its way through the lawmaking machine. On the other hand, Brussels-based journalists complain that it is hard to convince editors to report on stories that return year after year, whether to tax carbon or ban genetically modified crops. Alvaro Lopez Guicoechea, correspondent for Spanish broadcaster *TVE* in Brussels, says: 'The Spanish Parliament—like the British, French or Belgian national parliaments—debates an issue then it gets approved or rejected and that's about it. There is a beginning, middle and end to the story. The European Parliament is more bureaucratic, things are not so straightforward. This makes it more complicated and incomprehensible for citizens'.

WHERE DO THE STORIES COME FROM?

In terms of who pitches a story on an EU issue, the overwhelming majority of the respondents to our survey said they were responsible for proposing the subject from Brussels. Twenty-five replied 'always me' or 'most of the time me' to the question 'who initiates the topic of your stories?' with a further 10 saying, '50 per cent me, 50 per cent editor.'

Most of the news and events that Brussels-based correspondents propose to their editors and report on 'take place in a radius of less than one kilometre around the Rond Point Schuman,' a square in the heart of the EU district, explains *Frankfurter Allgemeine Zeitung*'s correspondent Michael Stabenow (Terzis, 2008, p. 358). Within close proximity to the Commissioners, MEPs, the Council of the EU and their staff, Brussels correspondents can also find NGOs, industry federations and many other journalists.

There are three principal sources of news in Brussels. First, the EU institutions themselves disseminate most EU-related news via press conferences and press releases (Siapera, 2004). During the 2000s, the European Commission also developed an 'Espresso' email system to alert journalists on upcoming events or to push press releases. Text messages and tweets are also being used more frequently to keep journalists up to date (Terzis, 2008).

As the EU's members and powers have increased, so has the number of its press officers and spokespersons. In the mid-2000s, the European Commission had 27 spokespersons and over 50 press assistants (Raeymaeckers, Cosijn, & Deprez, 2007). There are now 124 people in the Commission's Spokespersons Service, including 41 official spokespeople for different policy areas. In addition, each of the Commission's 33 directorate generals has a press officer or spokesperson, as do their offices in EU member states. The European Parliament has one spokesperson and 31 press officers in Brussels and a further 30 in member states. The Council of the European Union has 15 press officers. In addition, almost all the 139 EU delegations around the world, managed by the European External Action Service, have spokespeople or press officers.

Many journalists say that official communication from the EU institutions often lacks the 'essence of the story' and that personal contacts are much more useful and informative sources (De Bens, Paulussen, & Raeymaeckers, 2006, p. 14). The *FT*'s Peter Spiegel says: 'The most frustrating thing is the institutions don't know how to communicate what they decide. After an agreement [in the European Council], you get 28 different versions of the same event. Explaining what the deal was is seen as an afterthought.' Ann Cahill, president of the Foreign Press Association (API), says that although the EU's communications efforts have become more sophisticated, there is a tendency to sell stories instead of providing information. 'I can find my own information,' says the Irish journalist. 'I need information, not spin.'

Nevertheless, accredited journalists who are based in Brussels often attend the midday briefing of the European Commission, which often generates ideas for articles. Asked to choose three sources that provide the most story leads, 28 out of the 35 respondents in our survey mentioned 'government officials'; 11 ranked embassies and 10 other national sources. However, only one rated MEPs.

Second, informal contacts are vital sources of information. In a study carried out by APCO in 2008, journalists mentioned 'personal contacts' as their most important source for story ideas, with 85 per cent mentioning them as 'often important' or 'very important' (APCO, 2008). Brussels-based journalists often call on MEPs, parliamentary assistants, and Commission staff for anonymous quotes, which are found in almost a quarter of UK news reports (Price, 2010). They will also make full use of contacts in the plethora of lobby firms, think tanks, and nongovernmental organizations in Brussels. In our survey, 17 correspondents ranked NGOs as one of their top three news sources—second after government officials.

Third, Brussels correspondents rely on information services and international newspapers as additional sources. Although repeated Eurostat polls show that for the general public, television is by far the most important media for keeping up with EU affairs, Brussels-based journalists rely more heavily on newspapers to keep abreast of European news. Asked to name their primary news outlet, a third said newspapers, 22 per cent news agencies, 17 per cent online, and 13 per cent TV (APCO, 2008). Brussels-based news outlets such as *EUObserver*, *Europolitics*, and *EurActiv* are often mined for leads (De Bens, Paulussen, & Raeymaeckers, 2006).

The most influential media sources of information about the EU for Brussels-based journalists are European and international media, focusing on foreign policy and business. When asked in our survey how often they use such media—which includes publications like the *Financial Times*, the *Economist*, and *European Voice*, as well as online portals such as *EurActiv* and the TV station *Euronews*—19 out of 35 said 'every day,' while eight replied 'several times a week'. In addition, journalists use national newspapers—for example, *Le Monde*, *FAZ*, *The Guardian*, or *Libération*—to understand what is happening in other member states (De Bens, Paulussen, & Raeymaeckers, 2006).

Of these media, the *Financial Times* has a stable position as the leading news source—partly because of the quality of its reporting but also due to English increasingly outweighing French in EU circles, according to Stabenow (Terzis, 2008). In a poll of over 100 Brussels-based journalists,

46 per cent said they got their EU news from the *FT*—by far the largest percentage (APCO, 2008). In another survey conducted by the consultancy ComRes ZN in 2012, 65 per cent of correspondents said they read the *FT* at least once a week—higher than any other media outlet (ComRes ZN, 2012).

The second most influential media among journalists is *EUObserver*, a Brussels-based online news source. A third of correspondents said they got their EU news from the *EUObserver* in the APCO poll, while 53 per cent said they read news on the site at least once a week, according to the ComRes ZN survey. *EurActiv*, another Brussels-based online news source, was also read by 53 per cent of journalists, according to the same survey. However, only 23 per cent of APCO respondents said they got their EU news from the same source. Other influential media sources among Brussels-based journalists include *The Economist*, *European Voice*—a weekly newspaper about EU affairs—and the *BBC*.

In terms of which media are influential in Brussels outside the press corps, the *BBC* was cited as the most popular source of information in the ComRes ZN survey. It was the number one medium among MEPs (joint first place with the *FT*), MEPs' assistants, Parliament staff (together with *FT*), Commission staff, permanent representations, and EU agencies. The *Financial Times* topped the poll among EU representatives of business and think tanks, with the *Economist* also proving highly popular with Parliament staff, think tanks and academics. *EurActiv* was the most widely read among European trade associations and EU-level NGOs.

In terms of online presence, *Libération* correspondent Jean Quatremer—who writes only in French—has the most followers on Twitter among Brussels-based journalists. In late December 2013, the veteran journalist had 53,528 followers, compared to 22,947 for *BBC* Bureau Chief Gavin Hewitt and 21,908 for the *FT*'s Peter Spiegel. Quatremer's blog 'Les coulisses de Bruxelles' is highly influential and read by many decision-makers in the Brussels bubble. However, a survey into the most influential bloggers in Brussels carried out in 2010 by Waggener Edstrom, placed Gavin Hewitt's 'Europe' blog number one and the *FT* 'Brussels Blog' number two. The only EU official to make the top ten was EU Commission Vice President Neelie Kroes. A major flaw with this survey, however, was that it looked only at English-speaking bloggers.

Asked how often they use fellow correspondents as sources of information, out of 35 respondents in our survey, 10 said every day and 11 several times a week. Former *Radio France International* correspondent, Dominique Thierry says that some of his best 'professional friends' worked for the public radios of other member states. 'Many of the stories that we covered were the same, and because our audiences were very similar in all characteristics but the nationality we cooperated wonderfully since there was no direct competition. Sometimes you could have translated the story from the other language to French and it could have been almost as if I did it myself.'

HOW BRUSSELS NEWS IS FORMULATED IN DIFFERENT FRAMES

Despite much talk of the emergence of a European public sphere in academic circles, there is little evidence of it in the media. The most ambitious attempt to create a genuinely European media product—*The European*, which claimed to be 'Europe's first national newspaper'—lasted only from 1991 to 1998. Most other 'European' media are either aimed at the Brussels bubble—*EurActiv*, *EUObserver*, and *European Voice*—or are heavily subsidized by the EU (for example, *Euronews*).

There is also little enthusiasm for the idea among Brussels-based journalists, even those working for pan-European media. 'There is no European public sphere. It is a mirage,' says *Euronews*'s Bouchard. 'That is why it is necessary to bring European news to different TV audiences in national spheres, in national languages.'

Studies of foreign news coverage have found that geographic proximity and national links with politics and economics dictate the majority of news coverage, and regionalism and politics are the major factors influencing international news reporting, no matter which region of the world is examined (Stevenson, 1997; Koponen, 2003; Obijiofor & Hanusch, 2011). Therefore, it is unsurprising that De Bens, Paulussen, and Raeymaeckers (2006, p. 15) state, 'EU news must have national relevance or it must be directly relevant to the public.'

While EU news was first put on the 'international' pages, the growing importance of the *acquis communitaire* in the everyday lives of European citizens has shifted EU news reporting into 'national news' (Terzis, 2008). The tendency for media to present EU affairs with a national slant is usually most visible after a European Council meeting. At these summits of EU leaders, each story aims to show the public what their leaders did in their member state's interest (Kevin, 2003).

Editors have generally determined that the most relevant EU themes to the public include a link with domestic politics, security or daily life (de Vreese, 2005; Preston, 2009; Obijiofor & Hanusch, 2011). Journalists we spoke to tended to agree that audiences are more interested in the effects of legislation rather than in how it is arrived at. 'When we have an interesting story you have to show the human side,' says *Euronews*' Bouchard. 'When someone watches a European story, they have to be able to think it affects them.'

Indeed, audiences are perceived to be more receptive to EU news when it fits into domestic 'talking points' (Preston, 2009; Mörä, 2009). National media are also more likely to have an understanding of cultural traditions and 'social responsibility' within the nation state frame of reference (Mörä, 2009) and therefore an understanding on how to 'translate' EU news for a local audience.

How national media report EU news is largely dependent on public opinion in the countries where the media outlets are based. For example, polls show that Spaniards, Irish, Belgians, and Italians are traditionally positive about the EU, and this is reflected in their media—although less so since the start of the Eurozone crisis. However, in countries where EU support is more lukewarm—the UK, Denmark, Czech Republic, and Sweden—media are more hostile. When comparing the tone of reporting on the EU, British news sources are most likely to take a strong Eurosceptic approach (Preston, 2009). Indeed, reporting of the EU in the UK press is often so negative—and inaccurate—that the European Commission's Representation in London has set up a 'Euromyths' page on its website to counter tabloid scare stories.

Indeed, an overarching trend is that EU reporting often involves stories of negativity or conflict—domestic or international—which are almost always guaranteed to make it into the news (de Vreese, 2005; Franks, 2005; Joye, 2010; Obijiofor & Hanusch, 2011). 'The European Parliament is a classic example of no news is good news. Every time they do something they don't get enough coverage and attention. But whenever there is a scandal about their expenses or their privileges everyone is hurrying to write about them. I don't think that's fair,' said Irina Cristina, Foreign Editor of the Romanian daily *Jurnalul National.*

Perhaps echoing the public's growing disillusionment with the European project, Brussels-based journalists have also become more critical of the EU. Recalling his first year in Brussels in 2002, former *Financial Times* Bureau Chief George Parker recalls 'the bizarre sensation of being heckled by fellow journalists for asking irksome questions about the sacking of the EU's chief accountant,' (Parker, 2007a). Parker believes the 2004 enlargement of the Union 'brought a new generation of spiky, lively journalists from central and eastern Europe' and as a result the press corps, 'once dominated by veterans who viewed themselves as the praetorian guard of the federalist project is now younger, more pragmatic and more diverse' (Parker 2007b). One of those 'veterans', *Frankfurter Allgemeine Zeitung* correspondent Michael Stabenow, admits that in the 1980s and early 1990s, the Brussels press corps was more 'Europhile' (Terzis, 2008).

The Internet and the entry of Finland and Sweden in 1995—with their long traditions of transparency—have helped open up vast swathes of EU information to the public. This has made information easier to get for journalists—but also for everyone else. As a result, rewriting institutional press releases is no longer enough, says Jean Quatremer, the long-time correspondent of French newspaper *Libération.* 'More and more journalists in Brussels are reproducing the European Commission's own communication, and you can find the same story in 20 different newspapers. We are killing our work ourselves by doing this. We need to bring an expertise that you can't get in the capitals' (*EurActiv*, 2010).

Bouchard agrees: 'We do too much factual reporting and not enough analysis, commentary and investigation.' But as the EU's powers—and members—have increased, so has the workload of Brussels-based journalists. There are, quite simply, more countries to cover, more leaders' names to remember, and more issues on the table than a decade ago. 'We suffer from an overdose of information from the institutions,' says Bouchard, 'which drowns journalists.'

In addition to covering the European Union, most Brussels-based journalists are also expected to report on NATO proceedings and events in Belgium, the Netherlands, Luxembourg, and other European countries. In our survey, 22 said they covered Belgium, and 10 reported on affairs in the Benelux countries and other member states.

Another change is that journalists no longer have the luxury of working for one medium, with most required to blog and tweet about EU news and many expected to produce video and audio material in addition to written copy. One consequence of this is that reporters skim the surface of the news and have little time for research. According to a study carried out by the public affairs agency APCO in 2008, 39 per cent said they spent only one to two hours researching a story (APCO, 2008).

Another consequence of journalists having so little time and having to cover so much is a dearth of investigative reporting. With the notable exception of the resignation of President Jacques Santer and his college of European Commissioners in 1999—provoked by a series of media reports of cronyism and mismanagement—real scoops are rare in Brussels and investigative reporting almost nonexistent. 'There is a lot of money sloshing around here that nobody tracks,' says the *FT*'s Spiegel.

CONCLUSION

Brussels is not a dangerous posting, and there is no shortage of news to report. Nevertheless, correspondents we spoke with confirmed that covering the EU is a challenging task. Journalists have to grapple with explaining a political organization that has no national equivalent, fiendishly difficult decision-making procedures, and constantly changing aims, rules, and membership.

The main challenge correspondents face is 'trying to make "complex", bureaucratic or highly political issues interesting and relevant for a largely uninterested public' (Preston, 2009, p. 154; Kevin, 2003; de Vreese, 2005; Raeymaeckers, Cosijn, & Deprez, 2007; Price, 2010). Some scholars—and journalists—(Price, 2010) state that EU affairs are 'not sexy' and are therefore difficult to sell to their audience. 'The EU struggles to get media coverage because a lot of the work that goes on in this town comes under the heading of boring but important or important but boring,' says David Rennie, a former correspondent for *The Economist* in Brussels. He continues:

> European politicians often complain that we don't cover them the way we do national politicians. But look at some of the things national politicians get covered for: hospitals, schools, whether taxes will go

> up or down or your soldiers will go abroad to kill and fight and die. Well the EU doesn't really control those things. What it does control is issues like competition, consumer and environmental policy . . . rather technical and dull dossiers.

However, Mark Mardell, a former *BBC* bureau chief in Brussels, takes a different approach. 'I genuinely don't find Brussels boring. There are plenty of good stories here.' The key to making European stories interesting, he says, is to get out of the self-styled EU capital: 'What's worked best is not, or rarely, telling the story from Brussels . . . Tell the story from the individual countries and the point of view of the people affected by the EU. That's what's it's all about in the end.'

Another challenge for Brussels-based reporters is that the European Union is about finding consensus between 28 often divergent national viewpoints. But journalism is largely about conflict among ideas, states, and peoples. This can make life difficult for Brussels correspondents. 'In Westminster politics they are looking for a clash, to shout at each other,' says the *BBC*'s Mardell. 'You go to an EU summit and they are looking for consensus. Even if they have a bitter row it's pretty unusual they will come out and start condemning each other. That's not what it's about. It's about finding solutions. Does that make for great TV? No. But it's something we have to live with. It's a fact.'

In addition, there are few recognizable personalities for audiences to latch on to. For example, President of the European Council Herman Van Rompuy might be well known in his native Belgium, but it is unlikely he would be mobbed on the streets of Belfast, Bilbao, or Bucharest. 'Politics is very much about personalities. If you have a politician who doesn't speak your language and who doesn't feature in your media on a daily basis you are not going to know them and the media will lose interest,' said former MEP Michiel Van Hulten.

Other obstacles noted by Brussels-based journalists include deciphering and translating EU jargon into everyday speech, overcoming editors' resistance to stories about the Union, and reporting on an organization that is increasing in size and powers with smaller budgets and newsrooms.

Many journalists covering the EU are dissatisfied with both the quantity and quality of reporting on European affairs. Forty-eight per cent of the journalists questioned in a major survey on European journalism in 2011 described the quality of EU-related news as 'insufficient' (Economisti Associati, 2011). Christine Ockrent, the French former TV news anchor and head of *France 24*, says the level of ignorance about the EU is partly the fault of the media. 'If the media was more enterprising, more ambitious, and if they didn't hold their nose and say "Oh, everyone thinks Europe's boring so let's do nothing," we wouldn't be in this state'.

Despite these challenges, however, correspondents we interviewed and who responded to our survey remained relatively upbeat about their work.

The vast majority (21 out of 35) said they were not or not at all afraid their employers would cut their posts in the next two to three years to save costs. The same number disagreed with the premise that 'parachute journalists'—reporters who fly into a place to report an event and then leave again—are increasingly replacing traditional correspondents.

The feeling that the EU matters and that Brussels is still a major posting for foreign correspondents is also borne out by our analysis of accredited journalist numbers. There is little doubt that the economic crisis—and the existential crisis of the Eurozone—has helped keep the Brussels correspondents numbers relatively buoyant while media organizations have been shedding foreign correspondents elsewhere. For the fact remains that as long as Brussels maintains the headquarters of the European Union and NATO and these organizations keep growing in size and importance, then correspondents will continue flocking to the Belgian and EU capital.

REFERENCES

APCO. (2008). Media Relations and Europe—From the Journalist's Perspective. *Journalists at Your Service*. May.

CASTLE, S. (2010). As the E.U. Does More, Fewer Tell about It. *The New York Times* [Online]. 21 March.

ComRes ZN. (2012). *EU Social Media Monitor* [Online]. 10 May. Available from http://digitalpulse.eu/EUDigitalPulse_2012.pdf.

DE BENS, E., PAULUSSEN, S., & RAEYMAECKERS, K. (2006). The Case of Belgium. In AIM Research Consortium (ed.). *Understanding the Logic of EU Reporting in Mass Media: Analysis of EU Media Coverage and Interviews in Editorial Offices in Europe*. Bochum/Freiburg: Projekt Verlag, pp. 11–20.

DE VREESE, C.H. (2005). *Framing Europe: Television News and European Integration*. Amsterdam: Het Spinhuis.

Economisti Associati (2011). *Feasibility Study for the Preparatory Action 'Erasmus for Journalists' Part 2—Statistical Review*. Available from http://bit.ly/1rdgwt2.

EURACTIV. (2010). Brussels Press Corps 'Shrinking', Journalists Say. *EurActiv* [Online]. 22 March.

FRANKS, S. (2005). Lacking a Clear Narrative: Foreign Reporting after the Cold War. *The Political Quarterly*. 76 (1). pp. 91–101.

HESS, S. (1996). International News & Foreign Correspondents. Washington, DC: Brookings Institution.

JOYE, S. (2010). Around the World in 8 Pages? A Longitudinal Analysis of International News Coverage in Flemish Newspapers (1986–2006). Available from http://bit.ly/1eZtkkM.

KEVIN, D. (2003). *Europe in the Media: A Comparison of Reporting, Representation, and Rhetoric in National Media Systems in Europe*. London: Lawrence Erlbaum.

KOPONEN, J. (2003). The Structure of Foreign News Revisited. In MALMELIN, N. (ed.), *The Science of Mediation and Caring. Communicational Viewpoints of Society, Culture and Citizenship*. Helsinki: Helsingin yliopisto. pp. 144–166.

MCCORMICK, J. (2013). *Why Europe Matters: The Case for the European Union*. Palgrave Macmillan.

MOORE, M. (2010). *Shrinking World—The Decline of International Reporting in the British Press*. London: Media Standards Trust.

MÖRÄ, T. (2009). The European Union and Ideals of the Public Sphere. In SALOVAARA-MORING, I. (ed.), *Manufacturing Europe: Spaces of Democracy, Diversity and Communication*. Göteborg: Nordicom. pp. 81–96.
NOSTY, B.D. (1997). The European Union in the Press: Results of the Research. In ÁLVAREZ, C.L., & SCHWARTZ, P. (eds.). *The European Union in the Media: 1996*. Madrid: Fundesco. pp. 19–119.
OBIJIOFOR, L., & HANUSCH, F. (2011). *Journalism across Cultures: An Introduction*. London/New York: Palgrave Macmillan.
PARKER, G. (2007a). The Best Job in Journalism. *The Bulletin* [Online]. 6 September.
———. (2007b). Despatched from Brussels. *E!Sharp* [Online]. October.
PRESTON, P. (2009). 'Where's Europe?' Emergent Post-National News Cultures. In PRESTON, P. (ed.), *Making the News: Journalism and News Cultures in Europe*. London/New York: Routledge. pp. 144–161.
PRICE, J. (2010). A Tale of Two Cultures: A Comparison of EU News Reporting by Brussels-Based and National-Based Journalists. In VALENTINI, C., & NESTI, G. (eds.), *Public Communication in the European Union: History, Perspectives and Challenges*. Newcastle upon Tyne, UK: Cambridge Scholars Publishing. pp. 217–236.
RAEYMAECKERS, K., COSIJN, L., & DEPREZ, A., (2007). Reporting the European Union. *Journalism Practice*. 1 (1). pp. 102–119.
REESE, S.D., Rutigliano, L., Hyun, K., & Jeong, J. (2006). Mapping the Blogsphere: Professional and Citizen-Based Media in the Global News Arena [Online]. Available from http://bit.ly/PpMX9C.
RENNIE, D. (2010). The Incredible Shrinking EU Press Corps. *The Economist* [Online]. 15 March. Available from http://econ.st/1haEqSN.
SIAPERA, E. (2004). EU Correspondents in Brussels: Between Europe and the Nation-state. In HERRMANN, R.K., RISSE, T., & BREWER, M.B. (eds.), *Transnational Identities: Becoming European in the EU*. Lanham, MD/Oxford: Rowman & Littlefield, pp. 129–157.
STEVENSON, R.L. (1997). Remapping the World [Online]. Available from http://bit.ly/1haEwtT.
TERZIS, G. (2008). The EU Correspondent. *Journalism*. 9, pp. 537–550.
WAGGENER EDSTROM (2010). *Brussels Blogger Study* 2010. Available at www.jonworth.eu/downloads/Influen ce-Index-Report.pdf.

INTERVIEWS

1. Peter Spiegel, Brussels bureau chief, *Financial Times*. Interviewed May 2013.
2. Frédéric Bouchard, Brussels bureau chief, *Euronews*. Interviewed May 2013.
3. Ann Cahill, President, Brussels Foreign Press Association (API). Interviewed May 2013.
4. Jean Quatremer, Brussels correspondent, *Libération*. Interviewed April 2009.
5. Mark Mardell, Brussels bureau chief, *BBC*. Interviewed April 2009.
6. Irina Cristina, foreign editor, *Jurnalul National*. Interviewed April 2009.
7. David Rennie, EU correspondent, *The Economist*. Interviewed April 2009.

8. Michiel Van Hulten, former Dutch MEP. Interviewed April 2009.
9. Alvaro Lopez Guicoechea, Brussels correspondent, TVE. Interviewed April 2009.
10. Christine Ockrent, former director, *France 24*. Interviewed April 2009.
11. Michael Stabenow—Brussels correspondent, *Frankfurter Allgemeine Zeitung*. Interviewed 2007.
12. Dominique Thierry—ex-Brussels correspondent, *Radio France*. Interviewed June 2013.
13. Alexandros Koronakis—editor-in-chief, *New Europe*. Interviewed June 2010.
14. Vagelis Demiris, Brussels correspondent, Greek News Agency and Cypriot State TV. Interviewed April 2013.
15. Giuseppe Zaffuto, former Brussels correspondent, *La Repubblica*, and director of programmes at European Journalism Centre. Interviewed September 2012.

3 Foreign Correspondents in Bulgaria

News from the Eastern Frontier of the European Union

Lulivera Krusteva

INTRODUCTION

The media's interest in Bulgaria is due, first and foremost, to the geopolitical position of the country on the Balkan peninsula and in Southeastern Europe as a frontier of the European Union to the east and secondly to the fact that, since 2007, it is a comparatively new member of the European Union.

The interest of foreign media in Bulgaria dates back to the 19th century, with the investigative reports of American journalist Januarius Aloysius McGahan, a correspondent of the London newspaper, *Daily News*, during the April Uprising and the Russian–Turkish War. He was an ardent advocate of the Bulgarian national cause. Yet with the exception of individual dispatches, there have not been any more detailed publications about the role of foreign correspondents (FCs) in Bulgaria since. The literature quoted in this chapter is associated with the specificity of the individual problems mentioned in the course of the analysis, most of all those related to methodology and the different approaches to newsworthiness.

The oldest correspondents' office in Bulgaria is that of *Agence France Presse* (*AFP*), founded in 1945. The second oldest offices are those of *TASS* and *Xinhua*, and the most recent is where representatives of the Romanian *AGERPRES News Agency* work.

Today the curiosity of journalists in Bulgaria is provoked by the fact that, on the one hand, they know very little about the country and that, on the other, critical remarks about some processes in the country have been targeted at Bulgaria since it joined the EU. Bulgaria is frequently mentioned in the reports of the EU concerning the level of corruption, criminal offences, and nonreformed judicial system. Lastly, the 'older EU member states' fear that Bulgaria will import poverty, criminal offences, and corruption from the former Eastern Bloc, or that the workforce of Bulgaria and Romania will threaten the free movement of job seekers within the framework of the EU.

All these reasons account for the interest of foreign correspondents in Bulgaria, which figures in the EU reports with both positive and negative assessments. As a result, the nature of the journalists' interest in the country bears the imprint of this black-or-white polarity: interest is provoked, on the one hand, by a number of social problems holding back the development of the country and, on the other, by Bulgaria's remarkable natural and cultural sights, folklore, and beautiful nature.

With the exception of the end of the 20th century (the 1985–1990 period when the communist regime decided to give Christian names to people from Turkish origin), Bulgaria has never been such an object of interest as it has been since it joined the EU in 2007, particularly after the terrorist act against Israeli tourists in Bourgass in 2012.

THE WORK OF A FOREIGN CORRESPONDENT

The major differences between the foreign correspondents and the local media can be grouped along the following three major parameters:[1]

1. The journalist's idea about newsworthiness, that is, what type of news should be the focus of attention, with regard to its duration, size, novelty, predictability, continuity, relevance in terms of cultural proximity, nonambiguity, reference to elite persons and nations, and negativity (Montgomery, 1995; Reuters, 2008; De Maeseneer, 1978)
2. Their specific professional abilities and competence
3. Their awareness of the privileges they enjoy, their sense of independence, greater freedom and lack of limitations

Concerning the first parameter, it seems that the foreign correspondents working in Bulgaria try to find the news in all spheres of social, economic, and institutional policies, which inevitably leads to a variety of news stories. While for the journalists representing the local media the major parameter of newsworthiness seems to be 'negativity' (Krusteva, 2007, 2011; Lengauer, Esser, & Berganza, 2011).

The second major area is associated with the high professionalism of the foreign correspondents, which involves not only their specific sense and ability of finding the newsworthy event and thus avoiding what is less significant, but also their ability to write the story in the most attractive way. On the basis of their answers, we can also declare that the foreign correspondents have the command of a minimum of two foreign languages, enabling them to write their materials directly in French, English, or German.[2] They also have a deep interest in world politics and are open to other cultures; they have a sense of proportion and are always ready to look for a balance between different views.

The third area is associated with the greater political and economic independence that the foreign correspondents enjoy, because they are not hard-pressed by the same financial problems and self-censorship that typifies local journalists who are dependent on the economic interests of the owners of the media they work for. As a result of this, firstly, foreign correspondents can have access to all types of information from all types of institutions, and, secondly, they have an unlimited freedom to choose the topic, the approach to the problem, and the form of the text (newspaper article, Website, or a TV/radio program), that is, they are independent of 'a direct purchase of influence', which the experts in the field define as 'dark, under-the-counter media economy' (Association of European Journalists, 2011).

The data from the interviews suggest that two-thirds of their materials are published in parallel over three or four major media (i.e., as newspaper articles, Website materials, radio or TV programmes).

WHO ARE THE FOREIGN CORRESPONDENTS IN BULGARIA?

The methodology used here is based mainly on the questionnaire made for this book by the project partners, as well as on the basis of the content analysis method taking care of the foreign correspondents materials in terms of six quantitative and six qualitative indices. The data gathering is based on inquiries held with 54 journalists. The remaining 17 declined answering some of the questions (for example, about their marital status, the salary they receive, etc.). Interviews have been taken from about 30 of them, who have given answers to most of the 46 questions prepared by the project partners.

Information gathered in 2013 shows that Bulgaria has 37 correspondents' bureaus belonging to 48 foreign media. They include 19 news agencies (six of them international and 13 national); 10 print media (eight newspapers and two journals); and 14 radio and TV channels, as well as five online. The media is staffed by 71 accredited correspondents, who can be divided into 59 journalists, nine photo-reporters, and three camera operators. Fifty-four of the foreign correspondents are Bulgarians by nationality; the remaining are four Chinese, three Russians, three Arabs, two Germans, and a single Ukrainian, Italian, Spaniard, Estonian, and Austrian. Considering the news media that employ the 71 journalists, the interviews reveal the following data: 34 correspondents work for news agencies, 15 for broadcast media, 12 for print media, and 10 for online media. Countries with the largest number of foreign correspondents in Bulgaria include Germany (17 FCs), followed by the United States and Canada (13 combined), Turkey (9 FCs), China and France (6 each), and Spain and Russia (3 each).

All the foreigners—with the exception of two—speak Bulgarian. They do not have any problems with the language, nor do they have any with the local institutions. There is an obvious preference to having Bulgarians for correspondents representing foreign media because of the prevailing opinion that they are expected to have better inside information.

Men outnumber women in this profession: there are 51 males correspondents compared to 20 female. Yet women manage the offices of the largest global agencies in Bulgaria, for example *AFP*, *Xinhua*, and *Reuters*. With regard to age, the oldest correspondent is about 65, and the youngest is 26. The average age is 47.

Almost all the correspondents have an average of 15 to 20 years of professional experience as foreign correspondents. The person with the longest professional experience of 29 years is the manager of the Sofia bureau of the *AFP*, whereas the one with the shortest practice is that of *ITAR-TASS* (only five years). Most are professionals with a good command of English, German, or French. Each of the correspondents, apart from his or her mother tongue (the A-language), has a command of at least one foreign language (the B-language) and can also use another foreign language (a C-language). Fifty-two of the correspondents know English, with the second Western language being German, followed by French and Spanish. Also, a number of correspondents have graduated from social science institutes and have worked as translators but have later received the qualification of correspondents.

THE CORRESPONDENTS' OFFICES IN SOFIA

The present head of the *Agence France Presse* bureau in Sofia has been working there since 1995. Annually, the agency publishes over 365 stories about Bulgaria. Currently, four people work for the *Agence France Presse* bureau in Sofia (two journalists and two photo-reporters). From the remaining world-renowned agencies, one should mention the following: *Reuters* (with three reporters, two camera operators, and one TV operator), and *Associated Press*—with one correspondent and three photo-reporters. *Reuters* and the *Xinhua State Chinese Agency*, with five correspondents each, have the largest bureaus. The bureau of *Xinhua* in Bulgaria was founded in 1956, seven years after the establishment of diplomatic relations. Four journalists work for *Anadolu Agency* and as many for *Zaman* (a weekly that comes out on paper and has online versions in Bulgarian and Turkish). The bureau of the EU inside the Balkans, based recently in Zagreb, (Croatia) has three correspondents. The *Spanish State Information Agency EFE*, *DPA*, the *European Pressphoto Agency* (*EPA*), the *Polish Press Agency*, the Ukrainian *Ukrinform*, the *Cosmos Photo Agency*, the Greek *ATA* and *ITAR-TASS* have one correspondent each. The representative of the Russian news agency is the youngest FC, but in spite of this, he is given the chance to represent an agency with a long standing in Bulgaria.

The largest number of correspondents work for various German media, for example, the *ARD* Radio and TV, the *DPA Agency*, and *Deutsche Welle*. Eight people work for *ARD* Radio and TV and four for *Deutsche*

Welle (two of them are permanent correspondents, while the other two are columnists who write on demand about special events.)

Two Arabs work for the *BBC* and for a newspaper issued in the United Kingdom in English. There is also a separate office in Sofia representing the *Economic Daily*, published in Peking in English, covering issues related to industry, finance, and economy.

An interesting fact worth mentioning about the foreign correspondents in Bulgaria is that some of them have lived in Bulgaria for quite a long time and write also for the Bulgarian media.

Most of the correspondents work for the public media. Very few work for the commercial media. Most correspondents said they do not have political prejudices: they declare that they have liberal views and are members of the IFJ /EFJ (International Federation of Journalists/European Federation of Journalists).

THE MEDIA AGENDA: WHEN DOES AN EVENT BECOME NEWSWORTHY?

The public agenda of the correspondents is predetermined by the fact that Bulgaria is a more recent member of the EU. Most of the correspondents do their work following the guidelines of their own media; some of these guidelines are public, and others are only for internal use. The main selection comes at the initiative of the correspondent, not of the editor of the regional bureau, as the answers of 28 of the interviewed FCs suggested. In only one case was a top news item for Bulgaria (a bus crash with 18 casualties) proclaimed as irrelevant and unimportant for EU readers and viewers. No set number of dispatches are required to be sent to the respective bureaus. It depends on the nature of the events and the topical discussion going on at the moment. When there are important events, dispatches are sent everyday (for example, during the gas crisis in 2009).

On the basis of content analysis, one can sort out about 10 thematic spheres of interest. The first is associated with the political events and everything relevant to the EC and the EU (the level of criminal offences, the efficiency of the judicial system, the perspectives of Bulgaria in terms of its euro integration, etc.). Comparatively frequent is the discussion of economic topics and the quality of life. Lower down the interest scale are internal political scandals. All types of elections get good coverage, and the same goes for all issues associated with the energy projects. Economic topics that receive the most coverage are issues related to the generation of energy, followed by issues concerning finances (as 38 of the interviewed FCs suggested).

Concerning the number of covered events, the answers of the FCs suggest that the minimum is five stories per week while the maximum is 20. Apart from that, 70 per cent of them maintain that the stories they send are based on three sources at least (the highest percentage goes to government sources or other official national sources).

It is also worth mentioning that leading topics for both *Xinhua* and *Agence France Presse* are sports competitions, cultural events, and archaeological findings, as well as Bulgaria's problems about joining the Schengen area, foreign investments, and unemployment. The foreign correspondents provide good coverage of the demographic collapse, the aging of the population, the pension reform, and the state of the health services. In 2011, Bulgaria was the first country in which the census was taken via the Internet: 42 per cent of the population sent in their data via their computers, an event that also attracted the interest of the journalists. Additionally, the interest of some news agencies and more particularly—of the German media—in gypsy issues and the ethnic conflicts in general still persists.

In general, whether an issue is covered by a foreign correspondent is determined by the professional criteria of newsworthiness of the specific media and the personal preferences of the correspondent. The predominant part of the FCs suggest that they follow a special internal instruction concerning their professional criteria, which mainly follow the rules suggested by *Reuters*, *Agence France Presse*, and *Deutsche Welle*.

FOREIGN CORRESPONDENTS' BUREAUS

The decision to cover an event is taken by the FCs themselves. Stories may also be assigned if the head of the regional bureau has noticed an interesting topic published by either the local or other international media. In most of the cases, however, it is the task of a correspondent to arrange the events in terms of their importance and thus offer them to the regional bureau. Like their Bulgarian colleagues, foreign correspondents attend all the important press conferences organized officially by institutions, and their task is to select what they deem important and send it to the respective regional bureau.

Because the practice shows that the coverage of any topic is based on the collection of a variety of opinions coming from different types of people (politicians, experts in the political sciences, economists, experts in the respective field, ordinary people, or students), by interviewing them or organizing polls. For example, 50 per cent of those interviewed suggest that they obtain their information via direct participation in the event and not on the basis of materials from the local press. With regard to genre, the prevailing types are the reportage and the commentary; more rare is the profile type of writing, which is used mostly during elections for president or for local or the European Parliament. Also very rare is the practice of conducting interviews.

There is an obvious tendency for the correspondents to cover the events that would be interesting for their audience, and it is very rare that their output is a 'retold-and-translated' version of the ones published in the local press. The greatest number of publications express the correspondents' personal views; that is, they are commentaries, with a critical touch and negative analysis when necessary. There is a preference for materials created on the spot.

Two or three times in a year (usually before important events like elections), a journalist from the regional bureau arrives in Bulgaria. The most recent visit of this type took place before the elections on 23 October of 2011. There was a similar journalists' raid before the parliamentary elections in May 2013.

With regard to the problems the foreign correspondents may have in their work with the various institutions, the greatest obstacle is the difficulty they have in gaining access to the higher levels of power. Another problem the foreign correspondents may have is the organization of polls and inquiries; most Bulgarians are reluctant to speak to foreigners because of the prejudices and fears inherited from the communist past.

SOURCES OF THE MEDIA TOPICS AND HOW NEWS ITEMS ARE FORMULATED

The major sources for foreign correspondents are official press conferences, information from unofficial sources, and firsthand experiences from their travels in the country, as the answers of 33 FCs suggest. Of the utmost importance are the personal professional contacts of the correspondents, the social importance of these sources, and the regularity of using them.

The club of foreign journalists renders a great help to the foreign correspondents because it creates opportunities for organizing meetings and contacts with a variety of people. The club was set up some 30 years ago following an idea given by the Bulgarian Union of Journalists. The role of the club of foreign journalists is to help them in creating contacts and the organization of meetings with important people.

The relationships among the foreign correspondents can be defined as marked by professional cooperation and lack of unfair competition. There is a professional positive competition among the various correspondent bureaus, with strict observation of the journalists' ethical norms. The materials of *Deutsche Welle* and *Agence France Presse* are most frequently reprinted in the Bulgarian information sites. The commentaries of *Deutsche Welle* on different social problems are in high demand.

A rather interesting phenomenon is the local media reprinting what the foreign correspondents write, and not vice versa, as was the practice before the democratic changes in Bulgaria, when the foreign correspondents relied mainly on the local media, using the latter's materials and tailoring them according to the demands of the agency they represented.

CONCLUSION

The major conclusion to be drawn from this discussion is that the journalistic interest in Bulgaria will not decrease: on the contrary, it will continue to develop. On this basis, we can make the suggestion that the prospects for the future development of the correspondents' bureaus in Bulgaria's capital city will have to be looked for in the mastering and introduction of new media formats and spheres—in terms of range of coverage, contents, and further technological development, particularly by making greater use of TV and broadcasting formats. These new professional challenges are, on the one hand, due to the economic crisis in the Eurozone and, on the other, to a number of processes taking place in Bulgaria and holding back its development as a Balkan country and as a neighbour of new members of the EU.

By way of conclusion, we must underline the effort of the FCs to objectively and correctly inform the world about what is happening in the Eastern frontier of the EU. There are also sufficient data to suggest that there is a tendency toward a wider coverage of the variety of events taking place in the country, a variety that shows a more critical and more objective coverage of events than what is offered by the local media.

NOTES

1. The suggestions are based on data from my previous research (Krusteva, 2007, p. 127; Krusteva, 2012, p. 90) and the interviews with the FCs in Sofia.
2. A large percentage of the foreign correspondents are philology graduates as well.

REFERENCES

ASSOCIATION OF EUROPEAN JOURNALISTS (AEJ-Bulgaria). (2011). Results of the report Media and Democracy [Online]. Available from http://bit.ly/QfNrjq.

BERELSON, B. (1952). *Content Analysis in Communication Research*. Glencoe, IL: Free Press.

DE MAESENEER, P. (1978). Here's the News: A Radio News Manual. New York: UNESCO, pp. 22–34.

GITLIN, T. (1980). *The Whole World Is Watching: Mass Media in the Making and Unmaking of the New Left*. London: University of California Press.

GOFFMAN, E. (1974). *Frame Analysis: An Essay on the Organization of Experience*. London: Harper & Row.

KRUSTEVA L. (2011). *Bulgarian-Style EU Funding in the Mirror of National Press*. In *The Dialogue with the Other: Balkan Dimensions of European Identity*. Sofia: St. Kliment Ohridski University Press, pp. 381–389.

KRUSTEVA, L. (2012). *Медийна безконфликтност* [Conflict-Free Media] [in Bulgarian]. Sofia: Avangard, pp. 90–97.

KRUSTEVA, L. (2007). *Медийна ценностна пирамида* [Media Value Pyramid] [in Bulgarian]. Sofia: Gorex Press, pp. 125–134.

LENGAUER, G., ESSER, F., & BERGANZA, R. (2011). Negativity in Political News: A Review of Concepts, Operationalizations and Key Findings. *Journalism*. 13 (2), pp. 179–202.

MONTGOMERY, M. (1995). *Mass Media* [lectures]. Sofia: Sofia University, British and American Studies Department.

Reuters. (2008). *Handbook of Journalism*. Available from http://handbook.reuters.com/.

4 Foreign Correspondents in Cyprus
Tacking between Tradition and Change

Vaia Doudaki and Dimitra L. Milioni

INTRODUCTION

Academic literature on foreign correspondents revolves mainly around an ontological approach, attempting to paint a concrete image of who these people are (profiles), what they are doing (practices), and according to which professional logics (news values). This inquiry emerges as particularly important in times of radical change in the model of foreign correspondence, which is taking place in the 21st century, from a traditional single model to a plurality of types still under formation. The present study focuses mostly on foreign correspondents' profiles and practices, seeking to establish whether this shift has actually been implemented in countries of the periphery, such as Cyprus.

The traditional model of the foreign correspondent is often associated with quality reporting, namely the accurate, broad, and in-depth coverage of international news, which guarantees a well-informed public opinion (Hamilton & Jenner, 2004; Kester, 2010). Against this evaluative basis, recent radical changes in the nature of foreign correspondence, activated by economic imperatives and empowered by new technologies (Hamilton & Jenner, 2004; Sambrook, 2010), are lamented as potentially undermining quality journalism. For example, the decrease in the numbers of permanent foreign correspondents is considered to be accompanied by superficial factual news, produced mostly by news agencies, at the expense of in-depth background reporting and analysis based on eyewitness reporting in physical terms (Kester, 2010). In particular, the so-called parachute practice in journalism, where reporters are sent in to cover events temporarily, 'often produces news without context,' which is 'intrinsically misleading' (Perlmutter & Hamilton, 2007, p. 161).

However, from a different starting point, Hamilton and Jenner argue that the traditional idea of a foreign correspondent is 'anachronistic and static' because the systemic changes in the production of international news have given rise to new media environments, where new types of correspondents are flourishing (2004, p. 302). In this context, the emerging models for reporting foreign affairs are not always valued as threatening to the established one but are also seen as welcome alternatives. For example, the rise in freelance and specialist journalism is considered a response to an 'increasingly interconnected world' that needs a more contextualized journalism and a different style of reporting with more candid reflection, informality, and vividness (Sambrook, 2010, pp. 28–29). Also, 'parachute journalism' is viewed as allowing for more reporters on the ground that bring to the news the fresh perspective of the outsider (Hamilton & Jenner, 2004, p. 313).

IDENTITY OF THE STUDY

The Republic of Cyprus, a small Mediterranean country at the southeastern border of Europe, is a typical example of the periphery that does not attract international interest unless there is a major news event. For quite a while, that event was the so-called Cyprus Problem, the unresolved 40-year-long geographical and ethnic division of the island, consisting of the internationally recognized Republic of Cyprus in the south, hosting the Greek-Cypriot community, and the Turkish-held unilaterally declared Turkish Republic of Northern Cyprus in the north, recognized only by Turkey, hosting the Turkish-Cypriot community.[1]

Lately, the stagnation over any potential solution to the conflict and the outbreak of the financial crisis have shifted attention away from the Cyprus Problem and towards the economic deadlock of the country. According to the correspondents interviewed: 'Now it comes second due to the financial crisis, but it is also true that there are no developments' (FC10).[2] Similarly: 'We cover the Cyprus problem, but since June [2012] there is no Cyprus Problem' (FC11).

The present study looks at the profiles and working practices (Hamilton & Jenner, 2004; Hannerz, 2004) of foreign correspondents in Cyprus, together with the societal, organizational, and technological factors that shape, facilitate, or impede their work (Wu & Hamilton, 2004; Perlmutter & Hamilton, 2007). For this purpose, quantitative and qualitative data were collected through in-depth interviews, guided by a questionnaire designed for this book, which was enriched to allow for qualitative data gathering. The foreign correspondent is defined as a professional journalist reporting news for a host country to one or more news organizations, under various working contracts (e.g., full-time, part-time, freelancer).

Because no research on foreign correspondence on the island has been conducted before, it is extremely difficult to have a clear idea of the situation in the past. In any case, there have been references of correspondents based on Cyprus from the 1950s. *Associated Press* already had a correspondent (Alex Efthivoulou) in 1955. Also, the award-winning news photographer and journalist, Bob Egby, was based on the island working as a freelancer during the 1950s, covering the Cypriot independence struggle against the British. During the 1970s and especially the 1980s, Cyprus became a hub for foreign correspondents reporting on the Mediterranean region and the Middle East: in 1987, 110 foreign media from 32 countries were officially represented in Cyprus (18 news agencies, one photo agency, 20 radio/TV stations, 51 newspapers, and 20 magazines).[3]

The Press and Information Office (PIO) accreditation data for 2013 include 54 news agency journalists, 27 radio/TV journalists, 47 print journalists, and three Internet journalists, from 25 countries. Nevertheless, most news agency correspondents work for *Agence France Presse* (*AFP*), which has its regional hub in Cyprus, covering the Middle East.[4] Also, when contacted, many of the journalists—it was found—had either left or stopped working as correspondents, especially those from Greece. In addition, several journalists work for more than one medium type. Taking these into consideration, and after cross-checking with the PIO and individual correspondents, it is estimated that their actual number is 30–35. The total number of foreign correspondents interviewed during the period of December 2012–February 2013 was 18 (the rest either did not agree to the interview or were inaccessible).

PROFILE OF FOREIGN CORRESPONDENTS IN CYPRUS

Human Geography and Experience

Of the estimated 33 foreign correspondents working in Cyprus, most are male, middle-aged, European, married with children, and graduates of higher education but not of communication or journalism studies (see Table 4.1).

Regarding their language skills, eight correspondents speak two languages (their native language and English), six speak three languages, and four speak from four to six languages. While eight correspondents speak Greek well and can use it adequately to perform the main journalistic tasks, seven do not speak Greek at all. Unavoidably, issues involving access to sources, and firsthand experience from everyday life and local culture, are raised. However, only one correspondent acknowledges not knowing the domestic language as a restraint limiting her or his access to information. Also, only one correspondent speaks Turkish, which may point to poor information gathering in the Turkish-Cypriot community. Practically, although the correspondents interviewed claimed covering the Turkish-Cypriot community 'when necessary,' almost none has developed sources there.

On average, the correspondents interviewed have 29 years of journalistic experience, ranging from 12 to 54 years. The majority have been working for more than 20 years (only five have been working for less). Similarly, they have been working as correspondents for 18 years, on average, ranging from two to 41 years (only four have worked for fewer than 10 years). As most of them can be regarded as highly experienced, it is expected that they are part of a strong journalistic and correspondent culture.

Table 4.1 Sociodemographics of foreign correspondents in Cyprus.

Variables	Number (%)
Gender	
Male	11 (61)
Female	7 (39)
Nationality	
Double (Cypriot-British/American/Australian)	4 (22)
Cypriot	2 (11)
British	2 (11)
Greek	2 (11)
Russian	1 (6)
German	1 (6)
Portuguese	1 (6)
Belarusian	1 (6)
Swedish	1 (6)
Polish	1 (6)
French	1 (6)
Chinese	1 (6)
*Age**	
31–44 years old	2 (11)
45–55 years old	7 (39)
>55 years old	8 (44)
Family status	
Single	1 (6)
Married/ in a relationship	15 (83)
Divorced/widowed	2 (11)
With children	15 (83)
With more than one child	13 (72)
Education	
No university degree	3 (17)
Bachelor's Degree	12 (67)
Journalism/ Communication studies	
At university level	4 (22)
Only took some courses	3 (17)
No studies at all	11 (61)
Income	
Up to 1,000 euros	3 (17)
1,000–4,000 euros	9 (50)
RF	6 (33)

**N* = 17

Note: Throughout the text, the total number of respondents (*N*) for each question may vary due to missing values (no answer).

Half of the correspondents interviewed have worked only in Cyprus. The other nine have worked in two to four countries. On average, they have been reporting from Cyprus for 18 years, ranging from one to 36 years (only four for fewer than 10 years). Having been stationed on the island for a long time, one might assume that they enjoy the privileges of an extended stay, like developed networks of sources, familiarization with the culture and everyday life, and a nuanced firsthand experience of the country (which might be tempered in the case of correspondents who do not speak Greek). This is why, on the other hand, the risk of assimilation in the norms of the country is lurking. In any case, the great majority of correspondents in Cyprus (80 per cent, $n = 15$) claim that they manage to stay detached.

Media Organizations and Coverage Geography

Sixteen of the news organizations for which the correspondents work have their headquarters in Europe, five in America (three of which are in the United States), and three in Asia. Africa is absent; so is Oceania. Furthermore, with the exception of Brazil, all the other countries are from the northern hemisphere. Greek-based media have the highest number of journalists (5 total) working in Cyprus. The dominance of Europe and the North, possibly connected to geographical and cultural proximity as well as the allocation of the main news organizations internationally, is apparent.

Although half of the correspondents interviewed cover only Cyprus, the rest cover additionally one or more countries in the greater area of Middle East and North Africa (Lebanon, Syria, Israel, Egypt, Jordan, Iran, Iraq, and Turkey).

Employment Status

Full time ($n = 7$) and freelancer ($n = 7$) are the two dominant types of employment for correspondents working in Cyprus (three work on part-time contracts, and one is a stringer). This duality can be seen as evidence of two different trends in foreign correspondence. On the one hand, the full-time correspondent may be representative of a traditional model of foreign correspondence (Cole & Hamilton, 2008; Morrison & Tumber, 1985), working for big and prestigious news organizations: among the full-timers interviewed, four work for print media and three for news agencies. On the other hand, the equally high number of freelancers may point to the strengthening of a model of foreign correspondence that is based on nonexclusive working relationships between the journalist and the organization. Regardless of the model, the employment status of correspondents is fickle, subject to frequent changes. Several correspondents stated that they started working full-time, moved to part–time, and are currently working as freelancers. Some of them are also working in other jobs to make a living and, being unable to support themselves, two are considering changing their profession.

Foreign correspondents based in Cyprus work for up to 14 news organizations. Only six work for one organization in their home countries (one in a newspaper and five in news agencies, of which four are full-timers, one is part-timer, and one is freelancer). Twelve correspondents work for print media, three for television, seven for radio, six for online media, and eight for news agencies (the Internet is used as a publishing platform for 15 correspondents). Four work also as domestic journalists (for Cypriot media) and (at least) two more used to work for Cypriot media in the past. According to Hamilton and Jenner's typology (2004), they are 'local foreign correspondents' (local reporters who work also for media abroad as correspondents), a model that is gaining ground because it combines budget savings with the opportunity for contextualized journalism, by giving voice to local journalists (Sambrook, 2010, p. 49).

CORRESPONDENTS' REPORTING AGENDAS AND SOURCES

Unsurprisingly, politics (n = 15) and economy (n = 13), with news about the financial crisis, the presidential elections, and the Cyprus Problem, were the areas that mostly attracted the correspondents' interest at the time of research. However, because they are the only journalists of their home media on the island, they are ready to cover all news of importance working largely as generalists. Five of them answered that they cover all the beats. Thus, it is possible that their personality and value systems have some effect on the representations of Cyprus reaching their audiences through the news they produce. At the same time, however, any personal bias is likely tempered in the case of news agencies inasmuch as their content usually does not reach the audience unprocessed.

The predominance of institutional sources is more than apparent because both official sources and/or other media are the sources of information that all correspondents stated considering as most important (see Table 4.2). The institutional-only nature of sources is clear in one response: 'Nowadays there are the news agencies. Every topic has a source, that is, if it is, for example, economy, it's the Ministry of Finance. If it is unemployment, it's the Ministry of Employment. For us the Cyprus News Agency is a big help that covers all news in Cyprus, meaning that there isn't any political or social news [that it doesn't cover]' (FC10). As correspondents and their organizations attribute high credibility on other established media as sources, their need to cross-check information already published there is reduced. This practice points to intermedia agenda-setting effects and to the enhanced (symbolic) power of elite media organizations in this interplay (Golan, 2006).

When other types of sources are mentioned, they are usually positioned at the end, not challenging the hierarchy of official sources: 'The main

Table 4.2 The importance of sources for foreign correspondents in Cyprus as starting points to begin investigating a story.

Source	Mean (*n* = 16)	Std. Dev	Times Mentioned
Government officials	1.4	1.4	10
Other official national sources	0.3	0.6	4
Think tanks	0.2	0.5	2
Social networks	0.2	0.7	1
Alternative outlets/citizen journalism	0.2	0.6	3
Coverage of national media in my host country	1.4	1.1	12
Members of the opposition	0.2	0.6	3
Official sources from embassies	0.1	0.3	2
Academics	0.2	0.6	3
Twitter	0.0	0.0	0
Lobbies	0.2	0.5	2
NGOs	0.1	0.2	1
News agencies	0.8	1.2	6
Blogs	0.1	0.3	2
Average citizens	0.2	0.5	2

Note: Respondents were asked to rank the three most important sources with numbers from 1 [least important] to 3 [most important]). Two respondents did not answer this question, one ranked six sources, and one noted the most important but did not rank them.

sources are the government, the political parties, the universities, several other services, state organisations, society itself, civil society' (FC11). The institutional notion on sources exists also for correspondents having a broader network of information channels, attributing importance to experts and other 'illuminati' of the news system: 'It would be news agencies, publications (online and paper), and also VIP individuals and commentators in the area of news and world events' (FC18).

Also, when both official and unofficial sources are mentioned, they are equally bureaucratic: 'The official information provided by the government or the political parties, or the state organisations and . . . unofficial sources that may also come from the government or parties but mostly from officers and staff, from people that have some knowledge on certain issues' (FC18).

Institutional sources dominate the coverage of the Cyprus Problem as well, even more than other issues. One correspondent justifying the exclusive use of official sources said, 'This is a very sensitive issue . . . Only official sources. No think tanks . . . nothing else . . . that's probabilities. Because we are writing what is going on, not the idea of what can be' (FC17).

Most correspondents feel that access to first-hand sources is relatively easy in Cyprus, both to government and business (even though access to business is esteemed as slightly more difficult), with an average of 3.1 (n = 15). Access to citizens is rated as even easier, with an average of 4.4 (n = 13) (on a scale from 1 for very difficult access to 5 for very open access).

Ease of access is related to the organization they work for. According to the correspondents, working for established media can be the ticket to privileged information (see also Morrison & Tumber, 1985). Also, access becomes easier over time, as they develop further their networks of sources. Nevertheless, in practice there is some distance between access and actual or valuable information: 'The fact that you have access does not always mean that you have access to your questions. You might get nice smiles, might get free coffee . . . [I]t doesn't mean that you have answers to all your questions' (FC12). Especially in the case of news on the Cyprus Problem, access to 'real' information often becomes a challenge. Lack of transparency and the confidentiality frame of much of the related information often leave the correspondents with not much more than statements: 'You have to deal with statements and not with information. There is confidentiality, there is the UN, . . . and you try really hard to get the information on what exactly is happening behind the closed doors where the leaders of the communities talk' (FC11).

CORRESPONDENTS' SOURCES OF INFLUENCE

Time limits, availability of newsgathering resources, and access to information that emerge as the prime sources of influence in the work of foreign correspondents are related directly to the practice of the journalistic profession (see Table 4.3).

Working within time limits is not a new phenomenon for journalists and correspondents but rather a basic component of their work. However, additional time-related pressures also emerge: 'The new concept of 24-hour news creates a new pressure that does not allow many times to do the work properly and with your sources cross-checked' (FC14).

When correspondents are asked about the main difficulties in covering Cyprus, they rate access to information or sources as the greatest, which can be 'access to specific information, being able to cross check facts and figures, get quick response to breaking stories' (FC3) or 'lack of information flow, especially when you get PIO press releases without really news in' (FC4). Also, as one correspondent mentioned, 'Sometimes I know of things happening and is very difficult to find hard data on it,' which is attributed to 'lack of transparency and lack of availability' (FC18).

Media laws and editorial policy are considered quite influential in foreign correspondents' work, with the latter, however, having largely accepted their restrained freedom within the organizations they work for, adapting

Table 4.3 Sources of influence for foreign correspondents in Cyprus.

Sources of Influence	Mean (n = 17)	Std. Dev.
Your personal values and beliefs	3.5	1.5
Your peers on the staff	2.3*	1.5
Your editorial supervisors and higher editors	2.9	1.8
The managers of your news organization	2.5	1.8
The owners of your news organization	2.5	1.7
Editorial policy	3.4	1.6
Advertising considerations	1.9*	1.4
Profit expectations	1.8	1.5
Audience research and data	2.7	1.6
Availability of newsgathering resources	3.7	1.4
Time limits	4.1	1.4
Your friends and family	1.4	0.9
Colleagues in other media	2.0	1.2
Feedback from the audience	2.2	1.4
Competing news organizations	2.3	1.4
Media laws and regulation	3.4	1.7
Information access	3.8	1.3
Censorship	1.7*	1.3
Government officials	1.5	0.9
Politicians	1.3	0.6
Pressure groups	1.5	0.9
Businesspeople	1.8	1.2
Public relations	1.9*	1.3
Relationships with news sources	3.0	1.7
The military, police and state security	1.1*	0.2

Notes:

(a) Respondents rated sources on a scale from 1 (no influence at all) to 5 (extremely influential).
(b) For questions marked with an asterisk (*), n = 16.

to the 'rules of the game' by self-compliance: 'We are all dependent people. I think all of us are fine personalities but we are living in a world where we are not independent. We all have boundaries from many sides, from the law, from employers, from people who read us, from people who we write about . . .' (FC9). The contradictions that arise due to the opposing forces of organizational control and the ideal of professional autonomy are eloquent: 'You cannot enter into conflict with the medium you work for. That is, I cannot publish something they don't want me to. But to force me to write something that is against my principles, I will not do it. I may do it anonymously because I have to make a living, but with my signature, never,' (FC10).

Third-person perceptions of influence—that is, not recognizing direct or strong influence on their work while recognizing it in their environment—are also spotted: 'When you are in a private organisation, you cannot ignore it [advertising]. This basically does not affect the reporter, it affects the management. That is, they might tell you "do not do it because this particular person is being advertised and I don't want to lose the funding sources that I have, for a story" (FC10).

CHANGES IN CORRESPONDENTS' STATUS

Job cuts and increasing coverage of foreign news by headquarters are the current trends within the profession that stand out (see Table 4.4). One would expect that the scores recorded in the correspondents' responses regarding the changes and challenges within the profession would be higher. Actually, quite often their opinions were divided (as can be seen by the high 'Std. Dev.' values in Table 4.4), resulting in lower averages, which might be connected to the fact that several correspondents reported being witnesses to these trends but do not experience them personally (yet).

Resource cuts have affected mostly salaries and budget for travelling. For some correspondents, the level of cuts is so high that they cannot live on the money they earn from correspondence alone: 'up to the point . . . I have to stop . . . well, I have to start looking for other kind of activities precisely to be able to survive because they couldn't pay anymore the travel and things alike . . .' (FC12).

Increasing coverage by headquarters is attributed to the use of news agencies and the Internet, 'which gives direct access to the television stations, radios and newspapers of the country where the correspondent works' (FC8). Of interest is the diversified use of sources, the employment of different sources and newsgathering channels for different purposes: 'First-hand information is no longer needed, as the headquarters take available information from the Internet or they take just the international agencies' news without even editing them' (FC15). Similarly: 'Very often the headquarters uses the Internet and agencies for news reports but the journalist is there for in-depth stories' (FC4). The facilities offered by the Internet have seemingly the potential to change or take over some of the tasks employed by the correspondents: 'They use the Internet, Google . . . collect data and then do a writing there by themselves. Without asking me to review. This is the trend' (FC13).

Maybe surprisingly, more correspondents do not feel increasing time pressure at all (n = 7, 50 per cent), in relation to those who do (n = 5, 36 per cent). When experienced, time pressure is related to demands for quicker reflexes and

Table 4.4 Changes in the working conditions of foreign correspondents in Cyprus.

Questions	Mean	Std. Dev.	*n*
Has your employer—according to your knowledge—cut down the number of posts for foreign correspondents within the last decade?	3.2	1.9	16
Are you afraid that your current post as foreign correspondent in Cyprus may be cut down by your employer within the next two or three years in order to save costs?	2.8	2.0	15
Have the resources available to do your job been cut down (working equipment, budget for travelling, etc.)?	2.6	1.7	14
Within your media organization, have parachute journalists increasingly replaced traditional correspondents?	2.3	1.8	16
Within your media organization, have local journalists abroad been employed instead of traditional correspondents?	2.2	1.7	16
Within your media organization, is foreign coverage increasingly covered by headquarters?	3.1	1.9	16
Within your media organization, are amateur-journalists/ bloggers/ representatives of NGOs increasingly used as replacements for traditional correspondents?	1.3	0.6	15
Do you feel increasing time pressure on your job?	2.6	1.8	14
Do you feel that the audience today cares less about international news than in the past?	2.9	1.6	14
Overall, from your experience, has the job of the foreign correspondent changed for the worse or for the better in recent years?[b]	2.9	1.5	15

Notes:

(a) Respondents answered using a scale of 1 (does not apply to my working environment at all) to 5 (describes current changes/my working situation very well).

(b) The scale used for this question ranges from 1 (has changed for the worse) to 5 (has changed for the better).

higher productivity. Within this vein, increased pressure of time stems from 'the need to minimize cost, [the demand for] more work in less time, [for] more production' (FC8).

In general, time pressure is linked with competition and can hardly be regarded separately. The fact that eight correspondents replied that competition does not affect their work or that competition does not exist (absence of excessive competition is documented in other studies as well, e.g., Cole & Hamilton, 2008, pp. 463–464) may partly explain the low levels of increasing time pressure experienced by a large number of correspondents. The correspondents in Cyprus, being the only ones from their media—and often from their countries—on the island, are not exposed to direct peer pressure and thus generally do not experience strong competition.

Correspondents recognize both positive and negative changes in foreign correspondence, focusing, however, more on the deteriorating forces within the profession. The positive changes are connected to the facilities and the potential offered by new technologies, mostly easy access to information (see also Wu & Hamilton, 2004, p. 526). The negative developments mentioned are connected to budget and remuneration cuts ('Owners are looking for low paid staff instead of looking for reputable journalists' [FC16]), to increased time pressure and the 24/7 practice ('The 24-hours news, the reduced time that does not allow and does not even request in-depth analysis' [FC14]), to unprofessionalism or amateurism, which is considered an indication of gradual deterioration of work quality, and to more superficial coverage ('They give less space to serious stories' [FC7]) (see also Cole & Hamilton, 2008, p. 528).

CONCLUDING REMARKS

Foreign correspondents based currently in Cyprus find themselves in a bipolar situation. On one hand, the traditional model of foreign correspondence, privileging full-time employment for legacy news organizations, namely news agencies and newspapers, appears still solid. On the other hand, the equally high number of freelancers, working for a large number of media, may point to a model of correspondence of nonpermanent and flexible working relationships between the journalist and the organization. The changing working status of several correspondents—from full-time, to part–time, and then to freelancer—together with the trend toward increasing job cuts and coverage from headquarters may be supporting evidence for the new model. At the same time, however, other novel types of correspondents, like 'parachutist journalists,' seem to be absent in Cyprus.[5] Of course, such correspondents are difficult to locate due to high mobility, but in any case the dominant model in Cyprus is that of the correspondent based on the island for long.

The present study provides indications that older and arising models of correspondence will continue to coexist in Cyprus, at least for a while. There is also evidence that in countries of the periphery that are not primary news originators, some models might not be of high relevance (e.g., 'parachutist'). In addition, any special conditions prevailing in a country may lead to the promotion of several types of correspondence over some others. For example, the long-lasting conflict on the island may not privilege the model of correspondents who fly over for only a few days to cover individual events.

ACKNOWLEDGEMENTS

The authors would like to thank the foreign correspondents interviewed for their valuable assistance in this research project and Dr. Christophoros Christophorou for his generous help.

NOTES

1. The present study focuses only on the Republic of Cyprus.
2. Each foreign correspondent (FC) interviewed was given an identification code number.
3. Source: Press and Information Office (1988). *Yearly Press and Information Office Report for 1987*. Nicosia [in Greek].
4. *AFP* has currently 40–50 journalists. Only one correspondent covers Cyprus specifically for the news agency, 'but they do have journalists that will cover the odd event if it's important', according to the correspondent of AFP. These journalists are not calculated in the estimation of correspondents covering Cyprus.
5. According to one correspondent, the media prefer to work with a 'cheap' correspondent based on the island because the travelling cost is high.

REFERENCES

COLE, J., & HAMILTON, J.M. (2008). The History of a Surviving Species. *Journalism Studies*. 9 (5), pp. 798–812.

GOLAN, G. (2006). Inter-Media Agenda Setting and Global News Coverage. *Journalism Studies*. 7 (2), pp. 323–333.

HAMILTON, M.J., & JENNER, E. (2004). Redefining Foreign Correspondence. *Journalism*. 5 (3), pp. 301–312.

HANNERZ, U. (2004). *Foreign News: Exploring the World of Foreign Correspondents*. Chicago: University of Chicago Press.

KESTER, B. (2010). The Art of Balancing. Foreign Correspondence in Non-democratic Countries: The Russian Case. *International Communication Gazette*. 72 (1), pp. 51–69.

MORRISON, D.E., & TUMBER, H. (1985). The Foreign Correspondent: Date-line London. *Media, Culture & Society*. 7, pp. 445–470.

PERLMUTTER, D.D., & HAMILTON, J.M. (eds.). (2007). *From Pigeons to News Portals: Foreign Reporting and the Challenge of New Technology*. Baton Rouge: Louisiana State University Press.

PRESS AND INFORMATION OFFICE (1988). *Yearly Press and Information Office Report for 1987*. Nicosia [in Greek].

SAMBROOK, R. (2010). *Are Foreign Correspondents Redundant? The Changing Face of International News*. Oxford: University of Oxford Press, Reuters Institute for the Study of Journalism.

WU, D.H., & HAMILTON, J. M. (2004). US Foreign Correspondents: Changes and Continuity at the Turn of the Century. *Gazette*. 66 (6), pp. 517–532.

5 Foreign Correspondents in the Czech Republic

Coping with Social Transition and Financial Crisis

Alice Němcová Tejkalová and Filip Láb

INTRODUCTION

Finding a foreign correspondent in the Czech Republic (CR) is quite difficult. Official registration for foreign correspondents is not required, and there are no clubs or professional organizations for foreign reporters. To map the situation here, we searched major European and world media sources for authors of articles concerning the CR. In addition, we utilized a list of accredited foreign journalists (accreditation is optional) that is published regularly on the websites of the Czech Ministry of Foreign Affairs.

The Czech Republic, being a small country in Central Europe, does not receive much international press. According to Chang's (1998) classification of countries in relationship to their newsworthiness, the CR is a 'peripheral' country. Many news values must be involved in order for a story about the CR to make it into the international media. For example, in the international version of the news magazine *Time*, Czech topics appeared only three times in 2011 and 2012. The stories covered the deaths of comic artist Zdeněk Miler, former president Václav Havel, and novelist Josef Škvorecký.

The situation was different in 1989 after the Velvet Revolution. Journalists from afar flocked to the CR. More articles were published in the foreign press, and TV news broadcasts increased. The country, guided through dramatic transition by a charismatic president, became 'trendy'. After a year or two and the establishment of 'normal' politics and political wrangling, attention began to fade. International interest rose slightly in 2009 when the CR presided over the European Union, and the Czech government collapsed.

WHO ARE THE FOREIGN CORRESPONDENTS IN THE CZECH REPUBLIC?

In light of our country's position on the sidelines of the international media, we were surprised to find 104 foreign correspondents actively working in the CR. We interviewed 14 of them and promised them anonymity.

According to the works of Willnat and Weaver (2003) and Hess (2005), the per capita figures for correspondents working in the United States are almost the same compared with the numbers we found in the CR. This is quite startling considering the size of the United States and its prominence on the world's stage.

Considering the total number of FCs, the top countries of origin of the media they report to include Germany (14 FCs), the United States (10 FCs), Russia (six FCs), China (five FCs), the UK (4 FCs), Serbia (3 FCs), and Armenia, Austria, Denmark, and France (2 each). There are 73 male and 31 female correspondents. Individual information on the number of foreign correspondents working for each type of medium was unavailable.

Recent studies (e.g., Hess [2005] or Hamilton & Jenner [2004]) suggest that demographics have shifted significantly among foreign correspondents in general. The number of native, ethnic, and women correspondents has grown markedly in recent years. In the case of the CR, this is partially true. The majority of foreign correspondents are white men, and among them are found many Czechs who work for the foreign media and audiences as '*foreign* foreign correspondents' (Hamilton & Jenner, 2004).

Few surveys have been conducted that focus specifically on foreign correspondents in the CR. A handful of completed graduate theses look at journalists working as foreign correspondents for the Czech media (e.g., Sedláčková, 2009), but reporters working here for international media have so far remained unstudied. In September 2012, a conference titled 'Czech Republic in Europe Watched by Foreign Correspondents' explored the opinions of three reporters (two of whom we interviewed) regarding the manner in which the CR is evaluated by their home countries and the media outlets for which they work (Brezinová, 2012). The history and presence of foreign correspondence in the former Czechoslovakia and in the Czech Republic were not so far properly scientifically studied and described.

Some correspondents work for large news agencies like *AFP*, *AP*, *BBC*, *Le Monde*, among others. Other reporters (often from the former Eastern Bloc and Russia) are affiliated with smaller, sometimes business-oriented media. The larger news agencies usually use '*foreign* foreign correspondents' or, according to information culled from our interviews, foreigners living in the CR in order to be close to a Czech spouse or partner.

A unique group of foreign reporters works for *Radio Free Europe/Radio Liberty*. The organization has two bureaus, one based in Washington. D.C., the other in Prague. According to its website, the organization's motto is, 'Free Media in Unfree Societies'. *Radio Free Europe* broadcasts to 21 countries in 28 languages. These journalists are not foreign correspondents in the sense covered by this book (they do not broadcast primarily about the CR), but they do work as foreign correspondents for their countries, and some of them develop stories that are connected with both the countries they are covering and the CR.

One of the central goals of our research has been to explore the personal background of foreign correspondents. We were interested in their experiences as foreign correspondents, as well as their journalistic experience in general. We focused primarily on their work routines: journalists were asked about their reporting agendas, the sorts of topics they cover, how events become foreign news, and what sources had influenced them. We also looked at trends in foreign correspondence as well as the impacts of the recent financial crisis.

METHODOLOGY

To reach the goals of our inquiry, we used a common standardized interview format, which was completed with open questions that took into account the idiosyncrasies of the Czech context (whether correspondents sense a changing social and political climate often discussed by the Czech media or even consider moving elsewhere). The interviews were conducted in the CR with correspondents from various countries (all of them were, according to the typology of Hamilton and Jenner [2004], 'traditional foreign correspondents' and 'foreign foreign correspondents' and from different media organizations between 1 August 2012 and 31 May 2013. Keeping in mind that our sample is quite small, our research indicates that three types of foreign correspondents are in the Czech Republic: foreign journalists, expats, and Czechs working for foreign media organizations. (The difficulties involved in getting relevant answers from large samples of foreign correspondents are mentioned in Willnat & Weaver [2003] and Hess [2005].)

The challenges inherent in conducting a census of foreign correspondents in the CR has been already described As explained, we found 104 foreign correspondents active in our country, which represents the sampling frame for our research. We contacted 89 of these, and in many cases we were ignored or refused. In the end, we conducted 14 interviews with journalists representing different types of media organizations and based in different countries.

Three of the interviewed correspondents were from Germany, our largest and most important neighbour. Two of them were Central and East Europeans (Polish and Bulgarian), three were Czechs working for foreign news companies, two were Russians, two were from France, and two from the United States. Their average age was 45, and only three of the respondents were women. This number reflects the tiny percentage of women foreign correspondents found within our country's population. Slightly more than half of the correspondents work as freelancers, and the rest work under a full-time contract. Four of the respondents belong to journalists' unions. Their overall level of education was quite high. Most journalists had graduated from a university (13): two had received a bachelor degree, eight a master's degree, and three a PhD. Five majored in journalism and communication studies.

Our foreign correspondents had worked as journalists for an average of 20.5 years and as FCs for 9.4 years. They had worked in the CR for an average of 7.2 years. Almost half of our sample group worked as FCs in other countries before they arrived in the CR. Before they began work as correspondents, they worked at various other positions in media organizations (e.g., editors, moderators, feature reporters), and they covered fields ranging from economics and foreign policy to cultural affairs and education.

Czech language skills are required to work as a foreign correspondent in the CR. Most of our interviewees were fluent in three to four languages (in all cases, Czech and English, then German [five], Russian [five], French [five], Italian [two], Bulgarian [one], Chinese [one], Romanian [one], and Polish [one]).

We interviewed two expats who have been living here since the beginning of the 1980s, and because this was during the communist era, we were interested in what brought them to our country. Both came in order to be with family members. 'I came to the Czech Republic because of my wife. I was employed at the Czech Radio since 1981. Later I received an offer from Polish radio to work as a correspondent,' said FC2.

We were interested in whether foreign correspondents had witnessed changes in the Czech political and social climate. On the one hand, they seemed optimistic about the improved professional standards of the Czech media landscape. At the same time, they tended to have a sceptical outlook on developments in the political and social areas.

Here are some examples culled from our interviews. 'Definitely, the disillusionment of unmet expectations after November 1989 has deepened. On the other hand, the media quality has risen' (FC8). 'There have been better conditions for reporting in the last 10 years. It is easier to get accreditations. But the social crisis has deepened, which will also show in upcoming elections' (FC7).

> There were euphoric years before and after the Velvet Revolution until the middle of the 90's. Then a bad mood settled in society around '97 and it culminated with the Opposition agreement. Today, I feel that there is a shift of the Czech Republic into 'unimportance'. I feel that access to the European Union was a missed opportunity for the Czech Republic mostly because of the position of the Czech political leaders. I also think that most of the Czech people became cynical and lethargic toward sociopolitical issues in comparison to citizens in Germany, France or Italy. Italy is in a huge crisis but the public is still optimistic and many initiatives to better the political situation have emerged. In the Czech Republic there are a few such [initiatives], but public support is minimal.
>
> (FC4)

Despite maintaining sceptical views regarding the CR, most interviewees planned to remain in the country.

Most of our correspondents (10 FCs) worked for only one employer/media organization. These organizations usually have one correspondent in the Czech Republic, but in two cases they had three or more. Most of our interviewees worked for public radio stations (eight FCs), print (six FCs), online (seven FCs), or wire services (five FCs). More than half of them have jobs that combine several types of media. In addition, the majority worked for international media organizations (10 FCs).

Along with these trends, we were interested in the platforms our reporters use for publishing stories. All of the respondents use websites, and almost three-quarters use radio stations. Newspapers (eight FCs) and television (six FCs) are used frequently. When asked, four of our respondents said they do not use social media as a publishing platform. The others use Facebook (five FCs), personal websites (three FCs), Twitter (three FCs) and, in one case, YouTube.

WHAT MAKES IT INTO THE FOREIGN CORRESPONDENT'S REPORTING AGENDA?

Next we sought to discover which topics typically make it into correspondents' reporting agenda. All of our respondents cover politics, and most cover economic topics. Eight FCs report on cultural events, and the same percentage cover lifestyles. Seven of our respondents cover sport. We did not find strict specialization among the reporters we interviewed. Nearly half of them cover four types of stories, and all of them cover more than two kinds of stories. As is typical for foreign correspondents in the CR, the majority also cover Slovakia, especially because the CR and Slovakia were unified as Czechoslovakia over the course of the 20th century. The division of the country in 1992 did not change the fact that the two languages remain quite similar. Only two correspondents involved in our sample covered additional countries.

WHEN IS SOMETHING BECOMING FOREIGN CORRESPONDENTS' NEWS?

Most of the correspondents we interviewed choose their own story topics (eight FCs). Six of them consult with their editors in order to generate story topics. The average number of stories produced weekly is around six (ranging from five to 15). About 75 per cent of the stories reach publication.

Our respondents tended to favour the same types of news topics: those that have some impact on other countries (e.g., deaths related to the use of methanol and the alcohol's subsequent prohibition, the government crisis, church restitutions, etc.). As seasonal factors affect their work in the CR, foreign correspondents primarily list elections and sports events. Among the regular events that trigger their coverage are cultural happenings (e.g., the Karlovy Vary International Film Festival, the Prague Spring Festival, etc.), political affairs, economic issues, and sports events.

WHERE DO THE STORIES COME FROM?

Correspondents were also asked what sources they use for their stories. Most often they use official sources of information such as government officials, press releases, and national media coverage (*ČTK*, Czech News Agency; *ČT*, Czech Television). Slightly more than a third of the correspondents use average citizens as sources. ('The average citizens tell you the truth,' said FC7.) Three FCs use information generated by think tanks. The correspondents we interviewed rarely use information from NGOs (two FCs). All of them noted that, compared to other European countries, there is relatively open access to firsthand sources of information from the government and big businesses (an average of 3.7 points on a 1-to-5 scale—1 being very restricted and 5 representing very open access).

We also tried to discern who are the most influential foreign correspondents and local media outlets, as well as how often our respondents utilize other news sources to generate story ideas of their own. All of them use national and local Czech media on a daily basis. Several times a week, they use other foreign correspondents based in the CR, citizen journalism, blogs and social media, and the work of Czech journalists. Among the most important foreign media they use in their work are the large international news agencies (*Reuters*, *DPA*, *AP*, *Bloomberg*, *Xinhua*) and important newspapers such as *NYT*, *FAZ*, *International Herald Tribune*, and *SüddeutscheZeitung*.

We found it interesting that although correspondents know one another, they generally do not cooperate on stories. 'We communicate in our private lives, go out together, sometimes we help each other out (when someone needs a tape of an event) but we do not co-operate professionally on a larger scale' (FC3).

Correspondents were asked what factors influence the ways in which foreign news is selected and portrayed. Among the most influential factors are, in the following order: editorial policies, deadlines, personal values and beliefs, colleagues' ideas and opinions, and, finally, the sources for their stories. Other factors that influence their work are media laws and regulations, competition with new media, audience feedback, and colleagues involved in other media organizations. Far less influential are the owners of their news organizations, profit expectations, and advertising considerations. Among the factors with little or no influence are pressure groups, people in the business community, politicians, the military, police and state security, and censorship.

HOW TO COPE WITH SOCIAL TRANSITION AND FINANCIAL CRISIS

Finally, we examined recent trends in foreign correspondence. Half of our respondents said that their main employer had drastically cut the number of posts for foreign correspondents within the last decade. The same number of respondents feared that their current positions would be cut in the next two or three years in order to save costs. The same correspondents noted that their resources (equipment, travel budget, etc.) had been reduced. Four respondents stated that 'parachute journalists' (Hamilton & Jenner, 2004) have increasingly replaced traditional correspondents, and seven FCs believe that local journalists abroad have been employed instead of 'traditional foreign correspondents'. On the other hand, 11 foreign correspondents think that international topics are increasingly covered from media headquarters, and they dispute the idea that amateur journalists, bloggers, or NGO representatives are replacing traditional correspondents. Seven correspondents said they do not feel increased time pressure on their jobs. Five of them agree that today's audience cares less about international news than in past. Most of our respondents asserted that their job has changed for the worse in recent years. Considering the impact of the financial crisis on their profession, most of our respondents agreed that more articles on economics are being written. In addition, most think that the current crisis has caused average European citizens to pay attention to the internal politics of other European countries.

CONCLUSIONS

Journalists working as foreign correspondents in the CR face the conditions of a slowly developing, postcommunist, Central European country: for example, corruption, an unstable government, close relations between politics and the media, and the like. All these factors (and many others) influence the working conditions of foreign correspondents in our country. Using the typology of Hamilton and Jenner (2004) as a model, our research proves that most correspondents in the CR are 'traditional foreign correspondents', '*foreign* foreign correspondents', or 'parachute journalists'.

Overall, journalists interviewed by our research team were satisfied with their working conditions, even though they think things were better two or three years ago. The stories they write, once approved by an editor, are usually published and journalists have open access to the information they need. We were quite surprised that interviewees feel little influence from pressure groups, business interests, and politicians because from our experience, those pressures are quite high amid the Czech media. The reason for this discrepancy may be that foreign correspondents have the advantage of working for the foreign media and are not under the same pressures.

The biggest challenge for any foreigner coming to the CR is language. Foreign language proficiency is still low in the CR, even though it is much better than immediately after the Velvet Revolution. All of our interviewees can speak basic Czech at the very least. Others are fluent in the language. The language barrier is one of the most common challenges for foreign correspondents mentioned in Hannerz (2004).

Another challenge, as mentioned in the preface to Gross and Kopper (2011), is the ongoing media transformation and the use of so-called new technologies to attract a public that utilizes blogs, social networks, amateur videos, and photos as sources of information. Some foreign correspondents in the CR work exclusively in online media, and some include blogs and video-blogs in their 'standard' work. One such reporter is Danko Handrick (he declined to grant us an interview) who posts his video-blogs on German television ARD websites in the '*BöhmischeDörfer–Geschichte aus Tschechien*' section. There was generally low usage of so-called new media by our respondents, though this is not surprising given their average age. The younger people are, the more likely they are to use new media platforms.

It is advantageous for foreign correspondents to root themselves in a country so that they can compare the changes in its sociopolitical atmosphere over time. If they are sensitive, they can develop a perspective that differs slightly from that of their native colleagues and thus may offer valuable feedback for citizens of the country they are covering.

A final quote illustrates the insightful role often played by perceptive foreign correspondents: 'I just think that the rise of Klaus in the Czech government coincided with the end of the optimistic era of the Czech Republic,' said FC1, who had been living in the CR for 11 years. She continued: 'When I moved here from Russia, for example, people here did not speak Russian. They hated it. And now they are studying Russian. And when Havel died, I just got the sense that we lost the most powerful voice for reforms in the former communist bloc'.

REFERENCES

BREZINOVÁ, Z. (2012). Česká republika v Evropě očima zahraničních korespondentů (Czech Republic in Europe viewed by foreign correspondent) [Conference report]. Prague: Asociace pro mezinárodní otázky [Online]. Available from http://bit.ly/1gwFLTl.

CHANG, T. (1998), All Countries Not Created Equal to Be News. *Communication Research*. 25 (5), pp. 528–563.

GROSS, P., & KOPPER, G. G. (2011). *Understanding Foreign Correspondence—A Euro-American Perspective of Concepts, Methodologies, and Theories*. New York: Peter Lang.

HAMILTON, J.M., & JENNER, E. (2004). Redefining Foreign Correspondents. *Journalism*. 5 (3), pp. 301–321.

HANNERZ, U. (2004). *Exploring the World of Foreign Correspondents*. Chicago: University of Chicago Press.

HESS, S. (2005). *Through Their Eyes—Foreign Correspondents in the United States.* Washington, DC: Brookings Institution Press.
SEDLÁČKOVÁ, A. (2009). *Zahraniční zpravodajství jako životní styl* (Foreign correspondence as a kind of lifestyle). Unpublished thesis. Masaryk University, Brno.
WILLNAT, L., & WEAVER, D. (2003). Through Their Eyes: The Work of Foreign Correspondents in the United States. *Journalism.* 4 (4), pp. 403–422.

INTERVIEWS

FC1—12 August 2012.
FC2—28 September 2012.
FC3—10 October 2012.
FC4—12 October 2012.
FC5—5 November 2012.
FC6—4 November 2012.
FC7—4 November 2012.
FC8—5 November 2012.
FC9—5 November 2012.
FC10—11 December 2012.
FC11—11 December 2012.
FC12—10 April 2013.
FC13—29 April 2013.
FC14—15 May 2013.

6 Foreign Correspondents in Denmark

All Quiet on the Northern News Front?

Morten Skovsgaard and Arjen van Dalen

INTRODUCTION

> The Government Parties: Danish People's Party Has Scared Tourists Away

This headline appeared in the Danish Newspaper *Berlingske* in the early summer 2013 (Arnfred & Munksgaard, 2013). According to politicians from the three parties in the current centre-left government, Denmark's image abroad as an open-minded, cosy, and progressive nation suffered from the blunt rhetoric of the Danish People's Party, as well as from restrictions on immigration to Denmark put in place by the former bourgeois government with the support of the Danish People's Party. This has allegedly caused the decline in international tourism to Denmark.

But how can domestic politics and policies damage Denmark's image abroad? A necessary condition is that people abroad learn about these domestic Danish issues, and most often they do so from news reports from foreign correspondents. Of course, it was disputed whether it is true that international tourists have been scared away from Denmark because of the way that politicians have dealt with the immigrant issue. Nevertheless, there is little doubt that foreign correspondents play an important role with regard to which aspects of a small country like Denmark are emphasized in the international news and ultimately in people's perception of the country, especially those who have never visited the country.

This makes it relevant to study the foreign correspondents in Denmark. Denmark usually leads a quiet life in the foreign news around the world. With its 5.5 million inhabitants, the country is among the smaller ones in Europe, and when it comes to foreign news, size does matter (e.g., Wu, 1998). Denmark is a stable member of both NATO (since 1949) and the European Union (since 1973), and in general the country is politically, economically, and socially stable with a low conflict level and few disruptive events. This means that Denmark rarely stands out for negative reasons. However, sometimes the searching spotlight of the international press falls upon Denmark. This was the case with the Cartoon Crisis that erupted with full force in 2006 and made most Danes realize what international press coverage of the country potentially means for the image of the country abroad.

Inasmuch as foreign correspondents play a role in building Denmark's image abroad, it is interesting to know who they are, what their professional motivations and their working conditions are, and how they follow current affairs in Denmark and assess what is newsworthy. This chapter deals with these questions based on an online survey of the foreign correspondents in Denmark. In our analysis, we will pay special attention to the difference between full-time and part-time foreign correspondents. Over the last decades, news organizations worldwide have reduced the number of traditional foreign correspondents on full-time contracts in favour of freelancers or parachute journalists who are flown in to the international hot spots from their home country when a newsworthy situation evolves (e.g. Hamilton & Jenner, 2004). To be better able to judge the consequences of this development, we present the particular backgrounds and working conditions of full-time and part-time correspondents separately when doing so is relevant.

DATA COLLECTION

To investigate the characteristics of foreign correspondents covering Denmark, we conducted an Internet survey in the spring of 2013. To encompass the wide variety of journalists working as foreign correspondents (Hamilton & Jenner, 2004), we defined the population broadly as journalists who currently cover Denmark for one or more media outlets based in a country outside Denmark. This can include full-time and part-time journalists, as well as freelancers. According to our definition, Danish foreign correspondents also include correspondents located in another country who cover Denmark. Correspondents do not need to be trained journalists. Such a broad definition allows us to describe the increasingly diverse nature of foreign correspondents.

Following Nair (1991), Willnat and Weaver (2003), and Hess (2005), we categorize the population of foreign correspondents as members of the International Press Center (IPC) of the Ministry of Foreign Affairs and of the Foreign Press Association in Denmark (FPA). The IPC is an independent institution that provides professional assistance to foreign correspondents. The FPA represents the interests of foreign correspondents in Denmark. The websites of both organizations include lists with the names and email addresses of correspondents covering Denmark. Combining these lists, we identified 150 journalists.

At the end of April 2013, each of these journalists received an email with an invitation to take part in our online survey. Both the email and the survey were in English. We chose not to translate the survey to Danish, so the results can be compared to other countries that used the same master questionnaire. Translating the questions might have introduced biases (Wirth & Kolb, 2004). Over a five-week period, we sent out three reminders, including a letter by ordinary mail. Finally, the IPC sent out an email to their members who had not yet answered. In the process of data collection, we filtered out 15 journalists who we found out did not match our working definition of Danish foreign correspondents. A total of 43 journalists filled out our survey, which gives a response rate of 31.9 per cent of the population (AAPOR2, see AAPOR, 2008), a rate comparable to other journalism surveys (Donsbach & Patterson, 2004; Van Dalen, 2012). As a check for representativeness, we compared the geographical spread of the respondents in the sample. This was comparable to the geographical spread among the population of all foreign correspondents.

WHO ARE THE FOREIGN CORRESPONDENTS IN DENMARK?

Before analyzing the results of our survey, we first present some main characteristics of the whole population of foreign correspondents, 150 in total. Foreign correspondents who cover Denmark come mainly from countries that are geographically close or important trading partners. Sixty per cent of all the foreign correspondents in Denmark come from countries belonging to the European Economic Area (EEA). Denmark's neighbours and two main trading partners, Sweden and Germany (Denmark Statistik, 2013), have the most correspondents, respectively 18 and 17. Outside the EEA, the two countries with most correspondents are also important trading partners: the United States (15 correspondents) and China (12 correspondents).[1] Apart from these top countries, more than 20 other countries have media representatives in Denmark. Other top countries include Finland and the UK (10 each), Turkey (8 FCs), Norway and The Netherlands (6 each), Poland and Spain (5 each), Russia (4 FCs), and France and Pakistan (3 each). The majority of foreign correspondents cover Denmark for print media (46), followed by audiovisual mediums (29), press agencies (21), and online media (9).

We now turn to the results of the questionnaire. Thirty-eight per cent of the foreign correspondents in Denmark are female. Three-quarters of the respondents in our survey indicated that they live in Denmark, whereas most of the last quarter live in neighbouring Sweden. The majority of correspondents do not limit themselves to covering Denmark but also cover other areas, mostly the Nordic countries and the Baltic States.

Little over half of the correspondents work as full-time journalists (58 per cent). Journalists working part-time combine their journalistic work with a variety of jobs, ranging from translator to teacher or press officer at an

Table 6.1 Personal and professional characteristics of foreign correspondents working in Denmark.

	All Foreign Correspondents	Foreign Correspondent Working Full-time as Journalists	Foreign Correspondent Not Working Full-time as Journalists
Female	38%	35%	41%
Freelance contract	63%	48%	83%
Degree in journalism	30%	40%	11%
Located in Denmark	76%	67%	89%
Fluent in Danish	69%	64%	76%
Works primarily in Danish or other Scandinavian language	69%	68%	71%
Works primarily in English	26%	32%	18%
Journalistic experience (years)*	21	21	21
Experience as foreign correspondent (years)*	17	15	21
Correspondent in Denmark (years)*	17	14	21
N (lowest)	35	21	14

* Average

embassy. Table 6.1 shows the backgrounds and working conditions of the foreign correspondents in Denmark and reveals some clear differences between full-time and part-time correspondents. The majority of foreign correspondents have a freelance contract. This is especially true for correspondents who do not work full-time. These part-timers are also less likely to have a degree in journalism and have less experience as correspondents. On the other hand, they have a tighter bond with the country than full-timers: they have more experience covering Denmark, are more often located in the country, see themselves as more fluent in Danish, and are less likely to work in English.

Although full-time correspondents have covered Denmark for a shorter period than part-timers, they are generally not parachute journalists who are first journalists and second correspondents in Denmark: less than half of the full-time correspondents have a degree in journalism, and many of them speak Danish. Their average journalistic experience is 14 years, and their experience in Denmark makes up a large part of their experience as foreign correspondents. This seems to indicate that many news outlets do not use a rotating scheme to assign their correspondents to Denmark. This might be due to the language and to less competition for covering this relatively less newsworthy region.

PROFESSIONAL MOTIVATION

Self-realization is a more important motivation for foreign correspondents working in Denmark than motivations coming from their societal role as watchdogs and external rewards such as salary and prestige (see Table 6.2). The opportunity to have an interesting and exciting work life is by far the greatest motivation: to have a varied job where they work creatively is rated highest among the foreign correspondents in Denmark. Our analysis shows that this goes together with the chance to meet interesting people and participate in exciting events. Foreign correspondents are less motivated by fighting injustice and uncovering power abuse, although journalists often

Table 6.2 Foreign correspondents motivations in Denmark.

	All Foreign Correspondents	Foreign Correspondents Working Full-time as Journalists	Foreign Correspondent not Working Full-time as Journalists
*Personal realization**			
Have a varied job	9.1 (2.1)	9.3 (2.1)	8.7 (2.0)
Work creatively	8.8 (2.3)	8.8 (2.2)	8.9 (2.6)
Meet interesting people	8.3 (2.4)	8.6 (2.7)	7.9 (2.1)
Participate in exciting events	7.8 (2.3)	7.9 (2.6)	7.6 (2.0)
*Watchdog of society**			
Fight injustice	6.6 (2.9)	6.6 (2.8)	6.7 (3.0)
Uncover power abuse	6.4 (3.0)	6.3 (2.9)	6.7 (3.1)
*Personal status**			
Get a good salary	6.0 (3.0)	6.4 (3.1)	5.4 (2.8)
Get status and prestige	4.9 (2.8)	4.9 (2.7)	4.9 (3.1)
Lowest N	*40*	*22*	*17*

Note: Averages on a scale from 1 = not important to 11 = very important (standard deviations in parentheses).

Question wording: 'You can be motivated by many things in your job. To which extent are the following things important motivations in your job as a journalist?'

* A factor analysis (varimax rotation) resulted in the three dimensions—all with eigenvalues above 1.

refer to this role in democracy when they legitimize their work (e.g. Graber, 2003). External rewards, that is, salary and prestige, are the weakest sources of motivation. However, salary does come quite close to fighting injustice and uncovering power abuse. This picture closely resembles answers from Danish journalists who were also more motivated by self-realization than societal role and external rewards (unpublished data).[2]

Full-time correspondents are more motivated by salary than their colleagues who are not working full-time. We did not ask the foreign correspondents about their actual income, but it might be an explanation that the full-time journalists earn more and also have made a more conscious choice about the salary from their journalistic work because it is their only income. The full-time correspondents also indicated that they are more motivated by the chance to meet interesting people and have a varied job.

When it comes to their journalistic role, the foreign correspondents show awareness that their reporting on Denmark should be to the benefit of the public in the country they report to rather than to Denmark. Presenting a positive image of Denmark is by far the least emphasized role, and most respondents put more emphasis on describing the impact of developments in Denmark on the country they report to and drawing lessons from the developments in Denmark for their 'home' country.

The correspondents not working full-time find it more important than do full-time correspondents to present a positive image of Denmark, to create understanding of Danish society, and to provide interpretation and analysis of developments in Denmark. On the other hand, full-time correspondents are more inclined to draw lessons for their 'home' country from developments in Denmark. This illustrates that the correspondents not working full-time are more concerned with the way Denmark is presented than the full-time correspondents, who in turn are concerned with their home country benefiting from their coverage of Denmark. This might be related to the difference in connection with Denmark between the full-time and part-time journalists: correspondents not working full-time have a closer connection to Denmark than full-time foreign correspondents.

AUTONOMY

Traditionally, foreign correspondents have been considered to be among the journalists with substantial professional autonomy due to their prestigious position and distance from the newsroom (Hess, 1996). This means that it becomes harder for editorial supervisors to question their professional judgments of what to cover and how to cover it. However, efforts by media outlets to cut expenses and create value for money in terms of foreign news that attracts an audience put pressure on foreign correspondents (Skovsgaard & Van Dalen, 2013, p. 380). Despite such pressures, more than 90 per cent of the foreign correspondents in Denmark indicate that they have either a great deal of or almost complete freedom to make choices in the journalistic production process. This is close to, albeit a little lower than, how Danish journalists answered the same questions when their autonomy was studied (Skovsgaard et al., 2012). The foreign correspondents perceive their autonomy to be lowest in choosing the stories to work on and in the aspects of the story to emphasize, although they have more freedom in choosing sources for the story. This makes sense since editorial supervisors are more involved in the planning of a story in the initial phase than when the journalist actually gathers the research material, that is, chooses which sources to include.

To get further information on the limits on their autonomy, we asked about the influences on their work (see Table 6.3). They mostly feel the influence from space and time constraints, followed by the influence from

Table 6.3 Influences on foreign correspondents' work in Denmark.

	All Foreign Correspondents	Foreign Correspondents Working Full-time as Journalists	Foreign Correspondent Not Working Full-time as Journalists
Time limits (your time available to cover a certain issue)	2.5 (1.1)	2.7 (0.9)	2.2 (1.2)
Space limits (in the newspaper/news broadcast, etc.)	2.5 (1.2)	2.6 (1.3)	2.3 (1.2)
Your editorial supervisors in the newsroom	2.0 (1.1)	2.3 (0.9)	1.7 (1.2)
Coverage from competing news organizations	1.8 (0.9)	1.9 (0.8)	1.8 (1.0)
Audience research/ feedback from audience	1.7 (1.2)	1.7 (1.3)	1.6 (1.3)
The managers/owners of your news organizations	1.5 (1.3)	1.4 (1.4)	1.7 (1.3)
Advertising/profit considerations	0.8 (1.0)	0.5 (0.9)	1.1 (1.1)
Lowest N	*38*	*22*	*16*

Averages on a scale from 0 = no influence at all to 4 = extremely influential (standard deviations in parentheses).

Question wording: 'Please indicate how much influence each of the following aspects has on your work.'

editorial supervisors. They feel the least influence directly from profit and advertising demands and from the managers and owners of their news organizations. The impact of economic cutbacks seems to show itself as limitations in space and time rather than as direct pressure from the organization. It is noteworthy that full-time correspondents felt more pressure from time and space limitations and from their editorial supervisors than the correspondents not working full-time. They, on the other hand, feel more pressure from managers and owners as well as direct profit considerations. This might be due to their more insecure situation where they work on nonfixed terms and without full-time employment as journalists.

WHAT IS A NEWS STORY FROM DENMARK?

Given the importance of news coverage in shaping the perception of Denmark abroad, it is important to know what is actually covered by the foreign correspondents. When it comes to topics related to culture, Danish politics and business are the most covered by the foreign correspondents in Denmark, while crime and courts, as well as entertainment and the royal family, are covered less. The finding that traditional hard news topics are more covered than traditional soft news topics indicates that for news organizations in other countries, Denmark is interesting due to its relevance in other countries or in the international society even if it is rather small in an international perspective.

Interestingly, the full-time correspondents cover hard news topics, especially Danish politics and business, much more intensely than do the part-time correspondents, who in turn cover culture much more intensely than full-time correspondents. This makes sense, given that news organizations station journalists abroad to follow current affairs and societal developments in general, which will often result in a hard news focus.

In the literature on news values and news selection, it has been pointed out that journalists have ideals about what makes an event newsworthy, but because they do not have full autonomy, the actual selection does not always match these ideals (e.g., Shoemaker, 2006). To explore what constitutes newsworthiness among the Danish correspondents and the news organizations they produce content for, we asked the correspondents how important different attributes of an event should be for its newsworthiness and how important they are in the actual news selection.

Looking at the ideal news values, there is little doubt that relevance and exclusiveness are the most important to foreign correspondents, while dramatic appeal of the event should be less significant in their eyes (see Table 6.4). When it comes to the actual news selection, the picture is a bit more blurred. The most significant factor is that the event has consequences in the country that the correspondent reports to. But the dramatic

Table 6.4 Foreign correspondents' perception of actual and ideal news values in Denmark.

	Ideal Importance	Actual Importance	Difference
*Dramatic appeal**			
That the event is sensational and unexpected	3.7	3.6	−0.1
That the event is dramatic and thrilling	3.4	3.6	0.02
*Relevance**			
That the event has consequences in the home country of the media the journalist reports for	4.2	4.1	−0.1
That the event increases people's awareness of problems in society	4.2	3.5	−0.7
That the event increases people's insight and knowledge about society	4.3	3.4	−0.9
*Exclusiveness**			
That it is an exclusive news story	4.2	3.7	−0.5
Lowest N	*38*	*38*	

Averages on a scale ranging from 1 = not at all important to 4 = very important

Question wording: 'When deciding if an event should be covered, how important do you believe that the factors listed below *should be*, and how important *are* they in your experience as a foreign correspondent?'

* A factor analysis (varimax rotation) resulted in two dimensions—both with eigenvalues above 1 (the item on exclusiveness loaded moderately on both factors and is here treated independently).

appeal plays a much more significant role in the actual than in the ideal news selection and trumps the other aspects of relevance.

This is illustrated by differences between the actual and ideal significance of the different aspects of news selection in the third column in Table 6.4. It is clear that the biggest discrepancies between actual and ideal news selection arise when it comes to the question of whether the event increases people's awareness of problems in society as well as their insight on and knowledge about society. In the eyes of the foreign correspondents, these aspects should be much more important for news selection than they actually are. These results resemble the findings among both Danish and Swedish journalists (Skovsgaard et al., 2012; Strömbäck et al., 2012). It illustrates that foreign correspondents also feel their professional autonomy restricted, even though it has been argued that foreign correspondents have an elite status in the newsroom (Hess, 1996).

Earlier studies have pointed to several factors at the country level influencing foreign news selection, such as trade, cultural and geographical proximity, size, elite status, GDP per capita, the level of conflict or disruptive nature of events in the country (e.g., Wu, 1998, 2000). As mentioned, Denmark is politically, economically, and culturally a rather stable country with few disruptive events. This indicates that Denmark in general might not be the most newsworthy country in the eyes of the foreign press. But these studies work at the more structural level, and therefore it is interesting to ask foreign correspondents themselves what they actually find interesting to report on from Denmark. In an open-ended question, we asked the foreign correspondents to explain why they believe interest in Denmark either increased or decreased over the last five years.

As was to be expected based on previous research, several correspondents indicate that the newsworthiness of Denmark is limited because it is not the 'world's hotspot', 'has too little impact', and is 'one country among many' in the globalized world, where 'more and more decisions are made in Brussels'. Some correspondents mention the appointment of Anders Fogh Rasmussen as Secretary General of NATO, or Denmark as host of the COP 15 summit on climate change, as well as the Danish participation in the wars in Iraq and Afghanistan as some of the extraordinary events that increased interest in the country. These comments show that there are natural limits to the interest in Denmark due to the countries smallness, stability, and rather limited political power and impact.

Paradoxically this low level of conflict, openness, and social stability also make the country newsworthy. This happens in two ways. First, developments in Denmark can become news when they go against the general image of Denmark as a country that is firmly embedded in the international community. For example, the decision to reject the euro despite long-term EU membership was mentioned as a source for newsworthiness. Many of the correspondents mention that interest in Denmark increased during the previous bourgeois government, which based its majority in parliament on the Danish People's Party, which had strict immigration policies as one of their key issues. This resulted in increasingly restrictive policies on immigrant admission and at times in heated debates about the immigration issue.

Secondly, journalists cover Danish society because the way it is organized can inspire other countries and provide a model that others can learn from. Several correspondents, for example, point to Denmark's welfare model as a source of interest because it has been considered a role model worth spreading. The Scandinavian model apparently still attracts some attention, but maybe not as much as it used to.

It is not only policies and politics that make Denmark newsworthy internationally. Some of the correspondents mention the Danish way of life and especially point to the success of Danish chefs and their world-class restaurants or to the success of the television drama series *The Killing* and *Borgen*.

WHO ARE THE SOURCES?

Sources are important in determining which picture of Denmark foreign correspondents convey to news audiences in other countries. The most important type of sources for foreign correspondents in Denmark is the mass media, in particular newspapers (Table 6.5). This is followed by official sources, such as companies and politicians; finally, foreign correspondents rely on their personal network for information. There is no difference in rank order between those working full-time and part-time: for both groups, the Danish media are the most important source. When asked to rank the media outlets they use to be updated on the Danish news flow, they clearly prefer the national media. Among the five most mentioned media we find three omnibus newspapers (*Politiken*, *Berlingske*, *Jyllands-Posten)* and the two biggest national television channels (*Denmark's Radio* and *TV2)*.

Table 6.5 Most important source of foreign correspondents working in Denmark.

	All Foreign Correspondents	Foreign Correspondents Working Full-time as Journalists	Foreign Correspondents Not Working Full-time as Journalists
*Media**			
Danish newspapers	4.9 (1.4)	5.3 (0.9)	4.4 (1.7)
Danish television/radio	4.6 (1.5)	5.0 (1.1)	4.1 (1.8)
News agencies	4.0 (1.8)	4.3 (1.8)	3.6 (1.8)
*Official sources**			
Companies	4.1 (1.4)	4.2 (1.4)	3.8 (1.5)
Ministers	3.6 (1.9)	4.0 (1.6)	3.2 (2.2)
National politicians	3.5 (1.7)	3.7 (1.5)	3.2 (2.0)
Lobby groups and unions	3.2 (1.7)	3.4 (1.4)	3.0 (2.1)
*Network**			
Danish journalists	3.1 (1.4)	3.4 (1.7)	2.6 (1.6)
Social media	2.9 (1.7)	3.0 (1.7)	2.8 (1.8)
Other foreign correspondents	2.3 (1.8)	2.6 (1.9)	2.9 (1.6)
Blogs	2.2 (1.7)	2.3 (1.7)	2.1 (1.8)
N (lowest)	*40*	*23*	*17*

Averages on a scale from 0 = not important at all to 6 = very important (standard deviations in parentheses).

Question wording: 'How important are the following sources for your coverage of Denmark?'

* A factor analysis (varimax rotation) resulted in the three dimensions—each with an eigenvalue above 1.

The small size of the Danish country and relatively limited international interest seem to work to the advantage of foreign correspondents seeking access to Danish sources. The foreign correspondents are generally satisfied with the accessibility of firsthand sources. Around two-thirds of the respondents to our survey answered that they have easy access to Danish members of Parliament, companies, experts, lobby groups, and unions. This is the case for both full-time and part-time correspondents. It is more difficult to get in touch with ministers, but still around half of the foreign correspondents believe they are easily accessible.

CONCLUSION

The characteristics of Denmark as a relatively small and calm nation from a small language area clearly have an influence on the work of the foreign correspondents reporting from this country. In general, the foreign correspondents who report about Denmark cover the country for a relatively long period of time, often in combination with other Nordic or Baltic countries.

Only 58 per cent of correspondents work full-time as journalists. In our analysis we found some clear contrasts between full-time and part-time journalists. Part-timers more often work as freelancers, have less experience, and have a closer connection to the country. The part-timers feel more pressure from owners and profit considerations. These differences become increasingly important inasmuch as previous research suggests that media organizations worldwide seem to rely less and less on traditional full-time foreign correspondents.

The correspondents in Denmark are not primarily motivated by salary or prestige but rather by self-development goals. Only a minority of the correspondents have a degree in journalism. These journalists perceive a relatively high level of autonomy and believe that Danish sources are well accessible. This work situation is likely to be a completely different from that of journalists reporting from the world's power centres where pressure will be higher and access more difficult. On the one hand, the calmness and prosperity of Denmark make it less newsworthy than more turbulent places. On the other hand, it can also make developments in Denmark interesting because they can serve as an example for other countries, or when they seem to contrast with the general image of Danish as an open nation. Therefore, it is no surprise that when the government implemented harsh restrictions on immigrant admissions, the usually relatively quiet Northern news front was in the line of fire in the news abroad.

NOTES

1. These numbers are based on the 143 foreign correspondents of whom the country of origin is known.
2. Data collected in 2009 for the project 'The Danish Journalist'. See Skovsgaard (2010) for further information.

REFERENCES

AAPOR (American Association for Public Opinion Research). (2008). *Standard Definitions: Final Dispositions of Case Codes and Outcome Rates for Surveys*, 5th ed. Lenexa, KS: American Association for Public Opinion Research.

ARNFRED, C. E., & MUNKSGAARD, P. G. (2013). The Government Parties: Danish People's Party Has Scared Tourists Away. *Berlingske*. 3 July, p. 6.

Denmark Statistik. (2013). *Statistical Yearbook 2013* [Online]. Available from http://bit.ly/1qNQooo.

DONSBACH, W., & PATTERSON, T. E. (2004). Political News Journalists: Partisanship, Professionalism, and Political Roles in Five Countries. In ESSER, F., & PFETCH, B. (eds.), *Comparing Political Communication: Theories, Cases, and Challenges*. Cambridge: Cambridge University Press, pp. 251–270.

GRABER, D. (2003). The Media and Democracy: Beyond Myths and Stereotypes. *Annual Review of Political Science* 6: 139–160.

HAMILTON, J. M., & JENNER, E. (2004). Redefining Foreign Correspondence. *Journalism*. 5 (3), pp. 301–321.

HESS, S. (1996). *International News and Foreign Correspondents*. Washington, DC: Brookings Institution.

———. (2005). *Through Their Eyes. Foreign Correspondents in the United States*. Washington, DC: Brookings Institution Press.

NAIR, M. (1991). The Foreign Correspondent: Dateline Washington, D.C. *Gazette*. 48, pp. 59–64.

SHOEMAKER, P. J. (2006). News and Newsworthiness: A Commentary. *Communications*. 31, pp. 105–111.

SKOVSGAARD, M. (2010). The Danish Journalist. Unpublished PhD dissertation. Center for Journalism, University of Southern Denmark.

SKOVSGAARD, M., ALBÆK, E., BRO, P. & DE VREESE, C. H. (2012).Media Professionals or Organizational Marionettes: Professional Values and Constraints of Danish Journalists. In WEAVER, D. & WILLNAT, L. (eds.) *The Global Journalist in the 21st Century*. New York: Routledge, pp. 155–170.

Skovsgaard, M., & van Dalen, A. (2013). The Fading Public Voice. *Journalism Studies*. 14 (3), pp. 371–386.

STRÖMBÄCK, J., KARLSSON, M. & HOPMANN, D. N. (2012). Determinants of News Content: Comparing Journalists' Perceptions of the Normative and the Actual Impact of Different Event Properties when Deciding What's News. *Journalism Studies*. 13, (5–6), 718–728.

VAN DALEN, A. (2012). The People Behind the Political Headlines; A Comparison of Political Journalists in Denmark, Germany, the United Kingdom and Spain. *The International Communication Gazette*. 74 (5), pp. 464–483.

WILLNAT, L., & WEAVER, D. (2003). Through Their Eyes. The Work of Foreign Correspondents in the United States. *Journalism*. 4 (4), pp. 403–422.

WIRTH, W., & KOLB, S. (2004). Design and Methods of Comparative Political Communication Research. In: ESSER, F., & PFETCH, B. (eds.), *Comparing Political Communication: Theories, Cases, and Challenges*. Cambridge: Cambridge University Press, pp. 87–111.

WU, H. D. (1998) Investigating Determinants of International News Flow: A Meta-Analysis. *International Communication Gazette*. 60 (6), pp. 493–512.

———. (2000) Systemic Determinants of International News Coverage: A Comparison of 38 Countries. *Journal of Communication*. 50 (2), pp. 110–130.

7 Foreign Correspondents in Estonia

Representatives of the Nordic-Baltic region

Ragne Kõuts and Marju Himma-Kadakas

INTRODUCTION

Estonia is a small Baltic country (population 1.34 million) located on the eastern border of the European Union. The tradition of foreign correspondents (FCs) is not very old in Estonia because during the period in which Estonia belonged to the Soviet Union (1944–1991), the Communist Party and censorship institution, Glavlit, strictly controlled all foreign correspondents working in the Soviet Union, and FCs were only infrequently allowed to work on a republic's level (Veskimägi, 1996; Vihalemm & Lauristin, 1997). After the restoration of Estonia's independence, the changes at the end of 1980s attracted much interest from the rest of the world. The first foreign correspondents officially moved to Estonia after the nation acquired its independence from the Soviet Union, and the first international press cards were given to correspondents from Finnish *Yleisradio* and the Russian daily *Moskovskie Novosti* by the Estonian Foreign Ministry in October 1991 (Nõmmik, 2013). During the first year of independence, about 40–50 FCs were active in Estonia, with most of them hailing from European countries like France, Poland, Sweden, Germany, and Estonia's neighbouring countries, but there were also residing correspondents from Mexico and the United States. This was probably the period that saw the highest number of FCs working in Estonia; nowadays, usually no more than 30 FCs are on the list of accredited journalists, and not all of them reside in the country.

Although Estonia has been a member of the EU since 2004, events in Estonia are not normally of geopolitical influence or importance, while conflicts or high-profile events are seldom and do not appear to attract great interest from the audiences of other countries (Galtung & Ruge, 1965; Eilders, 1996). According to Galtung (1986)—who explained the global media pattern in terms of the 'centre–periphery' model, Estonia belongs to the second group of countries 'with a predominant flow of news from the former to the latter' (Aalberg et al., 2013, p. 390). Due to its size and peripheral location, the country is not represented in daily European news flow very often, but some aspects seem to attract heightened attention.

These include Estonia's geopolitical location (that is, its nearness to Russia), its stable economic development in the context of economic problems and the recession faced by many EU countries, and cyber innovations. The country is probably not big enough and the international events taking place in Estonia are not frequent enough to warrant sending an FC to Estonia for long periods; however, in this regard, we note that events in Estonia receive interest primarily from representatives of media organizations in neighbouring countries, who send a correspondent 'to the field', and that 'geographic proximity and national interest should also to be important factors in explaining the regional focus of foreign news' (Aalberg et al., 2013, p. 390). In addition to foreign correspondents who can be defined according to the traditional meaning of the term, many FCs also visit Estonia for short periods of time and are referred to as 'parachute journalists' or stringers (Hamilton & Jenner, 2004).

Economically, Estonia is ranked as one of the poorest EU countries—ranking 22nd of the 28 member countries (currently, the annual GDP averages at €12,700 per inhabitant)—and is the poorest member of the euro area (Eurostat, 2011). This said, living costs are not much lower than in other countries in Europe, which means that Estonia is not necessarily the cheapest country for residing FCs to live in. Furthermore, it is not valid to assume that working and living conditions in Estonia are very different and significantly cheaper from those in other European countries on the basis of its low economic ranking.

POPULATION OF FOREIGN CORRESPONDENTS

Given that the population of foreign correspondents in Estonia is rather small (approximately 30 persons based on the data of Estonian Foreign Ministry in December 2012), this chapter does not present extensive statistical analyses; however, the following observations regarding the presence and activity of FCs in Estonia can be made.

We have no grounds on which to claim that FCs working in Estonia belong to a different segment of journalists than other reporters working in the Estonian news media. If we make some preliminary conclusions based on the composition of accredited reporters, we find that the area is dominated by men—as has been the case in many other European journalistic organizations throughout history (Södertörn University, 2012). More than two-thirds (21) of the 30 FCs working in Estonia are men, and the remaining nine are women.

The majority of foreign correspondents (14) work for print editions (usually, this activity is combined with contributions to the web editions of print media), and eight journalists work for news agencies, and only a few (4) FCs in Estonia work for broadcasting companies. Of the latter group, only two journalists work specifically for web channels, while the principal medium of the remaining two journalists is unknown. In terms of broadcasting, all channels are those of the public service media (Finnish *YLE*, German *ZDF*, UK *BBC*, and Belarus's *Second National TV-Channel*); however, data on the countries of media origin were unavailable for Estonia.

In relation to news agencies, one finds representatives of the *Associated Press* (*AP*), *Deutsche Presse Agentur* (*DPA*), *Bloomberg News*, *Reuters*, and the *Xinhua*.

Foreign correspondents, accredited by the Estonian Ministry of Foreign Affairs, do not constitute a homogeneous group. Their working conditions and relation to the country differ on the basis of two defining characteristics: firstly, one must ask whether they are 'foreigners' and secondly, whether they reside in Estonia. Positive answers to these questions allow us to talk about traditional foreign correspondents, as defined by Hamilton and Jenner (2004), and according to this approach, we have grouped accredited journalist foreign correspondents into three groups:

- At least half of the 30 FCs accredited by the Ministry of Foreign Affairs do not reside in Estonia. Most of them live and work in neighbouring countries, such as Finland, Sweden, Latvia, or Poland, and cover events in Estonia via email, phone, and Skype, with occasional visits to Estonia (if an event of international significance takes place, such as an international cyber conference or a NATO meeting).
- About a quarter of accredited journalists work for local media organizations and have sufficient language skills to transmit news to the foreign markets. Some of these representatives belong to Estonian minorities, and, according to their cultural background, funnel select important information to the audiences of their countries of origin (e.g., Ukrainians who cover news from Estonia for their national media market).
- The third group (about seven journalists) can be classified as belonging to the traditional definition of foreign correspondents. These FCs are representatives of public service media organizations or bigger media organizations in neighbouring countries, like *ZDF*, *YLE*, *Helsingin Sanomat*, and are sent to Estonia by their organizations. However, about half of them have private links to Estonia, such as family in the country or other personal interests.

To arrive at an overview of the situation of FCs in Estonia, we used a standardized questionnaire and a few open-ended questions. This material was sent to all accredited journalists, but only six correspondents completed the questionnaire. Additionally, we interviewed the Press Attaché of the Estonian Foreign Ministry to obtain background information regarding the history of FCs in Estonia.

WHO EMPLOYS FOREIGN CORRESPONDENTS?

As Williams (2011, p. 24) argues, 'the largest employers of foreign correspondents have been the international news agencies'. The biggest news agencies, like *Reuters* or *Bloomberg* and the *Deutsche Presse Agentur* from the nations on the Baltic Sea, all have correspondents for Estonia. The majority of their correspondents do not live in Estonia, and those who do live in Estonia work mainly for the regional media organizations of neighbouring countries.

About one-third of FCs living in Estonia are from Finland. Some FCs cover all three Baltic countries. Hamilton and Jenner (2004) say that traditional foreign correspondents work mainly for the public service media. However, in Estonia, FCs work mainly for print or online news channels. Regional Scandinavian newspapers and magazines included *Karjalan Kuvalehti*, *Kaleva*, *Sjöfartstidingen*, and *Eesti Päevaleht* in Sweden. It is noticeable that many foreign correspondents cover many countries at the same time. There were correspondents who responded to our research, explaining that they had already participated in the same survey in another neighbouring country (e.g., Latvia or Sweden) and declined the offer to participate twice in the same study. It may therefore be useful to consider treating the region composed of the Baltic nations, and possibly also Scandinavian countries, as a whole when looking at the work of foreign correspondents.

Most FCs residing in Estonia live in the capital city, Tallinn. Only one correspondent lives in the countryside, covering news related to the southern parts of Estonia. FCs who live in Estonia full-time are usually here for personal reasons, as well as for work-related reasons. These include family relations or other occupational connections—for example, one correspondent worked as a media adviser for a law office.

Correspondents who cover Estonian topics can be considered as stringers who have contacts with local people. They can be foreigners living in Estonia but can also be foreign Estonians (e.g., descendants of Estonian citizens exiled during the World War II). Almost a third of the FCs working in Estonia are of Estonian origin. They work full-time, part-time, and as freelancers. Many work in other fields of occupation, and journalism may be just one of their sources of income.

This trend of having multiple occupations and sources of income may be a reflection of general trends in the media economy and the wider economic recession. The diminishing number of traditional journalists, or FCs, working according to the traditional profile of a FC, is further underlined by the fact that only one of the FCs in Estonia belongs to the journalists' trade union.

WHAT MAKES IT INTO THE FCS' REPORTING AGENDA?

It seems that in Estonia, international media organizations tend to use journalists of local origin. Even if their experience as journalists differs greatly (from 7 to 40 years), their experience as foreign correspondents (which ranges from 2 to 20 years) has mainly been for the local area. As local journalists, FCs can broaden their geographical coverage of news, and their work sometimes includes covering events in neighbouring countries, such as Latvia, Lithuania, Finland, and Russia.

Based on the extensive work by Williams (2011), we assume that the FCs living in Estonia are well settled in the country and can communicate in the national language. Based on survey data, we can conclude that journalists covering events in Estonia are multilingual and that the ability to communicate in four languages is not uncommon. These languages include Estonian, Russian, Finnish, Swedish, Norwegian, and Danish, as well as English and German. Only one journalist, originating from the United States, is monolingual and communicates in English.

The background knowledge and specialization of journalists are diverse. These fields of training and specialization include politics, current affairs, and economy, and some FCs began as writers for travel magazines. Even so, politics and economy are still the main topics covered due to the interest these subjects attract in international audiences, and, right from the start, journalists of Finnish origin have focused on 'serious' topics. Respondents to the survey felt that their audiences are still interested in foreign news.

FCs in Estonia tend to work independently. They decide what stories to cover for themselves. They are not specialists in one field; rather, they tend to act as generalists by covering different topics. The number of articles, between 10 and15 stories pitched per week, is around the same as that of journalists working in Estonian newsrooms, and nearly all of these stories are published by their home news organizations.

FCs frequently use local/native journalists as sources, who are often available and easy to contact. When comparing this factor to their experience in other European countries, they say that it is 'very good' (two journalists) or 'rather good' (four journalists), while two opinions given by FCs from foreign backgrounds regarding the availability of sources in Estonia reflect the obstacle of a language barrier.

Most official government press releases are published in Estonian. English versions have delays of between one day and one month, even if the story is of international interest. Moreover, press representatives who issue press releases of international interest media often do not make themselves available for any follow-up. Further delays arise as officials insist on responding by email rather than by phone. In one respondent's opinion, this both slows and degrades research efforts. This could be conditioned by the fact that the translation of official information takes time if one wishes to minimize the possibility of misinterpretation. One journalist from Finland wrote: 'Local media sources are low quality, leaving out or misrepresenting facts, so that a lot of effort is required to fill in the blanks and verify whether there is even anything to write about.'

This state of affairs makes it easy to understand why most FCs working in Estonia use local Estonian journalists to do their work. This may also be conditioned by the fact that—as mentioned by a journalist from a US background—'Officials may occasionally try to give different messages to local and international media; general lack of trust in international media in small countries as opposed to local press'.

CONCLUSIONS

Our study revealed that population of FCs in Estonia has rather similar sociodemographic characteristics to the general population of journalists in Estonia or in Europe. Foreign correspondents are mainly men who work for print media. However, a significant numbers of FCs also work for news agencies. Usually those who reside in Estonia (half of the accredited journalists) are local inhabitants or foreign journalists who have other reasons to be in Estonia—like family or occupational ties.

The definition of who is a foreign correspondent in Estonia is not entirely clear because FCs who correspond on topics related to Estonia are not necessarily FCs working in Estonia or covering only this country. The profile of FCs covering the region of the Baltic States and Scandinavia should be handled as an overlapping category. The situation seems to be less frightening for parachute journalists or local native journalists. This could be due to the fact that FCs residing in Estonia do not work exclusively as journalists but have the security of other sources of income. FCs active in Estonia have usually worked as journalists before arriving in Estonia, and their reason for settling permanently in the country as an FC is often dictated not exclusively by their work as journalists but also by family relations. The work profile of this type of correspondent has remained the same; however, this could also be conditioned by the fact that most of the FCs who work in Estonia work for newspapers, online editions, or news agencies. This said, the notion of increased time pressure was explicitly mentioned.

> International news is expensive to produce. . . . Keeping a network of foreign correspondents who speak the native language and understand the culture is also expensive; and maintaining a constant presence in a country, even when that country's events do not make international news headlines, requires an ongoing investment that does not consistently pay off. (Aalberg et al., 2013, p. 388)

Still, we believe that the role of FCs cannot be allowed to disappear because the ideal of the informed citizen has not changed in a democratic society: citizens still need relevant and up-to date information about current affairs in both domestic and international spheres in order to have (and act on) informed political preferences.

Finally, we identified the challenges faced by this kind of research in the future. Our study revealed that many foreign correspondents cover events from multiple neighbouring countries simultaneously. The analysis of working and living conditions of foreign correspondents should not be limited to just one country, and it could therefore be useful to consider treating the region of the Baltic countries and Scandinavian countries as a whole. Certainly, covering different countries at the same time presupposes a more complex and multinational approach.

REFERENCES

AALBERG, T., PAPATHANASSOPOULOS, S., SOROKA, S., CURRAN, J., HAYASHI, K., IYENGAR, S., JONES, P.K., MAZZOLENI, G., ROJAS, H., ROWE, D., & TIFFEN, R. (2013). International TV News, Foreign Affairs and Public Knowledge. A Comparative Study of Foreign News Coverage and Public Opinion in 11 Countries. *Journalism Studies*. 14 (3), pp. 387–406.

COLE, J., & HAMILTON, J.M. (2008). The History of Surviving Species: Defining Eras in Evolution of Foreign Correspondence. *Journalism Studies*. 9 (5), pp. 798–812.

EILDERS, C. (1996). *The Role of News Factors in Media Use*. Berlin: Wissenschaftszentrum Berlin für Sozialforschung.

EUROSTAT. (2011). *Statistics in focus* [Online]. Luxembourg: European Commission. Available from http://bit.ly/1jRykHt.

GALTUNG, J. (1986). On the Role of the Media in Worldwide Security and Peace. In Varis, T., & San Jose (eds.), *Peace and Communication*. Costa Rica: Universidad para La Paz.

GALTUNG, J., & RUGE, M. (1965). The Structure of Foreign News: The Presentation of the Congo, Cuba and Cyprus Crisis in Four Norwegian Newspapers. *Journal of International Peace Research*. 1, pp. 64–91.

HAMILTON, J.M., & JENNER, E. (2004). Redefining Foreign Correspondence. *Journalism*. 5 (8), pp. 301–321.

NÕMMIK, H. (2013). The First Foreign Correspondents in Estonia in the Beginning of 1990s. [Interview]. 13 November.

SÖDERTÖRN UNIVERSITY. (2012). *Journalism in Russia, Poland and Sweden—Traditions, Cultures and Research*. Research project. *Journalism in Change* (1). Stockholm: Södertörn University.

VESKIMÄGI, K.O. (1996). C (in Estonian). Tallinn: Tallinna Raamatutrükikoda.

VIHALEMM, P., & LAURISTIN, M. (1997) Political Control and Ideological Canonization. The Estonian Press during the Soviet Period. In Mühle, E. (ed.), *From the Instrument of Party to the 'Fourth Estate'. The Press of Eastern and Central Europe as the Source of Social History from 1945* (in German). Marbrug: Verlag Herder-Institut, pp. 103–109.

WILLIAMS, K. (2011) *International Journalism*. London: Sage.

8 Foreign Correspondents in Finland

News from the Fringe of Europe

Raimo Salokangas

INTRODUCTION

Seen from continental Europe, Finland is an island in the far end of the Baltic Sea. In the north, it has an open border with Sweden and Norway, and in the east is Russia. In the Soviet era, the 1,300-kilometre eastern border really was equivalent to an open sea, and still the crossing requires a visa both ways. There is also an ancient cultural divide inasmuch as, in the 12th century, what is now Finland was incorporated into the Roman Catholic sphere, with some Russian Orthodox influences in the east. In the16th century, Finland, as part of the Kingdom of Sweden, became Protestant (Lutheran), along with Denmark and Norway. So Finland belongs to the 'Western' cultural sphere, preserving and emphasizing those qualities even as a Grand Duchy (1809–1917) under Russia.

By area, Finland is wider than the UK or Italy, and only slightly smaller than Germany, but with a population (according to 2013 figures) of only 5.4 million, it is a 'small' country. In the coastal areas is a Swedish-speaking minority of about 300,000 people, and the Swedish language has a constitutional status as a second national language. Swedish is a compulsory subject in Finnish-language schools, as is Finnish in Swedish-language schools.

Because the Finnish language is unintelligible to anyone but Estonians, foreign correspondence from Finland has suffered from a linguistic barrier. However, it has been partially overcome with the help of Finland's Swedish language media. Traditionally, the Helsinki-based daily *Hufvudstadsbladet* has been an important source because foreign journalists are able to read Swedish more often than Finnish.

From a historical perspective, Finland is one of the cases where war has made the biggest foreign news. The very period when the country was in the focus of international attention was the Winter War (November 1939–March 1940). The war in Europe was at a standstill, and the numerous war correspondents moved themselves to countries where something was happening. According to Julkunen's (1975) study, the negotiations that the Soviet Union demanded in the autumn of 1939 brought a wave of correspondents to Helsinki.

After the Russian invasion and air raids on 30 November, the number of foreign journalists increased again, and by Christmas about 80 of them were in Finland. In the first phase, their remit was to cover the expected collapse of Finland under the attack of the Red Army, but eventually, as the defence held, their tone changed. The correspondents came and left, and Julkunen has calculated that about 300 foreign journalists stayed in Finland for some period, as many as 120 at one time. The largest national groups were Swedes and Americans. The big news agencies, as well as major American newspapers, had their staff correspondents in Europe, and now Helsinki was the place to be. More exactly, Hotel Kämp was the gathering ground. Julkunen quotes a Swedish journalist: 'It was a hotel, newsroom, information ministry, and centre of rumors. The most exciting languages, from continental European to Japanese, buzzed there as in a beehive' (Julkunen, 1975, pp. 47–62).

In the case of the Winter War, it is noteworthy that only a few of the international correspondents knew much about Finland, so it was natural to write their stories in the frame of Big always defeating Small and later of having the heroic David resisting Goliath.

On a more regular basis, foreign correspondence from and especially to Finland had its start in cooperation among newspapers in different countries and between newspapers and news agencies. In the years 1930–1941. *Helsingin Sanomat* and its editor/owner Eljas Erkko held the status of the Helsinki correspondent for the American news agency *International News Service* (INS): the agency wired enquiries on specific topics, and *Helsingin Sanomat* replied (Manninen & Salokangas, 2009, p. 400). This was the way international news agencies came to Finland. In the 1930s, Eljas Erkko made great efforts to make sure that *Helsingin Sanomat* had the best foreign news coverage in the country, and simultaneously he created close personal relations with leading personalities, especially at *United Press* (*UP*). *UP* established a bureau in Stockholm in 1939, also covering Finland. When *UP* opened a bureau in Helsinki in December 1945, it was prepared to negotiate with Erkko, and eventually a journalist from *Helsingin Sanomat* became *UP*'s Helsinki office. One reason behind this move was the rumour that *Associated Press* (*AP*) was planning to establish an office in the Finnish capital—which it had actually done earlier in the autumn of 1945, the base being the office of another Helsinki paper, *Hufvudstadsbladet* (Manninen & Salokangas, 2009, pp. 123–124, 522–523).

In both cases, the main objective of the bureaus was to serve their Finnish customers with foreign news, but the new branches also fed the agencies with news from Finland.

THE CORRESPONDENTS IN FINLAND IN 2013

In 2013, about 80 correspondents in Finland were working for foreign media, most of them in the Helsinki metropolitan area (Vehkoo, 2013). The Website of the foreign ministry's international press centre[1] lists

117 names, including journalists monitoring Finland from some other country, as well as wider variety of freelancers. Of the 117 persons, 24 had an address outside Finland: 14 in Sweden, four in Denmark, and one each in Estonia, Norway, Germany, France, Switzerland, and the United Kingdom. Additionally, some had only an email address, and most probably were not resident in Finland.

Not surprisingly, the highest number of resident correspondents served media in the neighbouring countries of Sweden (11) and Russia (10), followed by big countries like the United Kingdom, the United States, China (six each), and France (five). The total of 71 names included many who live in Finland for a shorter or longer period and whose activity as freelancers, for this or that reason, vary on a broad scale. As many as 13 of the 21 nonresident correspondents had Sweden listed as their base. Seven of the 21 served German media, which also had four correspondents living in Finland. The correspondents were typically men: fewer than a fourth were female (16 of the 71).

Correspondents living in Finland served news agencies, broadcast media and print media in quite similar numbers (19, 21, and 20 respectively), and even the number of correspondents working for online media was about half of the figures for traditional media (11 total). For nonresident correspondents, print media was the biggest employer.

Only some news agencies had offices and/or staff correspondents in Finland: *Bloomberg News*, *Associated Press*, *Reuters*, *Chinese Xinhua*, *Russian Itar-Tass*.

In an interview, *Xinhua*'s correspondent Li Jizhi said that the agency is concerned with items that somehow relate to China but also that softer topics may be of interest. The agency serves all kinds of media, so Li Jizhi both writes and makes videos and multimedia reports. *AP*'s television correspondent David McDougall was stationed in Helsinki but had all the Nordic and Baltic countries to cover. 'Many people believe that nothing worth reporting happens here. If you think that only terrorism and bombs are newsworthy, you should get another job. Interesting things about Finland for people who can hardly find it on the world map' are what he wanted to tell about. Many of the news agencies employ Finnish journalists. *Bloomberg* relied solely on native journalists, while *Reuters* had an American director and two Finns reporting on economy items (Vehkoo, 2013).

Not even Swedish media had staff correspondents in Helsinki anymore. The public service broadcasters in the two countries have a long history of cooperation, and now *SVT* and *Sveriges Radio* use some *Yle* journalists as their correspondents. The Stockholm newspapers had returned to a pattern of earlier history: one journalist of *Hufvudstadsbladet* was also the correspondent of *Dagens Nyheter*, and another of the tabloid *Aftonbladet*.

A German-born freelancer worked for the German public service TV channel *ZDF* and radio and TV network *ARD*, as well as for the French news agency *AFP* (Vehkoo, 2013).

The *BBC*'s freelancer Mark Bosworth said to Vehkoo (2013): 'The BBC has no staff correspondents in the Nordic and Baltic countries. I had to leave my job as I moved to Finland. My boss said that I should not expect to make a living as a freelancer with Finland stories. He and many others think that nothing happens here'.

THE FRAME: INTERESTING FOR THE CLIENT

The classical foreign news criteria by Galtung and Ruge (1965) are still partially relevant to Finland. Of their list of 12 factors affecting the newsworthiness of items, some fit the case of Finland better than others. 'The more the event concerns élite nations, the more probable that it will become a news item' (Galtung & Ruge, 1965, p. 56); this dictum reminds us that Finland is a small nation of which few know anything and that is far from the centres. In such countries international 'élite people' are also a scarce commodity. Another significant factor is that the news item should fit 'the mental image of what one expects to find' (Galtung & Ruge, 1965, p. 56) and that negative events are traditionally assumed to make better news than positive, although this 'mental image' can also be challenged. Asked in 2003 (Uskali, 2007, p. 28) whether his criteria still held water, Galtung added one more—entertainment value—and said that it probably had become the most important criterion.

Prakke's criteria, also from the 1960s, offers a concentrated view on the value of a news item as the interplay of three dimensions: temporal, cultural, and spatial distance (Hadenius & Weibull, 1999). For Finland, being spatially 'distant' from any 'centre', the event needs to be big or somehow interesting to overcome even the cultural distance.

Pietikäinen (2000) made a study of Finland as a news item in British and French quality papers (*The Times*, *The Independent*, *The Guardian*, *Le Monde*, *Libération*) in 1991–1992 and 1997–1998. The total number of articles in the five papers in four years was no more than 264. The spatial distance from 'peripheral' Finland to 'central' Britain or France was not great, but the cultural connections were thinner: no direct historical ties, linguistically alien.

When Pietikäinen conducted her study in late 1990s, none of the British or French papers had a permanent correspondent in Finland. *Libération* had a stringer in Stockholm, *The Independent* said its Scandinavian correspondent was in Bonn, Germany, and *The Guardian* was sending a reporter to Finland when necessary. Only *Le Monde* had a staff correspondent in Stockholm, speaking Swedish and covering Scandinavia and the Baltic countries. Pietikäinen refers to another thesis, based on interviews with correspondents resident in Finland: they all had emphasized the importance of insight into the culture, history, and contemporary political issues of the subject country, as well as mastering the language—which all in all required that the correspondent should live in the country (Pietikäinen, 2000, pp. 44–45).

Pietikäinen's own correspondence with the Stockholm-based *Le Monde* correspondent confirms the point. The correspondent said that he suggested about 80 per cent of *Le Monde*'s material on Finland, and if he did not actively look for news and suggest stories, there would be very few news items. He travelled to Finland about five times a year, read *Hufvudstadsbladet* and *Yle*'s Swedish language text TV on a daily basis, and monitored news about Finland in other Scandinavian papers (Pietikäinen, 2000, pp. 46–47).

In the 1990s, Finland became newsworthy. As long as the Soviet Union existed, Finland tended to be, to combine two contemporary catchwords, 'a Finlandized neighbour of the bear'. Still the deep recession of the early 1990s was usually credited solely to the abrupt fall of trade with Russia (which actually was one of the factors behind the crisis, but not the only one). The recession made news, and at the same time Finland was negotiating to become a member of the European Union, which it did in 1995 along with Sweden and Austria. In Pietikäinen's later period, 1997–1998, the recession was over and Finland was in the EU, so the number of news items was lower. But Pietikäinen concludes that even if there were fewer stories, the variety of items was broader, and the articles were longer and more analytic. According to her content analysis, in the late 1990s the news was also less stereotypical than in the early years of the decade, and Finland perhaps was getting a little bit out of the periphery (Pietikäinen, 2000, pp. 119–122). Lindberg's (2008) study, based on the Finnish foreign ministry's reviews of the German press in 1989–1998, also suggests that the frame for Finland changed from Russia's neighbour to a fellow member of the EU.

Finland and Sweden are neighbours and have a long common history, and Swedish is commonly understood in Finland or spoken as a first language, and in Sweden there are indigenous Finns in the North, and a large immigrant population in the country's industrial centres. Paakkunainen (2008) analyzed news about the neighbouring country on the Websites of the public service broadcasters *Yle* and *SVT* and of the leading newspapers *Helsingin Sanomat* and *Dagens Nyheter* over a period in the spring of 2007. The material consisted of 823 news stories, 71 per cent of which appeared in Finnish media. From Sweden to Finland, the linguistic and cultural barrier is higher than from Finland to Sweden, and according to the general pattern, the flow of news tends to be denser from a bigger country to a smaller. For Finns, Sweden is less of a foreign country than Finland is for Swedes. Paakkunainen also pointed out that the news items were rather versatile on both sides and that the differences in categories were small. The flow was dominated by positive and neutral news items.

WHAT: 'INTERESTING' NEWS IF 'NOTHING' HAPPENS

In the summer of 2013, Mark Bosworth initiated a story about the Finnish maternity package, babies who sleep in a cardboard box, on *BBC*'s Website, and it became one of its most ever read stories.[2] Soft stories are the recipe of Bosworth and many other freelancers: a Tango Festival in a small town in western Finland; Muslims living in Rovaniemi, Lapland; and, naturally, Santa, hosting visitors in the same town (Vehkoo, 2013; Mayow, 2013).

In recent years the biggest negative news from Finland has been two cases of school shootings within one year (Koljonen, 2013, pp. 208–220). Everyday hard news usually concerns the economy, and in the context of the Eurocrisis it is often negative. Even the former source of good news, Nokia, has been declining. An example of good news noticed by correspondents is the success of Finnish school children in the Pisa (Programme for International Student Assessment) studies. Finnish personalities are seldom newsworthy outside the country's borders, with a few exceptions. Generally, however, weird things make the news: such 'sports' as mobile phone throwing, wife carrying, or bog football, or a pop-up restaurant down in a mine (Vahtera, 2012).

CONCLUSIONS

For foreign correspondence, Finland really is a distant country in the north. Non-Finnish staff correspondents have become a rare phenomenon—the full-time staff of Western news agencies consists mostly of Finnish natives, but Russian and Chinese agencies have their own nationals. Sweden is culturally and politically close to Finland, but even the Swedish media has withdrawn from Helsinki, while Finland's biggest newspaper *Helsingin Sanomat* and the public service broadcaster *Yle* both have a staff correspondent in Stockholm.

Historically, small nations tend to be interesting mainly when they are in trouble, so from a national point of view the absence of correspondents may be interpreted as a good sign; the flow of economic news is business as usual. 'Interesting' is the key criterion for full-time freelancers, the lack of which does not mean that items are insignificant. The 'babies in a cardboard box' story is a parade example of an interesting story with substance.

NOTES

1. See: http://bit.ly/lnykiKd. Data from this source are incorporated into the figures in the Conclusions chapter. The standard questionnaire of this book was not used because quantitative information could be based on the source indicated here and sufficient qualitative material was available in published interviews.
2. See http://bbc.in/1eoq4Pq.

REFERENCES

GALTUNG, J., & RUGE, M. (1965). The Structure of Foreign News. Reprinted in Tumber, H. (ed.), *News: A Reader.* Oxford: Oxford University Press.

HADENIUS, S., & WEIBULL, L. (1999). *Massmedier: En bok om press, radio & tv.* Stockholm: Bonniers.

JULKUNEN, M. (1975). *Talvisodan kuva. Ulkomaisten sotakirjeenvaihtajien kuvaukset Suomesta v. 1939–1940*. Turku, Finland: University of Turku.

KOLJONEN, K. (2013). *Kriisi journalismissa. Kansakunnan katastrofit ja muuttuva professio*. Tampere, Finland: Tampere University Press.

LINDBERG, M. (2008). *Ulkoministeriön mediakatsaukset ja Suomi-kuva Saksan lehdistössä 1989–1998*. Turku, Finland: University of Turku.

Manninen, O., & SALOKANGAS, R. (2009). *Eljas Erkko. Vaikenematon Valtiomahti*. Helsinki: WSOY.

MAYOW, L. (2013). Laatikossa nukkuvien vauvojen isä. *Helsingin Sanomat*, p. C20 [Online]. Available from http://bit.ly/1jMrClF.

PAAKKUNAINEN, P. (2008). Suomen ja Ruotsin naapurisopua. Vertaileva sisällön analyysi naapurimaan uutisoinnista ja uutiskriteereistä Helsingin Sanomien, Yleisradion, Dagens Nyheterin ja SVT:n verkkouutisissa. Unpublished master's thesis in journalism, University of Jyväskylä, Finland.

PIETIKÄINEN, M. (2000). Pois periferiasta? Suomi uutisena Ison-Britannian ja Ranskan laatulehdistössä 1990-luvulla. Unpublished master's thesis in journalism, University of Jyväskylä, Finland.

USKALI, T. (2007). Ulkomaanuutisten uusi maailma. Tampere: Vastapaino.

VAHTERA, T. (2012). Mikä meissä kiinnostaa? *Helsingin Sanomat* [Online]. Available from http://bit.ly/RqUqHl.

VEHKOO, J. (2013). Sähkeitä Suomesta. *Journalisti*. September. Available from http://bit.ly/1nrY7Xc.

9 Foreign Correspondents in France

From Prestige Status to Changing Practices and Complex Perspectives

Jérémie Nicey[1] *and Antonella Agostino*[2]

INTRODUCTION

France has long been a hub for international news and several media innovations happened in Paris. In 1835, Agence Havas, the precursor of *Agence France Presse*, was the first modern news agency. It defined an initial 'model' of news correspondence (Palmer, 2011). France was also where photojournalism developed. As a hub, it was appealing because of the international role played by France and the attractiveness of its capital in several fields, as well as with the discourse of national political leaders, who emphasized the crucial role of foreign journalists in shaping the image of the country abroad and in diplomacy.

The situation has changed in the past 20 years. Paris is no longer as central in the production and circulation of international news as it was. This has an undeniable impact on the strategies of foreign bureaus, and this reflects on the transformations of news production and coverage, on journalists' career patterns, and on digital uses and practices in the past decade.

This chapter results from original research and interviews; it examines the profiles of foreign correspondents (FCs) in France, as well as their constraints and perspectives in a changing environment. The study seeks not only to depict the range of conditions in which FCs operate, but also to identify shared patterns and elements in their daily routines.

This study therefore intends to address the following issues: Within the context of economic pressure and of the redefined role of journalism, which strategies do newsrooms develop toward their FCs based in France? How are FCs' practices affected, and does the coverage of Europe from Paris function as a prism of interpretation and influence in similar ways to those it does for national breaking news?

Our hypothesis is that the changes observed in the activities of FCs correspond to both macro and micro sociological levels: they illustrate the reconfiguration of the media environment and media uses, as well as the modifications in their own professional practices and identities. To test and verify the latter, we will briefly map the landscape; then we will try to examine the significance of FCs in the French political and media landscape, as well as their various working practices; finally we shall discuss their role in addressing European issues and their own perspectives as producers of international news.

WHO ARE THE FOREIGN CORRESPONDENTS IN FRANCE? GAPS IN THE 'OFFICIAL' LANDSCAPE

With respect to quantitative analysis, research focusing on foreign correspondents, an activity marked by relative operational freedom, always risks being incomplete. FCs in France are represented by several associations, and many of them (945 in 2012) are accredited by an official entity: the *Centre d'Accueil de la Presse Etrangère* (CAPE), set up in Paris in 2001 under the aegis of the Ministry of Foreign and European Affairs. This shared space was removed and replaced by an ordinary office at the Ministry during the summer of 2013. But not all FCs request such an accreditation. Accordingly, available statistics are incomplete, but the data do help us to understand the origins of FCs (see Table 9.1): around 50 per cent are from Europe; more than 20 per cent from Asia; 20 per cent from North, Central, and Latin America; less than 10 per cent from North Africa and the Middle East; less than 1 per cent from Africa and Oceania. Countries with the most number of FCs reporting in France include the United States (143 FCs), Japan (115 FCs), Germany (111 FCs), the UK (92 FCs), and China (52 FCs). According to the CAPE, 442 FCs work mainly for print media, 277 for broadcast media, 193 for news agencies, and 33 for online media. There are approximately 566 male and 379 female journalists.

Table 9.1 Geographical distribution of accredited foreign correspondents in France.

Continent/Zone of FCs Accredited in France	Number of FCs (2011)	Proportion (2011) (%)	Number of FCs (2012)	Proportion (2012) (%)
Europe and Russia	544	52	**436**	**46**
Asia	213	20	**209**	**22**
Americas (North, Central, Latin)	209	20	**197**	**21**
North Africa and Middle East	78	7	**88**	**9**
Africa	8	1	**12**	**1**
Oceania	2	<1	**3**	**<1**
Total	*1,054*	*100*	*945*	*100*

Source: French Ministry of Foreign Affairs: Bureau de la Presse, de la Radio et de la Télévision Étrangère.

Three features stand out. The number of accredited FCs in France is still decreasing: in the 1980s, there were about 3,000. Asian correspondents are well represented; they were much encouraged by the French authorities in the 1980s, and they still consider Paris as a cultural and business international news centre. Despite historical ties between France and Africa, very few FCs are from African countries, mostly due to the financial situation of the African press.

Another difficulty that we faced was to identify the FCs. Official information says only that over 98 per cent are located in the Paris region, a reflection of the centralism of the country. Our study suggests that most FCs cover solely France. And as some of the media have separate journalists based in Brussels (who also work once per month in the French city of Strasbourg, the official seat of the European Parliament), the France-based FCs do not have to cover EU stories. There are exceptions: most Nordic FCs in Paris are in charge of Western and Southern Europe; many Asian FCs in Paris cover the EU and sometimes Eastern Europe and the Maghreb. In short, the geographical duties of FCs range widely; they depend on the past and present positions of their company in Europe and on personal factors of the FCs themselves.

Recalling that FCs in France form 'a segmented and heterogeneous group' (Ribadeau-Dumas, 2010, pp. 83–92), we sought to go over and beyond the global trends suggested by the official data. This chapter was thus inspired by the PhD work of Agostino (2006–2013) focusing on Italian and French foreign correspondents based in Brussels, Paris, and Rome and on their coverage of European issues. In the PhD study, she conducted 168 interviews, and we isolated one case; however, the elements provided by the 167 others are appropriate for the final discussion. The present study is based mainly on new in-depth interviews with 22 journalists (see Table 9.2). The sample was chosen to comply as much as possible with official lists (despite bias in referencing). The common survey instrument designed for the present book project guided our interviews.

Our research initially intended to be completed by the administration of the same questionnaire to 20 other FCs online, but this method was abandoned when noting that the richness and length of the questionnaire were quite inadequate to the full schedules of FCs (our first attempts showed that the journalists were not eager to spend time on the document and that they preferred face-to-face interviews to formulate precise and relevant answers). However, our sample managed to respect the geographical proportions of the official data, including oddities such as the over-representation of Japan, which has more than 100 accredited FCs (115 in 2012); the sample included several freelancers because the latter correspond to a strong and increasing trend (with the constraint of being paid piecemeal). These freelancers generally produce soft news and include nonprofessionals or retired correspondents who call on their network of contacts and their knowledge of the country. This enabled us to clarify our target

Table 9.2 Foreign correspondents in France: Interview data (2012–2013).

Correspondents	Country of the Media's Headquarters	Type of Media	Ownership
FC1	Italy	Press/radio	Private/public
FC2	Albania/Germany	Radio	Public
FC3	United Kingdom / Canada	Radio	Public
FC4	Germany	Press/photo	Private
FC5	Japan	TV/radio	Public
FC6	Romania	Radio	Public
FC7	The Netherlands/Belgium	Press/radio	Private/public
FC8	Denmark	Press	Private
FC9	United States	Press	Private
FC10	Switzerland	Press	Private
FC11	Colombia	Press/radio	Private
FC12	China	Press	Private
FC13	Norway	Press/radio	Private
FC14	United Kingdom	Press	Private
FC15	Canada	Press	Private
FC16	Japan	Print	Private
FC17	Mexico	Print	Private
FC18	Chile	TV/radio	Private/public
FC19	Turkey	Press / TV	Private
FC20	Russia	Press	Private
FC21	Israel	TV-radio/press	Public/private
FC22	Senegal	Agency	Semi-public

group in terms of the definitions of foreign correspondents (Hamilton & Jenner, 2004a; Gross & Kopper, 2011; Archetti, 2013). We focused on professional journalists who frequently collaborated with and produced for their home news outlets, whether they were registered as such by institutions, unions, or press clubs.

WHAT IS REPORTED? FCs' PRACTICES AND STORIES

This section analyzes the modus operandi of FCs in gathering and selecting news and in producing their outputs. First and foremost: the selection. FCs generally initiate 80–90 per cent of their stories, which could indicate a certain degree of autonomy, although this has decreased, especially for TV journalists (Foote, 2005). In the end, the foreign news editors, who have their own perception of what is newsworthy, have to agree on which stories are to be researched and published. This confirms Chang's earlier observations (1992). The editors follow agency copy or online stories. The increasing use of such sources at headquarters hastens the reduction in FC contributions, as noted by all interviewees. The consequence of such practices for FCs is that they often deal with predictable stories: accordingly, Strauss-Kahn's affair (in 2011) was highly covered, as well as the love affairs of the former and current presidents Sarkozy and Hollande (in 2008 and 2012). The majority of FCs mainly cover politics, economics, and society, but their duties also include typical stories about French culture, tourism, gastronomy, and women and thereby risk feeding and reinforcing stereotypes. Sports are seldom covered, save for feature pieces.

In the end, the practices and stories of FCs may be classified as the:

- Coverage of French breaking news stories;
- Coverage of news stories affecting the community of their home country;
- Comparison with France of stories happening in their home country (public debates, new laws, etc.) as directed by the headquarters;
- Investigation of feature/magazine stories.

Whereas the third case (comparative aspects) is driven mainly by accuracy and facts (reported by FC7, FC8, FC10, FC12, FC16, FC19), in the fourth case FCs operate as both ethnographists and sociologists and are therefore more subjective than in any of their breaking news stories coverage. Yet some assume that correspondents may often combine facts and comments (FC10). All interviewees denied censorship: stories are agreed to before production, and if some of their articles were not published, the reason was rather that there was no room left. By extension, the noncoverage of certain stories is problematic, especially in the case of news agencies (FC22) because it means that such stories therefore remain completely unknown by their customers and by audiences. Because of current and increasing budget pressure, many stories occurring far from Paris are not covered, unless they are crucial or financed via a press trip, which is ethically arguable. Finally, the coverage of the Europe Union's issues is itself specific (see infra: FCs and the Specific Coverage of Europe: A Critical Approach).

WHEN AND WHERE DO STORIES COME FROM? FCs' SOURCES AND ROUTINES

Despite nuances, especially between breaking news FCs and soft news FCs, the sources and routines appear rather homogeneous. Almost all, except for FC22 working for an agency, rank their consumption of French national media as their first source to be consulted (most of them cited regional

Le Parisien and 'real-time' TV broadcasting). An increasing trend emerges: some often produce 'second-hand' stories by adapting, if not simply translating, the material from national media. Whether this is specific to France and/or due to time pressure remains uncertain. Pressure of time was mentioned as the most signifying source of influence in their practices by 90 per cent of the interviewees (despite the relativity due to time zones); some even specifically pointed out that it gives them less time for reporting on the spot (FC6, FC8, FC17, FC19). Its corollary—that is, competition (at least for private companies)—was also often mentioned. But both factors need to be nuanced since 'the declining number of FCs has actually reduced the number of competitors' (F17). In passing, all correspondents underline the low possibilities of producing stories during the summer and the weekends. FCs all feel their mailbox is snowed under with public relations messages; many consider such communications as counterproductive and prefer to develop their own strategies. Surprisingly, the ordinary citizen is almost never mentioned as a primary source of alerts (except FC18 and FC22).

However, FCs themselves massively use the Internet, as an organizational, newsgathering, and verification tool. Some even wonder how they managed news stories before the Internet era (FC17, FC18), or they at least compare it to their ancient and complex practices. Among the practical changes are the disappearance of the price of transmission and the opportunity to read their own final production online, even on PDF versions of the newspaper. Digital communication is highly challenging because it has transformed both the work of FCs and their professional identity. The trend applies to Twitter, which FCs use opportunistically: half of them follow what is produced, but very few produce content because of the lack of time to deliver accurate news. Similarly, few frequently feed their own blogs (FC7, FC10, FC12, FC14, FC16, FC18).

Finally, the output of foreign correspondents remains influenced by their national journalistic cultures (Hallin & Mancini, 2004). Whereas the ambient environment of the French press is historically opinionated, the Anglo-American press is fact-centric. Another element: as the venue has lost part of its international and diplomatic influence, scoops and exclusive interviews are challenging for FCs in Paris, and they often occur when events are centered on their own nation, for instance, when politicians or celebrities from their home country happen to be in France before they are a top story in national news (FC2, FC15, FC20, FC21).

HOW DO FCs MANAGE THEIR MISSION? DIVERSE CONDITIONS AND POSITIONS

The working conditions of FCs in France are diverse. Some still have a bureau, but increasingly since the 1990s, more work from home because of economic reasons. The latter also affects the positions and job profiles, even for experienced FCs. In the past five years, several interviewees (FC3, FC7, FC13, FC15) were asked to transform their permanent and full-time assignment to freelance contributions, which they then need to multiply and diversify, thus producing far more stories to maintain their standard of living and 'developing [themselves] as their own brand' (FC7). The same trend applies to new FCs, who rarely have a permanent contract; there are exceptions in public service media, as well as for Asian FCs generally installed for three years, following the rules of diplomats.

Likewise, salaries of full-time FCs differ widely: they are indexed on age and experience, on type of media, and to a certain extent on the cost of living of their home country rather than of Paris, one of the highest in Europe. This is a problem for several interviewees (FC6, FC11, FC18, FC22) and is aggravated by the high rents in Paris; as a consequence, they do not all live in the same district but are spread throughout the Parisian region. This confirms that they do not form a homogeneous group.

All FCs identify the present decline of their significance to the digital shift (Wu & Hamilton, 2004). The Internet has increased the availability of documents and sources useful for FCs, but it has also brought competitors of a new kind, including nonprofessionals. Furthermore, the Internet turned the logics of time into the logics of the instant, and it transformed the logics of quality (understanding, interpreting, and providing context to news) into quantity (circumscribed to the news events per se). For instance, the work of FC5, a Japanese TV and radio journalist, nowadays often includes the production of textual short flashes for the Website of his company, before editing audiovisual material: this illustrates how 'close and competitive to news agencies the practices of FCs can be' (FC19), and this raises the challenging issue of whether this is an isolated case or a trend.

Hitherto, we briefly contextualized the identities and conditions of exercise of FCs. However, more obvious criteria lend significance and influence to some FCs and less to others. Their country of origin and the position/prestige of their media company are still strong variables. Correspondents working for Anglo-American news outlets (FC3, FC9, FC14) combine these aspects and therefore benefit from easier conditions of exercise: they find relatively open doors to political and business leaders. Yet this access to primary sources is said to be more difficult in French than in Nordic, German, and Dutch traditions (FC2, FC4, FC7, FC13). The networks that the FCs have themselves built over years or decades play a role (some senior journalists, for instance, admit that they personally know senior diplomats), as well as the mastering of the French language, in conjunction with the historical and cultural proximity of their country of origin.

Almost all interviewees, however, mentioned the same factor: most French politicians are not interested in giving time to foreign media, as they consider the latter's audience more or less useless for vote getting, or sometimes because they underestimate the skills of foreign journalists (FC13), despite the authorities' recurring reminders about the diplomatic influence and the image of France provided by FCs. Some see this as a challenge and develop their own strategies: FC15 mentioned that after identifying 'vanity as the Achilles heel of French politicians', he found that 'contacting their book publishers is often fruitful to obtain direct interviews'. Similarly, television foreign correspondents seem to have easier access because their medium is considered more influential.

FCs AND THE SPECIFIC COVERAGE OF EUROPE: A CRITICAL APPROACH

In recent years, the news coverage of the EU has often dealt with critical issues: the 'no-vote' of France and the Netherlands in the referendum about the European Constitution (2005), the critics of the Bolkenstein Directive on the European internal market and services (2004–2006), the record abstention rate for the European Parliament elections (2009), and the crisis of the Eurozone especially in some South European countries since 2011. The non-European FCs admit that they regularly point out 'the degradation of the welfare state' (FC16). We should also note the negative image of Europe among 28 per cent of citizens (European Commission, 2012a); 48 per cent of them claim they cannot understand the work of the EU, and 60 per cent blame the media for not being well-informed (European Commission, 2012b), despite the multiple communication strategies deployed by the European Commission (Agostino, 2014, pp. 29–61; Dacheux, 2004).

The image and knowledge about Europe thus depend on news reports, which do not evoke a sense of a common European identity: the coverage is generally limited to a comparison between social problems, in accordance with national interests, thus confirming the process of 'news domestication' (Clausen, 2004). As a result, the projected image of the EU is highly contrasted country by country (Baisnée, 2003b). This highlights the need for 'pedagogy by Foreign Correspondents' (FC13), although information about Europe is said to be 'difficult to sell and promote' (FC1). If the capacity of news users to 'think Europe' exists, it would comply with Anderson's observations (1991) about 19th-century newspapers enabling local inhabitants to imagine themselves as members of national communities or with Hannerz' assertions about international news stories making users feel cosmopolitan and thinking of 'the world as a single place' (Hannerz, 2004). However, there is a gap between citizens who do not appropriate the European ideals and issues, and the elites or journalists who do but who end up being 'the only E.U. public' (Baisnée, 2000). In other words, 'news about Europe is often ahead of a European identity' (Wolton, 1997, p. 316).

As already mentioned, when FCs in Paris have a colleague working in Brussels, they then are not in charge of European news. When this is the case, the practices of both FCs are separate and 'almost no type of contact or collaboration' (FC1) exists between them, even when EU events affect national affairs. As a result, the coverage from capitals such as Paris is either nation oriented or nonexistent (Baisnée, 2003a). Consequently, the idea of a 'public sphere' (Habermas, 1989) on a European level appears an illusion (Baisnée, 2007) or an 'unfinished project' (Trenz, 2009), and it seems to come down to a European '*media* public sphere' (Mazzoni, 2003; Dahlgren, 2005; Mazzoleni, 2004). Finally, if there exists a sort of 'eurojournalism'—although this is much debated (e.g., Baisnée, 2003a, 2003b)—this is nowadays to be found in participatory forms: some citizens, whether in individual or collective modes—such as the blog 27etc.eu (see e.g. Fougier, 2010, p. 8)—address online audiences with a certain neutrality, and their content aims to enhance 'Europeanness'. In the end, such nonprofessional contributors illustrate how correspondents, despite their number, face competition when they are too institutional, as well as how involved and indeed expert online citizen platforms can be.

CONCLUSION: UNCERTAIN ROLE AND PERSPECTIVES: FCs OR 'NEWS AGENTS'?

Traditional foreign correspondents are changing, and their very existence is under threat; this is true of FCs in France, after the disappearance in recent years of several foreign bureaus and correspondents in Paris, and the significant reduction of their available resources, as mentioned by our interviewees. This limits the attractiveness of foreign correspondence for young generations of journalists: assignments and salaries are unstable; budgets to cover events are declining; time pressure is added to that of increased output, in addition to the initial missions (e.g., TV journalists producing online texts). Therefore, several FCs—mainly those with a senior status—consider that being an FC in France has lost its prestige (FC1, FC4, FC13, FC20, FC21; see also Hamilton & Jenner, 2004a, p. 301): 'fewer resources and shorter time to produce stories make the job of a FC a little less fun' (FC9). In this context, together with the growing number of freelancers of all sorts, they predict that few permanent FCs will survive in Paris.

They indeed face competition from online contents. Editors at the headquarters therefore claim that 'they already know the news, which is disseminated anyway . . . but without a FC, this is an illusion' (FC21). Foreign correspondents may not be reduced to a role of 'content coordinators' (Bastin, 2005) or to the cynical position of, let us say, 'news agents'. FCs' added value comes from their experience on the field, as well as from their subjectivity.

FCs knowledge of the host country and their capacity to interpret events (FC1) cannot be replaced by news agencies or online distant reporting. FCs are supposed to play the role of 'cultural interpreters' (Mazzoleni & Splendore, 2007), 'fighting stereotypes, although sometimes feeding them in their articles or books' (FC1). For a few, this goes further: with experience, the FC may be affected by 'the diplomat syndrome': she or he may 'act as an ambassador defending his/her host country [France] and correcting negative and inaccurate French-bashing often read in the British press by editors at the headquarters' (FC21). In other words, experienced FCs are able to 'transform confusion into essential information' (F. De Bortoli, FC for *Il Corriere della Sera*, in Macri, 2011). FCs are of great use if their production is not limited to breaking news but rather enlarged to soft news and investigation. However, such practices become marginal, and FCs who have time for 'a wider look and a wider analysis' (FC16) consider themselves 'fortunate' (FC14).

In the past, the role of FCs could be defined as making the far near and the unknown known to media users. Nowadays, as news items circulate faster, the role of FCs may be to render intelligible what is confused and to bring nuances and distance to events. Whereas the trend is to employ technicians capable of fast transmission, some FCs claim this is not the same job and try to move to a different practice, consonant with slow journalism (FC18). Inasmuch as the FCs can no longer be 'the only eyes of readers and foreign editors abroad' (FC11, FC18), they may alternatively add value by providing their viewpoint based on experience. For all these reasons, most FCs in France predict not their demise but their 'evolution' (Hamilton & Jenner, 2004b). Practices have certainly changed and continue to do so, as did and do those of the actors they 'monitor'. Ultimately, this is a challenge for researchers as much as is the uncertainty of the results due to incomplete official data: in the end, FCs based in France have not lost all their mystery.

ACKNOWLEDGEMENTS

We would like to thank the correspondents who agreed to be interviewed for this chapter.

NOTES

1. Jérémie Nicey: Associate professor at the public school of journalism of Tours (University François-Rabelais), member of the media and communication lab. (CIM, team MCPN) of Paris 3 Sorbonne Nouvelle University; contact: jeremie.nicey@univ-tours.fr.
2. Antonella Agostino: Journalist; PhD, media and communication lab. (CIM) of Paris 3 Sorbonne Nouvelle University; contact: a_agostino@ymail.com.

REFERENCES

AGOSTINO, A. (2014). *Médias et institutions européennes: Discours des professionnels de l'information—De la presse écrite aux blogs (français et italiens) sur l'actualité européenne.* PhD thesis, Université Sorbonne Nouvelle Paris 3 (forthcoming), Paris.

ANDERSON, B. (1991). *Imagined Communities: Reflections on the Origin and Spread of Nationalism.* London: Verso (revised and extended, 2010).

ARCHETTI, C. (2013). Journalism in the Age of Global media: The Evolving Practices of Foreign Correspondents in London. *Journalism.* 14 (3), pp. 419–436.

BAISNÉE, O. (2000). Les journalistes, seul public de l'Union européenne? *Critique internationale.* 9, pp. 30–35.

———. (2003a). The (Non-) Coverage of the European Parliament. In Bond, M. (ed.), *Europe, Parliaments and the Media.* London: Federal Trust, pp. 77–104.

———. (2003b). Un impossible journalisme européen. *Hermès.* 35, pp. 145–51.

———. (2007). The European Public Sphere Does Not Exist (at Least It's Worth Wondering). *European Journal of Communication.* 22 (4), pp. 493–503.

BASTIN, G. (2005). L'Europe saisie par l'information (1952–2001): Des professionnels du journalisme engagé aux *content coordinators.* In Garcia, G., & Le Torrec, V. (eds.), *L'Union européenne et les médias. Regards croisés sur l'information européenne.* Paris: L'Harmattan, pp. 19–33.

CHANG, T. K., & LEE, J-W. (1992). Factors Affecting Gatekeepers' Selection of Foreign News: A National Survey of Newspaper Editors. *Journalism Quarterly.* 69 (3).

CLAUSEN, L. (2004). Localizing the Global: 'Domestication' Processes in International News Production. *Media, Culture and Society*, 26 (1), pp. 25–44.

DACHEUX, E. (2004). Le visage actuel de l'espace public européen. *Médiamorphoses.* 12, pp. 26–31.

DAHLGREN, P. (2005). The Public Sphere: Linking the Media and Civic Cultures. In Rothenbuhler, E., and Coman, M. (eds.), *Media Anthropology.* Thousand Oaks, CA: Sage, pp. 218–227.

EUROPEAN COMMISSION. (2012a). *Standard Eurobarometer 76.* Media Use in the European Union. Autumn 2011 [Online]. Available from http://ec.europa.eu/public_opinion/archives/eb/eb76/eb76_media_en.pdf.

EUROPEAN COMMISSION (2012b). *Standard Eurobarometer 77.* Public Opinion in the European Union. Spring 2012 [Online]. Available from http://ec.europa.eu/public_opinion/archives/eb/eb77/eb77_publ_en.pdf.

FOOTE, J.S. (2005). The Changing Role of TV Network News Correspondents. In Tunstall, J. (ed.), *Media Occupations and Professions: A Reader.* New York: Oxford University Press, pp. 158–160.

FOUGIER, E. (2010). '27etc' ou l'émergence d'un journalisme citoyen européen. In Fougier, E. (ed.), *Médias et Europe (2).* Paris: Institut de relations internationales et stratégiques (IRIS), pp. 7–8 [Online]. Available from http://bit.ly/1j54L2X.

HABERMAS, J. (1989). *The Structural Transformation of the Public Sphere.* Boston: MIT Press.

HAMILTON, J.M., & JENNER, E. (2004a). Redefining Foreign Correspondence. *Journalism,* 5 (3), pp. 301–321.

———. (2004b). Foreign Correspondence: Evolution, Not Extinction. *Nieman Reports,* 58 (3), pp. 98–100.

HALLIN, D. and MANCINI, P. (2004). *Comparing Media Systems: Three Models of Media and Politics.* Cambridge: Cambridge University Press.

HANNERZ, U. (2004). *Foreign News: Exploring the World of Foreign Correspondents.* Chicago/London: University of Chicago Press.

GROSS, P., and KOPPER, G. (2011). *Understanding Foreign Correspondence*. New York: Peter Lang.

MAZZOLENI, G. (2004). *La comunicazione politica*. Bologna: Mulino.

MAZZOLENI, G., & SPLENDORE, S. (2007) Italian Foreign Correspondents: Fashioning Representation of France. In Palmer, M., & Aubert, A. (eds.), *L'information mondialisée*, Paris: L'Harmattan, pp. 142–152.

MAZZONI, M. (2003). La sfera pubblica europea: concetti e problemi. In Marini, R. (ed.), *Comunicare l'Europa. Campagne elettorali, informazione, comunicazione istituzionale*. Perugia: Morlacchi Editore, pp. 15–53.

MACRI, P. (2011). La pubblicità non basta a sostenere il giornalismo online. *European Journalism Observatory* 6 May [Online]. Available from http://bit.ly/1gCKdgs.

PALMER, M. (2011). *Homo Informans: l'urgence des news au fil des millénaires*. Paris: L'Amandier.

RIBADEAU-DUMAS, V. (2010). *Le Centre d'Accueil de la Presse Etrangère: Un instrument de diplomatie publique?*, Mémoire de 4e année (supervised by D. Ruellan), Rennes: Sciences Po Rennes.

TRENZ, H-J. (2009). Uniting and Dividing. The European Public Sphere as an Unfinished Project. In Salovaara-Moring, I. (ed.), *Manufacturing Europe: Spaces of Democracy, Diversity and Communication*. Oslo: Nordicom, pp. 19–35.

WOLTON, D. (1997). *Penser la communication*. Paris: Flammarion.

WU, H. D., & HAMILTON, J. M. (2004). US Foreign Correspondents: Changes and Continuity at the Turn of the Century. *Gazette*. 66 (6), pp. 517–532.

10 Reporting Teutonia: Foreign Correspondents in Germany

Doing Well Despite Pessimistic Outlook

Oliver Hahn, Thomas Hanitzsch and Michael Brüggemann

With the support of:

Isabelle Brodeßer, Julia Eder and Stefan Kruschwitz

In modern, media-saturated society, foreign correspondents deliver us the world. They feed us with pictures from afar that often lie beyond the realm of our direct experience (Perry, 1985; Brewer, Graf, & Willnat, 2003; Wanta, Golan, & Lee, 2004; Ihlen, Allern, Thorbjornsrud, & Waldahl, 2010; Riegert, 2011). Furthermore, by way of reporting events and occurrences abroad, foreign news contributes to the cultivation of 'a sense of belonging in the world' (Hannerz, 2004, p. 34). The primary importance of foreign correspondents, therefore, lies in their power to shape our perceptions of other countries and cultures (Willnat & Weaver, 2003; Ihlen, Allern, Thorbjornsrud, & Waldahl, 2010; Gross & Kopper, 2011; Shoemaker, Cohen, Seo, & Johnson, 2012). Large-scale public opinion surveys have shown that foreign and international news can substantially affect the audience's knowledge, perception, and attitude toward other nations (Perry, 1990; Salwen & Matera, 1992). It is exactly for this reason that foreign news is 'a prime example of an area where most of us are reliant on what the media report' (Ihlen, Allern, Thorbjornsrud, & Waldahl, 2010, p. 31). Moreover, because international diplomacy and foreign policy making increasingly takes place within the media, foreign correspondents assume a key position in public conversation about foreign policy (Wu & Hamilton, 2004; Gross & Kopper, 2011).

The striking importance of foreign news notwithstanding, the proportion of news devoted to events and occurrences from afar seems to be shrinking in many countries, most notably in the United States (Carroll, 2007). This has become a matter of concern to media scholars and practitioners across the globe. Emery, for instance, has declared the international news hole to be an 'endangered species' (1989, p. 151), and a survey of US foreign correspondents conducted in 2001 indicated that the trend toward general neglect of traditional foreign newsgathering is not likely to be reversed in the near future.

At the same time, foreign correspondents today are facing manifold challenges, many of which result from the rapidly changing economic context of news production. Foreign news is one of the most costly news-gathering endeavors (Hamilton & Jenner, 2004; Sambrook, 2010), which is why news managers increasingly raise the question whether the fairly high costs of foreign reporting are justified by the audience's interest in foreign news (Hannerz, 2004). In response to the shrinking budgets allocated to foreign reporting, many news organizations have started to reduce the number of their correspondents and bureaus abroad (Meckel, 1998; Kumar, 2011; Willnat & Martin, 2012). As a result, fewer journalists are expected to work more (Archetti, 2012; Willnat & Martin, 2012). The remaining correspondents are concentrating around a few 'hot spots,' such as the Middle East (Hamilton & Jenner, 2004). One important trend in this context is the replacement of permanently employed correspondents by freelancers and so-called parachute reporters (Hamilton & Jenner, 2004; Archetti, 2012; Sambrook, 2010).

Foreign correspondents are a difficult object of scientific inquiry. They are almost constantly on the move, which is probably why we still know fairly little about this 'special tribe' (Hannerz, 2004, p. 3) of journalists (Hahn, Lönnendonker, & Scherschun, 2008). In this chapter, we will introduce the world of foreign correspondents operating from Germany. The study is based on online interviews with 119 correspondents and additional qualitative interviews with 98 journalists.

FOREIGN CORRESPONDENTS AS OBJECTS OF RESEARCH IN GERMANY

German researchers have devoted fairly little attention to foreign correspondents, which sets them apart from their American colleagues. It was Maletzke who, as early as 1966, demanded a broad study of the 'psychology and sociology' of correspondents, and yet there has not been much progress on the empirical front before recent years. Still, a quarter century ago, Marten characterized foreign correspondents as the 'unknown species' in communication research (1987, p. 23). There have been a number of small studies about German correspondents working abroad (Jürgens, 1974; Kirschstein, 1996; Siemes, 2000), as well as about correspondents reporting from Germany (Kluge, 1981; Sange, 1989; Piel, 1999).

Four major studies have been conducted in the more recent years: Junghanns and Hanitzsch (2006) conducted an online survey of 176 foreign correspondents working for German media. They concluded that foreign correspondents tended to be older and more experienced than their colleagues back home. Foreign correspondence was, more than other domains, dominated by men. Furthermore, foreign reporters were more likely to embrace role perceptions that emphasize context and analysis and that contribute to a better understanding of other cultures. Hahn, Lönnendonker, and Schröer

(2008) edited a volume for which qualitative interviews had been conducted on-site with approximately 300 foreign correspondents from Germany being based in various news places and regions to be reported around the world about their different working conditions and routines. Riesmeyer's (2010) study of foreign correspondents was based on qualitative interviews with 91 German journalists working from abroad. A major conclusion was that despite a deterioration of their working conditions, foreign reporters still feel privileged for pursuing a 'dream job'. This positive evaluation was largely driven by a relatively high professional autonomy.

The study that is perhaps most relevant in this context was carried out by Rothenberger (2009), who surveyed members of the Foreign Correspondents' Association in Germany (*Verein der Ausländischen Presse in Deutschland*, VAP). The association was founded in 1906 and had 444 members as of 2012, consisting of correspondents and journalists working for foreign media (VAP, 2012). An advantage of the VAP is that it maintains formal relations with the German Federal Press Office (*Bundespresseamt*, BPA) and the Federal Press Conference (*Bundespressekonferenz*, BPK). The BPK offers VAP members access to press conferences and grants them the right to ask questions (Rothenberger, 2009).

On the basis of 178 online interviews and eight additional qualitative interviews with VAP members, Rothenberger found 28.4 per cent of the respondents to be women and of an average age of 44.5 years for all members. Most of the interviewed journalists covered more than one country, with only 45.5 per cent of the respondents exclusively reporting on Germany. About half of the interviewed journalists were based in Germany for more than six years.

METHODS AND DATA SOURCES

Evidence reported in this chapter is based on a collaborative research project involving scholars from three universities: the LMU Munich/Germany, the University of Passau/Germany, and the University of Zurich/Switzerland. We applied a mixed-method strategy in order to gather meaningful information about foreign correspondents working in Germany, combining a quantitative survey with qualitative interviews.

The researchers conducted a quantitative survey as well as qualitative semistructured in-depth interviews between summer 2012 and spring 2013.[1] Altogether, we have approached a total of 357 journalists. Two messages were returned due to invalid email addresses, and 33 journalists said they were not any more working as foreign correspondents in Germany. The remaining, adjusted sample resulted in 119 completed questionnaires, which indicated an overall response rate of 37 percent.

In addition to the online survey, we conducted qualitative interviews with 98 correspondents from five continents and in all kinds of media. The interviews were carried out by students from the Universities of Munich/

Germany and Passau/Germany via email and telephone. Some of the correspondents wanted to stay anonymous during the qualitative phase; others agreed to being quoted.

The respondents for this study were obtained from the membership list of the Foreign Correspondents' Association in Germany (VAP). We recognize that not all foreign correspondents reporting from Germany are members of the VAP. However, due to the benefits VAP members get in terms of access to the Federal Press Conference, we assume that most permanent correspondents are enlisted in the organization. Freelancers and parachute correspondents, on the other hand, may be undersampled in this study. For the qualitative interviews, we drew a random sample from the VAP membership. All remaining correspondents were contacted for the survey. Journalists were provided with a personalized link to the survey tool, which allowed us to trace nonresponse during fieldwork. In the following section, the findings of quantitative survey and the qualitative interviews are alternately discussed.

FINDINGS

The Correspondents

Slightly more than half of the correspondents we identified through the roster of the Foreign Correspondents' Association in Germany (VAP) originated from Europe. Four major European nations contributed the largest numbers of journalists reporting from this country. These countries were France (38 FCs), Italy (26 FCs), Spain (16 FCs), and Great Britain (23 FCs). Another 68 of the correspondents were from the United States and 35 from Japan. Altogether, 36.5 per cent of these correspondents were female, which is a rather modest proportion of woman journalists in this particular field.[2] This comes without surprise: most studies have pointed to a heavy dominance of men among foreign reporters. The surveyed correspondents appeared to be relatively highly educated. Almost all of them (95.4 per cent) went through academic education, with 48.6 per cent holding a master's degree and 10.1 per cent being awarded a doctoral degree.

Also, two-thirds of the journalists (66.7 per cent) who responded to the online survey were married or lived in a partnership with their partners, also living in the country. This may be seen as an indication that assignments as foreign correspondents in Germany provide enough continuity and stability to strike a balance between work and life. This finding was endorsed in qualitative interviews: many correspondents stated that they are autonomous in scheduling their day and are very satisfied with the job as a correspondent as well as with the working and living conditions in Germany. The main problems for combining job and family are related to working until late at night due to time differences, and for some correspondents the job also implies a lot of travelling, which can be a problem.

Germany generates enough news and seems to be important enough to keep correspondents busy. More than half of the respondents (52.7 per cent) said they reported only about Germany. Other correspondents had to cover a larger territory. One out of five journalists (19.6 per cent) reported from two or three countries, while relatively few correspondents (8.9 per cent) had to cover ten or more countries. Popular combinations of covered countries are Germany and Austria, Germany, Austria and Switzerland, as well as 'Germany and the European Union'.[3]

The Stories

The journalists generally feel that stories from Germany are highly relevant to their audiences. Three out of four correspondents (75 per cent) even said that the interest in news from Germany had increased within their newsrooms and among the audiences. From the in-depth interviews, it becomes clear that the growing interest in news from Germany is mainly caused by the European crisis. Germany's role in the crisis has been absolutely central, and especially people living in Europe are highly interested in what is going on in Berlin. Up to 90 per cent of what the correspondents had to write about for the last two and a half years is connected directly or indirectly with the European crisis.

On average, the interviewed correspondents have reported about 9.8 years from their current post, which shows that being sent to Germany is a rather long-term assignment. Half of the respondents (50.9 per cent) have already spent seven years working in Germany when they responded to the survey, and more than one-third (35.3 per cent) said they spent 12 years or more.

Our results indicate that about two-thirds of the correspondents were employed by their news outlets, while the remaining 33.3 per cent said they work as freelancers. More than half of the interviewed journalists (54.4 per cent) work for a single news outlet, and another 20.2 per cent contribute to two media organizations. The correspondents work as journalists for 20.1 years on average and as foreign correspondents for 11.6 years. This indicates that many of them did not start their journalistic careers as correspondents but have worked as journalists in their home countries well before they were sent to assignments abroad.

The print media are still the prime sector for foreign correspondents, but online media are catching up fairly quickly. Most correspondents we interviewed work for print media (56.3 per cent, or 67 journalists), while the proportion of correspondents in online media (28.6 per cent, 34 journalists) was the second largest in the sample, followed by journalists working for news agencies (27.7 per cent, 33 journalists). Considering broadcast media as a whole, 58.6 per cent of correspondents (70 journalists total) could be broken down into the following categories: television reporters (public TV, 17.6 per cent [21 FCs]; private TV, 13.4 per cent [16 FCs])

Table 10.1 Reasons for working as a foreign correspondent in Germany.

Reasons	FC Agreement (%)
Personal interest to go abroad as a foreign correspondent	63
Offer by my media organization/post was available	44
Expertise / personal interest in Germany	43
Language skills	38
Personal ties/relationships to Germany	35

and radio journalists (public radio stations, 21.0 per cent [25 FCs]; private radio stations, 6.7 per cent [8 FCs]). These numbers indicate that a substantive number of foreign correspondents are already working across media. The data show that an impressive 51.3 per cent (61 FCs) of all interviewed correspondents produce content for more than one medium platform.

The Motivation

We also asked the journalists about their motives to work as foreign correspondents (see Table 10.1). Among the reporters we interviewed, the strongest motive was a personal interest to go abroad. Still, about 44 per cent said they took the job as it was offered to them by their media organization. Expertise and personal interest in Germany, personal ties, and relationships to the country, as well as German language skills, were other important motivating factors for a substantive proportion of the correspondents.

Another motive for correspondents to work in Germany is the contribution to intercultural understanding. Correspondents from the United States, Mexico, Japan, Egypt, Italy, France, and Britain said their job is to give people in their home countries an understanding of German culture and to explain German perspectives. Some of them also state that they are aware of stereotypes and clichés about Germany: they try either to use them only thoughtfully and in selected, mainly humorous contexts or to counteract them.

The Working Conditions

One important concern of this study was related to the conditions and constraints under which foreign correspondents work in Germany. Slightly more than half of the journalists interviewed said that they were the only correspondents reporting from Germany for their news organizations. Most of the correspondents describe the relation to German journalists and to other foreign correspondents in terms of networking, the exchange of opinions and information, and helpful contacts, but only rarely as a cooperation. The 'lone-rider' correspondents are usually covering a fairly wide area of issues and topics. Almost all of the journalists state that politics and economics are the most important German topics to cover, especially the Eurozone crisis. But, as some correspondents mention, there are also topics that the home office does not welcome, such as corruption in the Ukraine, prostitution in Sweden, criticism of the Islam in India, or royal families in Mexico. Overall, however, the data point to a rather fair workload for those covering the news from Germany. Most of the respondents (59.8 per cent) said they produce between one and five stories per week.

The Influences and Problems

Table 10.2 provides an overview of a number of factors that influence news work as perceived by the correspondents. The interviewed reporters were asked to rate the significance of their influence in their daily work on a scale ranging from 1 (no influence at all) to 5 (extreme influence).

Table 10.2 Influence on news work in Germany.

Influencing Factors	Mean Score
Time limits (your time available to cover a certain issue)	3.8
Peers in the newsroom and editorial supervisors	3.4
Personal values and beliefs	3.2
Resources limits (e.g., travel budget)	3.2
Access to sources and information in Germany	3.1
Space limits (in the newspaper, on the news broadcast, etc.)	3.0
Personal network of sources	3.0
Coverage from competing news organizations	2.9
Other foreign correspondents in the country	2.7
Audience research/feedback from the audience	2.5
Media laws and regulation in home country	2.4
The managers and owners of your news organizations	2.3
Politicians/governmental officials in Germany	2.2
Politicians/governmental officials in home country	2.1
Availability of press releases/PR material	2.1
Media laws and regulation in Germany	2.1
Business interests in home country	2.0
Friends and family	2.0
Business interests in Germany	1.8
Pressure groups home country	1.8
Pressure groups in Germany	1.8
Advertising considerations/profit expectations	1.4

Not surprisingly, the often limited time and resources allocated to the coverage of specific stories, along with limited space or airtime for foreign news items, put some major constraints on the journalists' work. These factors are of procedural relevance in that they have a direct impact on the conditions of news production. Another factor influencing the work of correspondents based in Germany is the authorization of interviews. This unique practice allows an interviewed person to change his/her statements afterward. For this reason, all journalists working in Germany are forced to send quotes or even the whole article to interviewees so that they may approve it for publication. The correspondents state that 'this is actually a totally self-defeating system,' (a reporter from the *Financial Times*, UK); it 'is completely archaic', 'makes work very difficult', and 'has to be cancelled the sooner the better!' (a correspondent from *Yedioth Ahronoth*, Israel).

Peers in the newsroom and editorial decision makers were also important in shaping the work of foreign correspondents. These are the people foreign correspondents have to deal with when they negotiate stories and angles of their coverage. Most of them confirmed working very autonomously, with freedom of selecting stories and with a regular, in most cases daily, contact with their home media organization. In only a few cases, the home office requests special stories from the correspondents, for example, when competing media pick up a newswire story. This agenda-setting function of news agencies can lead to conflicts between the correspondent and the editorial office, as one correspondent experienced.

At the same time, the surveyed journalists found their personal values and beliefs to be another important source of influence. Because many correspondents work rather independently from their newsrooms back home, they have probably more leeway in tailoring their coverage to some subjective views.

Many of the factors that often play out within the media organization and the newsroom seem to be of limited relevance to foreign correspondents. Competition among news media was still regarded a somewhat important issue, but other sources were of less concern to the interviewed journalists. These sources include audience research and feedback, media laws, politicians and government officials, as well as the managers and owners of the correspondents' news organizations.

Access to sources and information in Germany was rated fairly high among the factors that constrain the correspondents' work. However, this factor varies a lot depending on the home country and home media organization of the correspondents. Many correspondents from English-speaking countries (United States, Britain, India, South Africa) are content with the access to sources. Journalists from Switzerland, the Ukraine, Israel, Egypt, and Mexico expressed their dissatisfaction about the access to politicians and complained about long waiting times for information and appointments. Correspondents from Britain, France, and Switzerland especially recommended the *Bundespressekonferenz* (BPK). This is one way to easily get access to high-profile figures. An important source for story ideas, information, and hints for relevant topics are the German media, as the correspondents say. They explicitly name some nationwide newspapers and magazines, such as *Frankfurter Allgemeine Zeitung* (*FAZ*) and *Der Spiegel*, but no tabloid press.

Advertising considerations and profit expectations of the media company, on the other hand, had extremely little influence on foreign correspondents.

Recent Developments

Another important concern of the study was the transformation of foreign correspondence. We therefore presented the journalists with a list of statements about changes in their profession and asked them to indicate to what extent they feel these are true (see Table 10.3). Overall, one out of two interviewed journalist (47.2 per cent) believes that foreign correspondence has changed for the worse, while 20.8 per cent of the respondents think that things have improved. The remaining one-third of correspondents feel that the situation has not changed much. Consistent with a large stream of literature of foreign correspondence, this result indicates that job conditions in this field are indeed deteriorating.

A closer look at the journalists' assessments of specific trends within their profession, as reported in Table 10.3, helps identify some of the reasons

Table 10.3 Trends in foreign correspondence in Germany.

Trends	FC Agreement (%)
I feel increasing time pressure on my job	57
The number of correspondents has been substantially cut within the last five years	49
The resources available to do my job have been cut down (e.g., budget for travelling)	45
Parachute journalists have increasingly replaced traditional correspondents	39
Foreign coverage is increasingly covered from headquarters	39
There is reason to believe that my current post as foreign correspondent here may be cut in the near future	31
Local journalists are employed instead of traditional correspondents	26
Amateur journalists/bloggers/representatives of NGOs are increasingly used as replacements for traditional correspondents	20

why the overall trend is negative. Most journalists feel increasing time pressure in their work, and almost half of the respondents agree that editorial resources and the number of correspondents have been substantially cut down within the last five years. One reason for this development is that the importance of online media has increased. Today, people obtain their information very differently, so that journalists are being asked to use a wide variety of media channels. They have to write articles for the newspaper as well as for a Website or do a video broadcast. In addition, social media have had a big impact on the journalists' work. The speed of Twitter and the incredible engagement on Facebook present daily challenges that the correspondents have to master.

Still, more than one-third of all respondents believe that parachute journalists have increasingly replaced traditional correspondents and that foreign coverage is more and more covered from headquarters. And three out of ten correspondents even have reason to believe that their current post may be cut in the near future. Relatively few correspondents, on the other hand, see an increased use of amateur journalists and local journalists in foreign correspondence.

To sum it up, many correspondents feel that they have to deliver more stories with less time for research. This is for two major reasons: the increasing demand for cross-media reporting and the financial crisis. The latter had a huge impact on the work of the correspondents because it has been the most important topic to cover in recent years. But the topic also confirms the importance of on-site correspondents in Berlin. One unique problem in Germany is the peculiarity of having interviews authorized before publication, which not only complicates the FCs' job but also deteriorates journalism in Germany at large. However, the institution of the VAP helps correspondents in their daily work by getting access to sources, especially through the *Bundespressekonferenz* (BPK), and by arranging an exchange among the journalists. Although many correspondents in Germany feel working conditions have deteriorated in recent years, the majority of them are still very confident with their tasks and the relation to their editorial office.

CONCLUSIONS

We can draw a few conclusions from this review. First, the typical correspondent reporting from Germany is male, highly educated, and comes from a European country. Correspondents in Germany tend to be fairly experienced; the work as foreign reporter at their current location was a rather advanced step in their careers. Germany as a country seems interesting enough to keep journalists busy, which is why most of the correspondents can focus on a single country. The interviewed foreign correspondents even feel that the interest in news from Germany had increased during the last years, which is most likely an outcome of the

European financial crisis and the important role Germany plays in the political process. The correspondents we interviewed were strongly motivated by their personal interest to go abroad, but many of them also said that they simply took the job when it was offered to them by their media organization.

Most foreign correspondents still work for the print media, but online media seem to catch up rather quickly. Interestingly, about half of the reporters we interviewed already work across media. It is perhaps little surprising that foreign correspondents complain mostly about limited time and resources allocated to the coverage of specific stories, as well as about too little space or airtime for foreign news items. Quite peculiar for the German context is the culture of 'authorizing' interviews, which was seen by many of the interviewed journalists as an awkward practice.

Finally, our study found evidence for a rather substantive proportion of freelancers in foreign correspondence, but the good news is that about two-thirds of the correspondents are still employed by their news organizations. Nonetheless, the general outlook tends to be pessimistic: Nearly half of the interviewed journalists believe that foreign correspondence has changed for the worse, while only one out of five respondents think that things have improved. And here again, it is especially the increasing time pressure and limited editorial resources that have become a matter of concern.

NOTES

1. The authors thank master's students from the Universities of Passau/Germany and Munich/Germany for their support in collecting the empirical data.
2. Of all the journalists we identified in the list and for which we were able to determine gender, 277 were male and 159 journalists were female.
3. The latter is especially true for journalists from non-EU member states since many correspondents working with media inside the EU consider reporting about the EU (from Brussels) rather as domestic than as international correspondence (AIM Research Consortium, 2006, 2007a, 2007b, 2007c, 2007d).

REFERENCES

AIM Research Consortium (ed.). (2006). *Understanding the Logic of EU Reporting in Mass Media: Analysis of EU Media Coverage and Interviews in Editorial Offices in Europe* (AIM—Adequate Information Management in Europe, Working Papers, vol. 1). Bochum, Freiburg/Brsg.: Projektverlag.

———. (2007a). *Comparing the Logic of EU Reporting in Mass Media across Europe: Transnational Analysis of EU Media Coverage and of Interviews in Editorial Offices in Europe* (AIM—Adequate Information Management in Europe, Working Papers, vol. 2). Bochum, Freiburg/Brsg.: Projektverlag.

———. (2007b). *Comparing the Logic of EU Reporting: Transnational Analysis of EU Correspondence from Brussels* (AIM—Adequate Information Management in Europe, Working Papers, vol. 4). Bochum, Freiburg/Brsg.: Projektverlag.

———. (2007c). *Reporting and Managing European News: Final Report of the Project "Adequate Information Management in Europe" 2004–2007*. Bochum, Freiburg/Brsg.: Projektverlag.

———. (2007d). *Understanding the Logic of EU Reporting from Brussels: Analysis of Interviews with EU Correspondents and Spokespersons* (AIM—Adequate Information Management in Europe, Working Papers, vol. 3). Bochum, Freiburg/Brsg.: Projektverlag.

ARCHETTI, C. (2012). Which Future for Foreign Correspondence? *Journalism Studies*. 13, pp. 847–856.

BREWER, P.R., GRAF, J., & WILLNAT, L. (2003). Priming or Framing: Media Influence on Attitudes toward Foreign Countries. *Gazette*. 65, pp. 493–508.

CARROLL, J. (2007). Foreign News Coverage: The US Media's Undervalued Asset. Working Paper. Joan Shorenstein Center on the Press, Politics and Public Policy [Online]. Available from http://bit.ly/1fbvJUl.

EMERY, M. (1989). An Endangered Species: The International News Hole. *Gannett Center Journal*. 3, pp. 151–164.

GROSS, P., & KOPPER, G.G. (eds.). (2011). *Understanding Foreign Correspondence: A Euro-American Perspective of Concepts, Methodologies, and Theories*. New York: Peter Lang.

HAHN, O., LÖNNENDONKER, J., & SCHERSCHUN, N. (2008). Forschungsstand—Deutsche Auslandskorrespondenten und -korrespondenz. In HAHN, O., LÖNNENDONKER, J., & SCHRÖDER, R. (eds.), *Deutsche Auslandskorrespondenten. Ein Handbuch*. Konstanz: UVK Verlag, pp. 19–43.

HAHN, O., LÖNNENDONKER, J., & SCHRÖDER, R. (eds.). (2008). *Deutsche Auslandskorrespondenten: Ein Handbuch*. Konstanz: UVK.

HAMILTON, J.M., & JENNER, E. (2004). Redefining Foreign Correspondence. *Journalism: Theory, Practice & Criticism*. 5, pp. 301–321.

HANNERZ, U. (2004). *Foreign News: Exploring the World of Foreign Correspondents*. Chicago: University of Chicago Press.

IHLEN, Ø., ALLERN, S., THORBJORNSRUD, K., & WALDAHL, R. (2010). The World on Television: Market-driven, Public Service News. *Nordicom Review*. 31, pp. 31–45.

JUNGHANNS, K., & HANITZSCH, T. (2006). Deutsche Auslandskorrespondenten im Profil. *Medien & Kommunikationswissenschaft*. 54, pp. 412–429.

JÜRGENS, G. (1974). *Politische Auslandsberichterstattung im deutschen Fernsehen am Beispiel der Korrespondentenberichterstattung über die USA*. Berlin: Leitstelle politische Dokumentation.

KIRSCHSTEIN, F. (1996). Liveberichterstattung im 'Feuerwehrstil'. Auswirkungen neuer Technologien auf die Auslandsberichterstattung. In MECKEL, M., & KRIENER, M. (eds.), *Internationale Kommunikation. Eine Einführung*. Opladen: Westdeutscher Verlag, pp. 229–240.

KLUGE, H. (1981). *Die Bundesrepublik Deutschland als Objekt der Auslandsberichterstattung. Die Arbeit ausländischer Korrespondenten in der Bundesrepublik*. Münster: University of Münster.

KUMAR, P. (2011). Foreign Correspondents: Who Covers What. *American Journalism Review* [Online]. Available from http://bit.ly/1hOATv9.

MALETZKE, G. (1966). Interkulturelle Kommunikation und Publizistikwissenschaft. *Publizistik*. 11, pp. 318–331.

MARTEN, E. (1987). Zwischen Skepsis und Bewunderung. Zum Tätigkeitsprofil, Selbstverständnis und Deutschlandbild amerikanischer Auslandskorrespondenten in der Bundesrepublik Deutschland. *Publizistik*. 32, pp. 23–33.

MECKEL, M. (1998). Internationales als Restgröße? Zur Auslandsberichterstattung in Fernsehnachrichten. In KAMPS, K., & MECKEL, M. (eds.), *Fernsehnachrichten—Strukturen, Funktionen, Prozesse*. Opladen: Westdeutscher Verlag, pp. 257–274.

PERRY, D. K. (1985). The Mass Media and Inference about Other Nations. *Communication Research*. 12, pp. 595–614.

———. (1990). News Reading, Knowledge about, and Attitudes toward Foreign Countries. *Journalism Quarterly*. 67, pp. 353–358.

Pew Research Center for the People and the Press. (2002). Pew Research Center for the People and the Press Biennial Media Consumption Survey [Online]. Available from http://bit.ly/1gKR8Ed.

PIEL, A. (1999). *Niederländische Korrespondenten in Deutschland. Tätigkeitsprofile und Selbstverständnis*. Hagen: ISL-Verlag.

RIEGERT, K. (2011). Pondering the Future for Foreign News on National Television. *International Journal of Communication*. 5, pp. 1567–1585.

RIESMEYER, C. (2010). Traumjob oder Albtraum? Deutsche Auslandskorrespondenten im Zeitalter von Internet und Globalisierung. In HEPP, A., HÖHN, M., & WIMMER, J. (eds.), *Medienkultur im Wandel*. Konstanz: UVK, pp. 421–434.

ROTHENBERGER, L. (2009). *Aus Deutschland berichten. Entwicklung, Arbeitsweise und Mitgliederstruktur des Vereins der Ausländischen Presse in Deutschland*. Münster: Lit.

SALWEN, M. B., & MATERA, F. R. (1992). Public Salience of Foreign Nations. *Journalism Quarterly*. 69, pp. 623–632.

SAMBROOK, R. (2010). *Are Foreign Correspondents Redundant? The Changing Face of International News*. Oxford: Reuters Institute for the Study of Journalism.

SANGE, R. (1989). Japanische Auslandskorrespondenten in der Bundesrepublik Deutschland. Qualifikationsmerkmale, Arbeitsbedingungen und Berufseinstellungen. *Publizistik*. 34, pp. 62–77.

SHOEMAKER, P. J., COHEN, A., SEO, H., & JOHNSON, P. (2012). Comparing News on Foreign and International Affairs. In ESSER, F., & HANITZSCH, T. (eds.), *Handbook of Comparative Communication Research*. New York: Routledge, pp. 341–352.

SIEMES, A. (2000). *Auslandskorrespondenten in Polen. Nachbarschaftsvermittler zwischen Rollenverständnis und Arbeitsrealität*. Bochum: Bochumer Universitätsverlag.

VAP (Verein der Ausländischen Presse in Deutschland e.V.). (2012). *Mitgliederverzeichnis 2012/2013*. Berlin: Verein der Ausländischen Presse in Deutschland.

WANTA, W., GOLAN, G., & LEE, C. (2004). Agenda Setting and International News: Media Influence on Public Perceptions of Foreign Nations. *Journalism & Mass Communication Quarterly*. 81, pp. 364–377.

WILLNAT, L., & MARTIN, J. (2012). Foreign Correspondents—An Endangered Species? In WEAVER, D., & Willnat, L. (eds.), *The Global Journalist in the 21st Century*. New York: Taylor & FRANCIS, pp. 495–510.

WILLNAT, L., & WEAVER, D. (2003). Through Their Eyes: The Work of Foreign Correspondents in the United States. *Journalism: Theory, Practice & Criticism*. 4, pp. 403–422.

WU, H. D., & HAMILTON, J. M. (2004). US Foreign Correspondents: Changes and Continuity at the Turn of the Century. *Gazette*, 66, pp. 517–532.

11 Foreign Correspondents in Greece

Facing the 'Communication Deficit'

Stylianos Papathanassopoulos and Iliana Giannouli

INTRODUCTION

Greece, like many small countries, with the exception of the Olympic Games of 2004, usually goes unnoticed in the foreign press as a low-interest country mostly associated with specific types of stories, such as the terrorism, natural disasters (mostly earthquakes and fires during the summer), or other crises such as political upheavals (such as the dictatorship in 1967–1974). This 'model' has changed dramatically since the outburst of the global financial crisis, which sank the country and its economy into the deepest recession in its modern history. The Greek financial crisis exposed some of the frailties of the Eurozone financial framework as well. The fear that the Greek debt crisis might spill over into the Eurozone gave the country extensive coverage in the international news media (Papathanassopoulos, 2011). The scenarios of a Greek default, as well as the rescue by the European Union in relation to the wrath in the streets, have triggered worldwide media interest. Consequently, the number of foreign journalists in Athens has increased dramatically. Several journalists stated 99 per cent of their stories are about the Greek financial crisis. One said, 'If the crisis didn't happen, be sure that Greece would be reported once in a year' (FC7).

This chapter, based on original research, focuses on foreign correspondents in Greece with a goal of investigating their profile and exploring the way they choose and cover stories from the country. In addition, it attempts to highlight the problems correspondents encounter as they exercise their duties.

WHO ARE THE FOREIGN CORRESPONDENTS IN GREECE?

To shed some light on the work of the permanent FCs in Greece, the research collected information about the age, education, ethnicity, and experience of the FCs. The questionnaire also looked at the work routines of FCs, how they chose news stories, the impact of new technologies on their work, particular problems in their daily work, perceptions about their work, the future of foreign reporting, and whether they believed that the global crisis had affected their profession.

To investigate the proposed research questions, 26 semistructured, in-depth interviews were conducted in Greece with correspondents representing various countries and different types of news organizations from 2 April to 26 May 2013. A semistandardized interview format was chosen, which required the design of an interview guide but allowed freedom for open-ended questions and follow-up enquiries. The Foreign Press Association active members' list, totalling 124 names provided the sampling frame. The interviews conducted were analyzed according to the method of qualitative content analysis.

Our research showed that in Greece there are three types of foreign correspondents: foreigners, expatriates, and indigenous.[1] In our sample, the majority come from Southern Europe (30 per cent), as well as Central and Eastern Europe (40 per cent), while the rest come from Asia (20 per cent) and Western Europe (10 per cent). Of the 124 FCs, the top-represented countries include the UK (21 FCs), the United States (15 FCs), France (14 FCs), Germany and Turkey (11 each), Cyprus (9 FCs), and Serbia (6 FCs). The average age of FCs is 44 years, and, as expected, the average level of education is high: 61.5 per cent are university graduates; 30.8 per cent hold a master's degree, and 7.7 per cent have a PhD. However, only 23.1 per cent reported that journalism was their principal area of study at university. The majority studied the social sciences or economics. There are 71 male and 53 female correspondents.

Most of the correspondents in our sample (16) had worked as journalists at local media before they began their careers as FCs. This echoes findings of other international research focusing on foreign correspondents. These results, however, are inversely proportional when it comes to their experience as foreign correspondents; the majority (20) of the respondents stated that they started their careers as foreign correspondents from Greece, having no prior experience as FCs. Only six correspondents said that they had already covered other countries before their arrival in Greece. However, with a few exceptions the majority of correspondents (20) have covered Greece for a long period of time, resembling the 'long-timer' type of foreign correspondent according to Hannerz's typology (2004); the average time they have been covering Greece is 14.7 years.

The findings also indicate that the average foreign correspondent speaks at least two foreign languages. It is worth mentioning that despite the fact that the Greek language is not so common, all, apart from two, correspondents were able to speak Greek fluently. All of the correspondents in our panel speak English, and a high percentage speak French.

Regarding their experience abroad, before entering the journalistic arena, most of them (12 in our panel) reported that they had travelled mostly as students during their college years, and several (9) stated that they had no prior experience abroad.

In a breakdown of all FCs in Greece, 49 work for print media, 45 for news agencies, 26 for broadcast media, and 4 for online media. Most interviewed work exclusively for an agency; two work exclusively for radio stations and two for the press. Some work simultaneously for at least two media. In addition, the majority (17) of correspondents that participated in our survey work for national media, and only nine of them work for international news organizations, mainly for international news agencies. As expected, the major international agencies maintain a larger network of correspondents in Greece, compared to the national news organizations. More specifically, *Reuters* has 17 employees (reporters, photojournalists, cameramen) in Greece, *AP* 12 and *AFP* seven.[2] On the other hand, most national news organizations hire only one correspondent, who has to make the survey for his or her story, find the relevant audiovisual material, edit the story, and file it. As a correspondent put it bluntly, '[J]ournalism tends to become [a] one-man show'.

Moreover, correspondents working for national newspapers or TV stations are mainly freelancers who get paid by the stories they file. In our sample, only six of the 14 correspondents who work as freelancers stated that they have a steady income every month. Conversely, all the journalists (12) who work for news agencies are staff correspondents.

The geographical position of Greece seems to make it easier for foreign correspondents to cover neighboring areas either on a more permanent basis or in the form of special missions when significant events occur. Most of them (15) cover the so-called triangle of the Aegean (Greece-Cyprus-Turkey) and Balkan countries. Of the respondents, only 11 said that they cover just Greece.

WHAT MAKES IT INTO THE FOREIGN CORRESPONDENT'S REPORTING AGENDA?

Many correspondents pointed out that for a long time Greece did not produce stories of interest to the international news media. Things have changed since the financial crisis. As one correspondent comments: 'The picture they have about Greece is very short-sighted, that is to say only in peak periods, namely elections, fires, famines, earthquakes, financial crisis etc., that is where their interest is orientated, something that restricts us from suggesting stories of wider interest, beyond the political current affairs' (FC9).

However, all correspondents believe that FCs should cover everything that happens in the country where they are stationed. As a result, they are not specialized in particular types of stories. One FC said: 'A correspondent, who is specialized in specific issues, literally undermines his existence in a country. Thus, if you limit your options and say, "I don't cover cultural issues, I don't do stories about economy etc.", then eventually you will be of no worth to your boss and someone else might appear and steal your job' (FC24).

All the FCs agreed that they selected stories based on whether the news item will have interest for their national audience. As correspondents told us, most stories are assigned to the following categories: foreign policy, government (including major political events, such as elections), economy, terrorism and natural disasters, as well as culture (including museums, travel, and customs).

It became quite obvious that there is a major distinction between correspondents representing national media and those who work for international news agencies, concerning the definition of audience in each case. Correspondents who work for agencies tend to consider their audience as an international and heterogeneous audience: 'If you are writing for a news agency you are interested in stories with a universal appeal, stories in which more than one or two countries would be interested, you are looking for stories that will explain the country that you cover, human-interest stories, sad stories, funny ones, very unusual stories, which somehow tell a story about what Greece is' (FC26). Another said: 'You always have to think what might be interesting for a foreigner, what a particular story has to say to another country. Many times, when something happens in Greece I wonder—is this going to make a good story?' (FC20).

The correspondents who work for national news media look for foreign news stories that appeal to particular interests of their home audience. These stories usually have to match the audience conceptions of what is generally interesting about Greece, or they are about specific connections between home and Greece (FC23). In addition, these correspondents are usually asked to file a more comprehensive news item about a story that had appeared in a news agency or, more often. to write features stories. One told us: 'I file stories about the Greek current affairs but also stories that French people are interested in. For example, in France drought is a matter of public concern at the moment, so I was asked to write an article comparing the situation between Greece and France' (FC10).

WHEN IS SOMETHING BECOMING FCs' NEWS?

The Internet has had an impact on the work of FCs, especially on their relations with their home offices. Most of the interviewed journalists commented on the role of media competition as an important determinant of topic agenda. The Internet has helped correspondents monitor competitors' coverage. Several respondents admitted that at times they had to file a story simply because one major news agency had published a particular story and they know that their home editors always keep an eye on the work of the immediate competition.

FCs said that the Internet has had a major impact on the profession. Several reported that the Internet made it easier to get background information; some of them described the impact of the Internet on their job as a 'true revolution' or a 'miracle' that has changed their daily routine because they are able to file stories everywhere and at any time (FC2). However, it has created additional pressures: many FCs admitted that they had to file their stories more quickly than they used to, and they do not get the time needed to write a more thorough story (FC5).

Some correspondents also stressed the lack of 'in-depth reporting', resulting in the absence of thorough coverage in economic and social dispatches. Several correspondents believe that there is not enough time or space for their stories. 'The problem is that we are asked to do everything at the same time. When there is a protest on Syntagma Square and the number of protesters exceeds 15,000 and we have to file a story real time, the problem is that you don't have the opportunity to do enough 'digging'. You are not always given the time to go deep in your stories and this is a major constraint for my job', explained a correspondent who works for French media (FC14).

Correspondents who work for print media agreed that the visual clichés create additional problems because they emphasize specific aspects of a given event and sometimes create a distorted picture of a true situation. One FC explained:

> Snap-shot journalism is easy for foreigners. Our job is on some level determined by the airtime that major international broadcasters decide to devote to Greece. We have our opinion, we know the truth, but our home editors compare the news content we send to what foreign television networks broadcast. This is often a breaking point with our home editors. So, we are trying to find ourselves in the middle. The correspondents who are based permanently here are familiar with the protests, but if a foreigner comes in Greece and sees 10,000 protesters in the streets he will be shocked. There is a clash of cultures and that's where a balance is needed.
>
> (FC3)

The pressure for instant news is much more intense for journalists who work for the major international news agencies because they compete for news exclusivity. As a correspondent from *AP* put it: 'If there is a protest on Syntagma Square, the correspondent who gets first the shot wins a point in this stupid competition. In the end of time, it makes no difference, since somewhere you win, somewhere you lose' (FC22).

Nowadays, most news media try to reduce the cost of newsgathering, which leads to the emergence of a new type of FC: the 'multi-skilled staffer'.[3] Some reporters feel that they don't have the time to do the necessary research for their topics because they have to cover the technical aspects of the news transmission. 'Due to the global crisis a correspondent is expected to do pretty much everything himself. A person has to film a story, edit it and file it. Journalism tends to become 'one-man show', which would lead to the deterioration of journalism' (FC3).

WHERE DO STORIES COME FROM?

Most reporters rely primarily on official state sources like press conferences and press releases to fulfil their professional obligations. However, our survey indicated a heavy reliance on domestic news media as important sources, which requires the correspondents' ability to speak Greek. It is worth noting that all correspondents highlighted the significance of knowing the language of the country they cover. 'We always watch Greek TV stations and listen to local radio stations; we read the *Athens News Agency*'s outlets, because a foreign reporter always relies on the local media of the country that he covers' (FC20).

Another common characteristic is their advanced professionalism, since all emphasized that although they do get informed about what happens in Greece by the domestic media, they do not ever reproduce a story without having previously cross-checked it personally. All the correspondents rely mainly on public media, although noting that, over time, one learns to assess the validity and importance of each medium separately (FC17).

However, several correspondents pointed out that local media do not set their agenda, in the sense that correspondents might be interested in topics that are not of concern to the local press. One correspondent claimed that 'all foreign reporters should be very suspicious about the local media agenda-setting function, because they can easily be misguided' (FC15).

Hannerz notes that 'one's handling of foreign news beat will depend partly on one's interactive and communicative abilities and partly on the social characteristics of the place itself' (2004, p. 88). Most correspondents think their personal 'sources' are important channels of communication as well as an essential part of their job.[4] Agencies' correspondents indicated as a problem the issue of nominal source. As one correspondents put it, for a news agency the credibility of news is judged upon the importance of the "source". And even though many officials are willing to speak anonymously, officially they do not want to commit to the liability of their own declarations. Among other 'sources' reported by correspondents are diplomats, experts, and scientists, according to the type of story they have to cover, in addition to ordinary people.[5]

We must also note that Greek journalists are important news sources for the foreign press correspondents. Local journalists are truly helpful to their foreign colleagues, particularly when it comes to topics that require a minimum background (FC8).

Furthermore, foreign correspondents, like most journalists, build information networks with their counterparts in order to exchange information for their respective articles. It's a relationship built primarily on the logic of reciprocity. Nonetheless, competition emerges among agencies' correspondents because the speed of news coverage is the ultimate criterion for judging their work. In the same vein, journalists who represent national media feel competitive only with journalists from their home country.

A major cause of frustration among the interviewed journalists is the communication policy of Greece; almost all respondents felt at times that they were at a distinct disadvantage due to their professional role. As several correspondents told us, some government officials think of foreign journalists as 'spies', and they are very cautious with the information they provide to them. In addition, many journalists consider the Greek ministries' press material as vague (FC 19). Several correspondents are still excluded from official briefings granted by the Ministry of Defence, and they are facing difficulties in finding people in governmental positions who are eager to answer their questions officially. 'In Britain if I needed a piece of information all I had to do was lift the phone and someone in a supreme position in the governmental hierarchy would be eager to answer my questions. In Greece, nobody answers your phone calls. They keep sending you from one official to another, they are afraid of your questions, since they are not ready to give you some answers, given that they do not know how to manage a crisis' (FC18).

Several correspondents stated that bureaucracy in Greece is a major obstacle to a correspondent's work because changes in the press offices associated with the switching of governments are the impetus for a new circle of accreditation procedures for the foreign press corps. Many claimed that the foreign correspondents in Greece had less access than Greek journalists to government sources (FC7, FC10).

In addition, our research showed that the journalists shared common experiences with discrimination based on the importance and influence of their news organizations. *Financial Times*, as well as major German and British publications, emerged as the common example against which many journalists based their allegations of unequal treatment among the foreign correspondents. As correspondents told us, '[T]he reason for this discrimination is the fact that those media have a huge impact on the international market and Greece "needs" them, given the economic situation of the country'.

Despite these problems, all the respondents referred to work-associated problems that have a personal touch for each correspondent. Overall, most interviewees, when they talk about the daily obstacles of their work, refer to their lifelong study of Greek topics, and after the outburst of the financial crisis they had to gain knowledge in economic issues (FC5).

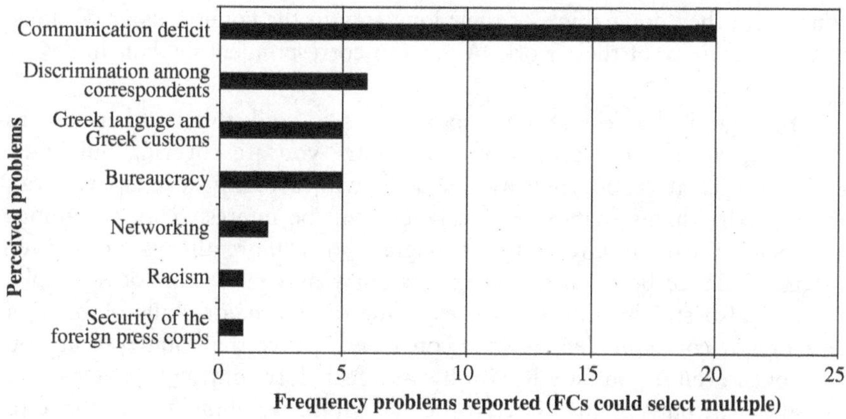

Figure 11.1 Perceived problems in correspondents' work in Greece.

HOW FOREIGN NEWS IS FORMULATED

Worth noting is that all correspondents, including those who have Greek roots, agreed that a correspondent's duty is the objective coverage of news. Several respondents pointed out that even if correspondents want to present the news in a more sympathetic tone, they will have to face their bosses' reluctance, who normally are more interested in negative news (FC18).

Some correspondents noted that some stringers, even after living in Greece for several years, turn to sensationalism in order to sell their stories and pointed out the obstacles created by the so-called easy journalism. Most reporters recalled the notorious articles that started the rumour that Greece had decided to sell some of its islands and stated that they had to put up a real fight with their home editors in order to convince them that these stories were not true. As one correspondent put it: 'Sometimes, our home editors monitor what the other foreign media distribute and they give us a hard time. For instance, when they read the article about Greece's intention to sell its islands they called us and asked why we hadn't filed the story. And we had to explain to them that there was no story. We have to be 100 per cent sure about a news item before we let it go public' (FC20).

An issue that is often associated with the objectivity of a correspondent's work is the risk of assimilation, resulting in the loss of the 'gift' of tracing stories. That is why many news organizations move their FCs every three to five years to new postings. However, the Greek case seems to escape this general rule inasmuch as most reporters have been covering Greece for a long time. Although many 'foreign foreign correspondents' felt that to some extent they have adjusted to the Greek way of life, as far as their daily habits are concerned, they don't think of their long stay in the country as an obstacle to the objectivity of their work. A veteran correspondent explained:

> Your goal as a foreign correspondent is to walk this line between as being close to the people of the country you are covering but when you look at them, you have to do it with a foreign eye, so you can spot the things that other foreigners will be interested in, the things that will explain Greece to a foreigner. So, you are always looking for this balance between knowing a country as well as the local people, and also still having 'fresh eyes'. One of the major skills of being a foreign correspondent is that you have to love the country that you cover, even if you hate it, you have to feel close to it, you have to care about it, but you also have to be very objective about it. You have to be an insider, *looking at it as an outsider.*
>
> (FC26)

Moreover, several correspondents claimed that travelling frequently in their home country and being informed about their country's current affairs help them maintain their 'foreign perspective' (FC5).

Furthermore, the majority of correspondents seemed to agree that their long stay in Greece has rendered them more autonomous because they don't have to rely on stringers. In addition, they feel that are capable of developing very deep local knowledge and therefore portray a more accurate picture about Greece: 'To live in the same country for many years, is a positive thing. It gives you the opportunity to learn the local language and become very knowledgeable about the country you cover', stated an agency correspondent (FC16).

What most respondents pointed out as a problem directly related to the long coverage of Greece, is that the correspondent starts losing his or her interest in the country when having to do the same story the second or third time (FC6).

CONCLUSIONS

As noted, the financial crisis has revitalized the foreign media's interest in Greece. However, correspondents seem to worry about their professional future because they believe that the global economic crisis has affected the media environment, resulting in job cuts (FC21). In addition, new technologies have contributed to the emergence of new types of foreign correspondence, such as 'citizen journalism'. In effect, agency correspondents consider themselves luckier than the freelancers. They believe that there are two classes of correspondents: on the one hand, staff correspondents who are well paid and who receive proper support from their news organizations and on the other hand, freelancers and stringers who are asked to do the same job for less money and in precarious working conditions.

One newspaper correspondent said:

> Foreign correspondence is a profession, which tends not to disappear entirely, but to shrink. The Internet is only one aspect of the coin. Major international news agencies have also rendered the foreign correspondent redundant, since the agencies cover everything. There is no need any longer for a news organization to maintain individual correspondents. Smaller news organizations are subscribed to agencies and they get to know everything that happens around the world.
>
> (FC1)

As several correspondents told us, the sustaining of foreign journalists in a foreign country depends on each news organization's financials situation, on the 'news beat', and on the particular interest that a country might have for the correspondent's home country. Greece seems at this period of time to fits these criteria.

NOTES

1. In our sample, the Greek foreign correspondents amounted to 13, of whom eight are expatriates and five indigenous. The other 13 correspondents come from the following 11 countries: Cyprus (2), Turkey (2), Spain (1), Germany (1), Egypt (1), China (1), Australia (1), Russia (1), Bulgaria (1), Romania (1) and Albania (1).
2. The numbers come from the list compiled by the Foreign Press Association of Greece.
3. For a description of the main duties of a 'multi-skilled staffer', see Reynolds (2010).
4. 'I read Greek newspapers, watch local TV channels, but I have my own sources as well. Since I work for a TV station I always have to put someone in front of a camera, who shares his opinion with the public, so I must have my own "sources"' (FC23).
5. '. . . The other is your personal effort; you should go outside your desk, speak to people and verify your information. If someone is able to read between the lines, he would have no difficulty in finding out the truth,' (FC25).

REFERENCES

HANNERZ, U. (2002) Among the Foreign Correspondents: Reflections on Anthropological Styles and Audiences. *Ethnos: Journal of Anthropology* 67 (1), pp. 57–74.

———. (2004). *Foreign News: Exploring the World of Foreign Correspondents.* Chicago: University of Chicago Press.

PAPATHANASSOPOULOS, S. (2011). The Greek Crisis and the European Media. Lecture presented at the International Conference, 'Soothsayers of Doom? Covering the Global Financial Crisis in Comparative and Historical Perspective'. City University of London, the Institute of Contemporary History, King's College, London, and the British Academy, London, 12–13 December.

REYNOLDS, J. (2010). Correspondents: They Come in Different Shapes and Sizes. *Nieman Reports.* 64 (3), pp. 8–11.

12 Foreign Correspondents in Hungary

Local, Glocal, Global Agendas

Jolán Róka[1]

INTRODUCTION

Hungary is a relatively small country with a population of fewer than 10 million. It has been a member of the European Union since 1 May 2004, and it joined NATO in 1999. The country has had a turbulent history indeed, with a democratic regime change taking hold in 1989. Since then, eligible Hungarian voters have been able to vote for winning party coalitions and in six parliamentary election campaigns: 1990, 1994, 1998, 2002, 2006, and 2010. In 2010, the Alliance of Young Democrats (FIDESZ), in coalition with the Christian Democratic People's Party (KDNP), won the elections and formed the government with an absolute majority, getting two-thirds of the parliamentary seats. In Hungary, two EP elections have been held, thc first in 2004, thc sccond in 2009.

Foreign correspondents (FCs) in Hungary have been able to report on several crucial social and political issues since the first democratic government. Since 2010, some of the most widely discussed topics have been the new media law and the setting up a new Media Council, Hungary's fiscal policies, the development of a new constitution, negotiations about financial aid from the European Union and the International Monetary Fund (IMF), a new central bank law, and education reform, just to mention a few.

> A deluge of new legislation approved at the end of 2011 by the two thirds parliamentary majority, controlled by Orban's Fidesz party, included a new central bank law and others linked to the new constitution which went into effect Jan. 1. While Hungary made many significant changes to the central bank law in order to more closely comply with the standards of the European Central Bank, some of the most disputed points, including new nomination procedures for top central bank officials, were passed without modification.
>
> (Gorondi, *Associated Press*, 2012)

The history of foreign correspondence goes back to the end of World War II. As Hamilton and Jenner state, nowadays,

> technology-driven changes are reshaping international news flows by lowering the economic barriers of entry to publishing and broadcasting and encouraging the proliferation of nontraditional international news sources. The audience—now fragmented and active—is far better able to choose and even shape the news. Consequently, a broader definition of foreign correspondence and of foreign correspondents is required to assess what consumers of news now know about the world.
>
> (2003, p. 132)

Due to the fast development of communication technology, the most widely used means in foreign correspondence are the news agencies, organizational in-house information, do-it-yourself reporting and editing, and some others (Hamilton & Jenner, 2003, pp. 131–138).

The history of Hungarian foreign correspondence should be thoroughly investigated. We know very little, in fact, about its history. The second Hungarian correspondent to the United States by *HVG* (*Weekly World Economy* magazine) revealed in a personal interview that *HVG* started setting up its correspondent network at the end of 1990s. At that time there were already two 'inherited' locations: Moscow from the 1970s and Vienna from the beginning of the 1990s. The *HVG* established its first correspondent position in Brussels, then in Berlin and New York. In 2005, the American position was closed, and all the other ones became stringers.

In the history of Hungarian foreign correspondence, one of the most significant events to have grabbed global attention was the 1956 Hungarian Revolution. The uprising broke out on 23 October, when there were just a few foreign journalists in Hungary. Most of the Hungarian correspondents were also out of the country, having been sent to Warsaw to report about the election of the new head of the Polish Communist Party. Right after 23 October, however, the number of journalists and foreign correspondents grew to more than 150; this was clearly a story to be covered.

> Most of the foreign journalists arrived in Hungary . . . a few days later. The majority represented the press in capitalist countries; those from the Eastern Bloc came mainly from Poland and Yugoslavia. . . . Most of those from the Eastern Bloc wrote anonymously and their work did not reflect their personal opinions. The press in most communist countries took over verbatim reports of the official Soviet news agency TASS or Pravda, central daily paper of the Communist Party of the Soviet Union (CPSU). Journalists elsewhere in the Eastern Bloc took a similar line, branding events in Hungary as counter revolutionary. Not so the Polish or Yugoslav journalists, though. The former rejoiced openly. Yugoslav reports were also enthusiastic until the official Yugoslav view emerged in early November.
>
> (Molnár, 2007)

WHO ARE THE FOREIGN CORRESPONDENTS?

For the purpose of this study, contact was made with the Hungarian International Press Association (HIPA), who provided me with the names of several journalists. Although this proved to be very helpful in establishing a group of journalists who would make up our focus group, we soon recognized that most of the foreign correspondents were reluctant to speak about their journalistic work in Hungary. The few correspondents whom we managed to meet and interview were asked about their personal background, their work routine in Hungary, their reporting agenda, the stories they report on, the sources of their stories, and the structure of their news stories.[2] The results of the focus group and several interviews form the empirical research on which this paper is based. The evaluation of the empirical data will hopefully contribute to a better understanding of the main competencies, responsibilities, working routines, and practices of foreign correspondents reporting about current political, economic, social, and cultural issues from Budapest (the capital city of Hungary) with special attention given to the European Union economic crisis. Furthermore, information regarding the newest trends in news coverage by foreign correspondents from Hungary and their impact on the local, glocal, and global mass audience will be discussed. It is also critical to discuss the role of HIPA in providing professional assistance to the foreign correspondents stationed in Hungary.

We have defined a population of 41 foreign correspondents representing news agencies and media organizations around the world. They are all registered by HIPA; a list of news agencies and foreign media with representatives in Hungary can be found in Table 12.1. They come from 13 nations, with most coming from the UK and the United States. Specifically, 11 of the correspondents come from the UK, nine from the United States, four from China, and three from Austria, France, and Germany, respectively. Twelve of the foreign correspondents based in Hungary work for news agencies, with the others working in various aspects of audiovisual media, press, newswires, or online media.

There are different foreign correspondent categories in Hungary, the first being that of foreign press agencies. All the large agencies are represented to some degree either with a full-time office or with at least a stringer or a correspondent. This includes the largest ones, which are the *Associated Press* (American), *Agence France Press* (*AFP*) (French), *Reuters* (British), *Dow Jones* (American), *Bloomberg* (American), *DPA* (German), *APA* (Austrian), *EFE* (Spanish). There are also agencies from Japan, China, and the UK (*BBC*).

Another large category includes correspondents who write for magazines and newspapers. Here one should mention *The Times of London*, *The Economist*, *Financial Times*, French newspapers like *Liberation*, and several German newspapers. These correspondents are either people residing in

Table 12.1 Countries, news agencies and media organizations with representatives (FCs) in Hungary (accreditations as of 2011).

Name	Country	Media	Ownership	Private/Public/Not-for-profit News Cooperative
FC1	Republic of Austria	*Wiener Zeitung*	Republik Österreich	
FC2	United States	*Bloomberg News*	Private	Bloomberg L.P.
FC3	Great Britain and Northern Ireland, United Kingdom	*Thomson Reuters*	Woodbridge Company	
FC4	French Republic	*Radio France Internationale*	State (Foreign Affairs)	Public
FC5	Kingdom of Belgium	*VRT Radio & TV*		Public
FC6	Israel	*JTA, Jediot Jewish Telegraphic Agency*		The JTA is a not-for-profit corporation
FC7	Great Britain and Northern Ireland, United Kingdom	*ITN, Gemini News Service*		
FC8	Federal Republic of Germany	*DPA, Der Standard (osztrák)*	*Der Standard* (Oscar Bronner)	Dessen Privatstiftung und Bronner Online AG
FC9	Great Britain and Northern Ireland, United Kingdom	*Thomson Reuters*	Woodbridge Company	
FC10	United States	*Dow Jones Newswires*	Private	Dow Jones, a subsidiary of News Corporation
FC11	Federal Republic of Germany	*Joker*		
FC12	Great Britain and Northern Ireland, United Kingdom	*Thomson Reuters*	Woodbridge Company	
FC13	People's Republic of China	*Economic Daily*		

(*Continued*)

Table 12.1 (Continued)

Name	Country	Media	Ownership	Private/Public/Not-for-profit News Cooperative
FC14	Republic of Austria	*ORF*		Public
FC15	United States	*Bloomberg News*	Private	Bloomberg L.P.
FC16	United States	*Associated Press*	Private	Not-for-profit news cooperative
FC17	Republic of Romania	*Roman Radio*	Public	
FC18	United States	*Dow Jones Newswires*	Private	Dow Jones, a subsidiary of News Corporation
FC19	Republic of Austria	*ORF*	state 97.3% county 2.7%	Public
FC20	Kingdom of the Netherlands	*Trouw*		
FC21	Kingdom of the Netherlands	*KRO Radio*	Public Catholic radio	Public
FC22	United Kingdom	*Financial Times*	Private	Pearson PLC
FC23	French Republic	*Agence France Presse (AFP)*	Public	Not-for-profit news cooperative
FC24	Great Britain and Northern Ireland, United Kingdom	*The Times*		
FC25	United States	*Atlantic News Service*		
FC26	French Republic	*Agence France Presse (AFP)*	Public	Not-for-profit news cooperative

FC27	People's Republic of China	*New China News Agency*	Republic of China	Public
FC28	Spanish Republic	*EFE*		
FC29	Federal Republic of Germany	*Frankfurter Allgemeine Zeitung*	FAZIT-Stiftung GmbH (FAZIT Foundation)	
FC30	Swiss Confederation	*Finanz und Wirtschaft*		
FC31	Slovak Republic	*Slovak Radio*		
FC32	United States	*Bloomberg News*	Private	Bloomberg L.P.
FC33	Great Britain and Northern Ireland, United Kingdom	*Thomson Reuters*	Woodbridge Company	
FC34	United States	*Bloomberg News*	Private	Bloomberg L.P.
FC35	Great Britain and Northern Ireland, United Kingdom	*Thomson Reuters*	Woodbridge Company	
FC36	Great Britain and Northern Ireland, United Kingdom	*Thomson Reuters*	Woodbridge Company	
FC37	United States	*Associated Press*	Private	Not-for-profit news cooperative
FC38	People's Republic of China	*New China News Agency*	Republic of China	Public
FC39	Great Britain and Northern Ireland, United Kingdom	*Thomson Reuters*	Woodbridge Company	
FC40	United Kingdom	*BBC*		
FC41	People's Republic of China	*New China News Agency*	Republic of China	Public

Hungary or those who come occasionally. Nevertheless it would seem that all of them know the country relatively well. There are also those correspondents who write for foreign newspapers—German, French, American—who don't live in Hungary but who travel to Hungary to find their stories. Most of the German newspapers work in this manner: they do not have an office in Hungary. Rather, they rely on news agencies like *AP* and *Reuters* to find out if something important is happening. The most significant news agencies mentioned were *Reuters*, *Bloomberg*, and *Dow Jones*, which cover issues having to do with the economy of Hungary, whereas others like the *AFP* and *AP* produce more general news. Most of these news agencies and bigger newspapers have had correspondents in Hungary since before the regime change. Some had offices (or at least a stringer or single representative) in Hungary during the communist era, but since 1990 all of these companies have established a presence in Hungary. Indeed, since the early 1990s, with the explosion of business in Hungary due to its extensive privatization process, many foreign agencies have been actively present in the country.

The bigger news agencies, mentioned earlier, like *AFP*, *Bloomberg*, *Reuters*, and *AP*, all have offices in Budapest. They employ at least two or three correspondents, usually Hungarian, including reporters, as well as photographers, and increasingly there is a large emphasis on video journalists because video and television markets are becoming lucrative for the agencies in comparison to print media, which is declining and, as a consequence, whose revenues are falling.

All the current correspondents have at least 5–10 years of experience working at news agencies, so they are a relatively experienced and knowledgeable group of journalists. In the past decade, most of the journalists working in traditional news agencies are Hungarian. This is less typical for newspaper and magazine correspondents, who often employ foreigners, British, American, French, or German correspondents who have lived in Hungary at least 10 years.

The typical age of the correspondents working in Hungary is between 35 and 45 years of age. It's a male-dominated profession, but nearly every office has a woman on staff; among news agency staff, the ratio is about two-thirds men, one-third women. With newspapers, the ratio is closer to fifty-fifty, but there are still more men than women.

Most of those working for agencies are full-time employees, whereas most of those writing for magazines and newspapers are usually stringers and often write for more than one publication at the same time. In this sense, the agency journalists are a bit more secure and more stable in their employment status because they get a salary every month no matter how much they write, whereas the stringers' income depends on their output.

Although the local language is not an issue for Hungarian-born correspondents, there is a growing tendency for foreign-born journalists working in Hungary, even among the stringers and those who write for magazines and newspapers, to speak Hungarian at least to some degree.

WHAT MAKES IT INTO THE FOREIGN CORRESPONDENT'S REPORTING AGENDA?

The organization for foreign correspondents in Hungary (HIPA) was founded in 1994. It has approximately 85 members, of which a little more than half are journalists, while the rest include mostly diplomatic representatives in Hungary. There are approximately 60 journalist members, 40 associate members, and two corporate members. HIPA regularly organizes meetings (press breakfasts) with politicians, researchers, and scientists. Sometimes the organization provides informative press trips. These activities are free of charge for HIPA members.[3] Especially in the past 10 years, HIPA has become very popular among journalists and embassies. Its leadership has good relations with the various governments and businesses, and it is seen as a serious organization.

HIPA has a five-member board and a president, today chosen from a small and rotating group of journalists vying for the positions. The board members represent a broad sampling of newspaper, agency, and magazine journalists. The members meet quite regularly, and at the meetings there are often invited experts on subjects as far-ranging as the Roma minorities to tourism, the arts, and business. They recently had a meeting with suicide experts because it is becoming a significant issue in Hungary.

In terms of any foreign correspondents' reporting agenda, it is in many cases much different from newspaper journalism. The reasons are many and may include the fact that FCs have a more universal audience and try to write articles that are interesting for as many people as possible. They also try to maintain a neutral political and economic point of view, and they don't consider themselves to be writing for specifically liberal or conservative media or for a particularly atheistic or religious audience, inasmuch as their main subscribers are the world's biggest newspapers and Internet news sites. They try to be as general as possible in their coverage to reach the local, glocal, and global audience.

The most immediate news FCs write about is what they call 'breaking news', usually a specific event. This can be a natural catastrophe, like the 2010 red-sludge flood in Hungary with its burst of red toxic mud from the alumina plant that flooded three towns.

FCs also report on the 'trend' stories: they try to discover and report on changes in social, business, or political trends taking place in the country being covered. Here in Hungary, some of the most recent trends being reported on is the rise of the far right and how the government specifically and society in general are dealing with this. Another trend at the moment concerns the Roma population in Hungary, with specific attention being paid to what actions have been or should be taken regarding Roma poverty and education. Business trends are also being written about. In particular, today there are many stories about the growing strength of the Hungarian economy and the far-reaching consequences of such growth.

Most of the FCs working for news agencies in Hungary rarely report on issues outside Hungary. In the case of large stories, such as the red-sludge story, colleagues from Vienna and Prague, for example, came to help out. The story was such an overwhelming one, with so many things to write about, including the concern over health issues because nobody knew exactly how toxic the sludge was or how many days you could spend up to your knees in it before there was a negative physical impact.

The work of newspaper and magazine journalists is a bit more regional. They usually cover two or three countries. As such, their beat might be not only Hungary but neighboring countries as well, such as Slovakia, Romania, Serbia, Croatia, or Slovenia.

WHERE DO STORIES COME FROM?

According to the results of my research with our focus group, breaking news is typically pulled up on a national news agency or from a TV broadcast or radio broadcast. Someone might call the journalist and report that something happened. Journalists get official press releases from governments, ministries, businesses, and NGOs. They monitor the local media, usually at least all the large daily newspapers and the important weekly magazines, and, of course, nowadays they use the Internet a lot. Social media in Hungary are probably less relevant than in the United States (at least as of this writing) because they are less frequently used as tools for newsmakers in Hungary. This, needless to say, is rapidly changing.

HOW IS THE NEWS FORMULATED

One big difference when journalists are writing as foreign correspondents is that they have to provide the readers with a lot of context because familiarity with all things Hungarian is still rather limited. For example, readers outside Hungary might need a better understanding of how many people live in a certain location or a few facts about history, not the least of which is that Hungary was a communist country until 1989. Sometimes it even goes as far as having to say in the foreign correspondent's story that Hungary is located in Eastern Europe. It depends on what the correspondent is writing about.

WHICH ARE THE MOST INFLUENTIAL FOREIGN CORRESPONDENTS?

In Hungary, the most influential international media are the British *BBC*, *The Financial Times*, and *The Economist*. As far as the United States is concerned, it's usually *The Wall Street Journal* and *The New York Times*, as well as—now to a lesser degree, but still important—*Time* and *Newsweek* magazines. There are also the large German newspapers, the weekly *Die Welt*, *Stern*, and the Frankfurt and Berlin newspapers.

Among the international news agencies, there is a lot of rotation of journalists, for example, people who have worked at *Bloomberg* and who previously worked at *Reuters*, *AP*, or *Dow Jones*. Consequently, they know one another, having worked together often or in many cases at the same organization. Even though they now write for another wire, they do not turn into enemies.

CONCLUSIONS

There are definitely fewer foreign correspondents in Budapest now than there were 15 or 20 years ago. This might be due to economic difficulties that so many news agencies are experiencing; it might also be due to a lack of a 'big' ongoing story, such as the war in Yugoslavia, when many journalists were based in Budapest to cover that conflict. There are fewer full-time correspondents for newspapers. There are also fewer journalists who are dedicated only to Hungary; today many of them cover a broader Central Eastern European region. In terms of the news agencies, there is relative stability. Numbers haven't changed that much during the last 10 to 15 years. There has been a reduction in the number of reporters but also a corresponding increase in video journalists. Ten or 15 years ago, there were very few video journalists. There may have been TV crews going from one country to another, whereas now we also have video journalists or a small video crew, mostly covering just one country. All the wires employ a minimum of two to three people: reporters, photographers, and video journalists.

Based on the focus group interviews with foreign correspondents stationed in Hungary, we might conclude that their profession is complex and diverse. As the data reflect, their job requires creativity, a sophisticated sense for news, and quick reactions to the latest events and happenings in a given country or countries. Nick Bryant summarizes this idea in a witty way:

> The news industry can be a little like the grand-prix world of Formula One, in that a travelling circus flies from country to country and from continent to continent investing an extraordinary amount of work, energy and ingenuity in order to keep one person ahead of the competition. Apart from the occasional use of flameproof underwear, there—alas—the comparison almost ends. But correspondents often end up popping the champagne corks—when it is truly our cameramen, producers, picture editors, assignment editors, drivers, local fixers and translators who are more deserving of the plaudits. My great fortune since joining the BBC has been to work with the best of them.
>
> (Bryant, 2012, p. 412)

NOTES

1. Jolán Róka is a professor and vice rector for international relations at BKF University of Applied Sciences, Budapest. She is the head of the BA and MA programs in communication and media studies at the College of Communication, Business and Art in Budapest, Hungary. She has participated in international research projects on political communication and journalism for 20 years.
2. Although the foreign correspondents did not choose to share their names, educational level, or income for this publication, they were willing to share general information about their job.
3. See www.hipa-hungary.com.

REFERENCES

BRYANT, N. (2012). Confessions from Correspondent Land. The Dangers and Delights of Life as a Foreign Correspondent. Oxford: ONEWorld.

HAMILTON, J.M., and JENNER, E. (2003). The New Foreign Correspondence. *Foreign Affairs*. 82 (5).

Hungarian International Press Association (HIPA). [Online]. Available from www.hipa-hungary.com.

MOLNÁR, J. (2007). Foreign Correspondents in the 1956 Hungarian Revolution. *The Institute for the History of the 1956 Hungarian Revolution* [Online]. Available from www.rev.hu.

13 Foreign Correspondents in Ireland

Close Neighbours, Global Agenda

John O'Sullivan

With special thanks to Cristopher Dougan for research assistance

INTRODUCTION

Foreignness and representation by a dominant foreign culture have been a defining part of the Irish experience, from fantastic medieval and Elizabethan accounts of wildness (Neill, 1994) to the birth of English newspapers and their coverage of war and resistance (O'Hara, 2003), to later British and American journalism and propaganda playing a part on both sides in the struggle for independence (Walsh, 2008).

In recent decades, the primary agenda from the Irish perspective has evolved from reporting of the Northern Ireland conflict and political relations with the UK (Miller, 1994) to the projection of the state as a strategic location in the European and global competition for direct foreign investment, primarily by US-owned multinational corporations. As part of this present agenda, a low and arguably lax corporate taxation policy has been jealously guarded in the face of mounting critical international political commentary, especially from within the European Union, and in opposition to increased political pressure for tax harmonization among member countries (Spiegel, Weismann, & Hall, 2010; Matlack, 2013). Similarly, following the public rescue of Irish banks in 2008, which prompted the national debt bailout by the troika of the IMF, the European Commission, and the European Central Bank, the official establishment has sought to restore the trust of bond markets and international ratings agencies by seeking to project the country as a model of austerity economics (Pollak, 2012), while striving in negotiations with the troika to mitigate retrospectively the scale and harsh conditions of their bailout. In this context, foreign coverage of Ireland, especially in elite publications or emanating from prominent international commentators, itself informs the domestic political and economic agenda and in particular the debate on the continued austerity measures (Krugman, 2009; Lewis, 2011).

In non-economic or business news, Ireland's religious-cultural inheritance also has been reflected recently in extensive international coverage of the death of Savita Halappanavar, an Indian woman denied an abortion in spite of acute illness, bringing the relative novelty of coverage in the Indian press in addition to more familiar sources of attention (Suroor, 2012).

Perhaps because of its cultural and linguistic assimilation with the UK and the United States, as most sweepingly expressed in the oft repeated notion of Ireland's cultural proximity to Boston, as opposed to Berlin, and the partial integration of its media system with Britain's (Foley, 2010), the state historically has seen itself as punching above its weight on the international stage, with such disproportion similarly extended to rates of foreign investment, especially from the United States.

Just as its economic posture is influenced greatly by external events and actors in the European Union and wider spheres of global competition, so also is Ireland's representation affected by and through the media of elite nations, especially Anglophone news agencies and other news organizations that have global reach, latterly extended and deepened via the Internet (Boyd-Barrett & Rantanen, 2004; Thussu, 2004; Hachten & Scotton, 2012).

No Irish media organization or state propaganda campaign is ever likely to challenge or vary significantly the external portrayal of the country contrary to the values and perceptions of the *BBC*, *Financial Times*, *The Economist*, *Reuters*, or *Bloomberg*. Because the country has featured in the Eurozone crisis and in international controversy over austerity and corporate taxation, it is timely to examine the detail of the work of foreign correspondents (FCs) in Ireland and the factors that shape the representation of the country to the rest of the world.

WHO

In total, 26 journalists were identified as foreign correspondents, in the sense that a significant part of their role is reporting on Ireland. This categorization is problematic, however, not least because some of those covering the Republic for media elsewhere do so from their posting in London, and in this fluid context it was not possible definitively to recognize each of these in order to arrive at a securely comprehensive population. Two of the group declared themselves as London-based, but this does not preclude the existence of others working in the same way and who have not been identified. The majority of FCs work for media based in the UK (11 FCs), followed by the United States (6 FCs), with one correspondent each from France, Germany, Italy, the Netherlands, Norway, Portugal, Qatar, Russia, and Spain. Of the total 11 journalists who represent UK media, further folds of complexity are added by dint of the fact that three of this group work in Northern Ireland for British news organizations and so arguably could define themselves as working on domestic stories. They are included here on the basis that they also are charged with covering all-Ireland and Republic of Ireland affairs for UK media. The group is overwhelmingly male, at 23 out of the 26. News agency journalists form the largest subgroup, with half the total, at 13, while nine represent print news outlets, three are broadcasters, and only one could be identified as an online (only) journalist.

Methodology

Even though the total population of Ireland correspondents is small, in order to connect more effectively with the wider European research, a survey method was chosen based on the questionnaire developed for the larger study and partially adapted to fit the Irish context. In all, 20 respondents from the 26 were identified and approached. The Irish Department of Foreign Affairs declined to provide access to its list of journalists, on the basis of data protection and confidentiality, as did the Foreign Press Association in London. However, the Irish Embassy in Britain attempted to assist by forwarding an email to its list, inviting participation from correspondents based in London but also covering Ireland. The FPA chose not to assist the study in this way. Ultimately, however, most correspondents were identified through scanning of media outlets and associated social media, local journalism contacts, an appeal on Twitter, and through participant references.

Respondents were given a choice of conducting a telephone interview or completing the survey form themselves. It was felt that the latter option would increase participation, as most of the target group were, as expected, extremely busy, as confirmed by the frequent necessity for reminders. This decision was guided by the judgement that maximizing participation would be preferable, in terms of reliability of data, even at the expensive of the reflective depth that might be afforded with a more targeted approach. Almost all journalists approached chose eventually to complete the questionnaire themselves.

While some Northern Ireland–based journalists actively assisted the study, two did not take part. The principal impact of this is that the study does not have a representative from the *BBC*, one of the most influential sources of news globally.

The research largely was conducted in late 2012 and early 2013. All respondents were guaranteed anonymity.

The data gathered are based on a small sample and therefore are in no way purported to be statistically sound. Much the data is reported in median values, often arising from a Likert scale question: where possible, care has been taken to account for occasional outliers or for misdirected responses. However, as the survey of a group of informed experts who are experienced journalism practitioners in a specialized field, the data afford a means of descriptively recording and interpreting the situation and conditions of foreign news production in Ireland.

Nationality

Of the 20 participants, 12 described themselves as Irish, one Northern Irish, and seven are from countries in Continental Europe. None, other than the Northern Irish participant, is from the UK. The most dominant base nationalities of the news outlets headquarters are Britain and the United States, at six each. There are 14 European-headquartered organizations, including non-EU, and six of these, excluding the UK, belong to EU member states. All but two of the organizations are from Western capitalist democracies.[1] While 15 journalists say that their audience is international, five of these say they also cater to national audiences, and three specify national-only audiences.

The group comprises journalists working for national newspapers and broadcasters, as well as major news agencies, covering both general and financial news, and for global news brands, as well as some smaller outlets. Of the journalists surveyed, 15 are based in the Republic, two in Belfast, and three in London.

Personal and Professional Profile

The Ireland correspondents have a median age of 41. They are bilingual, with all but one claiming at least a basic facility in a second language. They are more likely to have a master's degree (14) and to have formally studied journalism (12). They are relatively well paid: 10 earn between €4,000 and €8,000 a month, with eight in a lower band. They are most likely not to have a stated religion (13), and there is an even split between those married and not.

Most have extensive experience, having worked as a journalist for 16.5 years (including one career span of 42 years and another, the lowest, of three) and as a foreign correspondent, or in a role comprising reporting for a foreign audience, for nine. Although not all participants cite previous work in the role, those who do have a median stay in each country of 3.5 years, spread across locations that include war zones, such as the Balkans and Lebanon, but primarily outside Ireland, the United States, and the UK. Their work in previous roles reveals for the most part a conventional spread of politics, business, economics, and general news beats.

Most (14) of the journalists primarily work for a single organization, 13 of them full-time, and two have explicit titles as senior editors or news executives. However, the diversifying presence of five freelancers and stringers in the group is reflected in an average of employing organizations of 1.9, with some working for two to, at the outside, eight news outlets. Just over half, at 11, are members of a trade union.

Organizations and Platforms

Inasmuch as digital publishing has blurred the lines between news media platforms, nine of the journalists identify themselves as working for organizations with a print newspaper title, with seven employed by news agencies. All of the respondents working for Anglophone news agencies are full-time staff. It is interesting to note that, among types of organizations classified by medium (and allowing for multiple selections), by far the most common medium identified is print, at 12, even if included in this set are several news brands that have strongly developed global digital and online presences. In spite of convergence, only six participants choose to describe their medium as online, behind news agencies at seven. Publicly owned news organizations total seven, with five and two public radio and television stations, respectively.

However, even as 18 respondents identify print as a publishing platform (in contrast to organization type), Websites (17) also feature strongly in this category, and seven journalists say that they also publish on social media. It appears that, while they regard their organization primarily as a print one, they also recognize that it has extended to new platforms. In all, six TV stations and seven radio stations are represented. Several of the agencies are stated as having three or four correspondents in Ireland, but otherwise, by and large, the journalists in the study are alone in their roles.

WHAT

Topics

Asked what category of stories they mostly cover, the correspondents' responses are dominated by economics (16) and politics (15), with fewer reporting also on society (11) and culture (10). With respect to this question, several of the respondents conflate their reporting from Ireland with that from the UK in spite of the survey's focus on Ireland, indicating the strength of their perspective on beat as reporting on the UK and Ireland rather than as separate entities. For example, one of the four reporters who says that he also covers sport for a European media outlet is referring to the English Premier League. In all, eight correspondents are tasked with covering both the UK and Ireland.[2]

The most prominent topic covered by the foreign correspondents is the debt/Eurozone crisis, with most placing economics at the top of their ranking, followed by Northern Ireland. A typical listing from one of the financial journalists is, 'Irish economy and bailout; Irish business and banks; Irish politics/relationship with EU and society', and this pattern of coverage of Ireland within the context of European affairs and in particular the general economic crisis is echoed by several others. Several correspondents mention coverage of violence with respect to Northern Ireland, and this reflects the outbreak of street disturbances that broke out over limits on the official flying of the Union flag in Belfast, which raised concerns for the peace process. Although few specific stories are named, another reporter singles out for mention the controversy surrounding the death of Savita Halappanavar, who had been denied termination of her pregnancy in an episode that has prompted the rekindling of debate over abortion law. Otherwise, few of the journalists rank cultural or social stories among their typical set.

WHEN DOES A STORY BECOME INTERNATIONAL NEWS?

In the main, the correspondents are independent of their news desks in terms of deciding which individual stories they should cover: 12 report that they alone initiate story topics, with six saying that this privilege is shared with the desks. Only two say that stories are originated by desks or editors. They also are successful in their story choices, with eight saying that 100 per cent of their story pitches achieve publication, and most others reporting rates of 90 per cent, from a median number of pitches of 3.8.[3]

Journalists' influences in deciding what is covered follow a rather narrow pattern: government officials are cited by six correspondents as first in their ranked listing of sources most likely to be the main reason for initiating the investigation of a story, and Irish national media are cited by five in this respect: two rank non-governmental official sources first, and three see the public as most important. Business is considered the second most important story spark here. In spite of the volume of hype surrounding it, social media barely features, being confined to one mention in the second ranking.

In summarizing answers to a different but related question concerning how much influence is wielded by various factors and source types on journalists' work, we find relationships with news sources rank second, with a median score of 3.5 from a range of one to five, among 15 potential influences on the work of the correspondents, but the related issue of access to information tops the list at four. Censorship is seen as having little effect, at one, and the journalists do not rate the importance of public relations, businesspeople, and pressure groups much more highly. Along with these, politicians and official sources score two (the latter outcome contradicting somewhat the opinions just expressed, perhaps indicating an ambivalent attitude to such sources and a desire to express autonomy).

However, journalists' peers, their competitors, and media laws and regulation are seen as moderately influential, at three. Audience feedback, which has been the subject of so much debate and expectation around interactivity, is viewed relatively sceptically and rated at 2.5, in line with previous studies questioning the relationship between digital media affordances and journalism norms (O'Sullivan & Heinonen, 2008).

Ireland is considered to allow relatively open access to official government and business sources, at 3.6, with some of the journalists comparing it favourably to the UK and observing that this might be due to the smaller size of country. However, others make a distinction between politicians and less accommodating officials. One journalist said: 'It's easy to talk to the politicians in Ireland but far more difficult to speak to civil servants, whereas in Belgium/EU civil servants are much easier to talk to.'

WHERE DO STORIES COME FROM?

Within the media environment, asked to rate various sources with respect to frequency of use, other foreign correspondents rank highest, at a median of five, indicating that news is a collective rather than an individual phenomenon, in spite of the appearance of reporters working alone. Native journalists are rated at a neutral three on this scale, but so also are citizen journalists, blogs, and social media, while news media in the host country scores only two. However, asked which of these sources were most likely to be the principal reason for a foreign correspondent to begin to investigate a story, native Irish journalists along with the national or local media were strongly identified as most important, whereas other foreign correspondents and citizen journalists fell noticeably lower in the ranking, revealing a difference in priorities between the decision to cover a story and the business of finding information to complete it.

HOW

Reflecting the dramatic scale and depth of the financial calamity in Ireland, as well as the continuing fallout over its causes, consequences, and solutions, there is strong agreement, with a median of five, among correspondents that the Eurozone crisis has impacted heavily on the framing of news from this country. There is weaker but still positive agreement (four) among the journalists that their individual organizations' coverage has resulted in the audience caring more about European news. And the correspondents are neutral or noncommittal on the assertion that their coverage has helped to create a European public sphere that overcomes citizens' narrow national concerns.

Closer within the correspondents' own circumstances and institutional setting, as shown in Figure 13.1, they see their own editorial supervisors as most influential on their work, along with the familiar time limits of news routines. The availability of resources for newsgathering is also seen as somewhat relevant, at 3.5. Correspondents acknowledge but regard in neutral terms, at three, the roles of managers in the organization and editorial policy, as well as their colleagues' and their own personal values

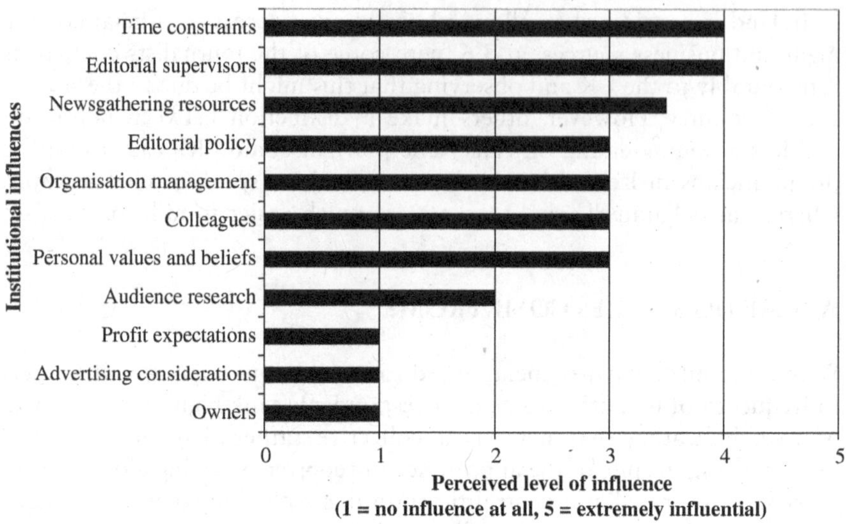

Figure 13.1 Institutional influences in Ireland.

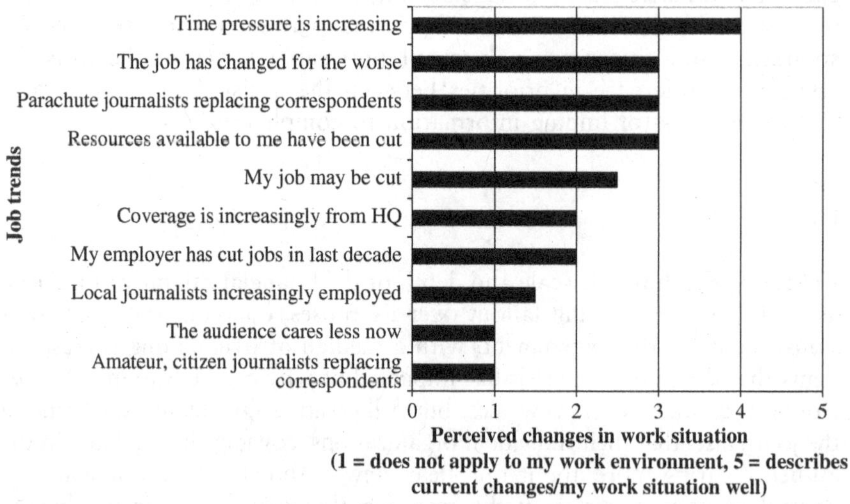

Figure 13.2 Trends on the job in Ireland.

and beliefs. They do not set much store by audience research, rating it at two, but, reflecting professional normative values and asserting journalistic autonomy, they are most dismissive (one) of the influence of advertising, profit expectations, and ownership.

Figure 13.2 shows the response to questions regarding trends in the correspondents' working conditions. The urgency of deadlines is reflected again, in the score of 4, indicating agreement with the sentiment that time pressure in the job is increasing. However, contrary to some of the more downbeat views of journalism employment in recent years, the correspondents broadly demur on most negative expressions of trends in conditions. Statements that so-called amateur journalists, citizen journalists, or representatives of NGOs are being used to replace traditional correspondents and that audiences now care less about international news are fully rejected. There is weaker disagreement that foreign coverage increasingly is covered from organizations' home headquarters, while statements that reporting resources are being cut, that short-stay, single-story parachute journalists are being deployed instead of regular correspondents, or that conditions overall have deteriorated recently are all met with neutral or ambivalent responses. This, it could be argued, may reflect the preponderance of staff journalists among the correspondents: for freelancers or stringers, the experience is different, as expressed by one such journalist:

> I do believe that foreign reporting is being undermined by increasingly provincial reporting by various news organisations. I have seen this happen with the exploitation of, for example, local stringers (paid too little), or by simply neglecting significant foreign coverage, which is a pattern within a major number of broadcasters. Funding is definitely on the decline in general across broadcasters and there is a tendency to snip where foreign coverage is concerned. Generally speaking, getting paid and or getting paid enough is a huge problem for people like me.

Overall, it would appear that, while feeling the pressures of deadlines familiar to most in the modern journalism habitus (Schultz, 2007), Ireland's foreign press corps largely is sanguine about prospects for the profession, at least in this specialized field.

WHICH ARE THE MOST INFLUENTIAL FOREIGN CORRESPONDENTS AND LOCAL MEDIA?

Perhaps contrary to the perception of them as an exclusive club, while recognizing one another's influence, foreign correspondents do not consciously cooperate, registering a median of just 2.5, on a scale of one to five. The group judges *Reuters* to be the most important foreign media organization in Ireland, named by seven in lists of up to three, followed by the *BBC*, at six, and *Bloomberg*, at five. *The Guardian* and *Financial Times* are rated in the top three by four individuals. These rankings do not correspond with the number of foreign correspondents employed in Ireland by the various organizations: for example, it may be that the Press Association, which has a number of correspondents based in both Dublin and Belfast and which is responsible for a high volume of stories from

Ireland, is tacitly excluded from consideration as a foreign news organization and instead is perceived as a domestic or quasi domestic operation, not only in Northern Ireland, but also in the Republic.[4]

CONCLUSIONS

This chapter has briefly outlined the descriptive data arising from the survey of the majority of foreign correspondents in Ireland. This discussion necessarily is tentative because of the small number surveyed. Further, there is some lack of definition around the role of foreign correspondent, both because some Irish correspondents are reporting from Northern Ireland and therefore within the UK and because some based in London also cover Ireland as part of their beat. Nevertheless, in spite of these caveats, a reasonably coherent picture emerges. Although there are important elements of European journalism from France, Germany, Spain, and other countries, overall, this group of journalists is dominated, both in terms of individual profiles and organizational identity, by the conventional protagonists of global Anglophone media, whether they be news agencies or global news brands, subscribing primarily (as do Irish journalists) to the North Atlantic Liberal press model (Hallin & Mancini, 2004) and with a pronounced business and financial orientation.

Ireland, primarily, is represented to the world by correspondents stationed here but directed from headquarters in Britain and the United States, and the advent of globally networked journalism is likely to reinforce rather than alter that pattern.

Within that paradigm, foreign correspondents show a largely conventional or standard reliance on government, official, and business news sources (Tunstall, 1971; Manning, 2001), although notably they show some regard for citizen journalists at the level of sparking interest in potential stories. By and large, they display adherence to familiar professional norms in their perceptions of influences and in their working priorities. However, it could be argued that theirs is a compressed and restricted news agenda, concerned less with the social and cultural aspects of Irish life than with the immediately political or with the grand sweep of the economic crisis. Ireland may enjoy some advantage, relative to its size, in the global news agenda because of its belonging to a certain journalistic culture and associated media networks and because of the evident goodwill of most of its foreign correspondents.[5] But, ultimately, its coverage is determined by the norms of that culture. As one correspondent taking part in this study puts it: 'Ireland has fallen off the world map as a result of the peace process in Northern Ireland. After all, we are a country the size of Greater Manchester. When the killing largely stopped, the newsrooms lost interest. There is a skeletal staff of stringers covering Ireland, and only for the major outlets. Specialist news aside, i.e. business, the bulk of copy comes from the wires'.

Seen especially in the light of the narrowing effect of coverage in European affairs, favouring official over civil actors (Koopmans, 2007), it is not clear that this media setting can serve fully to assist in communication between Ireland and other countries in Europe, concerning the immediate debate over its own economic interests vis-à-vis those of other member states and of the wider entity, but also at a deeper level of understanding as partners in any European citizen project.

NOTES

1. A correspondent for one of the 'non-Western' organizations says this distinction does not imply a different perspective for work done for other outlets.
2. Some reporters refer to Ireland as one entity, others as two split between Northern Ireland and the Republic, while another says that he covers four countries: England, Wales, Scotland, and Ireland.
3. One respondent, a senior editor, said that he pitched 'dozens', and this figure was excluded from the median calculation.
4. The Press Association has shareholders among both British and Irish media organizations. Irish newspapers historically have used PA copy on domestic and UK stories without a special credit or byline.
5. The *Financial Times* has recently appointed a full-time staff correspondent for Ireland, primarily because of the financial crisis and the bailout.

REFERENCES

BOYD-BARRETT, O., & RANTANEN, T. (2004). News Agencies as News Sources: A Re-Evaluation. In PATERSON, C., & SREBERNY, A. (eds.), *International News in the Twenty-First Century.* Eastleigh, Hants: John Libbey Publishing for University of Luton Press, pp. 31–45.

FOLEY, M. (2010). A Return to News? The Irish Press after the Crash. *Eurozine.* 31 December [Online]. Available from http://bit.ly/1iB54Vk.

HACHTEN, W. A., & SCOTTON, J. F. (2012). *The World News Prism: Challenges of Digital Communication*, 8th ed. Oxford: Wiley-Blackwell.

HALLIN, D. C., & MANCINI, P. (2004). *Comparing Media Systems: Three Models of Media and Politics. Communication, Society, and Politics.* Cambridge/New York: Cambridge University Press.

KOOPMANS, R. (2007). Who Inhabits the European Public Sphere? Winners and Losers, Supporters and Opponents in Europeanised Political Debates. *European Journal of Political Research.* 46 (2), pp. 183–210.

KRUGMAN, P. (2009). Erin Go Broke. *New York Times* [Online]. 19 April. Available from http://nyti.ms/1fbFZvI.

LEWIS, M. (2011). When Irish Eyes Are Crying. *Vanity Fair* [Online]. March. Available from http://vnty.fr/1nAJ9yo.

MANNING, P. (2001). *News and News Sources: A Critical Introduction.* London: Sage.

MATLACK, C. (2013). Did Apple Pare Its Tax Bill with a 'Double Irish?' *Bloomberg Businessweek* [Online]. 22 May. Available from http://buswk.co/1toNGYH.

MILLER, D. (1994). *Don't Mention the War: Northern Ireland, Propaganda and the Media.* London/Boulder, CO: Pluto Press.
NEILL, M. (1994). Broken English and Broken Irish: Nation, Language, and the Optic of Power in Shakespeare's Histories. *Shakespeare Quarterly.* 45 (1), pp. 1–32.
O'HARA, D. A. (2003). English Newsbooks and the Outbreak of the Irish Rebellion of 1641 [1]. *Media History.* 9 (3), pp. 179–193.
O'SULLIVAN, J., & HEINONEN, A. (2008). Old Values, New Media. *Journalism Practice.* 2 (3), pp. 357–371.
POLLAK, S. (2012). *Behind the Story: TIME's Catherine Mayer Discusses Irish Prime Minister Enda Kenny* [Online]. Available from http://ti.me/1lprIDN.
SCHULTZ, I. (2007). The Journalistic Gut Feeling. *Journalism Practice.* 1 (2), pp. 190–207.
SPIEGEL, P., WEISMANN, G., & HALL, B. (2010). Ireland Faces Corporation Tax Showdown. *Financial Times* [Online], 18 November. Available from http://on.ft.com/1heJjWQ.
SUROOR, H. (2012). Savita's Death Triggers Irish Backlash against Anti-abortion Law. *The Hindu* [Online]. 15 November. Available from http://bit.ly/RBdV00.
THUSSU, D.K. (2004). Media Plenty and the Poverty of News. In PATERSON, C., & SREBERNY, A. (eds.), *International News in the Twenty-First Century.* Eastleigh, Hants., UK: J. Libbey Publishing for University of Luton Press, pp. 47–62.
TUNSTALL, J. (1971). *Journalists at Work: Specialist Correspondents: Their News Organizations, News Sources, and Competitor-Colleagues.* London: Constable.
WALSH, M. (2008). *The News from Ireland: Foreign Correspondents and the Irish Revolution.* I. B. Tauris: London.

14 Foreign Correspondents in Latvia

Can a Small Country Have Big News?

Inta Brikše

INTRODUCTION

Since the 1990s, when the foreign media interest in Latvia increased due to the struggle for the restoration of independence that, in 1991, resulted in the country's becoming an independent state, foreign reporting about Latvia has varied in its contents and scale.

By its territory and population, Latvia is a small state—with 2 million inhabitants—while its capital city, Riga, is the third largest city in the Baltic Sea region after St. Petersburg and Stockholm. Thus, the location of Riga facilitates the establishment of foreign correspondents offices in Riga.

The financial and state administration crisis (2008–2010) has certainly attracted the interest of foreign media. Latvia's approach to overcoming the crisis has become the theme for reporting in the world media (Krugman, 2012) about the ways of overcoming the crisis and the evaluation of the results.

Economic emigration has grown rapidly in Latvia—experts estimate total net outflow of 250,000 people between 2000–2010 (Zepa, 2011)—and large Latvian communities have been established in the UK and Ireland. This might promote the interest of the indigenous population of these countries in the homeland of their new neighbours, thus possibly sparking greater international coverage of Latvia.

The division of the population by their ethnic affiliation and by language and media use into two communities (Latvian and Russian) is not only a problem of domestic national identity and for the integration of society, but it explicitly attracts the attention of the neighbouring state of Russia. Journalists from other post-Soviet states also regularly report from Latvia. A large study on the representation of Latvia in the Russian media (Muižnieks, 2008) showed that in many but not all the issues, Latvia is portrayed as an enemy of Russia.

Concerns are often voiced in Latvia that, for foreign media, Latvia is a small country and that its problems are not reflected either sufficiently or objectively without understanding their context and historical conditions. Yet as demonstrated by the Latvian Institute monitoring, in 2012, 74.2 per cent of the publications of foreign online media about Latvia have been positive, basically about domestic policy and economics. The largest amount of information has been published in the media of Estonia, Lithuania, Russia, and the United States. Large attention was focused on Latvia in February 2012 when the referendum on the status of Russian as the official language took place (Latvian Institute, 2013).

WHO ARE THE FCs, AND WHOM DO THEY WORK FOR?

To identify foreign reporters, we used information from the Ministry of Foreign Affairs, which gives accreditation to foreign media journalists and other representatives. Since the new accreditation regulations were introduced in Latvia in 2006, 129 journalists have been accredited from more than 20 countries. The largest number of accredited foreign reporters (with their staffs) during these years has been from Russia (with about 20 FCs), Germany (about 10 FCs), Azerbaijan (about five FCs), Belarus (about four FCs), and China (about three FCs).

The national or ethnic background of journalists is very diverse; for many FCs this factor is associated neither with the state whose media they represent nor with their homeland. The number of accredited journalists per year has decreased by half, but the number of female journalists has dropped even more—from 20 to four. Journalists are of different ages (from 27 to 55), with different professional experience in journalism (from two to 25 years).

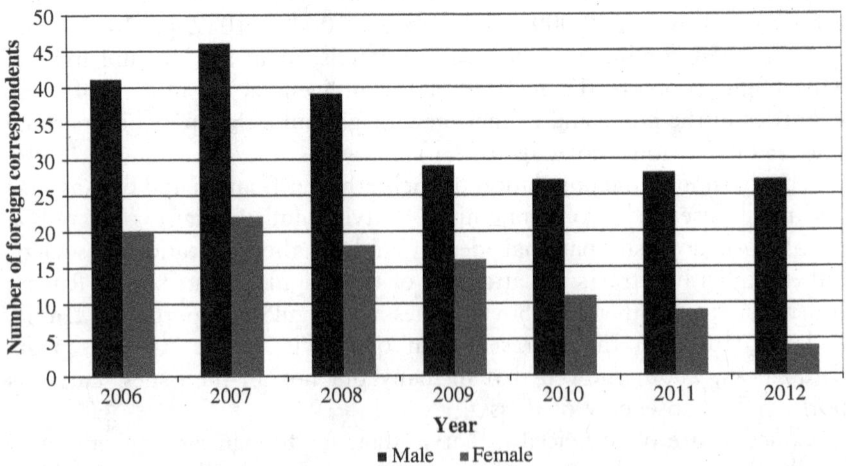

Figure 14.1 FCs' distribution by gender in Latvia (2006–2012).
Source: Data of the Ministry of Foreign Affairs of the Republic of Latvia, 2012.

In the past, about 100 media have been represented in Latvia. Permanent reporters have been from the news agencies: *Bloomberg*, *Reuters*, *Associated Press*, *Deutsche Presse-Agentur*, and *Xinhua News Agency*. The biggest interest in Latvia has been shown by Russian media (*RTR*, *NTV*, *Channel One Russia*, *RIA Novosti*, *ITAR-TASS*, *Lenta.ru*, and others) and by German media (*DPA*, *ZDF*, *ARD*, *DW*, *N-OST*, and others but they were represented by the same reporters). In general, the largest proportion of the FC community consists of representatives from news agencies and televisions, as well as from tourism and trade magazines.

The majority of the journalists were accredited in Latvia for one, two, or three years (correspondingly, 41, 22, and 11 per cent). Quantitative indicators of the presence of foreign correspondents are not high in Latvia, but it must be admitted that quality indicators are even lower for several reasons. First, many media whose representatives have been working in Latvia have little significance in their home countries because they have been representing niche or interest publications. Second, from all the correspondents, 10 per cent, on average, have represented *The Baltic Times* (independent pan-Baltic English-language newspaper covering regional events with headquarters in Riga).

The research data were collected using the information from the Foreign Affairs Ministry of Latvia about the journalists accredited in Latvia and the questionnaire developed by several authors for this book. Interviews were done in October 2012.

For this study, approximately 30 journalists were asked to participate. Eleven respondents were interviewed (about one-third of the original sample did not respond, and the last third represented the same media or media

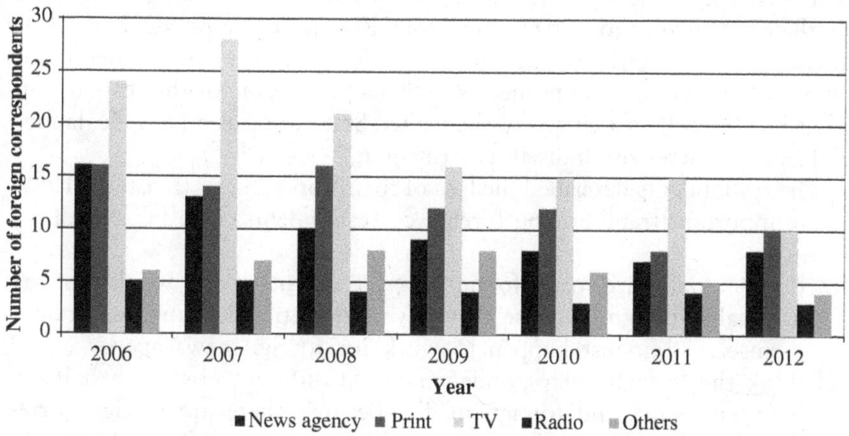

Figure 14.2 FC's distribution by type of medium in Latvia (2006–2012).
Source: Data of the Ministry of Foreign Affairs of the Republic of Latvia, 2012.

with low impact). Ten of the interviews were conducted face-to-face in Latvian and English and one with an interpreter in Russian. Five represent news agencies and three TV, but one respondent indicated that he prepares coverage for TV, radio, and press. Six journalists cover all the Baltic States, of which two also cover Scandinavia, the Russian border region (Kaliningrad) and one Poland. Six journalists work for only one medium (some specifically emphasized that the editorial board supports cooperation with others), but only four of them are employed full-time (one of them is a typical parachute journalist).

A typical characteristic feature for all the journalists is previous experience in covering political, economic, social, regional, cultural, and sports issues. Only a few of the reporters have been working abroad before Latvia. One of the journalists previously had been working in public relations and writing corporate publications.

None of the respondents displayed a clear belonging to their media organizations; one can conclude that the discourse of relationships is based on journalistic culture, news standards, and mutual trust.

As a reason for the choice of the work position, the respondents also mentioned greater independence compared to working in the media headquarters. The ways of arriving at and staying in Latvia had been diverse—both their own choice or appointment by the editorial office. The ways were supplemented by personal reasons; for example, the spouse is Latvian (FC1), or it is easier from Riga to visit the family living in another country (FC3). Several respondents emphasized the natural conditions of Latvia as an advantage in choosing their place of residence and work. Respondents saw also larger opportunities of creative freedom than in headquarters (FC7).

Four correspondents spoke English as their mother tongue; three others, Russian; two others German; and two spoke Latvian or Armenian as a first language. Eight of the journalists knew Latvian (as a foreign language). By their nationality (or citizenship), four Russian correspondents work in Latvia, two characterizing themselves as British and German, one identifying himself as Latvian, and another as 'half-Latvian'. One of the respondents described himself as a citizen of the United States, one as a New Zealander, and one characterized himself as Armenian.

The respondents described the loss of their 'foreignness' (Kristeva, 1999) as an important trend among foreign correspondents. One FC stated:

> there actually are many foreign correspondents that I would not say are really foreign, because they have family ties here or are Latvians themselves but just happen to work for foreign news agency . . . I think the foreign correspondent is quite different now, as a halfway between media and foreign media. Because there are foreign correspondents that come, do a story and then go away again. (FC1)

The majority of the respondents have an MA degree; some have two. It is characteristic that the range of their education is wide: ecology and geography, philology, sociology, economics, linguistics, and literature; only four of them have a university degree in journalism or have graduated from programmes that included journalism or media. Two of the respondents indicated that they had acquired journalism through learning in the field, two others mentioned short-term courses in journalism.

Foreign reporters' attitude to membership in professional organizations of journalists was radically different: some respondents are members of journalists' organizations in which the media they represent are located (FC4, FC11), or they are considering joining an organization (FC4) or they have not joined because they see no usefulness in such organizations ('What could they give to me? There is no particular need for them' [FC10]).

Cooperation with other correspondents and media is established only with separate TV journalists and camera operators, in order, for instance, to get some video footage (FC7).

WHAT IS THE AGENDA OF FCs?

The most important issues mentioned by the permanent media and news agency journalists included politics and economics, as well as social issues.

The journalists focus on a diverse audience for their material. Journalists working for news agencies perceive their audience as users and clients of their agencies ('Our clients can read everything we publish' [FC3]). Freelancers perceive media as users but also from the market perspective: 'I am selling me and I sell as much as I need to feed me' (FC4).

Journalists admitted how important it was to find the appropriate approach to get the interest of the audience:

> [A] large article needs an explanation about why we are writing about [an issue]. *Why do I care?* Facebook shares now are in the stock exchange, but they are not doing all that well. Therefore the question arises why the social network *draugiem.lv*[1] is doing so well compared to Facebook and why it is doing so well specifically in Latvia . . . [I]t is the only social network in Europe that did not lose its audience to Facebook . . . Two years ago I wrote an article about the Old-believers' village in Latgale region. Before that there had been another article about deserted villages in Latgale, we went there in the vicinity of the borders with Russia and Belarus. Immigration of people—that is [an agenda] issue. (FC3)

The opinions of journalists, what editors find interesting, and what would stimulate the audience's interest are different; some think that Ligo (the midsummer night) celebration is an interesting event: 'I had an article about Ligo, it was very interesting, many [of] my friends said it is [an] interesting celebration' (FC8]. 'We wrote about Ligo and Jāņi midsummer celebration because this tradition does not exist anywhere else in Europe' (FC3). But others do not find it of interest: 'Jāņi [Līgo] is not an interesting tradition either' (FC7). The theoretically highly evaluated stories about people in actual reality have no demand; besides 'you cannot do that very often, you always have to follow what happens very quickly and get on with all region' (FC6).

A different perception of audience is characteristic for journalists who are associated with specific national media because the choices of themes and events are linked by them with specific audiences (FC5, FC11), and it can be described as 'imagined community' (Anderson, 1991).

WHEN DOES SOMETHING BECOME NEWS FOR FCs?

Yet issues that are essential for Latvia get into the international news flow only if they have a possible international resonance. 'Anything that happens in Russia becomes an issue in Germany. Everything that is related to Russia and is happening here is always like [all] of a sudden interesting, because it is related to Russia' (FC6). Other FCs note, 'There is no particular interest about Latvia in Russia, besides the obvious facts that twenty years ago they were one country. And many Russians live here . . . [E]thno-politics is a huge topic in Russia' (FC2).

As for the balancing of their media with the agenda of Russia, several respondents made ironic statements that minus 30 degree weather in Moscow is interesting news because 'people get frozen in Moscow', and then it is usually reported that the temperature is 'minus 30 in the Baltic region' (FC5).

Thus the agenda is basically established depending on the media organizations' targets and not on those events that have real significance for Latvia and the countries of the Baltic region and for the people who live there: 'our company is interested in economic news, in almost all the economic data, inflation or retail . . . A large part of my work is to report on these data from the Central Statistics Office' (FC3).

Inclusion of the events from Latvia and the other Baltic States into international news agendas is essentially influenced by the traditional news values—if the event is exceptional or if it can be recognized by the local target audience and so on:

> I don't do many stories on economy or private business, because the size is often not that relevant. You have different perspective . . . [T]hey had a project in Estonia that offered electricity in each household, valued 90 million euros . . . I did not even ask, I just made up the story and sent it and I got feedback it was not a big deal. I was like—*what do you want more, all country is going to be covered, 90 million . . . that would be no big deal.* It depends on perspective. (FC6)

Several other respondents also admitted that, 'Latvia is tiny' and with its 'two million population is smaller than Berlin' (FC5).

The attitude to the traditionally significant events in the local context varies by different media. For example, the Latvia Song and Dance festival that takes place once every five years across the country over five days is reported extensively by the national media every day, but the foreign media view it differently: 'Song Festival certainly, that's almost like a seasonal thing . . . that attracts a lot of international interest. Because it is a unique event, there is nothing really like it' (FC1); '[the editor had heard] that there was a crowd standing there, some choirs and sing. I said—"yes, there are hundreds of thousands standing and singing there"' (FC5).

WHERE DO THE STORIES COME FROM?

For all the foreign correspondents, the process of producing a story is quite similar—getting in touch with the editors (Google chat, SMS, internal Web page, emails) and agreeing on the themes and issues, which, as the majority of the respondents admitted, are usually initiated by the journalists themselves. The basic sources for getting information about what happens in Latvia and the other Baltic States are the local media, followed by government officials, members of the opposition, and other official national sources, but as the second most important source of information, the respondents generally mentioned common citizens.

Only a few of the journalists gave their evaluation of information independence and credibility of the local media that everyone admitted as important sources. All the respondents positively assess the accessibility of high-ranking officials, stressing that they are easier to get access to compared to officials in other countries because Latvia is not a big country. It is characteristic that the businesspeople's openness to media had much lower

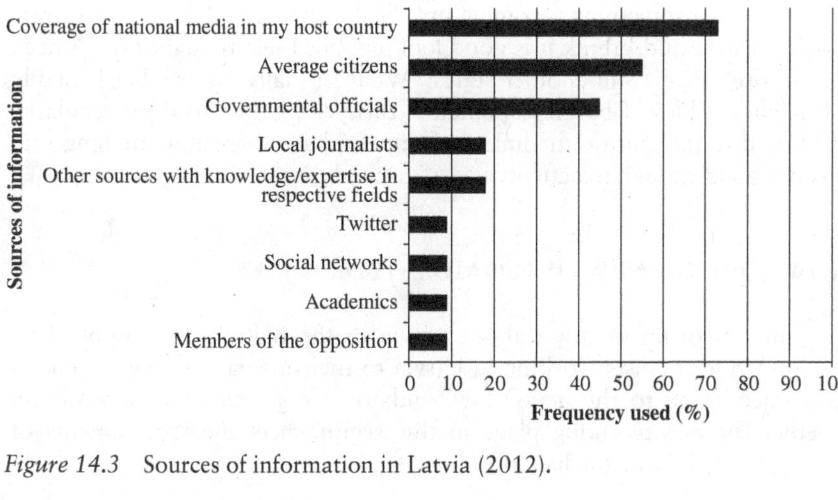

Figure 14.3 Sources of information in Latvia (2012).

evaluations. Average citizens as a source were evaluated by the respondents not as an independent source but rather as a balance to the information provided by the state power sources.

Respondents have little information about other foreign journalists working in Latvia and with local journalists. They do meet at press conferences and different events, but no professional community has been established in Latvia. Interestingly enough, when responding to the question of how many foreign reporters work in Latvia in total, the answers were on the scale of between two and eight. Some of journalists tried to network the small foreign correspondents community of Latvian and Russian journalists, but with no success. Yet respondents indicated that networking can be significant in achieving a successful outcome:

> When you go to the press conference or something and you know there is going to be only one question asked from the foreign correspondents, you all don't try to ask the same question, or you have a talk inside, what's the question one of us is going to ask that we could all end news on, or what do we think is the most important angle of the story . . . So that's part of why we were having a coffee a minute ago just to try to come up with the reasonable question. (FC1)

Different reasons are mentioned as to why contacts with colleagues are not established: competition among media (FC10, FC3), the heavy workload, as well as the fact that journalists work in different countries: 'I have to follow two other countries, I have many more events that have some relevance to me' (FC6).

Journalists have fairly diverse attitudes to the use of social networks, blogs, and Twitter; some treat them with caution: 'I use them in a passive sense, just checking and following, what people are saying, writing on Facebook . . . I use it in a sense if there are people using it then you just follow to see if something is coming up' (FC2). Others said: 'I have a website I once created, and I think it is good looking, but I just thought I don't need it anymore' (FC4). Still another states: 'What I usually do or what I usually did is have a blog. I haven't updated it this year, I used to do it regularly, but I used to just put on the link on features I have done and anything that was not good enough to actually use, so second rate stories in general' (FC1).

HOW FOREIGN NEWS IS FORMULATED?

The amount of information about Latvia or the Baltic States supplied by the foreign journalists working in Latvia to their media and news agencies varies according to the news flow, and to a large extent it depends on whether the events taking place in this region meet the requirements of the larger agenda of media or audience.

Journalists take a distanced position on how and where their work will be used, and often they even have difficulties answering where their stories were used (especially in news agencies and those media that work in different channels) (FC7, FC9).

Several respondents critically assessed the approach that the editors rely more on the hard news set in the agency agenda than on their own correspondents; therefore, they wait first for the agency news from Latvia: 'then my editors read this and ask me to do something. So there is a close connection—you must write as much as possible about the Baltics, then Baltics are on the minds of editors' (FC4).

When describing their relations with headquarters, journalists often use the discourse of 'they and me': '[f]or a feature, every couple of months I would make a list of possible features, you know, cover features I find interesting, I send that to *them*, *they* think about them as long as *they* want to think about them, and then tell me what *they* want me to do' (FC1, italics added).

One of the ways of getting into the news agenda of other countries is by means of renowned persons who are not known to come from Latvia. If, however, they are residing in a totally different part of the world, problems are created by the fact that they are then not significant enough to report on from Latvia .

The themes to which headquarters editors pay attention and on which they ask for stories often surprise the journalists themselves: 'I got a phone call "you've got those wolves there". I said, 'yes, that's normal', we have wolves living here who sometimes wonder across the borders, and at that moment it had not even occurred to me that there are no wolves in Germany' (FC5). '[T]here are offbeat or "finally-stories", because they usually go at the end of the newscast with *and finally* like "*and finally*, *the bear that was kept in Ligatne*, *bla bla bla*. . . ." and it is something you know is going to require an update until it comes to an end . . . I covered the bear twice' (FC1).[2] '[Boar] would probably make news too in Moscow. I don't know if it got published, it could be declined . . . Because, you know, it is an offbeat. Riga is the cultural capital of EU in 2014, and a boar goes on its streets' (FC2).

Journalists admitted that stereotypes have a big role in requesting news. The most frequent stereotypes they encounter from their media journalists mention 'Kremlin power' (FC2), post-Soviet countries, and so on Inclusion of the events from Latvia and the other Baltic States into international news agenda is essentially influenced by the traditional news values—if the events pass a certain benchmark in something, if they can be recognized by the local target audience and so on. Several respondents admitted that the theoretically significant stories about people and their daily realities have no high demand because media want to receive stories about people who are well-known to the audience.

In general, themes of the stories as seen by the respondents' answers are not particularly different from the local media news, yet the agenda is different. Several journalists also admitted that foreign correspondent's work and hence also their reports have changed because 'there are foreign correspondents that come, do a story and then go away again' (FC1), and that influences the story content.

CONCLUSIONS

The research showed that the activities of the FCs working in Latvia are influenced by economic changes that have caused instability (many are freelancers working for several media), the global context of media agenda formation (interest about Latvia is associated with the events that have regional, European or some other context). Although journalists admit that their ideas are very well accepted by headquarters and that they are able to implement most of their ideas, in actual practice they are confronted by dependence on agendas formed by the large news agencies and on the predisposition of editors to stereotypes. Many events that are essential not only for Latvia but for all the Baltic States are perceived by headquarters as too insignificant, compared to large states—for example, costs in currency and so on—to report about them to public. As a result, the 'subjective voice' of journalists decreases (Archetti, 2011, p. 8), along with their opportunities in the public space, which can possibly decrease diversity of information and opinions. But the majority of people form their insight about other countries certainly under the impact of the media.

Journalists' work is more and more associated with data collection and analysis but not with the classical event reporting that is facilitated by computer-assisted reporting. But the reporters working in Latvia are comparatively passive in the formation and dissemination of contents outside their direct professional duties, considering that the media represented by them provide wide opportunities for reaching audience and that they do not need self-promotion activities. Only some of them are creating their audience of followers on Facebook. This fact can be possibly explained by comparatively distant relations with their audiences. Journalists working for news agencies do not have bonds with their audience either; several of them stressed that they do not know how and by whom the materials prepared by them are perceived. Journalists' links with their headquarters are basically to do with the planning of the topics, but the sense of affiliation to the editorial boards is quite weak. And that influences the self-identification of journalists.

Foreign correspondents in Latvia are quite isolated, possibly because there are no strong local organizations, but one should point out that only two of the foreign reporters coparticipate in their homeland journalists' organizations. Foreign correspondents in Latvia can be characterized as individual authors who provide media with information in compliance with journalistic standards. Respondents expressed the opinion that they strongly follow standards set by journalism and their media, but, at the same time, they voiced the opinion that they sell their work. These features were less characteristic in the answers of those reporters who were full-time employees.

Most foreign journalists in Latvia are not 'foreigners' in the traditional sense because they perceive Latvia as a stable place of their residence—because they are Latvians, have been living in Latvia for a long time and having established families or a set of friends with the local population.

NOTES

1. A social network in Latvia, similar to Facebook.
2. The bear that was brought up in the national park (located in Ligatne, about 70 kilometres from capital) twice escaped from the pen and was wondering through the forest. To avoid threats to people, it was shot.

REFERENCES

ARCHETTI, C. (2011), Which Future for Foreign Correspondence? London Foreign Correspondents in the Age of Globalization. Unpublished article [Online]. Available from http://bit.ly/PpKX17.

ANDERSON, B. (1991). *Imagined Communities: Reflections on the Origin and Spread of Nationalism*. London/New York: Verso.

KRISTEVA, J. (1991). *Strangers to Ourselves*. New York: Columbia University Press.

KRUGMAN, P. (2012). 'Latvian Competitiveness' [Online]. 12 June. Available from http://nyti.ms/1myPDQK.

LATVIAN INSTITUTE (2013). 74,2% of Foreign Online Media Publications about Latvia in 2012—Positive [Online]. 30 January. Available from http://bit.ly/1i5bwo0.

MUIŽNIEKS, N. (ed.). (2008). *Manufacturing Enemy Images? Russian Media Portrayal of Latvia*. Riga: Academic Press of the University of Latvia.

ZEPA, B. (ed.). (2012) *Latvian Human Development Report 2010/2011. National Identity, Mobility and Capability*. Riga: Academic Press of the University of Latvia.

15 Foreign Correspondents in Lithuania

Between Glorious Past and Miserable Future

Gintaras Aleknonis

INTRODUCTION

Lithuania, along with its neighbours Latvia and Estonia, is slowly vanishing from the global map of news. Attempts by the Baltic States to present themselves as part of Northern Europe were successful but did not help increase worldwide visibility. However, the logic behind that outcome may be that the Soviet past and the success story of escape from the Communist Empire made the Baltic States distinctive, whereas the image of a stable democracy is boring and, while it helps attract investment, the media turn elsewhere. In the early part of the 20th century, Lithuania was known for its conflicts with Poland and Germany. During the Cold War, it was either an unknown Soviet province or a home of human rights activists. Lithuania enjoyed a moment as a media star in the late 1980s and early 1990s while being on the front line in the fight against Communism. The first decade of independence was marked by a race for the membership in the European Union and NATO. This helped Lithuania preserve a modest place on the news map, but only for a short time. The year 2004 marked its entrance into the EU and NATO and the loss of any remnant of interest from the international media.

JOURNALISM DURING THE SOVIET ERA

During the Soviet occupation, for more than half a century, Lithuania was a closed zone. To visit the country, foreigners needed special permission. Foreign correspondents were given no exception, about 20 permissions per year were granted, and the visits were carefully choreographed by the KGB. In 1977, David Satter, correspondent in Moscow for *Financial Times*, visited the three Baltic States. His trip combined official interviews, arranged with the help of the Soviet news agency *Novosti* and secret meetings with local dissidents (Satter, 2007). KGB officials managed to outplay the journalist. His notes from the interviews with Lithuanian dissidents were stolen. In Tallinn, Satter's meetings with dissidents were set up by the KGB, who successfully played the roles of fighters against communism. Henry Shapiro, another long-term foreign correspondent in Moscow, remembered that, over time, the dissidents got bolder, even answering telephone calls from foreign correspondents (Senn, 2006). For Lithuanian dissidents, international publicity was the primary weapon in their struggle, and any foreign correspondents' help was highly welcomed and appreciated. Despite severe risks, Nijolė Sadūnaitė, Kęstutis Jokubynas, Antanas Terleckas, and their fellows used all opportunities to inform the Western media about human rights abuses. On the other hand, foreign correspondents helped dissidents smuggle microfilms of the underground press to the West, where the Lithuanian diaspora printed, translated, and distributed uncensored news from the occupied country. Genuine support for the dissident movement by those few foreign correspondents helped create high respect for this profession. The information presented by foreign correspondents essentially differed from the news offered by the Soviet media. Obstacles created by the authorities for the dissemination of information from the West (radio broadcasts were jammed, newspapers could only be smuggled) just increased the significance of the foreign correspondents' reports.

Another side of foreign journalism in occupied Lithuania is communist counterpropaganda: articles about the prosperous and flourishing Soviet way of life published by communist newspapers outside the Soviet Union were reprinted in the local media. A typical example could be a book by Harald Kreft, *Mit den Augen eines Deutschen: Das schönere Memel heisst Klaipėda* (Kreft, 1970), which was published in Vilnius in both Lithuanian and German. The editor of the East German communist newspaper *Das Volk* wrote about Klaipėda, which was disputed by Lithuania and Germany between World Wars I and II. Such work by a 'foreign correspondent' was presented as an example of reconciliation of nations under the 'profound ruling' of the Communist Party.

The actual profession of a foreign correspondent was nearly unknown to Lithuanian journalists. A few received appointments as representatives of Soviet news agencies. One exception was the position of correspondent of the weekly *Moscow News* in New York, accredited at the UN. From 1960, this appointment was combined with the job of a correspondent for the Lithuanian daily *Tiesa* and reserved for Lithuanian journalists who simultaneously kept a close eye on the activities of the Lithuanian diaspora in the United States. The candidates for the job were carefully picked by the Lithuanian Communist leaders and screened by the KGB. After returning to Vilnius, former foreign correspondents occupied important positions in party media or propaganda headquarters.

Journalists working for Moscow newspapers and residing in Lithuania were called 'foreign correspondents' as well. The most important Soviet newspapers *Pravda*, *Izvestia*, *Komsomolskaya Pravda*, and others had their representatives in Vilnius. Journalists for the jobs were cautiously picked by the editors in Moscow and approved by party leaders in Vilnius.

Moscow's media played a very special role in the pyramid of the Soviet press. Only newspapers 'from the centre' were allowed to criticize local authorities, after publication officials usually were sacked. This created the illusion of effectiveness, and correspondents from Moscow newspapers became influential public figures.

MEDIA CHANGES FROM THE 1980s

The influence of foreign media dramatically increased during the disintegration of the Soviet empire (1988–1991). Gorbachev's policy of openness created a new environment, and foreign journalists were able to report outside Moscow. Lithuania was opened for foreign visitors; journalists used these new opportunities to report about the newly discovered land. Nobody knew for how long this Soviet openness would last.

'The Singing Revolution' in the Baltics was different from protests in other Soviet Republics, which often turned into clashes. Lithuanian Sąjūdis was able to gather in the hundreds of thousands for peaceful demonstrations; the restoration of national symbols or the demolition of Soviet monuments were attractive media events. Western journalists residing in Moscow hurried to recruit local stringers. Becoming a stringer was a good opportunity for local journalists, who were able to get in touch with Western media and received a comparatively high salary. Later, some worked for the foreign media in other hot spots of the disintegrating Soviet Empire.

'Classical' foreign correspondents were not in a hurry to settle in Lithuania, which proclaimed independence on 11 March 1990 but for more than a year remained under control of the Soviet military. Working from Lithuania was related to risks and offered limited opportunities. British journalist, Edward Lucas, former correspondent for *The Independent*, became some kind of iconic figure. He extensively reported about the Baltic freedom fight and was appreciated for his analysis and objectivity. Lucas was the first to receive a Lithuanian visa, a rather symbolic and brave step at the time of increasing Moscow repressions.

The Soviet military attack in Vilnius on 13 January 1991 marked a shifting point: news from Lithuania about the brutality of Soviet troops competed with the reports from the First Gulf War. Moscow falsely expected that international conflict would overshadow repressions in Vilnius. Western governments remained cautious and strategically supported Gorbachev. Public opinion in democratic countries became crucially important for the Baltic freedom movement, and foreign media were considered to be the main ally. Some sort of journalistic solidarity can be noticed: the Soviet military were targeting the media infrastructure; all casualties in Vilnius were at the TV tower and radio and TV buildings. On the other hand, foreign correspondents were not always understood by local journalists due to their scrupulous check of the detailed facts because the locals were fighting for their lives and saw information as a weapon of protection, which could only help if spread quickly.

As the Soviet military occupied media infrastructure, a large part of Lithuania remained without a source of information. At the time, the foreign broadcasts in Lithuanian language, especially by Radio Free Europe/Radio Liberty (RFE/RL) and Voice of America, played an important role, because it substituted the local media and helped raise journalistic standards. In these broadcasts, special attention was given to reviews of foreign press. RFE/RL established its bureau in Vilnius and employed a net of local correspondents, which served until the end of 2003, when broadcasts in Lithuanian were shut down.

THE CURRENT MEDIA LANDSCAPE AND FOREIGN CORRESPONDENTS[1]

Nowadays, the landscape of Lithuanian public life looks very calm and even boring; from time to time, it is shaken by elections, local scandals, or downfalls that have no broader than national impact and are common everywhere. Therefore, the foreign media feels no need to have a broader presence in Lithuania. In 2013, the Lithuanian Ministry of Foreign Affairs accredited 54 foreign journalists (12 Belorussian; eight Polish; seven Latvian; six Russian; five Kazakh; three German; two each Chinese, Norwegian, Swedish, Ukrainian; one each American, British, Canadian, French, and Iranian). The gender breakdown was 36 male and 18 female correspondents. Twenty-six journalists represented TV, 15 news agencies, five worked for magazines, four for newspapers, two for radio and other media. These modest figures do not reveal the real situation because accreditation does not mean that the journalists permanently reside in Lithuania. Correspondents from neighbouring countries and even other EU member states receive accreditation, but usually stay in their home country and visit Lithuania occasionally. Accreditation remains important for small media organizations and is still vital for journalists, who need residence permits in order to stay in Lithuania. Some foreign correspondents serve Lithuania from Warsaw or Riga, either of which is larger than Vilnius and better connected. At the end of 2013, we can notice a sudden increase of foreign correspondents in Lithuania. In November, the Lithuanian Ministry of Foreign Affairs had 76 foreign correspondents on their accreditation list. This temporary change should be linked with Lithuanian presidency of the Council of the European Union.

Despite the decline of accreditation, there are still remnants of old-fashioned media attitudes: a few Russian or Belarusian journalists in Lithuania were involved in Cold War–style games, which undermine the reputation of foreign correspondents. In 2011, a correspondent of the Belarusian state TV, Aleksei Mikhalchenko, was accredited for the coverage of the meeting of the Organization for Security and Co-operation in Europe (OSCE) foreign ministers in Vilnius. He received a Lithuanian visa despite being on the list of Belarusian officials banned to enter the EU. This controversy worried the democratic opposition in Belarus and pleased the Belarusian government. In 2012, the Lithuanian Ministry of Foreign Affairs withdrew accreditation for Russian news agency's *RIA Novosti* correspondent Irina Pavlova. This move irritated Moscow; Sergey Lavrov, Russian Minister of Foreign Affairs, personally mentioned the problem to his Lithuanian counterpart, and the accreditation was renewed. In 2013, Vladimir Ryzhkov, one of the representatives of Russian democratic opposition, publicly complained about spying during his stay in Vilnius. A small-scale conference about democracy was attended by an extraordinarily large group of Russian journalists, most of whom were suspected to be working for special services. According to an online source, 'even in Moscow there was not such spying like in Vilnius' (Ryzhkov, 2013).

It is difficult to use conventional classifications of foreign journalists (Hamilton & Jenner, 2004) for the few professionals residing in Lithuania, where 'traditional' foreign correspondents could be called an 'extinct tribe'. As international media organizations face everlasting funding problems, locations such as Lithuania seem like the right places to save money and resources because there is no need for a permanent high-profile presence. Modern communication technologies only boost this trend.

Starting from the late 1980s, stringers were and remain the 'core' group of foreign correspondents corps in Lithuania. Usually they work on a full-time basis for a local news agency or daily, and they report for foreign media on a part-time basis. This model is efficient: stringers, who report to regional bureaus, are highly trusted and professional. They consider themselves to be part of a global network and do not hesitate to use their contacts in order to do a better job for their Lithuanian employers. Stringers have a good understanding of what is important for their audience, but they lack a view from the outside, which is the core attribute of a foreign correspondent.

It is often difficult to draw precise boundaries between a stringer and foreign correspondent. Details of job contracts usually are kept secret, but a few foreign journalists in Lithuania receive regular salaries with an obligation to deliver a certain number of reports every month. Usually they are paid for every report; for some of them, it is not unusual to report to several media organizations simultaneously. The balance between being a stringer and foreign correspondent is most striking among those who could be called 'love migrants'. They are not necessary journalists by training but have come to Lithuania because of personal reasons and found a job for the media in their country of origin. Most of them are confident: '[i]f not [for] me, the media organization would not look for a correspondent in Lithuania' (FC7).

According to the Ministry of Foreign Affairs, which monitors foreign media reporting about Lithuania, every month the country is mentioned between 400 and 500 times. About 70 per cent of reports are considered to be 'neutral', the rest are split in nearly equal parts and rated as 'positive' or 'negative'. Such an official analysis should not be a surprise; the majority of reports about Lithuania are provided by the news agencies.

Routine economics and politics are the main topics of interest for foreign correspondents, but they differ from the stories in local media. 'Changes of foreign affairs or finance minister are a story, but nobody cares about the change of ministers of culture or education', says one of the journalists (FC5). For the last few years, controversies about closing the Ignalina atomic power plant and plans to build a new one were among the commonly discussed topics. Lithuania had a vast Jewish community that did not survive the atrocities of World War II, so Jewish heritage and the hunt for Nazi criminals are always noticed by foreign media. Foreign correspondents from neighbouring countries are interested in the activities of Polish and Russian communities, but this interest is controversial. 'Reporting about minorities is a bit formal, in reality, our readers are not interested in it', thinks FC3. His colleague from another country agrees: '[m]inorities are not important; readers prefer stories about places of interest for tourists' (FC2).

The economic crisis was a global event, and Lithuania was not a unique case and thus of no special interest to foreign correspondents. Even attempts to introduce common European currency in Lithuania are reported in contradictory manner. 'It is a story for Brussels correspondents, not for us', complains a journalist residing in Vilnius (FC7).

Being on the periphery of political and economic news creates a situation where Lithuania becomes a source of soft news. As the country lacks world-known celebrities, journalists are looking for 'strange' stories. An example could be the video, 'Vilnius Mayor Artūras Zuokas Fights Illegally Parked Cars with Tank', which was watched by millions on YouTube and was reported by the world media. A journalist by training, Zuokas was awarded the Ig Nobel Prize (the American parody of the Nobel Prizes), but photos of the event were deleted from the archives of the *Associated Press* because the photographs had been 'Photoshopped'. Among local stringers, such 'soft stories' cause conflicting feelings. 'I was upset when I couldn't write about [a] woman who eats sand', regrets one correspondent (FC1). His colleague says, 'I try to escape such topics as a woman who eats sand; I am working for respectable media' (FC3). Another journalist adds: 'I don't want to write stories about a woman who eats sand; I don't want my homeland to be seen as a crazy place' (FC5). Contradicting opinions show the rise of 'infotainment' as well as efforts to resist it.

Unlike the local media, foreign media presuppose the impartiality of stringers, which is difficult to achieve, as most work for both. On the other hand, some stringers try to escape controversial stories, which are complicated to explain to foreign audiences. This is understood as loyalty to the home country: 'I live here. My children live here. I am faithful to Lithuania', says one of the correspondents (FC3).

Despite the fact that Lithuania became a member of the EU and NATO a decade ago, foreign media depicts it as an 'ex-communist' or 'ex-soviet' country. Some Lithuanians consider such a label insulting. 'Why don't you describe Germany as a partially ex-communist and partially ex-Nazi country?' (Paulauskas, 2011). Similar problems are mentioned by foreign correspondents who remember their engagement in private battles with their editors: 'We agreed to write that Lithuania gained independence X years ago and not to use such words as ex-communist or ex-soviet,' says one former foreign correspondent (FC5).

Foreign media is not popular in Lithuania; it is complicated to speak about the direct impact of foreign correspondents reporting on local politics. Opinions, commentaries, and excerpts of the news reported by foreign media reach the Lithuanian audience usually as a second source through the local media. Thus, certain aspects are overexaggerated or lost in translation. An excellent example could be an essay by Lucas, 'End of Year Prizes for the CEE Region' (Lucas, 2010), published in the blog *Eastern Approaches* on the Website of *The Economist*. With delicate British humour, the journalist delivered so-called prizes to the politicians of the region. Nomination of Lithuania's President Dalia Grybauskaitė for The Foot in Mouth award in Lithuanian media was presented as the official *Economist* prize.

Foreign correspondents have no complaints about access to the government institutions. Direct comments from government ministers are available without difficulty. But journalists who work for local and foreign media simultaneously notice that politicians try to use different language while commenting to foreign and local media. 'Speaking to foreign audience, politicians try to be more balanced and mild', notes one former foreign correspondent (FC5).

Technological changes influence foreign correspondents' work in Lithuania. It is difficult to say which reports from Lithuania are published and which are declined. Although all reports are published on the Websites, the news from Lithuania cannot compete with information from Brussels or New York in other fields of the media. Some of the journalists have personal Websites and/or use Twitter or other modern technologies. As news agencies are increasingly involved in video production, in Lithuania they use different forms. The *Associated Press* occasionally sends professional TV teams from Warsaw, and local stringers only advise with the topics but do not participate in the production. *RIA Novosti* supplies their local correspondents with video equipment and expects them to deliver video material, but editing is left to Moscow.

CHALLENGES FOR THE FUTURE

Lithuania cannot expect an increase of interest from the foreign media, and 'classical' foreign correspondents will remain a glamorous figure. The hard news from Lithuania will remain at a deficit, and there is a risk for the country to become a source of soft news and strengthen its image as a nation of strangers. Worldwide decline of interest in foreign countries and the increase of 'infotainment' should support such tendencies. Modern communication technologies will only diminish the need and want of foreign media to have permanent correspondents in Lithuania. Stringers will likely remain the main source of news—they are already becoming the trusted sources who confirm the facts—but their role will weaken.

Social media allow foreign media to track local news and moods remotely. But the Lithuanian language remains a problem. Some hopes of an increase of professional coverage of local affairs could be linked with the expansion of modern technologies: data-gathering commentaries from local professionals could be received from a distance. But such a style of remote reporting undermines the very idea of foreign correspondence, which is based on interconnectedness between the view from the outside and a deep understanding of the local environment. As hard news about Lithuania in the international media becomes scarce, every mention in foreign media becomes a local event, and the importance of such an 'event' is exaggerated by the home media. This creates a divergence between the decline of the quality of foreign media commentaries and the exaggeration of their importance.

ACKNOWLEDGEMENTS

The author would like to thank the journalists who are or were working as foreign correspondents in Lithuania and who in June and July 2013 gave interviews for this research project: Liudas Dapkus, Agnieszka Filipiak, Vladimir Ivanov, Irina Pavlova, Artūras Račas, Romas Sakadolskis, and Marielle Vitureau. Special thanks to officials from the Information and Public Relations Department of the Lithuanian Ministry of Foreign Affairs, Giedrius Puodžiūnas and Gina Kazlauskienė, who provided statistical information.

NOTE

1. This section is partly based on interviews with foreign correspondents residing in Lithuania. At the time, Lithuanian Foreign Affairs Ministry was reluctant to provide contact details of accredited foreign journalists referring to the protection of personal data. With the help of foreign embassies, seven foreign correspondents were contacted in June and July 2013. Because of the modest number of the respondents, the method of in-depth interviews was applied. The structure of the interview was based on the survey questions designed for this book.

REFERENCES

HAMILTON, J., & JENNER, E. (2004) Redefining Foreign Correspondence. *Journalism*. 5 (3), pp. 301–321.

KREFT, H. (1970). *Klaipėda—pagaliau didelės ateities miestas: Lietuvos uostamiestis vokiečio akimis*. Vilnius, Lithuania: Mintis.

———. (1970). *Mit den Augen eines Deutschen: Das schönere Memel heisst Klaipėda: Schicksal und Aufstieg der litauischen Hafenstadt*. Vilnius, Lithuania: Mintis.

LUCAS, E. E. L. (2010). *End of Year Prizes for the CEE Region* [Online]. Available from http://econ.st/1hN2YC7.

PAULAUSKAS, K. (2011). Anti-communist. *Economist*. [Online]. Available from http://econ.st/1mfUx2s.

RYZHKOV, V. (2013). *Владимир Рыжков: даже в Москве не было такой слежки, как в Вильнюсе* (Vladimir Ryzhkov: Even in Moscow there was no surveillance as in Vilnius) [Online]. Available from http://bit.ly/P7aYSK.

SATTER, D. (2007). Never Speak to Strangers. A Memoir of Journalism, the Cold War, and the KGB. *Weekly Standard*. 12 (44) [Online]. Available from http://tws.io/1gKjmCr.

SENN, A. E. (2006). *Foreign Correspondent: Henry Shapiro in Moscow, 1933–1973*. Kaunas, Lithuania: Vytauto Didžiojo universiteto leidykla.

16 Foreign Correspondents in Malta
Peculiarities of a Small Nation State

Joseph Borg

INTRODUCTION

At face value, the small Mediterranean island of Malta, whose mediascape has interesting indigenous characteristics (Borg, 2009), should not make news beyond its shores barring some natural catastrophe. However, the country's news value is more important than its size for two reasons. Its membership in the European Union implies that events in Malta can have repercussions beyond its shores, particularly during the Eurozone crisis. Its geographical position as a frontier state of the EU, particularly during the uprising in Libya and the movement of irregular migration, also increased its news value.

This research was carried during August and September 2012 through a questionnaire and semistructured interviews with 12 foreign correspondents in Malta. This combination of a quantitative and a qualitative approach helps the researcher get a both wide and deep insight into the question studied. The structured interview technique implies the use of an interview guide used with all correspondents but enables the researcher to make follow-up questions (Langdridge & Hagger-Johnson, 2009). The journalists interviewed were identified after consulting several editors and examining the list of foreign correspondents on the Department of Information Website. This method ensured that the number of those interviewed were representative of FCs in Malta.

WHO ARE THE COUNTRY'S CORRESPONDENTS?

All those registered as foreign correspondents in Malta (12 in total) are in fact Maltese citizens. Most of them work with a Maltese newspaper but then also work as part-time foreign correspondents. Therefore, one cannot find among this corps the same characteristics documented in several studies (for example Hess, 1996; Hannerz, 2004). The nomenclature 'foreign correspondent' is therefore somewhat misleading. According to this research, seven correspondents have journalistic tasks, and five are photographers.

Hamilton and Jenner (2004) criticize Kalb's (1990) position that the genre known as foreign correspondent is becoming extinct. They state that it is in evolution mainly due to economic pressures, global interdependence, and technological innovations. They argue for a new model of foreign correspondence and propose a new typology that includes six categories of foreign correspondents alongside the elite/traditional foreign correspondent whose presence is on the decline in many countries. As noted, none of the foreign correspondents in Malta belongs to the elite/traditional type. Consequently, throughout this paper, the term 'indigenous foreign' correspondent (IFC) will be used, it being preferred to the appellative 'foreign, foreign correspondent' used by Hamilton and Jenner (2004).

IFCs generally work on their own, though three media organizations employ both a photographer and a journalist. Some of the correspondents work for more than one foreign media organization. The journalistic tradition runs in some families; in fact, three carry on the baton from their fathers. All IFCs describe themselves as stringers, albeit of different kinds. One IFC strings for a number of different organizations specializing in photographing visiting foreign celebrities. One photographer works on assignments supporting a local journalist. Another has a contract with three established media organizations. Commitment varies. Six pitch weekly, one pitches monthly, and five merely occasionally. Two are almost sleeper stringers who provide logistical support to visiting foreign staff or background information to the parent organization. This is reflected in the remuneration packet of the seven who answered that particular question: two earn over €4,000 per month, while two earn less than €1,000 per month, and the others in between.

The IFCs cover the whole gamut of media, from online to the more traditional media, from print to the broadcasting media, although there is a stronger presence in the latter. Seven work for news agencies, while three work for broadcast media and two for print media. With two exceptions, all media organizations represented are commercial ones, reflecting the contemporary commercialization of the media. Some, for example *Thomson Reuters* and *Associated Press* (both represented by a journalist and photographer), have been present in Malta for many years. The UK and United States have four correspondents each, France has two, and Australia and Germany one each. The interest of the Australian-based Special Broadcasting Services results from the great number of second- and third-generation Maltese in Australia. The English edition of *Al Jazeera* and the financial news station, *Bloomberg*, are comparatively newcomers.

Although all correspondents are Maltese, the first language of two of them is English, a reflection of Malta's bilingualism. Most also speak Italian, and a few also speak German, French, Spanish, or Arabic. All but three have university educations, and half have studied communication or journalism at university level, generally at the undergraduate level. Two have doctoral degrees, though not in communication studies.

In Malta all IFCs are males, reflecting the fact that all newspaper editors and almost all editors of broadcasting stations and the new media are male. The religious profile of the island is reflected in the composition of the group: almost all are Catholic. Nine are married, one is single, another widowed, and one divorced. The most senior foreign correspondent is 73 years old. The average age of the rest of the group is 41. They have been working as journalists for periods varying from 13 to 45 years. Half have been stringing as foreign correspondents for fewer than seven years, while others have been in the job for more than 10 years. Two IFCs did short assignments overseas, and one worked for an international media company. Only three said that they belonged to a journalists' trade union.

WHAT MAKES IT INTO THE FOREIGN CORRESPONDENT'S REPORTING AGENDA?

The debate about what is news has been part of the academic discussion at least since the seminal work of Galtung and Ruge (1965). Since then, many scholars produced lists of news value criteria. McQuail (2005) mentions 10 criteria, including drama, the large-scale nature of an event, relevance, proximity to home, and personification. Christians and colleagues (2012) list 16 professional news values, including proximity, impact, conflict, human interest, entertainment, novelty, immediacy, and independence. Boyd (2001) gives six elements: proximity, relevance, immediacy, interest, drama, and entertainment. These criteria are reflected in the statements of the IFCs who also refer to the policy of the parent media organizations and the nature of the medium used as factors that influence whether an event is considered newsworthy.

The criteria of relevance (McQuail, 2005) and potential impact (Christians, Fackler, Richardson, Kreshel, & Woods, 2012) are manifested through Malta's membership in the EU, which gave back to Malta, albeit for a different reason, its traditional strategic importance. As FC6 said, 'Whatever happens in Malta today can have an effect on the EU particularly in this time of economic crisis. Malta's importance is far larger than its size.'

FC7 added an example: 'The political instability that characterised our political scenario this year was of interest to our parent organisations. A change in government by a revolt of one back bencher in a one seat majority is interesting in itself. This becomes more so as it could change Malta's position in the EU institutions.' FC8 said that 'the stand of a Government MP against Malta's support for accession negotiations with Turkey interested people beyond our shores.'

The drama and personification criteria (McQuail, 2005) give news worthiness to the movement of irregular migration, which was mentioned by almost all IFCs. In line with the proximity criteria (Boyd, 2001; McQuail,

2005), the IFC representing US-based media said that this becomes news only when these migrants are accepted by the United States.

As irregular migration has been happening over many years, the innovation criterion wears off and compassion fatigue creeps in (Moeller, 1999). Most IFCs noted this element of news fatigue, adding that the arrival of migrants now becomes news only when the numbers are relatively large or when there is a particularly dramatic human interest element or when there is a stand-off between Malta and Italy about the port of welcome. Several IFCs noted an EU dimension since the subject is on its agenda. Malta's policy of detaining migrants before deploying them in open centres is deemed to have news value as, in the words of FC1, 'it had attracted criticism of several international NGOs or institutions'.

IFCs noted that Malta's geographical position was of prime news value during the uprising against Gaddafi. The conflict and impact criteria (Christians, Fackler, Richardson, Kreshel, & Woods, 2012) were buttressed by the large scale of the event (McQuail, 2005). Malta became a base for the coordination of humanitarian assistance as well as for journalistic activity. IFCs generally described it as the most important story for many years, but three said that they provided only logistical support for 'parachute' journalists. Some said that, thanks to their local contacts, they managed to file very important stories either from their base in Malta or from Libya itself where they were sent on assignment. Most foreign correspondents complained that their task was made more difficult when international agencies were broadcasting false reports about Malta. An instance mentioned was the untrue report in the international media that two Libyan warships had entered Malta's main harbour during the uprising against Gaddafi. 'My editor phoned angrily asking me why I did not file a story which was so hot on the wire. I had a hard time persuading him that the story was not true', said FC8.

News is also about what is out of the ordinary (Christians, Fackler, Richardson, Kreshel, & Woods, 2012). 'The May 2011 divorce referendum was of interest as Malta was the only European country without divorce legislation', said FC7. Most IFCs subscribed to this statement. Visits by international figures are always news, but their relevance is balanced by the proximity factor. Deutsche Presse-Agentur (DPA) considers visits by German politicians to be of importance; *Agence France-Presse* (*AFP*) gives more prominence to French personalities, while *Associated Press* (*AP*) goes more for American public figures. IFCs said that they were bypassed during the visit of US Secretary of State Hillary Clinton because the press corps that habitually accompanies her took precedence. The same thing happened during a visit by Pope Benedict in April 2010. Others were given specific briefs; for example, they were asked to frame the visit within the clerical child abuse scandal that was rocking the Catholic Church locally and internationally. On the other hand, FC3, who was stringing for an Italian magazine, said that his brief was to film Pope Benedict with the people.

International showbiz celebrities are also news worthy (Golding & Elliot, 2000). The IFCs said that this was mainly the domain of photographers who, in turn, lamented big competition from the foreign paparazzi. However, as FC3 said, their local knowledge and contacts enabled the Maltese to outdo the foreign photographers on several occasions. Tailing celebrities can be problematic; FC3 was beaten by an actor's bodyguards.

Proximity is one of the most important characteristics of newsworthiness and is not just about physical distance. FC4 files more weekly reports for the Australian Special Broadcasting Services than the others. The presence of a very large audience of Maltese migrants in Australia makes Maltese news close to people who are physically very far away. The proximity criterion is evidenced in sports. ICF photographers said that parent organizations are interested in photos of international football matches, particularly when the result makes a difference to who qualifies in the European Nations or World Cup competitions.

What makes it to the news pages or programmes is also medium influenced. Photojournalist FC5 said that 'a good picture can be accepted and distributed internationally even if it does not fulfil the ordinary characteristics of news value. Journalists have to meet stricter criteria'.

With the exception of the correspondent of *SBS*, the other correspondents file from twice a week to occasionally. Generally, the decision to file is taken by the IFC based on his knowledge of the company's news culture. Rates of acceptance vary from 90 to 100 per cent. This gives credence to Harrison's (2006) hypothesis that news is what journalists judge to be worthy of putting in the media within the confinements of the news organization for which they work. In a minority of cases, the editors ask for something specific or for a particular angle to the story. The IFCs said that this generally happens when editors have prior knowledge of an event, such as a visit by a foreign dignitary, or because they want to place it in the context of other stories they are covering.

WHEN IS SOMETHING BECOMING FCs' NEWS?

The IFCs said that two main annual seasons provide a pattern of news picks and lows. FC8 summed the collective position: 'Summer and early autumn gives [sic] us the news about illegal migration'. The photographers said summer presents most photo opportunities for traditional occasions like the village *festas*, the international jazz festival, and the Isle of MTV music festival.

The IFCs said that political developments provide most news material during the winter/spring season. The news value of the political scene was greater during the researched period because the government's one-seat majority was threatened by its own back bench. The correspondents of *Thomson Reuters* and *Bloomberg* also mentioned the news value of the annual report and comments made by the Governor of the Central Bank, who is also a member of the board of the European Central Bank.

WHERE DO STORIES COME FROM?

Journalists are as good or as bad as their sources, which have been described as a journalist's bread and butter (Christians, Fackler, Richardson, Kreshel, & Woods, 2012). Their importance and the complexities that arise from their relationship to journalists explain why sources have been studied so much (Hachten, 1998; Norris, Kern, & Just, 2003; Marken, 2007; Beales, 2009). The IFCs said that government officials are their most important source of news. Both the national media and 'other official national sources' concurrently came a very distant second as the most important sources of news. The members of the opposition, lobbies, and official sources from embassies trail far behind; none of them was mentioned by more than three IFCs. Only one correspondent mentioned social networks as a source. A minority of IFCs said that they are treated in the same way when they approach government sources either as Maltese journalists or as foreign correspondents. However, most said that they notice a marked improvement when they present themselves as IFCs. 'Doors open up when I mention the international media organization I work for', said FC6, echoing the position of most others. Politicians seem to be more open to journalists than civil servants. FC6 mentioned an incident when the deputy prime minister immediately agreed to be interviewed, even though the regulatory authority was very reluctant. Several interviewees said that ministers use the IFCs to pass on messages to the international community. FC7 explained: 'Government officials contacted me on migration issues telling me "this is the message we want to get out there." And because I am Maltese, in a case like this, I oblige'.

HOW FOREIGN NEWS IS FORMULATED IN DIFFERENT FRAMES

This raises important questions about journalistic independence and sources of influence.

'Being Maltese does not make a difference. I report something even if it embarrasses my country', commented FC6, echoing replies by all respondents. However, on further prodding, a number of 'ifs' and 'buts' emerged. For example, one photographer decided to send the picture of a hooded demonstrator burning an EU flag, but FC2 refused because it 'would have given a wrong impression of Malta'. Journalist IFCs would report about Malta's policy of detaining irregular immigrants and their conditions, whereas the photographers were split. FC2 would send photos showing bad conditions inside these camps because these 'do not respect human dignity'. FC3 disagreed because he 'will never embarrass the country by photographing these camps since Malta is doing a lot for these migrants'.

In recent years, journalism has been moving away from a normative to a market-driven concept wherein news is based mainly on its saleable value

(McManus, 1994; Croteau, Hoynes, & Milan, 2012). Most Maltese IFCs differ from this model, stating that advertising considerations, profit expectations, and businesspeople are the least favored sources of influence. Moreover, even politicians and government officials are identified as sources of minimal influence.

Journalists are not independent professionals. Their actions and judgements are exercised within organizational parameters (McManus, 1994). Unexpectedly, the IFCs said that they give more importance to their own personal values and beliefs than to organizational factors, both editorial and managerial. IFCs said that family and friends influenced them more than peers on the organization's staff and colleagues in other media organizations. Besides, an analysis of the institutional factors of influence shows that IFCs give more importance to editorial policy and editors than to managers and owners. All said that time limits and the competing news organizations are the factors that influence them most. 'You have to be very quick and file before everyone else', said photographer FC3.

WHICH ARE THE MOST INFLUENTIAL FOREIGN CORRESPONDENTS AND LOCAL MEDIA?

Half the IFCs consider *Reuters* the most important foreign media organization in Malta, while one-fourth opt for *AFP*, *AP*, or *CNN*. This shows that judgement about importance is given independently of one's belonging to a particular organization.

Three-quarters of IFCs said that their main sources are both the local media and the local journalists. One-third use these sources every day, and one-half several times a week. The IFCs also refer to the local media as the main reason to start investigating a story. Just over half the respondents mentioned blogs/social media and other foreign correspondents as the sources most frequently used, though the former are more often used on a daily basis. Both sources receive equal mentions as being the main reason for initiating a story.

All IFCs bar two said that there is cooperation between them, particularly when nonexclusive stories or logistical reasons render cooperation to be mutually beneficial. However, as FC8 emphasized, there is competition when an exclusive story is in the offing.

CONCLUSIONS

It is a known fact that the cost-cutting exercises of many media organizations have negatively impacted foreign bureaus (Croteau, Hoynes, & Milan, 2012) and that this has had an effect on peoples' understanding of what happens in other countries (McChesney, 2008). The Maltese experience seems to be different. The majority of IFCs, while fully conscious of the cost-cutting and job-shedding exercises by their foreign employers, are not afraid of meeting the same fate because their resources have not been cut down. Several said that the effect of the Euro crisis was mainly editorial; that is, there is more interest in European affairs. Most IFCs also said that their work has not been affected by an increase in the use of parachute journalists. Opinion is equally split on whether news is being increasingly covered by headquarters, and a slight majority does not feel that the audience cares less about international news. The employment of amateur journalists is not considered to be a problem.

This paper's starting point was the compositional difference between the Maltese corps of IFCs and several foreign ones: it is a very small corps, and all foreign correspondents are Maltese! This paper ends by pointing out another difference between the Maltese corps of IFCs and other foreign ones: two-thirds do not think that their job has changed for the worse. The indigenous nature and small size of the corps enable it to perform with resources that were so rudimentary that they are now not negatively impacted by the economic downturn. It seems that the limitations of the local situation turned out to be its strength.

REFERENCES

BEALES, I. (2009). *The Editors' Codebook. The Handbook to the Editors' Code of Practice*, 2nd ed. UK: Newspaper Publishers Association [Online]. Available from http://bit.ly/1m9fnD3.

BORG, J. (2009). Malta's Media Landscape: An Overview. In Borg, J., Hillman, A., & Lauri, M. A. (eds.), *Exploring the Maltese Media Landscape*. Malta: Allied Publications.

BOYD, A. (2001). *Broadcast Journalism. Techniques of Radio and Television News*, 5th ed. Oxford: Focal Press.

CHRISTIANS, C., FACKLER, M., RICHARDSON, K. B., KRESHEL, P. J., & WOODS, R. H. (2012). *Media Ethics: Cases and Moral Reasoning*, 9th ed. White Plains, NY: Longman.

CROTEAU, D., HOYNES, W., & MILAN, S. (2012). *Media/Society. Industries, Images, and Audience*, 4th Ed. London: Sage.

GALTUNG, J., & RUGE, M.H. (1965). The Structure of Foreign News. The Presentation of the Congo, Cuba and Cyprus Crises in Four Norwegian Newspapers. *Journal of Peace Research*. 2 (1), pp. 64–90.

GOLDING, P., & ELLIOT, P. (2000). News Values and News Production. In Marris, P., & Thornham, S. (eds.), *Media Studies: A Reader*. New York: New York University Press.

HACHTEN, W. A. (1998). *The Troubles of Journalism: A Critical Look at What's Right and Wrong with the Press*. Mahwah, NJ: Lawrence Erlbaum.

HAMILTON, J. M., & JENNER, E. (2004). Redefining Foreign Correspondence. *Journalism*. 5 (3), pp. 301–321.

HANNERZ, U. (2004). *Foreign News: Exploring the World of Foreign Correspondents*. Chicago: University of Chicago Press.

HARRISON, J. (2006). *News*. London: Routledge.

HESS, S. (1996). *International News and Foreign Correspondents*. Washington, DC: Brookings Institution Press.

KALB, M. (1990). "Foreword." In SERFATY S. (ed.), *The Media and Foreign Policy*. New York: St. Martin's Press, 1990.

LANGDRIDGE, D., & HAGGER-JOHNSON, G. (2009). *Introduction to Research Methods and Data Analysis in Psychology*, 2nd ed. London: Prentice Hall.

MARKEN, L. (2007). The Real and the Right: Journalistic Authority and the Coverage of Judith Miller. *Journalism and Mass Communication Quarterly* [Online] 84 (2), pp. 265*ff*. Available from http://bit.ly/1m9fpuR.

MCCHESNEY, R. W. (2008). *The Political Economy of Media*. New York: Monthly Review Press.

MCMANUS, J. H. (1994). *Market-driven Journalism. Let the Citizen Beware?* London: Sage.

MCQUAIL, D. (2005). *McQuail's Mass Communication Theory*, 5th ed. London: Sage.

MOELLER, S. D. (1999). *Compassion Fatigue*. New York: Routledge.

NORRIS, P., KERN, M., & JUST, M. (2003). *Framing Terrorism: The News Media, the Government and the Public*. New York: Routledge.

17 Foreign Correspondents in The Netherlands

Anything That Would Be of Interest for Our Readers[1]

Bernadette C. M. Kester and Mirjam Goudswaard

INTRODUCTION

This chapter maps the journalistic practices of foreign correspondents based in The Netherlands. How interesting can one of the smallest countries in Europe be in light of international news coverage? Interesting enough for international correspondents to make it their residence. It isn't terribly obvious that this small country was once a world power. In the 17th century, the then Dutch Republic was a large colonial empire (controlling Indonesia, Suriname, and The Netherlands Antilles), a thriving trading nation famous for its religious and diversity tolerance and for its high degree of freedom of the press. Free spirits from all over Europe were looking to reside in this country. In the 19th century, The Netherlands, by then a parliamentary constitutional monarchy, developed a unique social-political system where parallel ideological currents coexisted. This rather unique constellation was called 'pillarization,' a form of 'organised pluralism' (Hallin & Mancini, 2004, p. 53). From the beginning of the 20th century, this constituted the basis of the Dutch (mass) media system. In the context of Hallin and Mancini's media systems theory, the Dutch media system is in compliance with the parameters of the democratic-corporatist model. It is characterized by external pluralism in the national press, a strong party press, and a high level of professionalization, among other features. The Dutch media landscape has 'depillarized' rapidly since the 1970s due to secularization, individualization, and commercialization.

During that same period, The Netherlands began to behave more and more like a moral pioneer. The country took on a leading role (*gidsland*) particularly in regard to social and ethical issues concerning soft drugs, abortion, euthanasia, and same-sex marriage. Many countries still observe how the Dutch manage these matters and how their politics deal with related issues. However, the image of The Netherlands as one of the most tolerant and free nations changed drastically in 2002 after the populist politician Pim Fortuyn was murdered in broad daylight by an environmental activist (Lechner, 2008). As one German correspondent states, 'From a political viewpoint The Netherlands was a bit dull, but since 2001/2002 with Pim Fortuyn a lot has changed and the country [is] became more interesting'.

After the murder of the critical and provocative filmmaker and publicist Theo van Gogh two years later, the situation became even more interesting for newsmakers. This time a young Islamic man was the assassin. Both victims were anti-Islam or, at the very least, critical of the multicultural society the country had become. For some opinion makers (Paul Scheffer, Ayaan Hirsi Ali), this meant the end (or failure) of multiculturalism. It also led to the emergence of a climate where an anti-Islamic attitude could easily thrive. This development was reflected in the immense popularity of the extreme right-wing populist Geert Wilders and his political movement, the Party of Freedom (PVV). As his one-man/member-party became part of the Rutte II cabinet (in a complicated structure in which Wilders' party, without being a member of the cabinet, supported cabinet decisions), Dutch tolerance and open mindedness toward foreign cultures and 'non-Western' inhabitants (from first to third generation) seemed to come to a halt. This was the situation at the time this research was conducted. Today, now that a liberal-social-democratic cabinet has been installed, Wilders' movement still has a large following and is therefore a force to reckon with.

For a long time (1839–1940), The Netherlands' position in matters of international affairs was characterized by a neutral status. After World War II, this position was no longer realistic, and The Netherlands became an ally of the United States and a NATO member. The Netherlands drew the interest of many foreign correspondents because of the Peace Palace in The Hague, where the Permanent Court of Arbitration has been located since 1913. Also, the International Court of Justice (formerly Permanent Court of International Justice) has resided in The Hague since 1946; it is also the city where the national Parliament presides and the home city of the International Criminal Court (2002). During the 1990s, various international war crime tribunals took place in The Hague, such as the International Criminal Tribunal for the former Yugoslavia (ICTY). Evidently this attracted the international press corps. Near The Hague, in Scheveningen, is the United Nations Detention Unit (UNDU) where (suspected) war criminals such as Slobodan Milosevic, Radovan Karadzic, Ratko Mladic, Laurent Gbagbo, Charles Taylor, and Bosco Ntaganda were or are imprisoned during their trial.

Very conveniently (and to no one's surprise), The Hague also hosts the Foreign Press Association of The Netherlands (FPA), which most correspondents who arrive here join. The Netherlands has a long tradition of being a guest country for foreign correspondents. In 1925, the FPA was founded and is still an active organization to this day. During our research, Kerstin Schweighöfer (*ARD Radio*) acted as president (2008–2012); Jan Hennop (*AFP*) succeeded her. The FPA offers excellent opportunities for correspondents to build or extend their network. The association regularly organizes field trips to universities, major companies and other institutions, and cultural organizations; also, working lunches with the prime minister, prosecutors of the tribunals, and ministers or other officials are highly appreciated.

THE RESPONDENTS

To obtain insight into the world and professional profile of foreign correspondents (FCs) based in The Netherlands, consulting the membership list of the FPA (which included the member's email addresses) was a discernable point to begin. The 85 members of the FPA were sent an email with a request to fill out an attached questionnaire. The chair of the organization informed us that of the 85 members, only 75 per cent are still active correspondents. Of the members, about 55 are male and 30 female. They are from 28 different countries; the most significant numbers represent Germany (13 FCs), the United States (eight FCs), Russia (five FCs), and the UK (four FCs).

Because the response rate was very low at first, we consulted the chairwoman, who kindly decided to disseminate our survey through the organization's internal mailing list. She also sent a message herself to encourage the FPA members to participate. Two reminders were sent around. In the end, one-third (N = 21) filled out (most of) the survey, and eight of them participated in in-depth interviews conducted by telephone. Some respondents did not fill out the form completely. We presume the questionnaire was too extensive and time-consuming for them. It will be mentioned in the text whenever results are based on the answers of fewer than 21 respondents. The response rate should be taken into account when consulting the results.

WHO ARE THE CORRESPONDENTS? *DEMOGRAPHICS*

The group of correspondents who filled out the survey was rather homogeneous, particularly concerning age. Only two are below 30 years of age, and four younger than 40. With four correspondents of over 60 years old, the average age was 47 years. Although this is in line with older research (Hess, 1996), more recent research shows that the age is lowering (Wu & Hamilton, 2004). Correspondingly, we observed that many (Dutch) correspondents are indeed quite a lot younger.

The average age we found could be one explanation as to why the respondents are generally on the job for a long time—22 years on average. This is very long compared to current policies in many newsrooms, which send reporters abroad for four or five years at the most.

Less in accordance with former research is the division regarding gender. Although correspondence is still considered a male-dominated profession (Hess, 1996; Wu & Hamilton, 2004), 53 per cent of our respondents are male and 47 per cent are female.

Concerning other sociodemographic aspects, we noticed the following outcome: 69 per cent are married or in a relationship; 39 per cent consider themselves affiliated with a religion (Christian). Most are well educated, with 68 per cent having obtained a master's degree. One has a doctoral degree, and one did not attend university at all. Only 42 per cent studied journalism on a vocational or university level.

The monthly salary of the majority of correspondents lies between €1,000 and €4,000; five earn up to €1,000 a month and two bring in €4,000–€8,000 a month. While in most professions women still earn less than men, it was rather surprising to find female correspondents occupying only the highest income category.

Where Do Correspondents Come from and What Languages Do They Speak?

Most foreign correspondents in our research sample are originally from European countries, such as Germany (seven), France (three), Italy (two), Poland, Russia, Spain, and the United Kingdom. Only three are from outside Europe, coming from South Africa, the United States, and China. Two correspondents are Dutch by origin but work for foreign news outlets.

On average, foreign correspondents in general are fluent in two or three languages, alongside their mother tongue. Although it is generally admitted how important it is for correspondents to master the language of the country they are based in, only 13 of the 21 correspondents speak Dutch (71 per cent), including the two Dutch reporters. The next important language to master in most European countries is English, and indeed almost every correspondent mentions this language as his or her second language. Surprisingly, though, three journalists mention that they are not able to speak English (two Italians and one German).[2] On average our respondents have mastered about four languages outside their mother tongue.

Professional Experience

Respondents have been working as journalists for 22 years on average before becoming a correspondent (not necessarily in The Netherlands). Only three of them started working as a correspondent immediately. Almost 50 per cent of the respondents have been working as a correspondent for 10 years or more. This confirms research that states becoming a correspondent often happens in a later stage in one's career and after having built up many years of experience (Hess, 1996). Therefore, we concluded that correspondents working in The Netherlands are very qualified. However, it might be even more important to know how well correspondents know the country they report from. They seem to be very qualified in this area, as well. The average number of years correspondents have been reporting from The Netherlands is 15 (the highest number of years being 42; the lowest, two).

Nine correspondents worked in another country outside their home country before coming to The Netherlands. Most of these countries are rather different from The Netherlands, culturally and geographically. Our respondents were based in non-European countries such as South Africa, Vietnam, India, Brazil, Singapore, Peru, UAE, Turkey, Eastern Africa, and the United States. The other correspondents worked from European countries like Germany, Belgium, Switzerland, Poland, Denmark, and the former Yugoslavia.

On average, correspondents stayed three years in each foreign country before coming to The Netherlands. That is not anywhere near the average number of years they are reporting from The Netherlands, but much more in line with current practices, as we have already indicated.

WHOM DO THEY WORK FOR? NEWS ORGANIZATIONS

All Dutch-based FCs work as freelancers (62 per cent) or full-time (38 per cent); not one of the respondents has a part-time job. This explains why most of them have several employers; working full-time does not necessarily mean working for only one news organization. Eighteen correspondents (86 per cent) work for one to five different employers, and three work for seven to 15 employers. Each news organization's headquarters is located in the correspondent's home country. Only three correspondents work for a news organization that has its headquarters outside of Europe: the United States, Singapore, and China. Seven reporters work for a German organization, and two each for a French, a Belgium, a Polish, a British, and a Swiss news organization. The other three correspondents work for Italian, Russian, and Spanish news organizations.

A small majority of the correspondents work for a news agency (52 per cent) and/or several other media types like print media (52 per cent), followed by online media (43 per cent) and/or public radio stations (33 per cent) and public TV (24 per cent). A minority (10 per cent) work for private radio or for other than the aforementioned media outlets (10 per cent). None of the FCs are employed by a private TV station.

No less than 62 per cent of the correspondents' articles reach an international audience (outside the country they come from). The rest work only for national media (nationwide). None of the correspondents work for local or regional media.

The Internet has become a big player in the news business, which is corroborated by this survey and the interviews. Because most correspondents ($N = 19$) work for different types of media at the same time, most of their stories are published on different media platforms, particularly on Websites (89 per cent).

Working for different media types helps correspondents to survive. One respondent stated, 'You can sell your story twice if you work for radio and print. The radio wants to be first, but you can use the same news in an article for a newspaper or magazine'. Even though one of the correspondents claims that working for radio is very time-consuming, nine of the correspondents do so. The reason may have something to do with payment. Several correspondents mentioned that they usually make more money with television or radio reports than with reports for print media and Websites.

Social Media

Our correspondents ($N = 16$) say they do not use social media platforms on a regular basis for publishing their stories, even though social media have become much more prominent as a source for news and information (for consumers as well as producers). Facebook, Twitter, and YouTube are popular ways of expressing oneself in The Netherlands, but only three correspondents publish on Facebook, four on Twitter, two on YouTube, and none on Google+. Where Facebook is concerned, 44 per cent of the Dutch own a Facebook account, 30 per cent of Germans, and only 5 per cent of Russians (Socialbakers.com). That might explain why some correspondents ignore social media as a publishing platform. On the other hand, some of the correspondents do write on a personal page (eight FCs) or a blog (six FCs).

WHAT TOPICS ARE COVERED? *THE NETHERLANDS (AND OTHER COUNTRIES)*

The correspondents' main focus is reporting about The Netherlands; however, 29 per cent also cover more countries, like, in most cases, the neighbouring countries: Germany, Belgium, or Luxemburg. Nevertheless, one correspondent reports European-wide on a specific topic only (vegetable oil), while another covers the Middle East and Africa as well. Sometimes the choice for covering countries is determined by language. One correspondent from Germany covers not only The Netherlands but also all German-speaking countries (Germany, Austria, Switzerland, and Luxemburg). He says, 'When writing for an international market, a correspondent has to make sure that his story is understood in countries worldwide. Which can be challenging because of all the national and cultural differences'.

Table 17.1 Topics covered in The Netherlands.

Type of story	Number	Per Cent
Politics	17	81
Economics	14	67
Culture	16	76
Sports	6	29
Society	13	62
Other:	7	33
Royalties		
Justice—mostly international (considering location in The Hague)		
International Courts and tribunals		
Fashion, Lifestyle, Art, Design		

Question wording: 'What type of stories do you mostly cover? (several may apply) $N = 21$'

On the other hand, as an *AFP* correspondent states, 'That makes this news agency so interesting and nice to work for. I mean, there is no difference in writing a story that will go in a European or an African newspaper. We try to write to the highest standard'.

Table 17.1 summarizes the topics covered.

Main Focus

Politics, culture, and economics are, in general, the most popular topics covered. All interviewed correspondents mention the International Criminal Court (ICC) and the tribunals as one of the topics they write about the most. The French news agency *AFP* is even stationed in The Hague because of the ICC. Sessions of the court of tribunals with the aforementioned war criminals always draw a lot of international media attention.

Until recently, when a new cabinet took office (this time without the populist political party PVV), Dutch politics received worldwide coverage because of the extreme statements made by the Populist Party leader Geert Wilders. Apart from that, The Netherlands is irrelevant in international politics and too small to play a major role in Europe. Nevertheless, the Germans keep their eyes on The Netherlands because the Dutch are one of their last allies in the European Union. The correspondents confirm that The Netherlands is often seen as exemplary for countries struggling with moral issues like abortion and euthanasia. These are interesting topics to report about for correspondents, but on a party level, Dutch politics is not considered of interest for the other countries within or outside Europe.

Correspondents clearly also keep their focus on Dutch events that are interesting, particularly for the home country of the correspondent. This domestication or localization of international news is a common practice, as various research has indicated (Clausen, 2004; Ruigrok & Van Atteveld, 2007; Kester, 2011). Notably, Germans seem to be particularly interested in the ins and outs of the Dutch royal family because of its popularity in Germany.

All correspondents try to avoid and take the edge off existing stereotypes like The Netherlands being a country where everyone likes drugs and is really open-minded. Over all, correspondents take a positive stance toward the Dutch and say they want to do them as much justice as possible.

Most correspondents (90 per cent) initiate topics for stories themselves; their clients do not request specific stories. On average, the correspondents pitch seven stories a week. Five reporters pitch only one story a week, but some even 15 to 20. This means the number of stories produced every week differs considerably per correspondent. The correspondents employed full-time tend to pitch more stories per week than the freelance correspondents do. This might have to do with the kind of coverage. Many full-time correspondents work for news agencies and have to write a lot of stories at a high pace on the latest news topics. Some of the interviewed freelancers mentioned they work on these current news reports also, as well as on background stories. The background articles in particular are of an additional value to the news desks back home.

For news organizations other than agencies, correspondents are not really needed, with news available 24/7 on the Internet and via the wire services. But correspondents are requested to dig for more and interesting quotes or facts. That takes more time than most current news stories do. Almost all pitched stories are published. Only a few correspondents have percentages below 90 per cent of pitched stories that get published. Most of the interviewed correspondents do not see any clear seasonal factors that influence their coverage.

WHERE DO THEIR STORIES COME FROM?

Correspondents were asked which three resources were the main places to start investigating a story and to rank them from one to three. Government officials and media content in the host country are considered the most important resources for correspondents. The interviewed correspondents all read the major Dutch newspapers, particularly the largest, more popularly oriented newspaper, *De Telegraaf*, as well as the two quality newspapers, *de Volkskrant* and *NRC Handelsblad*, on a daily basis. Some also read more specialist newspapers like *Financieel*

Dagblad. They all visit Websites of the major newspapers and receive RSS feeds of newspapers as well. Moreover, they watch the eight o'clock news (NOS) and current affairs programs. In addition, important sources are other official national sources, NGOs, academics, and even average citizens.

About half of the correspondents rated access to first-hand sources of government or big business with a three on a one–to-five scale, meaning it is not too easy to get in touch with those sources; only one correspondent rated access with a two. Others seem to have better access to these sources and rated it a four. Only two correspondents experience very open access in The Netherlands to first-hand sources.

Social media such as Twitter and blogs are not among the three most important sources. The interviewed correspondents hardly ever use Twitter or Facebook as a source for keeping up with Dutch current affairs. If they do use them, it is mostly to follow the accounts of other correspondents or important institutes like the ICC or government organizations. However, about half of the interviewed correspondents do not see the value of Twitter. One correspondent uses Twitter sometimes as a means to get in contact with someone to talk to about a certain topic. As one of the German correspondents told us, 'I wrote a piece about the '*langstudeerboete*' and wanted to talk to some students. Using Twitter was a nice and easy way to get in touch with them'.

Some do follow specific blogs to keep up-to-date, but they do not really use it as a source. Correspondents follow social media and blogs only when they come from a trusted source, for example, government institutions, experts, or the ICC. They are a starting point for further investigation, but almost never a source that stands on its own. Correspondents try to verify information that is tweeted or posted on a blog.

HOW ARE NEWS STORIES FORMULATED?

News is supposed to be objective or neutral, and correspondents thrive to live up to that expectation. However, there are always some influences that could alter the content of an article, or certain frames are used to put events in perspective. A lot of factors can leave a mark on coverage (Shoemaker & Reese, 1996). We asked correspondents to rate potential sources of influence on a scale from one to five. Table 17.2 summarizes professional sources of influence.

Editorial supervisors and higher editors are the biggest influence on correspondents, followed by time limits and editorial policy. This means the news desks in the home countries have a large influence on the way the correspondents work and create their stories. This is not surprising. In many cases, especially concerning freelance correspondents, correspondents

Table 17.2 Professional sources of influence within the news organization for FCs from The Netherlands.

Rank	Professional (Internal) Sources of Influence	Rating (mean)
1.	Your editorial supervisors and higher editors	3.2
2.	Time limits	3.1
3.	Editorial policy	3.0
4.	Availability of newsgathering resources	2.8
5.	Your personal values and beliefs	2.7
6.	The managers of your news organization	2.6
7.	Audience research and data	2.2
8.	The owners of your news organization	2.1
9.	Your peers on the staff	2.0
10.	Profit expectations	1.9
11.	Advertising considerations	1.7

have to sell their articles or broadcasts to their editors. Overall, correspondents don't seem to care about their own profits or advertising considerations. Those got the lowest ratings.

Sources from Outside the Professional Network (Outside the News Organization)

Correspondents experience other influences in their professional environment as well. Pressure groups (extra media) may try to get their viewpoints published, business companies circulate press releases with new products. All those influences can lead to bias or to a certain image of The Netherlands. The ratings show that the foreign correspondents in The Netherlands do not seem to be easily influenced by certain sources such as pressure groups, businesspeople, the armed forces, or by censorship from the government in general. The level of access to information does matter, though. However, inasmuch as The Netherlands is a very open country with easy access and hardly any serious restrictions for journalists, there seems to be no problem in this arena. Table 17.3 summarizes sources of influence from outside the professional network.

It is also important to mention in this context a Dutch act (1980), called the 'Wob', which is an 'Act on public access to government information'. In the exercise of their duties, government bodies shall observe the right of public access to information in accordance with rules to be prescribed by the Act of Parliament (Buitenlandse Zaken, 2008). This means anyone can make a request for information on issues regarding the administration of government institutions. Information is therefore in principle easily accessible in The Netherlands for journalists, although sometimes one has to be patient.

Table 17.3 Sources of influence from outside the professional network (outside the news organization) for FCs in The Netherlands.

Rank	Other (External) Sources of Influence	Rating (mean)
1.	Information access	3.1
2.	Relationships with news sources	2.8
3.	Feedback from the audience	2.7
4.	Competing news organizations	2.4
4.	Media laws and regulations	2.4
6.	Colleagues in other media	2.2
6.	Public relations	2.2
8.	Government officials	2.0
8.	Politicians	2.0
8.	Your friends and families	2.0
11.	Businesspeople	1.7
12.	Censorship	1.5
12.	Pressure groups	1.5
12.	The military, policy, and state security	1.5

CONCLUSION

As the case of foreign correspondence in The Netherlands clearly shows, it truly does matter whether a country harbours international institutions. The country itself is not considered very interesting for foreign news organizations, but its international relations are. The portrayal of foreign correspondents working in The Netherlands displays on one hand a conventional image: over 40, well educated, and very experienced, and, in accordance with the current trend, most of them are freelancers. They usually pitch their own stories, but the influence of editorial supervisors is strongly felt. Their main news sources are government officials and media content. On the other hand (although it is difficult to estimate whether this is representative), correspondents show a balance regarding gender, and female reporters occupy the highest-income positions. Conspicuous is the over-representation of German correspondents, as well as the fact that only half of the correspondents have learned to speak Dutch. Taken together, our respondents happen to cover almost one hundred different news organizations (correspondences). How important they are for the media representation of The Netherlands abroad shows their interest in recognizing stereotypes and in taking efforts to nuance them.

NOTES

1. From the interview with an AFP correspondent.
2. Presumably the question was misunderstood; the three respondents could have thought it referred to their mother tongue.

REFERENCES

CLAUSEN, L. (2004). Localizing the Global: 'Domestication' Processes in International News Production. *Media, Culture & Society*, 26 (1), pp. 25–44.

HALLIN, D., & MANCINI, P. (2004). *Comparing Media Systems: Three Models of Media and Politics*. New York: Cambridge University Press.

HESS, S. (1996). *International News & Foreign Correspondents*. Washington, DC: Brookings Institution Press.

KESTER, B.C.M. (2010). The Art of Balancing. Foreign Correspondence in Non-democratic Countries: The Russian Case. *International Communication Gazette*, 72, pp. 51–70.

LECHNER, F. (2008). *The Netherlands. Globalization and National Identity.* New York: Routledge.

RUIGROK, N., & VAN ATTEVELD, W. (2007). Global Angling with a Local Angle: How U.S., British, and Dutch Newspapers Frame Global and Local Terrorist Attacks. *The Harvard International Journal of Press/Politics*, 12 (68), pp. 68–90.

SHOEMAKER, P.J., & REESE, S.D. (1996). *Mediating the Message.* White Plains, NY: Longman.

SOCIALBAKERS.COM [Online]. Available from http://bit.ly/KhJuHu.

WU, D., & HAMILTON, J.M. (2004). US Foreign Correspondents; Changes and Continuity at the Turn of the Century. *International Communication Gazette.* 6, pp. 517–532.

18 Foreign Correspondents in Norway
Covering a Small, Rich Country near the Arctic

Sigurd Allern

INTRODUCTION

The relevance of the international debate about the future of foreign correspondents and foreign news must—in the case of Norway—be discussed in relation to two trends. In a debate about correspondents working for Norwegian news outlets in other parts of the world, the concept of 'endangered species' (Emery, 1989) is highly relevant. As in many other Western countries (Hamilton & Jenner, 2004; Sambrook, 2010), the number of full-time foreign correspondents working for Norwegian media has been decreasing during the last two decades. The public service *Norwegian Broadcasting Corporation* (*NRK*) is an important exception.

However, if we change the perspective and ask about the number of foreign correspondents *located in Norway*, there has been an increase over the last few decades. In 1993, the Foreign Press Association (FPA) in Norway (founded in 1990) had 37 members, and in 2000 the membership had grown to 52 (Lindahl, 2001). Moreover, in the autumn of 2012, the FPA had 85 names registered on their official membership list. In the autumn of 2013, the number of registered members was 88. The members include both full-time and part-time journalists—and even include a few who, for different reasons (like maternity leave), are inactive. According to the board of the FPA, the number of full- and part-time foreign correspondents has been relatively stable for the last five years. Aside from the largest news agencies, today there is little economic room for traditional full-time correspondents, the type who were sent out from a media organization's headquarters for years to cover another country or a larger geographic region. However, a new breed of foreign correspondents with different backgrounds and contracts seems to have taken their place (Archetti, 2012).

The first organization for foreign correspondents in Norway was the International Press Club of Oslo, founded in 1959 by journalists from news agencies like the *UPI, AP,* and *Reuters.* At its largest size, the club had 22 members (Lindahl, 2001). However, in the 1970s and 1980s, in contrast to the other Nordic countries, the Norwegian government and the

Foreign Ministry did not support a press centre for foreign correspondents. One reason was political strain related to the Cold War. Norway was a member of the NATO alliance, and a border country to the Soviet Union, and thus the political authorities looked with suspicion on correspondents from East European Warsaw Treaty countries. Such suspicion was fuelled by events in 1977, in which a correspondent from the Soviet news agency *TASS* was forced to leave Norway after attempting to gather military information (Haarstad, 1988, cited in Lindahl, 2001).

In the 1980s, correspondents from Nordic countries founded their own organization. This organization became popular but was put to an end in 1997 primarily due to the establishment of the Foreign Press Association in 1990, an organization that gradually grew in membership and became the common organization for correspondents from around the world. In 1991, the Ministry of Foreign Affairs established Norway's International Press Center, which eventually allowed for foreign correspondents to rent and use the space as offices. Today, up to 10–12 journalists use the Press Center daily as a workplace. The Center is also used for meetings with invited members of the government, politicians, and others. Foreign correspondents in Norway do not need an accreditation from the Ministry of Foreign Affairs to work as journalists. However, if they have an assignment lasting longer than three months, they need a residence permit from the Norwegian Directorate of Immigration. To be granted this permit, they must have received a concrete and relevant offer of employment from a foreign media institution.

The aim of this chapter is to map the field of foreign correspondents based in Norway and the news organizations they work for, as well as to illuminate the types of journalism they produce.

WHO ARE THE FOREIGN CORRESPONDENTS?

Several factors have contributed to the growing number of foreign correspondents in Norway. The country has only 5 million inhabitants but is technologically developed and wealthy—with vast energy and fishing resources. Norway lies on the northern periphery of Europe, and the country's central role in the Barents Euro-Arctic Council are of news interest for the international media. The large surplus from the petroleum sector has been used to establish a state-owned fund, which invests both in the international stock market and in real estate. Norway is a member of NATO and the European Economic Area but is not a member of the European Union (EU); it has its own currency and an independent central bank. These political and economic factors have contributed to placing Norway 'on the map' for international news agencies and other large media organizations. Norwegian governments are also historically known to have an active presence on the international scene in relation to conflict negotiations and development projects. The Nobel Peace Prize, which is decided by a committee appointed by the Norwegian Parliament, is an example of an annual event that receives international attention.

The number and types of correspondents are also influenced by external factors related to new media technologies and a changed media landscape. The Internet has lowered the barriers for publishing and broadcasting, and new global actors—like *Al Jazeera*—have entered the media scene. Further, global news bureaus are not always, as some decades ago, headed by Americans, Britons, or French nationals (Boyd-Barret, 1980, p. 49; Boyd-Barret & Rantanen, 2001, p. 139). Finally, financial reporting plays a much more important role in the modern media landscape, both as specialized news in real time and via traditional media organizations.

Based on the official membership of the Foreign Press Association in November 2013, the 88 members represented media organizations from all continents except Oceania; 62 are men and 26 are women. For international news agencies, one's nationality is here defined by the location of their media organization's headquarters. The largest group (14 foreign correspondents) comes from the United States, and the majority of them are full-time correspondents representing international news agencies like *Bloomberg News* and *Thomson Reuter*. Each of these two agencies has five correspondents based in Oslo. In addition to the United States, the countries with the most FCs include Germany (eight FCs), the UK and Sweden (four each), and Poland and Iraq (three each). Several members of the FPA (nine FCs) represent media organizations with Norwegian headquarters, most of which are magazines or newsletters published in English for an international audience (including expats). The majority of correspondents are working for European media organizations (55.7 per cent). However, rather few come from other Nordic countries. Especially noteworthy is the lack of correspondents representing Finnish and Danish media. In contrast, 9.1 per cent of correspondents work for transnational Arabic media—most of them located in Iraq, Qatar, and Egypt. Correspondents from Arabic countries are a relatively new phenomenon in Norway and in the Nordic region. Some of the members of the Foreign Press Association (7.9 per cent) are freelance journalists and photographers who take jobs for several news organizations (without any information in the membership list about the media's national location).

Twenty-two members of the Foreign Press Association in Norway work for news agencies, including many leading Western international agencies, like *Bloomberg News, Thomson Reuters, Associated Press* (*AP*), and *Agence France Presse* (*AFP*), as well as journalists from expanding agencies like *Al Jazeera* (Qatar), *Xinhua* (China), and *ITAR-TASS* (Russia). Thirty-two foreign correspondents work for newspapers and newsletters (including both printed and online media), while 17 correspondents work for TV and radio (broadcast media).

The membership list of the Foreign Press Association does not, however, give any information concerning whether foreign correspondents are full- or part-time employees. To gain knowledge about correspondents' work situation and journalistic priorities, this study is based on a two-pronged research design, combining six semistructured, qualitative interviews with correspondents and an online survey. The interviewees were selected strategically in order to get a varied sample of correspondents and stringers with experience from different types of news organizations: *Al Jazeera* (Qatar, Arabic-speaking countries), *Xinhua News Agency* (China), *Bloomberg News* (the United States), *Associated Press* (the United States), a news agency representing Swiss and other media, and a freelancer with different engagements, including her own English-language news site. In addition, the author of this chapter received valuable background information from the Swedish newspaper correspondent Björn Lindahl, a veteran foreign correspondent based in Norway and the author of a brief historical survey of the foreign press in Norway (Lindahl, 2001).

The survey was sent to 47 of the then 85 members of the Foreign Press Association in Norway. The criteria for this selection were that these members were known by the board of the Association to be present in the country and also actively working—either full- or part-time—as correspondents. The board of the Foreign Press Association was asked to prepare an address list, which excluded 38 formally registered members who belonged to one of the following four categories in the fall of 2012: (1) persons known not to be living in Norway, (2) persons known by the board to be away from correspondent work in Norway for other reasons, (3) part-time photographers, and (4) members known to be only occasionally engaged in professional journalistic work. Thirty-four correspondents answered the survey. One reason for the high response rate (72 per cent) was undoubtedly that the survey was sent only to active correspondents, not to passive or peripheral members of the association. This selection must be taken into consideration when analyzing the data.

The traditional elite foreign correspondent 'no longer has hegemony over foreign news,' as discussed by Hamilton and Jenner (2004, p. 312). Based on developments in the US, this new brand of correspondent presents a new typology of foreign correspondents, which also has some relevance for the situation in the Nordic region. Several of their categories, like the parachute journalist who is sent temporarily to cover an event in a foreign region, fall outside the scope of this analysis.

Only nine journalists (27 per cent) of the 34 members of the Foreign Correspondents Association who answered the survey have a full-time contract with a news organization, and nearly all of them work for news media with an international reach. Among them we find reporters from the international financial news services who are characterized as 'premium service' foreign correspondents in Hamilton and Jenner's typology (2004, p. 314). *Bloomberg*, as an example, has an office with three journalists and two editors in Oslo, news about oil and energy questions being one of their specialties.

A majority of the correspondents working in Norway either have a part-time contract or work as freelancers and stringers. Half of the correspondents without a full-time contract state that they have no other work than journalism, while the others combine journalism with other occupations. If the 'inactive' members of the Foreign Press Association had been included in the survey, the percentage of freelancers and stringers would have been much higher.

Overall, correspondents are very well educated; nearly all have a master's or bachelor's degree, and 62 per cent have studied journalism/media and communications at the university level.

Most of the journalists who answered the survey have worked as foreign correspondents for a long time, the mean being 11 years. Forty-one per cent have been based in other countries as foreign correspondents prior to their present position. However, only one-fourth of them came to Norway for professional reasons. For the majority of correspondents, personal and private reasons—like a spouse with a job in Norway—motivated their relocation. Only two journalists (6 per cent) have always lived in Norway. Many correspondents work for more than one type of medium, most typically for print newspapers and online news services. Thirteen (38 per cent) of the thirty-four correspondents answering the survey work for news agencies; one-third work for television, and one-third have radio engagements. One of the members of the Foreign Press Association, a freelancer for several news organizations, also runs her own news site and describes her editorial position as 'a freelancer for myself' (FC3).[1]

REPORTING AGENDA: WHAT BECOMES NEWS AND WHEN?

Full-time correspondents must accept being sent away on assignment. Around half of the correspondents who answered the survey stated that they also have to cover various neighbouring countries. For example, an *Al Jazeera* correspondent estimates that about half of his team's reports come from Norway, 20 per cent from Sweden, 20 per cent from Denmark, and the rest from other countries (FC2). The correspondent interviewed from *Bloomberg* stated that, because her news agency also has offices in Stockholm, Copenhagen, Helsinki, and Reykjavik, she basically covers Norway but has also been sent to Brussels on several occasions to help cover EU affairs (FC4).

Freelancers and stringers have additional considerations because they must, to a greater degree than full-time correspondents, take travel expenditures into consideration. A Swiss freelance journalist affiliated with a European news agency stated that he has travelled on reportage tours with a colleague from a Swiss radio channel because '[t]hen we can share the costs. And two journalists operating together can sometimes get interview engagements easier than one. It is both practical and social' (FC5). Such cooperation among foreign correspondents is not unusual if the news organizations serve different markets.[2]

International news agencies like the *AP* and *AFP*, and financial agencies like *Reuters* and *Bloomberg*, are competitors. However, even in such a competitive environment, colleagues may give each other help to cover a story. The head of the Foreign Press Association, a former stringer for the *AP*, stated, 'I once came late to a press conference, and later could borrow the tape belonging to my colleague from the AFP' (FC6).[3] As a service to their members, the board of the Foreign Press Association regularly arranges briefings and breakfast meetings with Norwegian experts and top politicians. Table 18.1 summarizes the types of stories that FCs cover in Norway.

Concerning the type of stories covered, politics is mentioned by 80 per cent of the respondents. Other categories with a high score are the yearly Nobel Peace Prize, economics, crime and terrorism, energy and the environment, social questions, and culture. However, such broad categories represent important differences among news organizations that serve different audiences and markets.

Most foreign correspondents in Norway routinely report on an institutional news event such as the Nobel Peace Prize, but the interests of different audiences and politics may influence the amount and type of coverage. The Peace Prize is normally given high priority by general news agencies like the *AP* and *AFP*. According to the correspondent from *Al Jazeera* (Qatar), 'It is a big news event for us as well, especially for *Al-Jazeera English*. We report the event, but for *Al-Jazeera Arabic Channel*, it is a little bit different . . . Perhaps more interesting is the person who was

Table 18.1 Types of sources covered by FCs in Norway.

Type of Stories	FC Agreement (%)
Politics	80
Nobel Peace Prize and other institutional events	71
Economics	69
Crime and terrorism	66
Energy and environment	63
Social issues	60
Disasters and accidents	51
Royalty	34
Other	31

Question wording: 'What type of stories do you mostly cover?'

N = 34. It was possible to select more than one topic; therefore, the percentage sum will be more than 100.

nominated for this award' (FC2). His colleague from the state-owned *Xinhua News Agency* (China) is even more reluctant, stating, 'I came to Norway just before Obama got the prize in 2009, and reported that. But since the Dalai Lama got the prize in 1989, *Xinhua* has not given much priority to the Peace Prize. I made a report after Liu Xiaobo got the prize in 2010, but I don't think it was published. China is, as you know, very critical of the Nobel Peace Prize Committee' (FC1).

The main reason why 'crime and terrorism' is mentioned by many correspondents is undoubtedly the terrorist acts by Anders Behring Breivik on 22 July 2011, which included a bomb directed at the executive government quarter of Norway and a massacre at a youth camp on a small island, Utøya, organized by the AUF, the youth division of the Norwegian Labour Party. Because the month of July is typically a holiday time with little political activity in Norway, many of the foreign correspondents stationed in Oslo were away on vacation when this happened. However, since the terrorist act immediately became 'breaking news' all over the world, news agencies and other news organizations sent correspondents or parachute reporters from other offices to Oslo to cover the case and, later, to report about the court proceedings against Breivik. *Al Jazeera English,* for example, sent 12 reporters from London to Oslo to cover the killings. 'But luckily such events are [a]typical,' stated the correspondent for *Al Jazeera* (Qatar), who added, '*Al Jazeera* knows that the Nordic region normally is a place without bombs and without war, without very dramatic events. We of course make regular news reports from many areas, but in our daily work, feature stories are also important, including features of positive things that may interest an Arabic public' (FC2).

The *Al Jazeera* correspondent goes on to state that stories about how public money is spent are important because they illustrate increased equality. 'Everything does not go to a King and his family or to a small segment of the population' (FC2). One of his specific examples is Norway's policy for people with Down's syndrome, which consists of attempts to enable them to live active lives: 'Here our public can learn something'. Another of his examples is Norway's public and tax-financed system for taking care of elderly people. 'In Arabic tradition this is a responsibility only for the family. We try to show our audience that a social system with public responsibility can have many good sides, and that old people can enjoy living together with other old people and have a guarantee for good medical service' (FC2).

For the financial agencies, Norway is given news priority mainly because of its large oil and gas resources and the international investments related to the petroleum fund (from 2006, named the 'Government Pension Fund—Global' in official rhetoric). Everyday politics is not that important, but the political and economic consequences of elections may be newsworthy. 'We write extensively about Norway's currency and the central bank's interest rate policy. The oil fund is also of great interest. We cover the money market—and follow some of the most important government ministers', says FC4 from *Bloomberg News*.

The *Xinhua News Agency*'s office in Oslo, established as late as December 2009, is staffed by two correspondents. The Chinese agency is today one of the expanding global media actors. Yet everyday politics in Norway is given low priority, both by *Xinhua* and other foreign correspondents, but major government reshuffles and national elections are reported. Economic questions play an important role in the type of coverage a story receives. 'We are interested in oil and gas, the shipping industry, science and technology—and in Norway's investments abroad', the *Xinhua* correspondent says. He also mentions income policy as an area for feature stories:

> A question we plan to take up, and I am doing research on this now, is the political attempts in Norway to avoid too high income gaps in the population. Of course, there will always be income gaps, but in China the development is extreme, which is bad. So maybe Norway has done something concerning regulation and taxes to avoid such development, policy attempts that will be of interest in today's China. (FC1)

An example of an interesting feature story for a Chinese audience, outside the realm of conventional news events, is a report *Xinhua* recently generated about children's safety in cars:

> Traffic accidents are a major problem in China, many children and youngsters are killed yearly. But we also know many Chinese tend to pay less attention to road safety, there exist no laws and regulation making it mandatory to use baby car seats, and besides that, baby car seats are expensive. By making this report, showing what has been possible to do in Norway, we hope both to put pressure on authorities to amend traffic safety regulation and laws, and to inspire families to take safety more seriously. (FC1)

Audience and market interests will always be of importance. A freelance journalist from Switzerland, working mostly for a small Central European news agency, says that one of the regular beats he tries to cover is Norway's relations to the EU—which is of special interest in Switzerland since both countries are nonmembers (FC5).

One of the more exotic aspects of being a correspondent in Norway is the chance to travel to the far north and write features from the Sami areas, which several of the correspondents have done. The Foreign Press Association has also—in cooperation with the Foreign Ministry—organized a study and reportage tour to Murmansk in northern Russia for its members.

News about the Royal family in Norway is mentioned as important by only 11 (33 per cent) of the 34 survey respondents. 'Of course I write about the Royals', says the one who runs her own English language news site about Norway and adds, 'When Princess Märtha Louise started talking to angels, I wrote about it (for a former employer), and our international traffic skyrocketed. Royal news, for better or worse, always generates a lot of traffic' (FC3).

SOURCES: WHERE DO THE STORIES COME FROM?

An important part of the role and work of a foreign correspondent is to establish a network of good sources in prioritized areas of work—and to be a witness of newsworthy events. One of the questions in the survey concerned which sources (out of a set list) the correspondents regarded as most important (several may apply). The answers showed a classical elite media and elite-oriented picture: 28 (82 per cent) of the 34 respondents mentioned news stories in the national news media, 27 respondents (82 per cent) mentioned government officials, and in third place (mentioned by 24 people, 70 per cent) were academic experts. A majority of the correspondents use social media in their work, but only 40 per cent rank social media as one of their important sources. The *Xinhua* correspondent says that his news agency has given the reporters a directive to be active on such platforms: 'I am very active on Weibo, the micro-blog that is the Chinese version of Twitter, but also on YouTube and Facebook. I publish some mini news reports, but also ask for help and ideas when I need it. The Chinese resident in Norway I interviewed about car safety was recruited as a source through Weibo' (FC1).

The importance of the national news media does not mean that the correspondents spend most of their time in front of their laptops searching for online news from other news organizations. It is more a question of getting easy access to the overall 'news picture'—being aware of what is going on—and getting ideas to follow up stories from other angles.

The *Bloomberg* correspondent underlines the importance of knowing enough of the national language, both because it is necessary not only to be able to read the national press and to listen to news broadcasts, but also to use it in interview situations. 'We interview economists, policy makers and politicians. It is important to know the local language because people often feel uncomfortable speaking English and prefer to use their mother tongue. Some reporters ask questions in English and get answers in Norwegian' (FC4).

In most cases, the correspondents, regardless of their contracts, have to take the initiative on their news stories. They know that some type of news can be covered from a home office relatively easily and that many news organizations are cutting down travel to save money. To represent the added value of their work, correspondents are now required to generate fresh ideas, angles, and sources, aside from what can be found via mainstream online news.

CONCLUDING REMARKS

Norway is a country that seldom attains massive, international media coverage, and the mass killings in July 2011 remind us that the lack of such breaking global news is a good thing. However, in spite of the reduction of foreign correspondents in most Western news organizations, the corps of foreign correspondents in Norway is larger today than it was in previous decades.

One reason for recent growth is the expansion of new TV channels and news agencies with a base outside the Western hemisphere, as well as the emergence of specialized financial news agencies. However, another factor is Norway's economic and social development. When 'follow the money' is used as a journalistic slogan, the financial strength of Norway has increased its market value for international and commercial media organizations

NOTES

1. The news site, *Views and News from Norway,* is according to the editor, read by foreigners interested in Norway and foreigners living in Norway who do not read Norwegian.
2. In Brussels, correspondents from small news organizations, like the Nordic news agencies, often join forces to get easier access to top leaders. Correspondents from Nordic financial dailies, serving different national markets, sometimes make common interview appointments (Allern, 2007, p. 115)
3. Amland is now the editor-in-chief of *Development Today,* an independent newsletter on development assistance, business, trade, and environmental affairs.

REFERENCES

ALLERN, S. (2007). The Case of Norway. In AIM Research Consortium (ed.), *Understanding the Logic of EU Reporting from Brussels: Analysis of Interviews with EU Correspondents and Spokespersons.* Bochum: Projectverlag.

ARCHETTI, C. (2012). Which Future for Foreign Correspondence? *Journalism Studies,* 13 (5–6), pp. 847–856.

BOYD-BARRET, O. (1980). *The International News Agencies.* London: Constable.

BOYD-BARRET, O., & RANTANEN, T. (2001). News Agency Foreign Correspondents. In Tunstall, J. (ed.), *Media Occupations and Professions: A Reader.* Oxford: Oxford University Press.

EMERY, M. (1989). An Endangered Species: The International News Hole. *Gannet Center Journal.* 3 (4), pp. 151–164.

HAMILTON, J.M., & JENNER, E. (2004). Redefining Foreign Correspondence. *Journalism.* 5, pp. 301–321.

LINDAHL, B. (2001). *Foreign Press in Norway.* Oslo: Foreign Press Association.

SAMBROOK, R. (2010). *Are Foreign Correspondents Redundant? The Changing Face of International News.* Oxford: Reuters Institute for the Study of Journalism.

INTERVIEWS

FC1—Guorong Li. Interviewed 20 November 2012.
FC2—Samir Shatara. Interviewed 21 November 2012.
FC3—Nina Berglund. Interviewed 22 November 2012.
FC4—Josiane Kremer. Interviewed 22 November 2012.
FC5—Thomas Hug. Interviewed 23 November 2012.
FC6—Bjørn Åmland. Interviewed 23 November 2012.

19 Foreign Correspondents in Portugal

News from Portugal: Thanks to the Debt Crisis

Carla Baptista and Cláudia Henriques

INTRODUCTION

The Foreign Press Association in Portugal (AIEP) represents foreign journalists. Founded in 1975, in the aftermath of the revolution of April 1974, it congregated reporters covering the lively end of dictatorship. It promotes regular meetings with Portuguese experts from various fields, organizes working visits, and assigns the Person of the Year Award.

Although some foreign correspondents (FCs) currently working in Portugal are still the same young reporters who arrived in the 1970s to follow the democratization process, the country lost the former appeal to attract foreign media attention. The Spanish *El Pais* is the only remaining quality European newspaper maintaining a reporter based in Lisbon. Other newspapers, which use to have correspondents in Lisbon since the 1960s, like the French *Le Monde* or the German *Frankfurter Allgemeine Zeitung,* are now using freelancers or charging the correspondent based in Madrid to cover Portugal. *Time Magazine* and *The Times* didn't fill the position left vacant when the former veteran correspondent, Martha de la Cal, passed away in 2011.

The *Comissão da Carteira Profissional de Jornalista* (Professional Journalist Commission, CCPJ) is the entity that regulates the activity of professional journalists, including foreign correspondents in Portugal. Its main function is to assign, renew, or suspend the professional journalist's card, which enables journalists to legally work within the agreed journalistic ethical standards. Since 2004/2005, fewer professionals have been registered as foreign correspondents, but 2012/2013 slightly reversed this decline, due to the venue of many Brazilian journalists and a timid appearance of reporters coming from countries that weren't represented before, like China, Morocco, Iran, and Pakistan.

WHO ARE THE FOREIGN CORRESPONDENTS?

We have defined a population of 89 correspondents, from which 71 are CCPJ members and 18 are AIEP members. They come from 27 nationalities, with Spanish and Brazilian the two largest groups.

The five most prominent countries of foreign correspondents' media origin are Brazil (19 FCs), Spain (17 FCs), France (eight FCs), United Kingdom (seven FCs), and China (six FCs). These countries correspond to the most relevant FCs' nationalities in Portugal.

Foreign correspondents based in Portugal work mainly for news agencies (26 FCs), followed by broadcast media (24 FCs). The press follows closely (23 FCs), while online media are the least represented with six FCs. Fifteen correspondents work across platforms, or a 'principal medium' cannot be identified.

The FCs are still predominantly a male group (with 55 total male FCs and 34 female FCs).

The questionnaire designed for this book project was adapted to the Portuguese reality and sent out to 40 foreign correspondents. The 17 answers that were obtained were later supplemented with 13 in-depth interviews. Participant observation also enriched the research, namely attending some of the AIEP briefings.

The predominant age group is from 51 to 65 years of age. The age groups up to 50 years old are predominantly female, and the older groups are composed mostly of males.

Most correspondents have extensive professional careers: on average, 18 years of journalistic activity, from which 13 years have been as foreign correspondents. Family relationships with children help to explain the average of 12 years of career as residents. About 36 per cent have been living in Portugal for over 20 years, and they belong to the group of journalists whose roots go back to 1974/1975 (Rodrigues, 2007, pp. 65–69). According to Jair Rattner, who describes correspondents of the Brazilian newspaper *Folha de São Paulo*, 'They are not the typical foreign correspondent sent on duty for a limited period of time. Instead, they decided to stay and have a family here'.[1]

The group, however, does change: one-third of them have currently been working in the country for fewer than five years. But mobility is reduced: more than half of the correspondents worked only in Portugal, and just two reported working in more than two countries.

This is a highly educated community: over 90 per cent attended university, 35 per cent of them graduates and more than half of them with master's degrees. They all speak Portuguese at a native or fluent level, followed by English as their second language.

The correspondents who answered our survey work mainly for the press and the radio, followed by television, online media, and newswires, although the different picture presented earlier based on the general data. Only five correspondents work for a single employer. The remaining ones have jobs at more than two media organizations. The former president of AIEP (Marie-line Darcy), fulfils the multitasking-oriented profile. 'You must be versatile in order to earn a living. I work for *Radio France* and *Radio France Internationale*, for the newspapers *La Croix*, *Ouest-France* and *La Tribune de Genève*

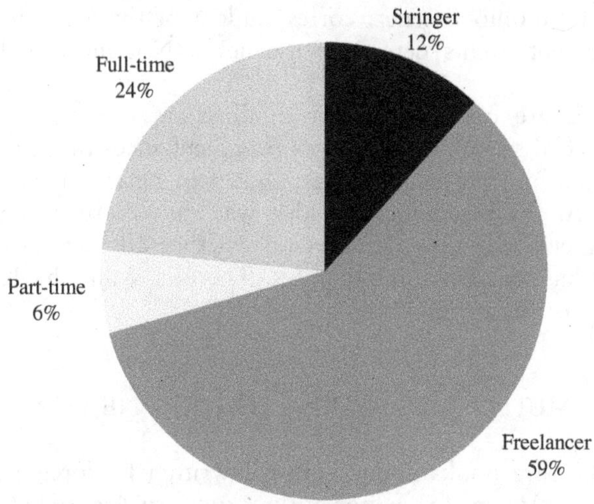

Figure 19.1 Types of FC employment in Portugal.

and I also collaborate with three news websites. Occasionally, I work for some television stations'.[2] (See Figure 19.1.)

The majority of FCs work as freelancers. More than half have no fixed contractual relationships with their employers. Belén Rodrigo has been a freelancer for 12 years: 'The *ABC* [Spanish newspaper] is where I send daily information. At first, I asked if there was any possibility of joining the company, but the truth is that, if I had been admitted, I probably would be out of a job today. My newspaper has a large network of correspondents, but only two from the in-house team are still with us. The others have been fired or sent back to Spain'.[3]

About half of the correspondents are not full-time journalists. Translation is the second most listed activity, among public relations, cultural programming, or academic studies. The average news production is two pieces, performed daily. More than half earn a monthly income between €1001 and €2000, and about 20 per cent receive between €2,001 and €4,000.

WHAT IS THE FC's REPORTING AGENDA?

The news agenda is diverse. None of the FCs are specialists, and they all consider themselves generalists, even if some have greater expertise on a particular issue (like environmental policies, renewal green energy sources, literature, or football). Politics (26 per cent), society (24 per cent), and economy (23 per cent) are the most covered areas. The interviews revealed a general concern about the need to address the issues in a broad perspective.

According to Antonio Jimenez, correspondent of the Spanish newspaper *El Pais:* 'Current events determine the news. Not individual journalist interests'.[4]

Life stories are commonly used to illustrate the worsening of the Portuguese social situation. This news frame enhances the real side of the crisis, as stated by Peter Wise, correspondent of *Financial Times* and *The Economist:* 'At the beginning, the idea was that Portugal could not do without financial aid. Now, I reflect on whether austerity is being exaggerated and has negative consequences. There is sympathy for the pain and suffering of the people'.[5]

WHEN IS SOMETHING BECOMING FOREIGN NEWS?

In one of the rare books about Portugal written by foreign journalists, Barry Hatton (2011, p. 15), editor at the *American Associated Press* (*AP*), in Lisbon, wishes to 'shed some light on this enigmatic corner of Europe, describing the idiosyncrasies that make this a unique, lovely and, sometimes, aggravating country'. These musings belong to a time where a watchful and bewildered eye struggling with the details of the Portuguese identity could still fit in. It defines the gaze of the original FCs' community (Rodrigues, 2007), a mix between the love for the country and the knowledge of its history, editorial autonomy, and professional seniority. The dominant framework of today's reporting is the impact of the financial crisis process initiated in May 2011, when Portugal, following Greece and Ireland, become the third Eurozone country to be 'rescued' by the International Monetary Fund, the European Commission, and the European Central Bank.

The economic situation became the focal point attracting international media attention and, in some cases, was the reason preventing FCs from leaving the country. Alison Roberts summarizes the pervasiveness of this context: 'I use to joke and say that any new idea has to be about the crisis, or despite the crisis. We have to find a connection. Any news piece starting with "in Portugal," immediately arouses associations in the listener and nowadays these associations refer to the crisis. The connection creates empathy with the listener'.[6]

The austerity program constrains the news and pushes aside the optimistic visions that have been built since the 1990s. Thomas Fischer, correspondent of the Swiss daily *Neue Zurcher Zeitung* and stringer at television station *Zweites Deutsches Fernsehen* (*ZDF*), recalls that period in which 'Portugal had some sex appeal. It began in 1991 with the opening of the Ford factory in Palmela Volkswagen, the largest foreign investment of all time. In 1992, there was the first Portuguese EU presidency, and many people came to see that Portugal was no longer the country of barefoot fishermen and *fado* singers'.[7]

The crisis promotes news coverage and is perceived as transcending an isolated country. According to Peter Wise: 'The *Financial Times* claims to be an international journal and demands an illustration of the main human and factual issues of the day. Its concerns are how austerity reflects in people's lives, in the emigration, in the state of the companies, how young people see the future. The idea is to illuminate a theme common to Europe. They often see themselves as the "owners" of the stories about the European crisis'.[8]

The crisis account shares the traces of 'global journalism', as defined by Peter Berglez (2008, pp. 848–849): 'This method of reporting interlocks peoples worldwide and their practices worldwide, by connecting events and processes of worldwide organizations, identities and political and economic institutions . . . is the natural consequence of increasing connectedness, boundarylessness and mobility in the world'.

Although the crisis kicks indebted countries away from the market capital flows and the table of political decisions, the journalistic narratives connect the people from both debtor and creditor nations. The experience of the former is offered to appraise the fear of contamination sensed by the latter. Journalists use the metaphor of the 'mirror' to justify how important their stories are to foreign audiences.

Globalization connects political and cultural unfamiliar spaces without displacing former rooted forms of articulation. Antonia Jimenez, from *El Pais,* claims how Spain, the country next door, closely follows the Portuguese evolution. 'The economic situation in Portugal is a mirror of what is happening or will happen in Spain'.[9]

The economic framing is also impacting the foreign correspondents reporting for the Portuguese language countries, whose coverage traditionally included more cultural and political news. According to João Carlos, correspondent of the broadcaster *Deutsche Welle*, 'We used to work much more focused on our African territory, while Europe was always important. Portugal became more news worthy after the request for financial foreign aid'.[10]

The *Mozambique News Agency* (*AIM*) has only three international offices: London, Johannesburg, and Lisbon. For Domingos Mossela, delegate and reporter at *AIM,* the presence in the Portuguese capital is important because of the risk perception regarding Mozambique banking system. 'We mainly provide economic and political information. The crisis is global. When Portugal returned to the markets, it was interesting news, because Portuguese banks operate in Mozambique. All type of turbulence affecting one side is also affecting the other side'.[11]

Journalists hired by non-European media use similar arguments, like Barry Hatton, editor at the *Associated Press.* 'Nowadays you cannot escape economics. Portugal won this relevance because the fate of the Eurozone is tied with the fate of Portugal. It is easier to sell news about the economy, because it could affect other countries. Previously, it was a rather indifferent country'.[12]

WHERE DO STORIES COME FROM?

Despite the importance given to the human side of news, journalists prefer to use official information sources, including members of the government and the opposition, followed by citizens and scholars. Institutional sources are quoted from secondary sources, such as the local media or press releases. FCs share the view that getting access to political sources is frustrating and time-consuming and resent the fact that Portuguese politicians are careless about the importance of foreign news. According to Alison Roberts, *BBC* stringer, 'When the country is seen in a poor, pitiable way, there is a great need for governments to project a better external image. We are the ones building this image every day. However, it seems that we don't even exist'.[13] (See Figure 19.2.)

Parts of a daily mandatory routine for FCs in Portugal include reading the local newspapers, accessing the national newswire service (Lusa), and following the news on the Portuguese radios and television. FCs label the information they produce as relevant and believe there is an increasing interest about Portugal among the international media. Some are invited to public events and debates, but their public visibility and social prestige are perceived as low.

All foreign correspondents have a traumatic experience dealing with Portuguese government sources. The main complaints refer to exclusion from informative email lists and briefings by communication agencies and press officers, as well as excruciatingly difficult access to politicians. The

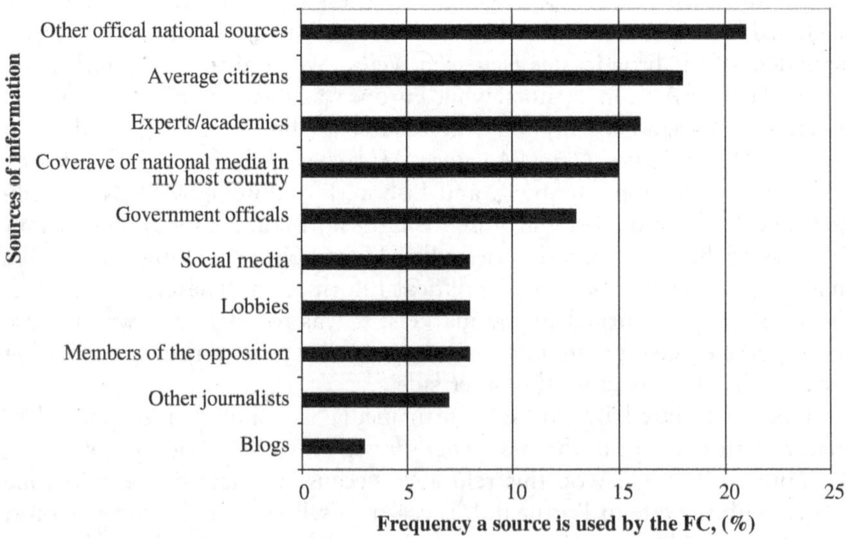

Figure 19.2 FCs' sources of information in Portugal.

phrase 'send an email' circulates playfully, parodying the typical response obtained from an official institution, whenever someone asks for a comment or a clarification. Emilio Crespo, *Agencia EFE, S.A.*'s (*EFE*'s) delegate, tells a story that is indicative of the official press culture: 'When Paulo Portas [Foreign Affairs minister] officially visited Spain, I called a week before to the press officer with two issues. He replied, "*Send an email*". Meanwhile, Paulo Portas went and returned. I think it's bad for the minister; he could have appeared in more newspapers. In Portugal, the press officers do not exist to facilitate, but to prevent access. In Spain, we expect them to tell what they want to sell'.[14]

FCs are guided by the values of timeliness and public interest to select the news. But their audiences' characteristics require a specific storytelling purpose. The fact that the people receiving the information 'do not know (almost) anything' restrains the use of ellipses, literary expressions, and rhetorical resources and dismisses inefficient newsworthiness values, like the presumption of the protagonist's notoriety or the familiarity with the subject.

The public attention is better captured when FCs propose the classical hard news format, a narrative essentially informative, analytical, and centred on topics that fit the cognitive construction of social relevance produced for enlightened publics. Peter Wise summarizes the requirements when the pretension is to provide a brief and insightful explanation about events and people remotely located. 'Although foreign correspondents are obliged to have the deepest knowledge possible about the country, what they can write is limited. Our readers do not know much about Portugal and we cannot go into details'.[15]

The narrative coherence ensures the circulation of the news stories from the production site to a range of diverse social environments. Quoting Peter Dahlgren and Sparks (1992), 'one can say that "storyness" both enhances and delimits the likely range of meaning. Audiences can take the stories and "run" with them, in many directions. Yet, the patterns and structures of stories also work toward cultural cohesion'.

HOW IS FOREIGN NEWS FORMULATED?

The nature of the international coverage about Portugal changed in the last decade, being mainly provided by a group of freelance journalists working simultaneously for various news organizations and performing journalism along with other activities. The older professionals—full-time journalists—are also subjected to the precariousness of the labour market. They are usually paid accordingly to the number of news pieces they are able to produce, even if their expertise is praised and meritorious. The Spanish newswire *EFE* closed the office at Porto, the second largest city in Portugal, considering it 'an eccentricity'. The

AP and *AIM* currently employ a single journalist after staff cuts were applied.

All respondents referred to travel restrictions (due to budget limitations) and editorial constraints. The kind of work that is requested, or that they anticipate editors will more easily accept, is focused almost exclusively on current political and economic affairs. The journalists working for news agencies reported a slowdown in the production of features outside the crisis theme and an increase of spot news fit to update the information, briefly and factually, precisely on this topic.

One can hardly continue to label this group as 'an elite of international reporters', and the need remains to 'redefine' the position, as pointed out by John Maxwell Hamilton and Eric Jenner (2004). Foreign correspondents continue to enjoy a high level of autonomy regarding the proposal of journalistic articles, but experience strongly encourages them to funnel these wide choices into the mainstream agenda. With imagination and persuasion, other frameworks can still be accepted, as told by Marie-line Darcy: 'They [the employers] are open minded but we are very dependent on negative news. I have to feed my media because they are feeding me. But I always try to do different things: I did a story about the crisis related to the popular assemblies and the exchange markets. These original ideas work well, along with presenting the crisis through people's stories'.[16]

Richard Sambrook (2010), from the *Reuters* Institute for the Study of the Press, identifies the key factors explaining the 'wrenching swiftness' of overseas newsgathering:

> Social media are leading, supplementing and complementing what professional news organizations offer, providing fresh source material for reporters, but also competing with them for public attention. Many other organizations have taken the opportunity to contribute directly to public debate by introducing their own information services—from governments, to NGOs to commercial companies—speaking directly to the public in favour of their own interests . . . International and domestic news agendas have merged to a significant degree. More organizations are relying on local staff—with advantages and risks attached.

The changing frames of foreign news reflect the contradictions implied in the globalization process. The FCs' community is experiencing the same effects they are telling the world about in Portugal: about becoming poor and about being uncertain of future survival. According to Stephen D. Reese (2010, p. 345), 'The very concept of 'media globalisation' suggests that we are not quite sure if media lead to globalisation or are themselves the result of it'.

CONCLUSION

One should be very sceptical concerning the future of foreign news about Portugal in a postcrisis scenario. Once the various historical circumstances that attracted international media attention are overcome—including the democratization that followed the revolution in 1974; the Europeanization driven by joining the EU in 1986; the economic growth (and the underlying indebtedness) that marked the cycle following the entry into the single currency from 1999; the financial crisis that led to the troika intervention in 2011—is it possible that the country can build up the conditions to enable it to be visible in the global media space?

Over the last few years, Portugal has returned to its eternal peripheral space. The absence of large European and American newspapers titles; the dwindling resources of the international newswires; increasing labour insecurity and a weak capacity for renewal among foreign correspondents; the preference given to Madrid as the Iberian basis for most foreign press offices and the low diversity of the news frames provided—are all signs of a coverage dynamics moving far away from the Portuguese seafront coast.

NOTES

1. Jair Rattner. Interviewed 2 April 2013, Lisbon.
2. Marie-line Darcy. Interviewed 9 May 2013, Lisbon.
3. Belén Rodrigo. Interviewed 26 March 2013, Lisbon.
4. Antonio Jimenez. Interviewed 15 April 2013, Lisbon.
5. Peter Wise. Interviewed 20 March 2013, Lisbon.
6. Alison Roberts. Interviewed 25 March 2013, Lisbon.
7. Thomas Fischer. Interviewed 22 March 2013, Lisbon.
8. Peter Wise. Interviewed 20 March 2013, Lisbon.
9. Antonio Jimenez. Interviewed 15 April 2013, Lisbon.
10. João Carlos. Interviewed 28 March 2013, Lisbon.
11. Domingos Mossela. Interviewed 9 May 2013, Lisbon.
12. Barry Hatton. Interviewed 18 May 2013, Lisbon.
13. Alison Roberts. Interviewed 25 March 2013, Lisbon.
14. Emilio Crespo. Interviewed 8 March 2013, Lisbon.
15. Peter Wise. Interviewed 20 March 2013, Lisbon.
16. Marie-line Darcy. Interviewed 9 May 2013, Lisbon.

REFERENCES

BERGLEZ, P. (2008). What Is Global Journalism? *Journalism Studies*. 9 (6), pp. 845–858.

DAHLGREN, P., & SPARKS, C. (eds.), (1992). *Journalism and Popular Culture*. London/Thousand Oaks, CA/New Dehli: Sage.

HAMILTON, J. M., & JENNER, E. (2004). Redefining Foreign Correspondence. *Journalism*. 5 (3), pp. 301–321.

HATTON, B. (2011). *Os Portugueses*. Lisboa: Clube do Autor.
REESE, S. D. (2010). Journalism and Globalization. *Sociology Compass*. 4 (6), pp. 344–353.
RODRIGUES, A. L. (2007). *Aos Olhos do Mundo. Portugal e os Portugueses Retratados por Correspondentes Estrangeiros*. Lisboa: Livros Horizonte.
SAMBROOK, R. (2010). *Are Foreign Correspondents Redundant? The Changing Faces of International News*. Oxford: Reuters Institute for the Study of Journalism.

20 Foreign Correspondents in Serbia

What Happens When a War Ends?

Verica Rupar and Sonja Seizova

INTRODUCTION

Serbia emerged on the international news agenda in early 1990 and immediately positioned itself very high on the list of newsworthy places in the war-torn former Yugoslavia. The media spotlight may have moved away from the other new small Balkan states in the mid- or late 1990s, but this was not the case with Serbia, where a volatile internal political situation continued into the 21st century. An army of foreign correspondents was kept busy by landmark events that ensued: a three-month long grass-roots protests against the regime of Slobodan Milosevic in the winter of 1996–1997, a three-month long NATO bombing of the country in 1999, the toppling of the regime in 2000, and the assassination of Prime Minister Zoran Djindjic in 2003. For some, Serbia became a low-interest country only after 2008, when it formally stepped on the European Union accession course. By then, occasional hiccups, mostly linked to arrests and extradition of those indicted for war crimes or the Kosovo issue, could not reverse the firmly established decline in foreign media coverage that the country was receiving.

This is the experience that colours the testimonies of foreign correspondents based in Belgrade. It is intertwined with the outburst of the global economic crisis and its notorious consequences for the media industry. Commercialization of the media; the impact of market forces; audiences' decreased interest in traditional news outlets; preferences for a short, digested format of news; and most of all limited financial resources have led to the prioritization of local news and shrinking media space for foreign news (Obijiofor & Hanusch, 2011). Foreign news from the Balkans in the aftermath of war shares this fate, in sharp contrast with the 1990s, when breaking news about the war was the most valuable media currency across the world.

Focusing on the cultural dimension (journalists) rather than on the structural dimension (the media) of foreign correspondence,[1] this chapter looks at the difference in the war/peace placement of the news. It asks what happens to foreign correspondents when a war ends and a country drops out of the international media spotlight? How does the end of war affect the work of foreign correspondents? How do they manage to run stories that are not about war, conflict, and crisis but about society in transition toward democracy? We examine what the most significant challenges are and the work-related problems of foreign correspondents in the light of the interests, affiliations, and preferences of their media and audiences.

WHO: FREELANCERS ON THE RISE

Long gone are the days of the 1990s when the foreign press corps rushed through the leafy streets of Belgrade to get to the Writers Club and share the war news. The once reserved seats of the Club nowadays host a different clientele. If and when a foreign correspondent comes, she or he is likely to be a local, home-grown journalist working for an international news organization. Naming this new breed of newsmakers 'foreign foreign correspondents', Hamilton and Jenner point toward hired foreign nationals who work and report for a foreign news organization (2004, p. 312).

Almost 15 years after the last of the four civil wars in former Yugoslavia ended, the snapshot of foreign correspondents based in Belgrade has dramatically changed; they are likely to carry Serbian citizenship, have worked in the region for more than 10 years, and, unless permanently employed by a news agency or a public service broadcaster, are on a casual contract with the foreign news organization. The average foreign correspondent from Belgrade struggles to negotiate a need to explain a complex set of ethnic, religious, and political relations in the region with the audience's decreased appetite for foreign news.

The process of foreign correspondents' accreditation in Serbia is run by the Ministry of Culture. The most recent list includes 82 accredited news organizations and 178 names of journalists, camera operators, producers, photo reporters, and support staff, some 30 per cent of whom are women. Correspondents work for media based primarily in Germany (38 FCs), the United States (24 FCs), Bosnia and Herzegovina (21 FCs), France (14 FCs), FYROM and Russia (13 each), the UK (nine FCs), and Austria (eight FCs).

This list, however, does not reflect the actual number of correspondents permanently based in Belgrade and reporting regularly, which is much lower. An official from the Ministry explains[2] this difference by the huge number of temporarily accredited journalists covering specific events or staying just for a couple of weeks. Other registered foreign correspondents just come and go, depending on their priorities at the time. A network of stringers and fixers—which constitute foreign correspondents—are included in the same Ministry's list, as are some 20-plus staffers of a Serbian online media outlet, which is based in Germany but actually addresses Serbian audiences within the country and abroad. A number of correspondents

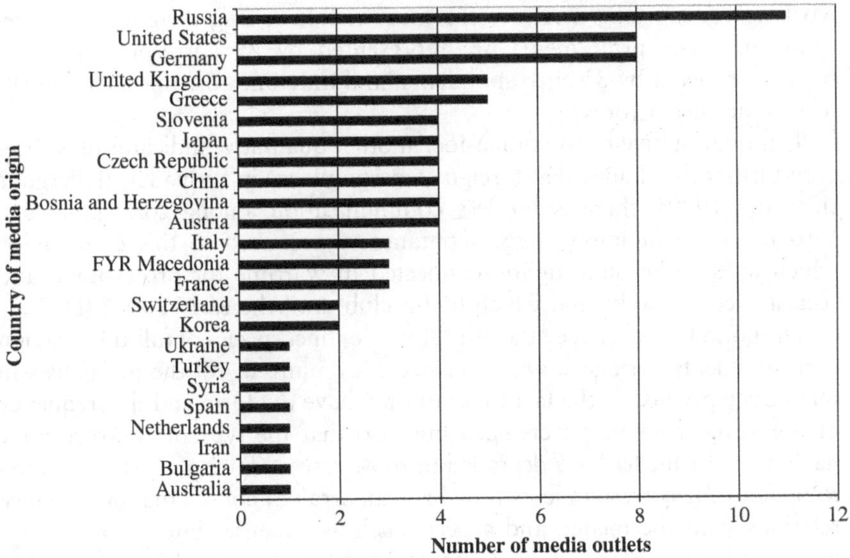

Figure 20.1 The number of media outlets in Serbia per country.

have accreditation from one media outlet but work freelance for many more, usually covering the region spanning the Balkans and the Middle East, all the way to Southeast Asia in some cases. 'There are a lot of clients that I have that would only need one story a year' (FC6).

Figure 20.1 shows the distribution of country interest in news from Serbia, with Russia, Germany, and the United States leading.

The sheer number of registered correspondents can be misleading, particularly in comparison to the 1990s, and not just because of several changes in the accreditation procedure, authority, and rules that have taken place since then. From 1990 to 1995, in the time of war in Slovenia, Croatia, and Bosnia, on average 87 permanent correspondents were registered per year (435 for five years). Today, journalists interviewed in this study could not name more than 15–20 correspondents whom they see reporting from Belgrade regularly. 'You have 15 people literally' (FC1). They do not know the others; neither are they aware of the overall size of the foreign correspondents' community. At one of the meetings with the president of Serbia, only 10–15 foreign correspondents were present, and although the officials might had been 'selective' in sending invitations, it is still an illustration of the size of the foreign press representatives in Belgrade. Inasmuch as the number of foreign correspondents translates into the expression of news interest in a country, this anecdotal evidence—rather than the Ministry's list—is another indication that the interest in the news from the Balkans has significantly fallen since the end of the war. 'They just don't publish enough from here', a freelancer (FC10) said. The 20 correspondents working for news agencies are the most visible among their fellow correspondents. The print media are represented by 29 correspondents, the broadcast media by 31 correspondents, and only one correspondent works for online media (only).

This quantitative fluctuation aside, another qualitative indicator illustrates even further the change that foreign correspondence in Serbia has undergone since the 1990s: there is far less communication among correspondents. Virtually none of interviewees spontaneously referred to this community, which used to be quite tightly connected in wartime for professional and security reasons alike and which had a club until the early 2000s (FC7).

The boundaries between the now almost extinct species of full-time foreign correspondents, stringers, and freelancers are blurred. All the journalists in our survey pointed to the fact that not only have the form and the frequency of reporting from Serbia changed but also that the type of contracts they have with the media have degraded in most cases. Many of those who used to be full-time correspondents now have an array of contractual or freelance relations with the media, and aspects such as expenses budgets for things like travel have been cut back. In some cases, bureaus have closed but retained the same staff under different contracts, while in others the staff has been reduced to one-fifth or less of what it was in 2000 (FC9). By 2004, Belgrade was no longer the regional hub. Some central offices were merged with the wider region and moved to Vienna and Budapest, or the region covered by Belgrade's office was reduced to Bosnia, Kosovo, Montenegro, and Macedonia.

Figure 20.2 illustrates the technological differences between various types of media and shows that audio-visual media require more staff than news

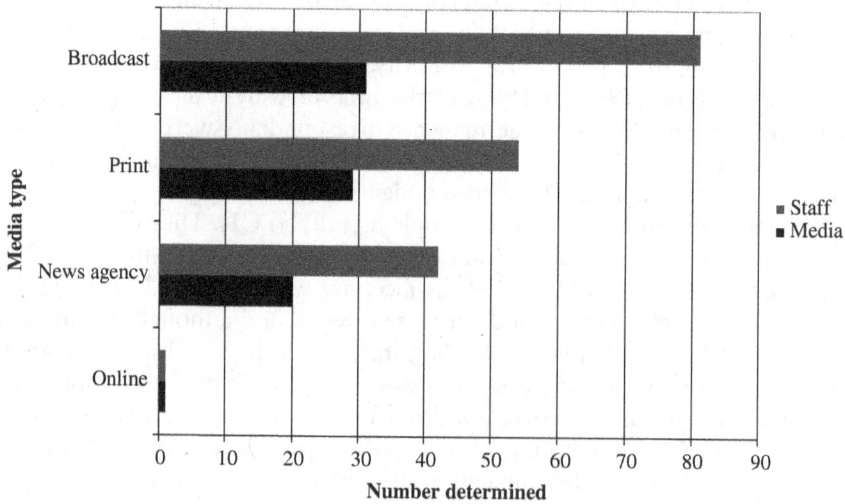

Figure 20.2 Number of media and number of staff in Serbia, per media type.

agencies or print media. Journalists, producers, camera operators and technicians are all registered as correspondents, averaging 2.6 correspondents per audio-visual media outlet, as opposed to 2.1 for news agencies and 1.8 for print media. This is why the number of accredited media is a more accurate indicator of the interest in news from Serbia than is the number of accredited individual correspondents.

WHAT: POLITICAL THEMES STILL DOMINATE

Political themes still dominate the coverage of the region (75 to 80 per cent of the stories are political), and the initiative for the story still comes mainly from a correspondent. The more tuned in s(he) is to the priorities of the home office, the higher the percentage of pitches that get accepted. By now, reluctantly or not, most FCs are well aware of what kind of stories they should offer.

Correspondents from Belgrade are cautious when it comes to official sources, stressing the unprofessional approach some media advisors take—there have been attempts to influence or censor questions in prearranged interviews (FC2)—and a shift toward the domestic audience. Foreign correspondents were important to Serbian politicians during the war, but nowadays politicians care more about home media. 'Officials are not interested in foreign media, maybe in big international agencies like *Reuters* but not in the others. They respond only when you push them and even then reluctantly' (FC5).

In terms of quality, a seasoned TV correspondent stated that a combination of factors influencing foreign correspondents in general, coupled with reporting from a postconflict country, has one devastating result: one has far less opportunity to report on the development of events, having to chose between a statement and a stand-up for the 70 seconds available in the main news and therefore living with polarization, incident reporting, and not reporting nuances in a story (FC2). The number of filed stories has decreased too, significantly so from the year 2008 and the financial crises that affected news organizations. A television journalist who produced 20–24 hours of programming annually in 2000–2001 is now producing 12–13 hours a year from a bigger region. 'Balkan is not sexy anymore', he says.

In parallel with the reduction in time and space available for stories from the Balkans, the structure and prioritization of issues have changed, and the 'division of labour' among news agencies, individual correspondents, and freelancers took a new form. Whereas political stories accounted for most of the reporting in the 1990s, the economy started creeping in during the early 2000s with the onset of transition and emerging markets, to be followed by human interest stories, culture, sports, and incidents. Come 2008, and the 'soft story' becomes a visible trend. 'Demands for entertainment, entertainment, entertainment are freaking us out; you were a political journalist all your life and now all of a sudden they want you to write about vampires in Valjevo', a news agency correspondent says (FC4). When it comes to sources for their stories, the only real change was brought about by the advent of the Internet which, together with satellite, plays a significant role in correspondents' daily routines.

WHEN: MORE DEMAND FOR FEATURES AND ANALYSIS

This doesn't mean that politics is off the agenda for a news agency; to the contrary, the daily news may have gotten shorter and scarcer, but there is more demand for features and analyses. They provide the background to reports filed by other correspondents and help explain to editors at home: 'why does it matter?' However, the first filter remains with correspondents working from the postwar region. How do they decide on how much background is too much for an otherwise relevant story? The range of responses to this question illustrates the spectrum of options. 'If a background has to be 2/3 of the text, I give up and [do] not run a story' (FC7). FCs are aware that '[news] has to be explained why it matters' (FC9). But this is not always possible, as: 'since the fall of Milosevic, any news that consists of one line of new information and nine lines of background, is not worth sending—it's getting too complicated to explain what is going on' (FC8).

Some of the constraints described by correspondents on contracts are not shared by freelance foreign correspondents who appear to have more independence in choosing the story and the angle but who also depend more on the strength of their network and ability to pitch a story well. The example of a freelancer who published 50 stories on 24 themes over two months is striking: most of the 'doubles' were follow-ups, some were the same theme for more clients. Of these 24 themes, seven themes were covered 'in depth', ranging from one big story to 12. The interviewed freelancer was on the road for 15 days. 'By and large, this sample is representative', he says and explains his take on a placement of stories from the Balkans:

> Cutting right to the 'post-crisis' angle, I feel newsrooms tend to be more conservative than my audience and me when it comes to story selection. For the current generation of journalists in my 'home country' the Yugoslav wars were a formative experience, whether covering them directly, indirectly or reading about it as a teenager. That goes for me too. I hardly remember reading about anything else in the early nineties and by the time I started working, the Kosovo war was my first big news story. I see a background like that all around me, and there is still a tendency to instinctively reach for that angle when it comes to reporting from this region, though I think it is diminishing. It all

> depends on the framework in which you look at developments around the former Yugoslavia, and on your best guess of the framework in which the audience sees them. In messy practice, newsrooms tend to impose their framework on the audience, and I think we see quite a bit of that when it comes to this region.
>
> (FC10)

The relationship between journalists' and editors' judgements about the newsworthiness of events and the audience's interests and preferences is complex. A comparison between *AP* surveys of news editors and Pew Research Center audience polls in terms of the top news events of the year indicates more divergence than convergence of perceptions between news editors and the audiences (Tai & Chang, 2002). In Doris Graber's (1988) seminal study of what information gets people's attention, the foreign news appealed only to a very small and selected group of the audience. Our research showed that a new generation of freelance correspondents from Serbia is less inclined to conform to the often commercially driven demands of newsrooms.

WHERE: AUTONOMY RECLAIMED

Provided they can make a living on more commercial stories, freelancers with a drive for a particular project are great believers in niche markets for their independent understanding of what's going on after the war. 'That's a motivation to be a journalist, a journalist from here. There is a market for that, I wouldn't say necessarily a commercial editorial market, but in the marketplace of ideas, people want that kind of interpretation. There are people who want to hear from correspondents' (FC6).

The knowledge and values of a journalist play a role in the way events and issues are selected and represented in the news (Entman, 2007). In the years marked by less autonomy of individual foreign correspondents to decide what is newsworthy (Foote, 2005), our research reveals freelancers are on the way to reclaiming the lost territory. FC6 recalls:

> One of the first things that I thought of when I was offered an opportunity to come here as a young journalist, young photographer, was that a lot of the work that I saw in the late 1990s that was really inspiring, all famous journalists, photographers, they were all in the Balkans in the 1990s. I saw these pictures, and I was wondering—what is it like now? We heard all about these conflicts at the time, nobody in America really understood them in depth, and it dropped off the radar in American media to the point that—in 2007, when I came, and I told friends that I'm flying to Belgrade next week, and they went—isn't there a war going on there? They heard about the conflicts

> starting, but there was never really a story about the aftermath, and it was forgotten, like—there is no more war in Bosnia, it's solved. I'm still interested in the stories that still aren't covered a lot by the mainstream media. I am interested in the aftermath.

The issues the people in Serbia are facing today, such as the lack of jobs or infrastructure, are consequences of the conflict, either directly or as a result of the economic collapse of that era:

> you can't talk about youth unemployment without considering that business, economy is still lagging from that era, delayed transition. So I don't see a lot of correspondents doing these kinds of long-term stories, who are aware of this, so I think that's a benefit of staying here, and trying to communicate this (FC6).

Somewhat unexpectedly, a generational shift imposed itself in this study in more than one way: in relation to the new breed of inexperienced editors in home offices, as a factor in the self-perception of the role of foreign correspondents, and in their detachment from the war. The most prominent is the change our interviewees describe as 'dramatic mistakes' committed with the replacement of 'old wolves' by young editors, under the pressure of financial constraints and technological demands. 'The continuity of knowledge was lost,' expresses a seasoned correspondent not directly affected by the change. 'Many of those people do not have the experience and education that we had' (FC2). 'Young people came to the foreign desk who know very little about foreign policy, very little about journalism. They would be happiest to get a report in a form of a text message' says a senior colleague (FC7).

'I was surprised when one of my editors asked me to state in the second paragraph who Milosevic was. I looked at him and asked: what do you mean who was Milosevic? But he was 35 at that point, and he said: "With all due respect I was 25 when there was a war in Bosnia, I've heard something but you know . . ." So I think we have to explain more because time has passed and even our editors don't know anymore what it was all about' (FC4). On top of that, 'other regions are getting a spotlight, so the audience does not know it either' (FC3).

HOW: THE POWER OF WAR MEMORY

The memory of the war colours correspondents' everyday work. Journalists stationed in Belgrade in the 1990s were witnesses to atrocities and civilian suffering the likes of which Europe had not seen since World War II. While some correspondents questioned the notion of objectivity by suggesting a 'journalism of attachment' (Bell, 1998), others looked at the war as a human misery.

'I had come to Bosnia partially as an adventure', reads the opening of Anthony Loyd's (2001) autobiography *My War Gone By, I Miss it So*. 'But after a while I got into the infinite death trip. I was not unhappy. Quite the opposite. I was delighted with most of what the war had offered me: chicks, kicks, cash and chaos; teenage punk dreams turned real and wreathed in gunsmoke'.

Memoirs like Loyd's offer an exciting taxonomy of journalists' fears in the face of 'the pointlessness of existence, the basic brutality of human life and the godlessness of the universe' (Loyd, 2001), but not all journalists have an opportunity to distance themselves from the region that shaped these experiences. Those who stayed after the wars ended have faced the environment of an ongoing reminder of the war times.

Paradoxically, and often lacking new framing of reports from a country in the aftermath of war, newsrooms also contribute to the perpetuation of the same interpretation. Many of the news reports coming from Serbia still call for some background on the war because it shapes the region in many ways. What is necessary, though, is 'a sober assessment on a per story basis what the war has to do with it', according to a correspondent who came after the war.

FC10 attempts to find a balance and gauges the audience regarding war-related stories:

> I frown on stories that drag the war in unnecessarily but I don't shy away from pointing out ways in which it is relevant to the story at hand. This is trial and error, give and take, and from time to time it involves a discussion with the newsroom, which generally tends to emphasise the war angle more than I do. I usually convince them, so I don't really feel censored in this respect. In my first few months here I noted a worrying phenomenon with clients to go for war stories. If I sent out five pitches of which one was a 'war topic'—defined in my dictionary by either highlighting ethnic divisions—that would be the one that got a response. I have been logging this and I must say it's getting a lot better. I still pitch this type of story when I think it's relevant, but they get 'taken' more or less proportional to other stories.

WHICH: DECLINE OF THE ELITE AND THE RISE OF NEWS AGENCIES

This study of foreign correspondents based in Serbia confirms the trend of the decline of elite foreign correspondents (Hamilton & Jenner, 2004) as 'sense makers' of international politics. It is the news agencies' correspondents that take on the role of, 'filtering material, providing an explanation and a background so the office can have a context and decide what to do, explaining [to] editors there "what" is relevant and why' (FC8).

News agencies produce more features and more analysis on a variety of topics in their reports from Belgrade now (FC3, FC9). Although there are fewer stories and fewer hours of work invested, journalists working in the news agencies feel they are doing a better job by providing more in-depth stories than before. 'In the past, editors in the main office would monitor what news agency got the story first, there would be feedback to the correspondent and praise when a job was well done. Now, not so much, only for breaking news' (FC4). The emphasis is now on quality. The problem is that this quality, framing, and interpretation of events in the international market increasingly come from a limited number of sources. This correspondent is very blunt about the process on the other end: 'I have noticed that the stories I file with the news agency, and which have more background, get republished more than short news. So that newsrooms do not have to pay journalists to write backgrounds' (FC3).

This is why the shift in the position of news agencies in the global media market is more significant than a change in the way foreign correspondents operate. Competition among gatherers of international news—journalists, politicians, nongovernmental organizations but also foreign correspondents and political reporters within the same newsroom (Williams, 2011)—leads to the emergence of new, transnational forms of reporting with ambiguous results. Looking at the work of two international news agencies, *Reuters* and *AP* television news, both during the crisis such as war in the Balkans and in a regular exchange of news, Paterson (2012) argued that, despite all grand expectations, the process of globalization did not bring more diverse journalism but instead a new form of media imperialism with a monopoly on images held by only two companies.

CONCLUSIONS

Some researchers indicate that the huge tide of available information highlights the increasingly important role of foreign correspondents as 'sense makers' (Archetti, 2012). When it comes to the Balkans though, this projected role is not accompanied by tangible circumstances of their work—budget constraints, smaller offices, fewer reporters, less travel, less interest in the region condition and framing of how they represent events and perceive their role. While experts on the Balkans may still be needed, the long-term correspondents from the Balkans see the signals that this expertise is of a limited value. Between a rock and a hard place, the power to resist this sweeping trend was found only with a strong public broadcaster of a European state less affected by economic crisis, and which has political interest in the region.

Overall, our findings reveal how the country of origin of a particular medium, type of media, and its ownership structure define news demand. As for the stories, they are a reflection of journalists too. In other words, 'the style of work may come to resemble that of correspondents themselves' (Hannerz, 2004). A generational gap among foreign correspondents, identified here, raises a question about whether an attachment to dramatic events that had moulded one's professional life, and often personal life too, can become an obstacle for embracing a postwar environment. A complex relationship between media and conflict, defined both by the representational and performative functions of the media (Cottle, 2006), outlives war circumstances and becomes intertwined into the daily life of postconflict society.

NOTES

1. The study is based on interviews with 10 foreign correspondents in Belgrade and a survey of 27 accredited journalists conducted February–March 2013 (response rate of 14.5 per cent).
2. Email correspondence, 28 March 2012.

REFERENCES

ARCHETTI, C. (2012), Which Future for Foreign Correspondence? London Foreign Correspondents in the Age of Global Media. *Journalism Studies*. 13 (5–6), pp. 847–856.

BELL, M. (1998). The Journalism of Attachment. In KIERAN, M. (ed.) *Media Ethics*. Abingdon, UK: Psychology Press.

COTTLE, S. (2006), *Mediatized Conflict: Developments in Media and Conflict Studies*. Maidenhead, UK: Open University Press.

ENTMAN, R. (2007), Framing Bias: Media in the Distribution of Power. *Journal of Communication*. 57 (1), pp. 163–173.

FOOTE, J.S. (2005). The Changing Role of TV Network News Correspondents. In Tunstall, J. (ed.), *Media Occupations and Professions: A Reader*. New York: Oxford University Press, pp. 158–160.

GRABER, D. A. (1988). *Processing the News: How People Tame the Information Tide*. New York: Longman.

HAMILTON, J. M. and JENNER, E. (2004). Redefining Foreign Correspondence. *Journalism*. 5, p. 301–321. doi: 10.1177/1464884904044938

HANNERZ, U. (2004), *Foreign News: Exploring the World of Foreign Correspondents*. Chicago: Chicago University Press.

LOYD, A. (2001). *My War Gone By, I Miss It So*. New York: Penguin Books.

PATERSON, C.A. (2011). *The International Television News Agencies: The World from London*. New York: Peter Lang.

TAI, Z., & CHANG, T. K. (2002). The Global News and the Pictures in Their Heads. *Gazette: The International Journal for Communication Studies*. 64 (3), pp. 251–265.

WILLIAMS, K. (2011). *International Journalism*. London: Sage.

INTERVIEWS

FC1—newspaper journalist. Face-to-face interview, 5 March 2013
FC2—TV and radio, Face-to-face interview, 12 March 2013
FC3—news agency, TV, radio. Face-to-face interview, 13 March 2013
FC4—news agency. Face-to-face interview, 13 March 2013
FC5—print media. Face-to-face interview, 20 March 2013
FC6—freelancer. Face-to-face interview, 25 March 2013
FC7—news agency, radio, TV. Face-to-face interview, 27 March 2013
FC8—news agency. Face-to-face interview, 15 April 2013
FC9—news agency. Face-to-face interview, 16 April 2013
FC10—freelancer. Online interview, 16 March 2013

21 Foreign Correspondents in Slovakia

Economy, Minorities, and Sometimes Politics

Andrej Školkay[1]

INTRODUCTION

This chapter presents an analysis of the work of foreign correspondents in Slovakia. The findings are based mainly on interviews with the majority of currently active foreign correspondents (FCs) and some of the FCs who were previously assigned to Slovakia (12 out of approximately 20). Additional sources included a few partial studies related to this topic. Research focused primarily on the professional and personal background of foreign correspondents, resources, their major challenges, the methods of work, and the lessons they learned while working as foreign correspondents in Slovakia. This chapter also focuses on the framework of the international news produced by FCs reporting from Slovakia, including how agendas are set and how news is processed.

In terms of population (5.4 million) and geographical size (48,000 square kilometers), Slovakia is a rather small country. Being one of the few countries in the world with a flat tax rate until 2012, Slovakia has been of interest to financial journalists. Nevertheless, it has never lost the image of a less important country compared to many of its European Union (EU) fellows and neighbours.

Slovakia's ethnic composition is fairly mixed. The country has a significant Hungarian ethnic minority of about half a million (8.5 per cent). The second largest ethnic group are the Roma people, estimated to be between 350,000 and 500,000 people. Other, smaller ethnic minorities in Slovakia include Czechs, Ruthenians (a minority from the northeastern border regions of Slovakia historically belonging to the peoples of Ancient Russia), Ukrainians, Germans, Poles, Croats, and Jews, among others. Generally, three of these minorities attract the attention of FCs.

First, Hungarian media have been long focusing on the life of ethnic Hungarians in Slovakia. The international media have occasionally addressed instances of political tension between Hungary and Slovakia, stirred by the rhetoric of some Slovak or Hungarian politicians as well.

Another ethnic group that attracts foreign media attention is the Roma population in Slovakia. Although in the 1990s, local Slovak media paid little interest to Roma issues, this changed significantly around 2000. One of the key factors for this was the foreign reporting about the Roma situation and the efforts toward full integration of this underprivileged social group in Slovakia as well as the related EU integration efforts of Slovakia. Nowadays, Roma issues represent a newsworthy topic on regional level and occasionally rise to a wider international issue (e.g., when France reported problems with Roma migrating from Bulgaria and Romania in 2011–2012).

Finally, the Jewish minority occasionally stirs up the interest of foreign media. This can be explained mainly by the historical legacy of the Nazi protectorate, Slovak State, for its contribution to the Holocaus, and by the significant intellectual influence of the Jewish community in the Slovak and international media.

Migration has been a marginal issue with negative connotations in Slovakia. The long-term structural unemployment has forced many Slovaks to look for jobs abroad, and this has been a trend for the past 20 years. This has created occasional opportunities for media to report on Slovakia as the country of origin of these migrant workers, usually in a negative light.

There is usually a correlation between a country's gross domestic product (GDP) and its international reputation. According to the World Bank, Slovakia's GDP per capita ranks at around 40th place in the world in 2012. Regionally, Slovakia has lower GDP per capita (US $16,856) than its former partner in the federation the Czech Republic (US $18,690) but higher than its southern neighbour Hungary (US $12,560), as well as its northern neighbour Poland (US $12,710). Slovakia is almost four times wealthier than its eastern neighbour Ukraine (US $3,867) and more than two times poorer than its western neighbour Austria (with a GDP of US $46,822). These data may help to explain, together with historical and present geopolitical factors, why issues happening in Ukraine are of little interest in Slovakia and, similarly, why events happening in Slovakia are of little interest in Austria.

WHO ARE THE COUNTRY'S FCs, AND WHOM DO THEY WORK FOR?

The number and status of FCs based in Slovakia are not very high. As a small and relatively new country, Slovakia initially lacked permanent offices of major news agencies, and even today its presence on the foreign media landscape is uneven. Until 1998, only two major international news agencies had their correspondents in Slovakia: *Reuters* and *Associated Press*. Apart from this, a journalist from the Slovak daily *Pravda* worked as a stringer for the *AFP*. Since 1999, most major news agencies (except Chinese) established their permanent offices in Slovakia, as well as two agencies specializing in financial news reporting: *Bloomberg* and *Bridge*.

It is almost impossible to identify all foreign correspondents reporting from or on Slovakia. The Ministry of Foreign and European Affairs (MFEA) in Slovakia keeps a list of the officially accredited foreign correspondents in the country. However, as it turns out, this list does not cover the majority of journalists actually working as foreign correspondents in Slovakia. The list of accredited foreign journalists includes 13 journalists, with some duplication for certain agencies and includes rather bizarre agencies like *Agentura DADU* (for which a Webpage could not be found). Considering these factors, an estimated 20 foreign correspondents are covering Slovakia. In general, it can be concluded that there are two groups of foreign—or better said—international correspondents in Slovakia. The larger group consists of those who are permanently or temporarily based and resident in the country. More than half of them are local journalists (mostly native Slovaks, ethnic Czechs, or ethnic Hungarians). Some of these journalists are accredited through the MFEA; however, it was virtually impossible to contact them based on the official limited data from the MFEA.

Then there is a second group of foreign correspondents who report about Slovak issue, but who reside in one of the neighbouring countries, with their base being, in most cases, Budapest or Prague. Be that as it may, it is possible that most correspondents from the previous subgroup (accredited journalists with MFEA) belong to this category as well. This means that it appears the majority of journalists accredited by MFEA actually reside abroad.

Of course, especially newsworthy events in Slovakia draw in more foreign correspondents. For example, during the vote on the European Financial Stability Facility (EFSF) in the Slovak Parliament at the end of 2011, four *Reuters* correspondents and three *Reuters* photographers were in Slovakia (in addition to other short-term FCs). In 2005, Slovakia was closely watched as presidents George Bush and Vladimir Putin met in Bratislava and heads of state attended the conference New Quest for Democracy. The MFEA issued 1,600 journalists' accreditations for this event.

The majority of FCs represented larger media companies, which seems logical, inasmuch as Slovakia is a small country, which at the time of the survey, did not have any significant newsworthy events (no war, no ethnic or social conflicts, and no significant threats to democracy).

In most cases each media company was represented by a single reporter. The rare exception was the Czech public television, which employed two local reporters until the summer of 2012. According to Palata (2012), in the mid-1990s, reporting was used as a convenient tool to support justification of the Federation split. Later, the media presence was interesting for Czech public service media (PSM) because Slovakia suddenly became a positive inspiration for the Czech audiences as a result of the economic and social reforms.

Based on official and unofficial data, one can say that about 10 correspondents work for print medium, five for broadcast mediums, and four for news agencies. Some journalists work for more (and different) media. The majority of reporters are men (13 vs. six women).

WHAT MAKES IT INTO THE FCs' AGENDA REPORTING?

Generally, FCs appear to be independent in their news selection. Some general journalistic news criteria are used (e.g., disasters or stories of strange phenomena are always covered) or some specific professional criteria (e.g., economics/financial issues in the case of a news agency or issues that are either very similar to what is happening in the world or, on the other hand, very different). The latter criteria include country specific issues (e.g., news involving Hungarian minority in Slovakia in the case of Hungarian correspondents and Hungarian media [FC10] or of Slovakian developments as a Eurozone member [FC11, FC12], or issues related to the country of the agency's origin [FC12]), and of course, regional issues (e.g., freedom of the press). When Slovakia joined the Eurozone, some traditionally important economic indicators lost some of their previous importance (e.g., GDP, foreign trade, and inflation). From this point, reporters became more interested in fiscal data and the situation of the banks. At the same time, the unanimity needed to pass some political and economic decisions at the European Council and other EU bodies has led to an increased role of this small country in the EU. In other words, without this EU rule, Slovakia would be even less important for FCs.

In general, a big part of the reported news comes from official reports and regular events (e.g., Agenda of the Cabinet). A lot of news in Slovakia is based on media/wire agencies' reports, and a small number come from readers' ideas or articles found in some obscure or local magazines (FC8)

Foreign media, especially wire agencies, also report on issues that are not so much of interest to local readers. For example, typically, these are issues related to the international agreements or to the broader activities of international companies with branches in Slovakia (FC4, FC8, FC9, FC11).

On the other hand, foreign media, especially wire agencies, do not pay as much attention to the issues exclusively related to local politics, unless these issues or protests cross a certain (hard to define) threshold of intensity. Even some issues with a strong domestic resonance such as the controversial process of repeated election of the prosecutor general in the Slovak Parliament in 2011 or huge street protests against allegedly corrupt politicians and business groups in late 2011 and early 2012 (Codename: Gorilla) received only limited international coverage.

WHEN DOES SOMETHING BECOME NEWS?

Because it is known from experience and previous studies and because it was also confirmed in interviews, the most important factors that influence FC reporting are the institutional ones. Firstly, it is crucial whether the media company belongs to the group of public service media or is privately owned. Their foreign coverage is focused either on different topics (e.g., more politic and less gossip in the case of PSM), or the news is presented in a different way (less emotionally in the case of PSM). Secondly, it obviously matters whether the correspondent represents a television, radio, paper, or a news agency because all these traditional media have their specific features that influence selection of the topics to be covered and their presentation (e.g., radio needs voice, TV needs pictures). Thirdly, it matters whether a medium or a foreign correspondent focuses on specialized coverage or covers everything. Obviously, specialization by definition limits focus of reporting but also increases its quality.

There have been cases when political affiliation of the medium (usually a liberal one) has influenced the selection of FC topics. For example, the Hungarian liberal daily, *Népszabadság*, is interested in issues pertaining to Hungarian minority in Slovakia. However, its viewpoint is from in a liberal angle, where the daily is interested in issues that 'cross the threshold of tolerance of people of Budapest' (FC10).

In the case of Slovakia, an important external factor shapes news coverage. The overall news coverage has been impacted for years by the access to official information and the helpfulness of the governmental press departments. This has changed significantly in the last decade toward more openness. The more difficult the access is to the official information or key political figures, the less willing journalists are to write about the government in positive terms.

The FCs also acknowledge that international readers are usually not exceedingly familiar with a small country like Slovakia and in particular that international readers do not follow the local media. This means that FCs in Slovakia are not under such pressure to write highly original stories, as, for example, FCs in Austria or Switzerland may be (FC8, FC12).

WHERE DO THE STORIES COME FROM?

The newly established FCs rely initially on their contacts among other FCs in the country. Later on, those FCs who more or less permanently reside in the country develop their own networks of sources. Those who do not have such extensive network rely only on official news, local media reporting, and a few outside contacts. The most difficult aspect of the work of FC in Slovakia has been establishing whom can be used as a reliable source (FC9).

The most important source of information for correspondents based in Slovakia is the local media, while stories brought by the news agencies are the primary source for the correspondents based in neighbouring countries (FC8, FC12). Some FCs claim that it is enough for them to follow the local media (most of them understand the language) because there seems to be too much information to cater to the sporadic interest among foreign audiences in news from Slovakia. Social media are used almost exclusively by a few specialized FCs, who use it to find contacts to specialists or to find original opinions and comments (FC7, FC9, FC12).

HOW FOREIGN NEWS IS FORMULATED IN DIFFERENT FRAMES

Several studies have analyzed how various foreign media reported Slovak issues since 1993. These studies are presented here in chronological order. This approach allows us to better illustrate the changes that have taken place in Slovakia in the international news.

The first analysis covers the most prestigious international media and two international news agencies (*Thomson Reuters* and *Associated Press*) in the years 1993–1998 (Beblavý & Salner, 1999). All these media 'personalised politics, put emphasis on visual or textual symbols, especially personalised stereotypes'. The second group of issues stemmed from substantial but often underlying issues like 'nationalism versus tolerance' (Hungarian minority, controversial historical figures, Roma minority). The third focus was represented by a single construction activity: a dam on the Danube between Slovakia and Hungary. In addition, soon after the country became independent in 1993, the foreign correspondents started to pay special attention to signs of the concentration of power and problems in the economy. Thus, the word 'instability' became the key term of reference, associated with unpredictable politics based on authoritarian personalities.

A more detailed study by Burgess (1997) focused on the image of Slovakia in the British press from 1993 until August 1994. Burgess concluded that, overall, the British press was not biased in its reporting on Slovakia. However, he also noted that the British press followed the discourse rather than real events in the country.

Neither the Canadian nor the US press showed signs of evident bias in the 1990s reporting on Slovakia, according to Kirschbaum (2004). However, Kirschbaum seemed to be surprised by the fact that the Canadian and the US press focused on problems and expressed its worries regarding the further developments in Slovakia, instead of showing more understanding for the new state and transition economy.

With the German press, there was some bias established even before the birth of independent Slovakia, claims the author of another study, Vergesová (2004). She argues that the German print press framed Slovakia's move toward independence as an effort of the communists, nationalists, and other negative social and political forces to strengthen their position in the country. However, Vergesová acknowledges that unbiased articles were published in the German press from the first year of the Slovakia's independence. As in the British, Canadian, and US media, ethnic Hungarians (especially in 1995 and 1997) and Roma were the focus of occasional German media attention. The early years of independence brought lowered interest of German media in Slovakia. Occasional reporting mentioned various progressive reforms, corruption, and weak integration of Roma minority.

Duleba (2000) suggested that perhaps the best empirical categories of the framing and priming of Slovakia's news can be demonstrated with the example of Russian media reporting. Firstly, Slovakia was an unknown country in Russia, and therefore there was virtually no image of the country. Secondly, it was the Czech image of Slovakia in Russia. Thirdly, there was the official image of Slovakia among the members of the Russian elite. This image was fully associated with the official political establishment in Slovakia. And, finally, there was also the critical image of Slovakia in Russia, presented by several independent media.

The tone of reporting on Slovakia in the foreign media changed very soon after Vladimír Mečiar (who was perceived as autocrat and populist) lost the elections (or, more precisely, when he won, but was unable to form working government). While the first and the second governments of Mikuláš Dzurinda (1998–2006) were mostly celebrated in the foreign media, sometimes with slight criticism, the first government of Robert Fico (2006–2010) was seen in the foreign media much more negatively. However, there was also a new attempt to differentiate between the country itself and the government in power (Žilinský, 2007). It was acknowledged later by some of the FCs that both the local media and some FCs demonized Robert Fico and uncritically glorified the next Prime Minister Iveta Radičová (2010–2012).

CONCLUSION

It seems that Slovakia is a country too small to have an established network of FCs. Except for its minorities, it does not have any specific feature or regular events important for the foreign media audiences. Many 'in-country' correspondents are local journalists who occasionally or permanently do work for the foreign media. Most of the 'out-of-the-country' correspondents reside in one of the neighbouring countries and cover Slovakia amongst others in the region. The officially accredited journalists on the list of the MFEA were mostly out of the reach. On the other side, some of the working FCs have never applied for an official accreditation.

The main resource of information for the majority of working correspondents is the local news and personal contacts. The most important and long-time foundation for an ongoing international media interest in Slovakia has been its mixed ethnic composition. Occasional and temporary media attention from abroad has been recorded in a number of disasters or scandal cases and one parliamentary vote threatening the Eurozone stability.

Since country's creation in 1993, the framing of international news about Slovakia has gone through many phases from being very negative and connected to a small group of active politicians; through the discovery of a flat tax haven in the middle of Europe; to pictorial and narrated reports about the knotty relationship between the major Slovak population and the two main minorities, Hungarians and Roma.

As our research found out, there are several trends in current reporting on Slovakia for foreign media. Firstly, there have been some structural changes, which reflect the move toward covering more countries by a single reporter; covering a single country in more tabloid-like style; using shorter stories (radio); and reporting less about local politics and covering popular or sensational topics or issues of broader relevance.

Although the foreign media have never paid extensive attention to Slovakia, in their reports they have used different frames and have chosen very distinctive topics over the past 20 years. Because Slovakia, as a country, is less known and many international readers who know Slovakia have a preconceived view of it, its foreign media images are based mostly on the personal opinion and attitudes of the reporting correspondents. Yet in the foreign press, one could find in the last 20 years information about Slovakia as a successful frontrunner in the emerging European economies; as a country struggling with racism; as a country with great educational challenges for minorities; as a country with dictatorial political leadership and limited human rights; or as a country with smart cabinet members.

Slovakia reached its most recent international media stardom in late 2011, when many foreign media followed the ongoing process of the Euro crisis (EFSF). The sharp division of opinions on this issue among coalition parties brought down the cabinet of Iveta Radičová. However, this issue drew international attention not because of the faith of the Slovak government but as a possible veto for an early version of the EFSF impacting the Eurozone. In this sense, it was a typical sign of what matters in international news reporting from a small country: issues that challenge or impact politically, economically, or socially (including sports) other, usually bigger countries.

NOTE

1. This work was partially supported by the Slovak Research and Science Agency under contracts no. DO7RP-0022–10 and DO7RP 0039–11. The author is thankful to Mária Hong and Vladka Bukerová for critical comments on earlier versions of this chapter.

REFERENCES

BEBLAVÝ, M., & SALNER, A. (1999). *Tvorcovia obrazov a obraz tvorcov. Vnímanie Slovenska v západných krajinách 1989–1999*. [Creators of Images and the Image of Creators. Perception of Slovakia in the Western Countries in 1989–1999]. Bratislava, Slovakia: Centrum pre spoločenskú a mediálnu analýzu.

BURGESS, A. (1997). Writing off Slovakia to 'The East'? Examining Charges of Bias in British Press Reporting of Slovakia, 1993–1994. *Nationalities Papers*. 25 (4), pp. 659–681.

DULEBA, A. (2000). Obraz Slovenska v súčasnom Rusku [Image of Slovakia in Contemporary Russia]. *OS*. 6, pp. 27–30.

KIRSCHBAUM, S. J. (2004). Tlač USA, Kanady a Veľkej Británie o desiatich rokoch Slovenskej republiky [The Print Media of USA, Canada and Great Britain during the First Decade of the Slovak Republic]. In Rolková, N. (ed.), *Desaťročie Slovenskej republiky* [Tenth Anniversary of the Slovak Republic]. Martin, Slovakia: Matica slovenská, pp. 520–523.

PALATA, L. (2012). Mečiara sme sa báli viac ako rozpadu [We Were More Afraid of Mečiar Than the Dissolution]. *SME Daily*, p. 13.

THE WORLD BANK. 'GDP per Capita' [Online]. Available from http://bit.ly/1ppRpWw.

VERGESOVÁ, D. (2004). Prehľad spravodajstva o Slovensku v nemeckých médiách [Overview of Reporting on Slovakia in German Media]. In Rolková, N. (ed.), *Desaťročie Slovenskej republiky* [Tenth Anniversary of the Slovak Republic]. Martin, Slovakia: Matica slovenská, pp. 527–541.

ŽILINSKÝ, J. (2007). *Obraz Slovenska v zahraničí* [Image of Slovakia Abroad] [Online]. Available from http://bit.ly/PsEqm8.

INTERVIEWS

FC1—Olga Baková, foreign correspondent for the Czech TV, Slovak native. Interviewed 18 July 2012 by Andrej Školkay.

FC2—Tatiana Bednáriková, *AFP*, Slovak native. Interviewed 8 August 2012 via email by Kristína Morávková.

FC3—Vojtěch Berger, foreign correspondent for the *Czech Radio*. Interviewed 12 June 2012 by Andrej Školkay.

FC4—Adrián Bobok, *CTK News Agency*, Slovak native. Interviewed 20 August 2012 via email by Miroslava Kernová.

FC5—Susan Greenberg, foreign correspondent for *The Guardian* covering both Czech and Slovak news from November 1990 to January 1994, based in Prague. Interviewed 9 August 2012 via email by Klaudia Lászlóová.

FC6—Renáta Havranová, independent correspondent for various Czech media, Slovak native. Interviewed 16 August 2012 by Andrej Školkay.

FC7—Ladislav Kerekeš, foreign correspondent for the *Czech TV* (*PSM*), Slovak native. Interviewed 17 July 2012 by Andrej Školkay.

FC8—Bernhard Odehnal (Tages Anzeiger). Interviewed 12 June 2012 by Andrej Školkay.

FC9—Karin Rogalska (*Wiener Zeitung*). Interviewed 12 May 2012 by Andrej Školkay.

FC10—József Szilvássy, Czech and Slovak correspondent for the Hungarian daily *Népszbadság*, since 2004 based in the Slovak town Šamorín, visiting

Prague several times a month. Interviewed 30 August 2012 by Klaudia Lászlóová.
FC11—Martin Šanta (*Thomson Reuters*), Slovak native. Interviewed July 2012 by Klaudia Lászlóová.
FC12—Christoph Thanei (*Die Presse*, *DPA*). Interviewed 14 May 2012 by Andrej Školkay.

22 Foreign Correspondents in Slovenia

A Small Country Neglected by Foreign Media

Marko Milosavljević and Gašper Završnik

INTRODUCTION

Slovenia became an independent state in 1991. Previously, it was a part of the former Socialist Federal Republic of Yugoslavia (SFRY) for almost five decades. Its declaration of independence was followed by a limited conflict with the Yugoslav People's Army that is known as the Ten-Day War, after which it was internationally recognized in 1992. Slovenia became a member of the European Union and NATO in 2004, implemented the Schengen regime, and entered the Eurozone in 2007 (Milosavljević & Kerševan Smokvina, 2012). It is geographically situated between Italy and the Adriatic Sea on its western border, Austria in the north, Hungary in the northeast, and Croatia in the southeast. Slovenia has a population of just over 2 million, of which more than 80 per cent declare themselves Slovenian, so the country is relatively homogeneous in terms of ethnic and linguistic composition ([0]Milosavljević & Kerševan Smokvina, 2012). Its per capita GDP in 2012 was €17,244, and the economic growth figures were positive for the first time after eight consecutive quarters in the last quarter of 2013 (2.1 per cent) (Statistical Office of Republic of Slovenia, 2014), with positive predictions for 2015, when the annual growth is forecast at 0.5 per cent (Institute of Macroeconomic Analysis and Development, 2014).

WHO ARE THE COUNTRY'S FCs, AND WHOM DO THEY WORK FOR?

According to information that we collected mostly from the journalists and editors, only seven foreign media correspondents are based in Slovenia. Five of them were included in our survey. Only one of them is actually a foreigner, and one has dual nationality: Slovenian and Italian. Slovenian journalists mostly work full-time as foreign correspondents, but there are also cases when they work part-time for foreign media and have full-time employment in Slovenian media, as in the case of the editor of the *Domestic*

Politics department and *Sobotna priloga* (Saturday supplement) at the Slovenian media group *Delo*, who occasionally acts as a so-called stringer reporter for the *Associated Press* (*AP*). As he put it, there is very little interest from *AP* in Slovenia and the region, so he does not report very regularly.

Croatian Press Agency (*Hina*) is the only media that has a permanent foreign correspondent based in Slovenia. Its office is in Kranj, the fourth biggest city in Slovenia. In 2010, another Croatian media, *Croatian Radiotelevision* (*HRT*), closed its correspondent office in Ljubljana, citing economic pressures (Delo, 2010). For now, *HRT* covers Slovenian affairs from neighbouring Zagreb, Croatia. The Croatian national broadcaster is not the only media organization in Croatia that does not have a correspondent in Slovenia anymore. Until 2009, the Croatian commercial television *Nova TV*, owned by the *Central European Media Enterprise* (*CME*), used to have an occasional collaborator in Slovenia, who also works for Slovenian television *POP TV* (owned by *CME* as well). She mentioned that there is not much interest in Slovenian affairs in Croatia lately and that whenever something really important happens, they send their own (parachute) reporters to Slovenia, but they mostly report on Slovenia from their headquarters in Zagreb. Until quite recently, one Slovenian journalist was a correspondent for the Spanish daily *ABC*. Due to the lack of interest in Slovenia, as well as the recession and structural issues that the Spanish media are facing lately, Spain does not have a correspondent in Slovenia anymore.

With few correspondents based in Slovenia, so-called parachute correspondents are common. During the last presidential elections in November 2012, some 40 foreign journalists were accredited, among them reporters from Russia (*Izvestia*, *Itar Tass*), Croatia (*HRT*, *RTL*, *Nova TV*, *Jutarnji list*, *Novi list*, *Objektiv*), Italy (*Il Piccolo*), Japan (*Asahi Shimbun*), China (*Xinhua*), France (*AFP*), Austria (*APA*), Serbia (*Tanjug*), Bosnia and Herzegovina (*Al Jazeera Balkans*), and international broadcaster *Reuters* TV (Dnevnik, 2012). In March 2013, Slovenia, according to prominent Slovenian journalists, was probably given the biggest foreign media exposure in its independent history (Jenko, 2013). After the Cypriot bailout, many speculations occurred about Slovenia being the next Eurozone country that will be forced to ask for a bailout. Therefore, a large majority of the most influential world media—*New York Times*, *CNN*, *BBC*, *The Guardian*, *Frankfurter Allgemeine Zeitung*, *Der Spiegel*, *Wall Street Journal*, *Al Jazeera*, *The Economist*, *El Pais*, among others—reported on Slovenia as the next European country in trouble. Some of them even sent parachute correspondents to Ljubljana, while others reported from Brussels or elsewhere.

Whereas most of the media are cutting down the net of correspondents, the case of Italian agency *ANSA* (*Agenzia Nazionale Stampa Associata*) is rather unique. The *ANSA*'s plan is to expand the net of correspondents to the so-called New Europe and the Balkan region (including Slovenia).

Apart from the previously mentioned *Hina*, *ANSA*, and *AP*, other news agencies, *Reuters* and *Bloomberg* have correspondents based in Slovenia. One Slovenian is a contributor for the Serbian press agency *BETA* and Bosnian agency ONASA, in addition to contributing to the Radio and Television of Bosnia and Herzegovina (*RTVBiH* and *BHRT*) and writing a blog on *Al-Jazeera Balkans*' Webpage. The correspondent for *ANSA* occasionally also collaborates with the Italian newspapers *Novi Glas* (*New Voice*) and *Primorski dnevnik* (*Primorska Daily*), which are published in Slovenian and are read mostly by the Slovenian ethnic minority in Italy. All of them, except a correspondent from *Bloomberg*, who refused to be interviewed due to the media's policy, and a correspondent for Croatian daily *Novi List* (*New Paper*) participated in our research. Although most correspondents work for more than one medium, we tried to determine a principal medium of employment. We can conclude that five correspondents work for news agencies and one each for print and online media. Based on this, we can conclude that the reach of (foreign) correspondents in Slovenia is regional (*Hina*, *Al-Jazeera Balkans*, *RTVBiH*, and *BHRT*) and international (*Reuters*, *Bloomberg*, *Ansa*, and *AP*). Most of the stories they work on are published online or in print media and in one case also on public radio and television.

The five correspondents included in our survey are all experienced journalists, who have been working as journalists between 11 and 30 years and as correspondents (based in Slovenia) from several months (the correspondent for *ANSA*) to 22 years (the correspondent for *Hina*). They all speak Slovenian fluently, and, with the exception of one respondent, they have all been correspondents only in Slovenia. In the past, The exception was a correspondent in Paris who was a parachute reporter in Portugal, Afghanistan, Russia, Algeria, and some other French-speaking African countries for various media in ex-Yugoslavia. Before becoming correspondents, they worked for Slovenian or regional media and some still work for them. Two correspondents have full-time contracts (*Reuters* and *Hina*), one has a part-time contract (*ANSA*), and the other two report for foreign media as freelancers or stringers. Three of them do not belong to any media or journalist union. On the other hand, two of the correspondents included in the survey are either members of an Italian journalistic association or members of Društvo novinarjev Slovenije (Slovene Association of Journalists).

Regarding the sociodemographic information of the respondents, four of the five correspondents based in Slovenia included in our survey are males. The average age of the all five of them is a 50.6 years, the youngest is 31 and the oldest is 68 years old. Four of them are married; one is single. Three of them do not consider themselves affiliated with any particular religion or religious denomination, meanwhile two do (one declared himself as Catholic). Regarding the highest level of education that they have completed—two of them have doctoral degree while the others had a bachelor's degree. Three of the correspondents who participated in the survey studied journalism or communication at university level, and two of them did not.

WHAT MAKES IT INTO THE FOREIGN CORRESPONDENT'S REPORTING AGENDA?

According to the answers that we were given, correspondents for foreign media mostly cover stories related to politics and economy, followed by sport events and stories related to society and culture. Their stories are pitched or initiated by themselves, by their editor, or by the news desk in the country where the medium is located. In the case of *AP*, it is often the editors who direct the story, whereas in the case of *Reuters* and *ANSA*, it is the correspondents who pitch their stories autonomously.

The *BETA* and Bosnian agency *ONASA* journalist contributes to agencies on a daily basis and less regularly for other media like *Al-Jazeera Balkans*, stating that reporting for other media depends on the nature of affairs in Slovenia. He mostly works on stories that are related to elections, the financial crisis, and important cultural events in which the Bosnians and the Serbs participate. The typical stories that *ANSA*'s reporter covers are austerity measures that Slovenian government embraces or the so-called stability program; analyzing the grounds of the financial crisis and the breakdown of data of economic development in Slovenia in recent years; and problems in the Slovenian banking sector and holes in the banking system. The *AP* correspondent works mostly on stories associated with the financial crisis, elections, and main international sports events. The same can also be said for the *Reuters* correspondent, who covers mostly economics and politics.

WHEN DOES SOMETHING BECOME FCs' NEWS?

The seasonal factors that affect the coverage of foreign correspondents based in Slovenia are elections, the releases of economic indicators and, according to *ANSA*'s correspondents, the development of economic crisis (for which Slovenia was getting real international repercussions in 2013). *AP*'s, *Hina*'s, and *Reuters*' correspondents say that there is no yearly, monthly, or weekly pattern of news picks due to the lack of interest in Slovenia. On the other hand, *ANSA*'s correspondent and the Slovenian FC believe that there are patterns; for example, the elections could be considered a yearly news pattern. The regular events that trigger their coverage are economic conferences, elections, releases of economic indicators, main sports events, bilateral events between Slovenia and the country where the medium is based, incidents (in the case of Croatian–Slovenian relations), the financial crisis, Slovenian measures against the recession, international responses to the financial crisis in Slovenia, and internal dialectics related to the issues of the Slovenian economic crisis.

WHERE DO STORIES COME FROM?

The key sources that could be the main reasons to start investigating a story are government officials, members of the opposition, and other national sources. Respondents also mentioned lobbies, think tanks, blogs, average citizens, nongovernmental organizations (NGOs), and coverage of national media in Slovenia. In the opinion of correspondents based in Slovenia, sources such as academics, Twitter, and other social media are not that relevant to starting to investigate a story. Correspondents rated their access to first-hand sources—from government and big business—in Slovenia as quite difficult in comparison to other European countries. On a scale from one to five, where one means very difficult access and five very open access, 'access to first-hand sources' was rated as an average of 2.75.

From the potential sources of influence that affect the work of correspondents, the most influential according to them are (in order of decreasing importance) their personal beliefs and values; their editorial supervisors and higher editors; their peers on the staff; editorial policy; the availability of the newsgathering resources; and time limits. As the least influential, they chose profit considerations and advertising.

As the most influential factors on the other list of potential factors of influence were chosen (in order of decreasing importance) competing news organizations; feedback from the audience; information access; government officials; colleagues in other media; relationships with news sources; media laws and regulations; businesspeople; the military, police, and state security; public relations; politicians; censorship; pressure groups; and their friends and family.

HOW FOREIGN NEWS IS FORMULATED IN DIFFERENT FRAMES

The correspondent for *AP* pitches one story a week, of which half are published. The correspondent for *Reuters* generally writes about seven stories a week, and almost all get published (98 per cent in her opinion). The reporter for the Croatian press agency *Hina* usually writes from 10 to 30 stories per week, and, according to his answers, around 70 per cent of his stories end up published. *ANSA*'s correspondent usually sends two or three short stories (from 10 to 15 lines) per day and once or twice a month pitches longer analysis, comments, and features on Slovenian affairs (around 40 lines). The vast majority of them are also published.

RECENT TRENDS

Most of the correspondents believe that, according to their experiences, the job of FCs has changed for the worse in recent years. This opinion seems to be more prevalent amongst the more experienced correspondents. Correspondents for *AP* and Bosnian and Serbian media said that their employers have cut down the number of posts for foreign correspondents in the last decade. On the other hand, *ANSA*'s correspondents have the opposite experience because it has increased the number of its journalists in the Balkan region. Therefore, the *ANSA* FC is not afraid that his current post as foreign correspondent in Slovenia may be cut down within the next two or three years in order to save costs. The *BETA* and Bosnian agency *ONASA* journalist was less optimistic. He thinks that there is a huge probability of cutting down the post of correspondent in Slovenia by some of the media he works for. The *AP*'s and *Reuters'* correspondents stated that in their cases the resources available to do their job have been cut down to a great extent (more so in the case of *AP* than of Reuters). *ANSA*'s correspondent has to cover any additional expenses himself. In *ANSA* and *AP* and, to a lesser extent, in the case of *Reuters*, parachute journalists have increasingly replaced traditional correspondents. Most of them agree to quite a great extent (four on the scale from one to five) that, within their medium, local journalists have been employed instead of traditional FCs. The majority of correspondents thought that amateur journalists/bloggers/representatives of NGOs are not increasingly used to replace traditional correspondents in the case of their media. Two of the correspondents do not feel increasing time pressure on their job at all; meanwhile, others feel increasing time pressure a bit more. Apart from the *Reuters*' correspondent, who does not agree with it at all, others believe to quite a great extent that the audience today cares less about international news than in the past. (*Hina*'s correspondent did not want to answer the section of questions related to trends in FC.)

IMPACT OF THE EURO/FINANCIAL CRISIS

In the terms of the quantitative and qualitative impact of the Euro financial crisis on their job, the *Reuters*' correspondent said that she writes more stories and longer ones. Both the quantitative and the qualitative effects are substantial, according to the experiences of *Hina*'s correspondents as well. A similar opinion is shared by the *AP* correspondent, who said that there is more news on specific Slovene financial situations, or as he called it 'troika issues'.

There was a difference of opinion regarding the question of whether they thought the current crisis helped to create a European Public Sphere where larger numbers of European citizens cared more about other European countries. The correspondent for *ANSA* thought that the countries do not care much more about each other now. He thinks that the reporting on the financial crisis is more about generating drama about which country will be the next one to fall. The correspondent for *AP* also thinks that the current crisis has not helped to create that kind of public sphere. The correspondent for Bosnian and Serbian media said that his audience had less faith in the EU's ability to solve the crisis. Only *Hina*'s correspondent agrees that countries now care more about each other's national politics.

WHICH ARE THE MOST INFLUENTIAL FOREIGN CORRESPONDENTS AND LOCAL MEDIA?

The foreign media organization that is the most influential, according to the FCs, is *Reuters*, followed by *Bloomberg*. One of the correspondents said that as far as he knows, there are no foreign media in Slovenia. There is not much cooperation among correspondents according to the information we gathered. If there is, it is mostly about the exchange of information.

FCs based in Slovenia use Slovenian national media and local journalists as sources several times a week. To a lesser extent, they use other FCs based in Slovenia and even less citizen journalists/blogs/social media. Some of correspondents do not even use social media, blogs, and citizen journalism, whereas others use those kinds of sources once a week or once a month.

CONCLUSIONS

Slovenia, due to its smallness and the lack of conflict, is an example of a country that receives very little attention from foreign media. It is not surprising that according to our findings, only seven FCs are based in Slovenia, of whom only one is a foreigner and one has a double nationality; the rest are Slovenians. Probably the most influential media that have FCs in Slovenia are *Reuters*, *AP*, *Bloomberg*, and *ANSA*. Meanwhile, others have more regionally limited reach (*Hina*, *ONASA*, *Beta*, *RTVBiH*, *BHRT*, *Al Jazeera Balkans*). Due to the small number of FC in Slovenia, parachute correspondents are common, especially during the elections, bigger sports events, and other unprecedented events—such as recent speculation about a Slovenian bailout. In recent years since the beginning of the finical crisis, some—especially Croatian media—closed their bureaus or stopped collaborating with their correspondents based in Slovenia. FCs predominantly cover political and economic stories and to lesser extent stories related to sports, culture, and society. The seasonal factors that influence their agenda are elections, the releases of economic indicators. and recently the development of the economic crisis. According to their answers, the key sources that represent the main reason to start working on a story are government officials, members of the opposition, and other national sources. Some FCs also pay attention to lobbies, think thanks, blogs, average citizens, NGOs, and the Slovenian media.

Most of the correspondents who participated in our research believe that their profession has changed for the worse in recent years. They explain it in terms of the cutting down the number of posts for foreign correspondent in the last decade. The case of *ANSA*'s correspondent is, therefore, rather unique in that *ANSA* has expanded its correspondent web in the region.

To sum up, there is not much interest in Slovenian affairs, so the FCs based in Slovenia work from the world's biggest press agencies or media from the neighbouring countries (Croatia and Italy) or from countries that have been culturally and historically close to Slovenia (Bosnia and Herzegovina). Slovenia comes to the limelight very rarely; on those occasions, foreign media send parachute journalists to Slovenia or report on Slovenian issues from neighbouring countries. The lack of interest in Slovenia in the times of financial crisis contributed to closing the bureaus in Slovenia (the case of *HRT*).

REFERENCES

DELO. (2010). HRT (začasno) brez dopisnika iz Slovenije [Online]. Available from http://bit.ly/1gOKkFJ.

DNEVNIK. (2012). Za predsedniške volitve precejšnje zanimanje tudi med tujimi mediji [Online]. Available from http://bit.ly/1nE5E5x.

INSTITUTE OF MACROECONOMIC ANALYSIS AND DEVELOPMENT. (2014). Pomladanska napoved gospodarskih gibanj 2014 [Online]. Available from http://bit.ly/1jurLax.

JENKO, M. (2013). Ko te oplazi CNN. *Delo* [Online]. Available from http://bit.ly/PpStsS.

MILOSAVLJEVIĆ, M., and KERŠEVAN SMOKVINA, T. (2012). *Mapping Digital Media: Slovenia*. London: Open Society Foundations. Available from http://osf.to/1nE5JpK.

STATISTICAL OFFICE OF REPUBLIC OF SLOVENIA. (2014). Bruto domači proizvod, Slovenija, 4. četrtletje 2013 [Online]. Available from http://bit.ly/1nE5MlB.

23 Foreign Correspondents in Spain

Facing the Economic and Professional Crisis

Ramón Salaverría

INTRODUCTION

The international media have always been slow to show much interest in Spain—at least, as regards upbeat news stories. When interest rises, the media attention tends to be drawn to the downbeat. Indeed, the first time a significant number of FCs visited Spain was the relatively brief, three-year duration of the Spanish Civil War (1936–1939). The war made the front pages of the main international newspapers and prompted some of the most preeminent journalists of the time to come to Spain: writers such as Ernest Hemingway and Arthur Koestler, and photographers such as Robert Capa and Gerda Taro, among others, came to the country to report to an international audience on a conflict that was to presage World War II (Preston, 2009).

Following the end of the Civil War, the Franco government enforced a strict regime of media control, which led to a decline in interest in Spain among international media outlets. Such news media indifference ended with the death of Franco in 1975 (Sinova, 1989; Barrera, 1995; Moreno Cantano, 2006). International press interest in Spain was revived by the dynamics of the transition to democracy. The turbulent development of Spanish political life at that time, punctuated by the attempted *coup d'état* in 1981 and bedeviled throughout by ETA terrorist violence, gave rise to greater interest in the country among foreign media organizations. Such interest was secured by Spain's accession to European Union membership in 1986 (Haubrich, 1999). This gradual process of increasing foreign news media interest may be said to have reached a peak in 1992, when two major international events were held in Spain: the Olympic Games in Barcelona and the World Exhibition (Expo '92) in Seville. In the 20 years since those highlights, when the country shone in the full glare of global media attention, Spain has retained its relatively significant status in international news media terms, receiving attention due to being the world's twelfth largest economy (according to the figures for 2011 issued by the World Bank).

The economic strength of Spain during the 1990s and into the early 2000s enabled the launch of foreign press outlets within the country in order to target a large immigrant population (López Romero, 2009). For the purposes of this paper, however, the most important outcome of Spain's economic power during that period was the stable establishment of international media organizations in the country. Besides certain specific events—political and economic summit meetings, major exhibitions, international sports competitions—that may draw special correspondents for a fixed period of time, Spain became a centre for news reporting that required the ongoing presence of foreign correspondents in situ. This journalistic interest has been reinforced since the outbreak of the global economic crisis in 2007, Spain being one of the countries to have suffered the worst of the fallout. The question of how the status of FCs has changed in recent years arises in this regard: how has the role of FC changed given the complex financial context in which media organizations are currently operating?

WHO ARE THE FOREIGN CORRESPONDENTS?

The first response to this question requires a reading of the figures for the number of FCs based in Spain over time. Such figures are recorded in the main directory of media outlets and journalists in the country: the *Agenda de la Comunicación* (Communication Directory), issued by the Ministry of the Presidency (2008, 2012). Published annually by the Spanish government, this register comprises the official list of state institutions and embassies, as well as both national and international print, radio, and TV media outlets based in the country. Needless to say, an unknown number of journalists do not apply for registration in this directory, especially those who work only occasionally for the international media; however, almost all of the main international media outlets and their correspondents are listed. Hence, a comparative historical overview of this directory will enable the analysis of how the number of foreign media outlets and journalists based in Spain has changed over time, as well as the various professional profiles, media, and other related characteristics involved.

The figures recorded in the 2008 and 2012 editions of the *Agenda de la Comunicación* have been compared for the purposes of this study.[1] A comparative reading of the two editions issued five years apart discloses significant differences in both the numbers and profiles of foreign correspondents in Spain.

In 2008, 235 international media outlets had correspondents and stringers or freelancers in Spain on an ongoing basis. The breakdown of these media outlets was as follows:[2] 92 newspapers, 64 radio and television stations, 43 news agencies, and 36 magazines. By 2012, the figures had changed significantly: the number of media outlets had declined by 14 per cent, yielding a new total of 202. The detailed breakdown comprised 89 newspapers (–3.3 per cent), 49 radio and television stations (–23.4 per cent), 40 news agencies (–7.0 per cent), and 24 magazines (–33.3 per cent). These figures show a variety of shifts depending on the type of media involved: while newspapers and news agencies experienced a slight decline, both radio and television stations and magazines saw a substantial numerical fall.

However, this decrease in the overall number of foreign media outlets was not mirrored in the proportional representation of countries with at least one media representative based in Spain. In 2008, 44 countries had accredited media representatives in Spain; five years later, in 2012, this figure had increased slightly to 45.[3] Although the overall number remained more or less unchanged, there was some internal variation: Bolivia, Lithuania, Nicaragua, and Senegal were among the 44 countries registered in 2008; these four countries were not on the 2012 list, but the following five countries had been added: Guatemala, Moldova, Serbia, Sweden, and Thailand. As far as continents are concerned, Europe topped the list in both editions: 19 countries in 2008 and 21 in 2012; followed by the Americas (16 countries in 2008 and 15 in 2012), Asia (five countries in 2008 and six in 2012), and finally Africa (four countries in 2008 and three in 2012). No media outlet from Oceania had a correspondent resident in Spain in either 2008 or 2012.

According to the 2012 edition of *Agenda de la Comunicación*, the overall number of foreign correspondents and stringers working in Spain was 258, with 188 male correspondents and 70 female correspondents. A total of 113 FCs were working for print media, 89 for news agencies, and 56 working for broadcast media.

WHICH COUNTRIES DO THE FOREIGN CORRESPONDENTS COME FROM?

Which countries had the highest rates of media representation in Spain? The top three countries on the list in 2012 were Germany, with 30 media outlets and 36 journalists; the United States, with 20 media outlets and 48 journalists; and France, with 16 media outlets and 22 journalists. The rest of leading positions, with at least 10 foreign correspondents, were for Mexico (13 media outlets and 16 journalists), Russia (11 media outlets and 13 journalists), the United Kingdom (10 media outlets and 13 journalists), and Morocco (five media outlets and 10 journalists). The top-five list in 2008 was slightly different, although the top three remained unchanged over the five-year period: first Germany, second the United States, third France, fourth the UK, and fifth Mexico.

There were no surprises on the list of cities in which media outlets or representatives were based. In 2008, 189 media outlets had a correspondent's office in Madrid (83.3 per cent), 20 in Barcelona (8.8 per cent), and

13 in other cities (5.7 per cent); the other five media outlets (2.2 per cent) did not indicate the city in which they were located. In 2012, the number of outlets based in Madrid had fallen to 149 (71.6 per cent); the number in Barcelona remained unchanged at 20 (9.6 per cent); there were 19 (9.1 per cent) in other cities; and finally, 20 media outlets (9.6 per cent) did not indicate their geographical base. It may be inferred that a significant number of the latter category had correspondents based in Madrid, which implies that the primary base for foreign correspondents and stringers is the capital of Spain.

Another key aspect in this analysis is the development of the professional profile of FCs. In relation to international media outlets, the *Agenda de la Comunicación* distinguishes between foreign correspondents and stringers. The former are staff journalists on a fixed salary, whereas the latter are paid on a per-item basis for each news story published or broadcast. The figures in this regard disclose a decline in job security among foreign media personnel based in Spain. Of the 235 media outlets in the country in 2008, 147 had correspondents and 88 used stringers; of the 202 outlets in the country in 2012, only 119 had correspondents and 83 relied on the services of stringers. In other words, while 62.6 per cent of the foreign media outlets had correspondents based in Spain in 2008, this number had fallen to 58.9 per cent by 2012.

A further indicator of the professional context in which FCs are working is the number of journalists based at the correspondent's offices. This figure is also available in the *Agenda de la Comunicación*, which lists the journalists working for each international media outlet with a base in Spain. In 2008, 24 of the 235 media outlets (10.2 per cent) had more than one correspondent or stringer to cover the news about Spain (four newspapers, seven radio and television stations, 13 news agencies, zero magazines). In 2012, the overall percentage rose slightly to 11.3 per cent; 23 international media outlets (out of the total of 202) had more than one journalist in Spain (four newspapers, nine radio and television stations, 10 news agencies, zero magazines). In 2012, the ranking of international media outlets with most employees in Spain was led by news agencies: *Reuters News* (United States, 11 journalists), *Bloomberg News* (United States, seven journalists), *Agence France Presse* (France, seven journalists), *Associated Press* (United States, six journalists), *Maghreb Arabe Presse* (Morocco, six journalists), and *Dow Jones Newswires* (United States, five journalists).

In light of this general overview of international media outlets in Spain, an in-depth account of the professional profiles of FCs and the typical features of their work are now presented. The data discussed are taken from the same questionnaire used to generate information for the other country-specific chapters in this book. The information relates to a total of 29 completed questionnaires,[4] as well as two in-depth interviews.[5]

As regards linguistic proficiency, all of the respondents claim to have either native-level (17) or at least a fluent (12) knowledge of Spanish. This response is significant, especially given the fact that only nine of the correspondents involved are from Spanish-speaking countries.[6] Thus, it is clear that advanced competence in the language of the host country is vital. English ranked second in the list of languages correspondents could use proficiently, followed in descending order by French, German, Portuguese, and Italian. The lack of proficiency in Portuguese is striking not only because Portugal borders Spain but also because 13 of the questionnaire respondents said that they cover news events in both countries. Indeed, such multijurisdictional coverage is standard practice: only 10 of the respondents said their remit was limited to Spain; the responses offered by the others varied: in addition to news coverage on Portuguese events, they covered stories in the Maghreb (three), France (two), and the rest of the EU (one).

In general, those interviewed had well-established careers in journalism: on average, 17 years of journalistic experience. The average time the journalists had spent working in the role of foreign correspondent was 11.4 years, and, more specifically, they had worked for 10.8 years in Spain, on average. Only three of the 29 respondents said they had fewer than five years of journalistic experience; 12 of the respondents had more than 20 years of such experience.

A variety of reasons were cited for having chosen Spain as a professional base: the most common were that the media outlet they worked for had proposed the move (10), followed by experience or a personal interest in the country (nine). Only one respondent referred to salary as a prime reason.

FCs based in Spain tend to be involved in a range of media roles: while just over half of those surveyed (15) said they work for a single media outlet, the rest responded that they work for two outlets (two journalists), three outlets (four), four outlets (four), and even five or more media outlets (four). In in-depth interviews, the journalists confirmed this increase in multitasking. 'You have to work for several media outlets at the same time to earn a wage you can live on', one of the interviewees remarked. However, it was also noted that greater instability in working practices does not affect all correspondents in the same way. One said that 'there are generational differences: veteran journalists long established in their media organisation have experienced no change in terms of standard of living, whereas those starting out now have to work for several media outlets at the same time'. The other interviewee noted that such instability has also had an impact on personnel in correspondent's offices through 'cuts in the number of journalists in the office and an obligation to produce more; stringers have been affected more by pay cuts'. Nevertheless, the two interviewees agreed that the working conditions of foreign correspondents—above all, in terms of salary—are better than their Spanish counterparts. The following figures issued by *FAPE* (*Federación de Asociaciones de la Prensa de España*, the Federation of Press Associations in Spain) are relevant in this regard: between 2008 and late 2012, over 10,000 journalists lost their jobs in Spain, and approximately 70 communication media organizations were closed down (*ElMundo.es*, 2013).

By far the most common type of media outlet foreign correspondents work for is newspapers (20 of the 29 respondents), followed by magazines (nine), online media (seven), news agencies (seven), public television (six), and radio stations (four). Most of these media outlets have an international remit (17), although there are also a significant number of national media (12); in contrast, however, none of the questionnaire respondents worked for local or regional media outlets. The in-depth interviews, however, disclosed the growing rate of online publication in work commissioned from correspondents: 'it's become more and more common for the newspaper to ask you to submit an article but, because of cutbacks in spending on paper or the need to inform the public immediately, in the end the report appears only in the online edition'.

WHAT STORIES DO THE FOREIGN CORRESPONDENTS COVER?

A reading of the study also discloses a set of professional patterns among foreign correspondents in Spain as regards work practices. Most of those surveyed said that they cover news stories relating to politics (25), the economy (24), and, to a lesser extent, society (20) and culture (19); other areas are of much less importance: sports (seven), science and technology (one), travel (one), and history (one). The correspondents who were interviewed cited increasing interest in economic news about Spain, in light of the ongoing financial crisis. 'In the past, news about the economy came in a distant second place, but now it's regarded as equally important or even more important than news about politics'. The decision to cover a particular news story was said to be the prerogative of the FC him-/herself always (six) or 'almost always' (19); only four respondents said that approximately half the time the idea of covering a particular story came from the media outlet's central newsroom.

HOW OFTEN DO FOREIGN CORRESPONDENTS FILE STORIES?

There was significant variation among FCs in terms of the number of news stories to be covered per week. Although the average ranged between four and five items per week, five correspondents stated that they were required to file only one story per week, and four journalists said that they publish up to—and even more than—25 items per week. However, it should be noted in this regard that the latter were likely to be full-time employees of news agencies, whereas the former tended to be part-time stringers or freelancers.

The percentage of news stories filed that went on to be published was high: half of the respondents (14) said that 100 per cent of the news stories they submitted were published by their media outlet(s). Only six correspondents said that the figure fell below 70 per cent. When asked about the significance of news items about Spain for the target audiences of their media outlets, the FCs responded with a relatively high importance rating: 3.5 on a five-point scale.

WHERE DO THE FCs GET THEIR STORIES?

As regards the sources consulted in drafting news stories, the most commonly cited were as follows: national media in Spain (21), government spokespeople (18), researchers and academics (14), NGOs (11) and other Spanish sources. In relation to the accessibility of such sources, researchers and academics were rated most accessible, followed by trade union representatives; by contrast, the least accessible were representatives of the government and, to a lesser extent, of the opposition parties.

The internal factors exerting the most influence on the work practices of foreign correspondents were deadlines, the availability of budgets and resources for reporting, and the views of editorial supervisors; on the other hand, the least influential factors were advertising concerns, the profit motive, and the views of media outlet owners. External factors (such as pressure from government representatives, political parties, trade unions, the business community, etc.) were generally regarded as having relatively little influence.

HOW DO FOREIGN CORRESPONDENTS REGARD THEIR PROFESSION?

By and large, FCs were somewhat pessimistic regarding professional prospects and expectations: the overall view was that the quality of working life for FCs had deteriorated in recent years and that media outlets had imposed budget restrictions on such work. At the same time, most of the correspondents said that they felt under greater pressure in their jobs and that cutbacks in the number of foreign correspondents over the last decade were now an established trend.

CONCLUSIONS

Finally, the data in the study allow us to trace a general portrait of FCs in Spain, who tend to be male; with an average age of 39; married; of no declared religious affiliation; with university training in journalism, educated to the master's level; and earning an average net monthly salary of between €2,000 and €3,000 per month for their work as journalists. In this regard, it should be noted that the calculation of the average monthly wage was based on the earnings of both journalists on full-time contracts (14) and freelancers and stringers (15).

In relation to working conditions, it should also be noted that of the 29 correspondents who filled in the questionnaire, half (15) said that they belong to a trade union or a professional association for journalists either in Spain or in their home countries. In 2013, there were three organizations in Spain related in one way or another to the work of FCs. Two of these were specifically for journalists from overseas based in this country: the *Círculo de Corresponsales Extranjeros en España* (the Association of Foreign Correspondents in Spain; www.corresponsales.com), which has 87 members, and the *Asociación de Corresponsales de Prensa Extranjera* (ACPE: the Association of Foreign Press Correspondents; www.corresponsales.org), which has 89 members. The third organization is the *Asociación de Periodistas Europeos* (APE, the Association of European Journalists; www.apeuropeos.org), which was founded in 1981 as the Spanish branch of a preexisting European association. The members of APE, which had a membership of 134 in 2013, are Spanish journalists for the most part, but a significant number of FCs are also involved.

NOTES

1. These two editions were carefully chosen for three reasons: (1) the five-year gap enables some insight into long-term development and (2) a comparative account of the situation at the start (2008) and height (2012) of the economic crisis; and (3), the 2012 figures are the most up-to-date available at the time of writing.
2. Neither the 2008 nor the 2012 edition of the *Agenda de la Comunicación* includes a specific category for online media; nor does either deal with radio and television stations separately: both radio and TV are listed under the same heading.
3. The list is composed of the following 45 countries: Algeria, Argentina, Austria, Belgium, Brazil, Bulgaria, Canada, Chile, China, Colombia, Cuba, Denmark, the Dominican Republic, Ecuador, Egypt, Germany, Finland, France, Greece, Guatemala, Iceland, Iran, Israel, Italy, Japan, Mexico, Moldava, Morocco, the Netherlands, Paraguay, Peru, Poland, Portugal, Qatar, Rumania, Russia, Serbia, Sweden, Switzerland, Thailand, Turkey, the United Kingdom, the United States of America, Uruguay and Venezuela.
4. Data collection for Spain was carried out using an online questionnaire sent to each of 194 foreign correspondents individually in February 2013. The addresses were taken from the 2012 edition of the *Agenda de la Comunicación*. At the same time, the *Asociación de Corresponsales de Prensa Extranjera* (*ACPE* [Association of Foreign Press Correspondents]) also contributed to the project by distributing the questionnaire among their 89 members via a private mailing list. Despite these various efforts, the response rate was quite low: 29 correspondents or stringers filled in and returned the questionnaire

(that is, 14.9 per cent of 194 journalists listed in the *Agenda de la Comunicación*).

5. These interviews were conducted in April 2013 with two of the 29 foreign correspondents who had submitted the online questionnaire. So as to prompt interpretations of the data obtained in the previous stages of the research, the interviewees received a summary of the findings a few days prior to the interview. The profile of the interviewees was as follows: the first is a French national, male, 30 years old, who works in a regular way for a newspaper and for a public radio station in France; the other interviewee is a journalist from Colombia, male, 36 years old, who works as a freelancer for a newspaper in the United States and who works occasionally for four other media outlets in different countries.
6. The nationalities of respondents were as follows: five from Spain, five from France, three from Germany; and one journalist from each of the following countries: Algeria, Argentina, Austria, Brazil, China, Colombia, Denmark, Finland, Guatemala, Italy, Mexico, Morocco, Portugal, the Netherlands, the United Kingdom, and the United States.

REFERENCES

BARRERA, C. (1995). *Periodismo y franquismo. De la censura a la apertura* [Journalism and Francoism. From Censorship to Liberalization]. Barcelona: Ediciones Internacionales Universitarias.

ElMundo.es. (2013). El periodismo español ha sufrido más de 10.000 despidos en cuatro años [Spanish Journalism Has Seen More Than 10,000 Layoffs in Four Years] [Online]. Available from http://mun.do/1l0Q9XY.

HAUBRICH, W. (1999). Corresponsales extranjeros: En la España de Franco y de la transición [Foreign Correspondents: In the Spain of Franco and the Transition]. *Claves de Razón Práctica.* (December), pp. 67–71.

LÓPEZ ROMERO, L. (2009). Prensa extrajera en España. La integración social a través de los medios escritos [The Foreign Press in Spain. Social Integration through Print Media]. *Telos: Cuadernos de comunicación e innovación*, 80 [Online]. Available from http://bit.ly/1toa1pB.

Ministerio de la Presidencia. (2008). *Agenda de la Comunicación 2008*. Madrid: Ministerio de la Presidencia.

———. (2012). *Agenda de la Comunicación 2012.* Madrid: Ministerio de la Presidencia.

MORENO CANTANO, A.C. (2006). El control de la prensa extranjera en España y Alemania durante la Segunda Guerra Mundial [Foreign Press Control in Spain and Germany during the Second World War]. *Historia Contemporánea.* 32, pp. 311–334.

PRESTON, P. (2009). *We Saw Spain Die: Foreign Correspondents in the Spanish Civil War, revised and expanded edition.* London: Constable and Robinson.

SINOVA, J. (1989). *La censura de prensa durante el franquismo* [Press Censorship under Franco's Regime]. Madrid: Espasa-Calpe.

24 Foreign Correspondents in Sweden

Professional Challenges and Strategies of Domestication

Jessica Gustafsson and Andreas Widholm

INTRODUCTION

In recent years, news organizations across the world have undergone significant changes due to technological developments and increased economic pressures. As a consequence, newspapers as well as broadcasters have been forced to cut budgets and decrease the number of foreign correspondents (Hamilton & Jenner, 2004). This process has taken place in a time marked not only by extended political integration but also by severe economic crises across Europe. Most studies devoted to international news conclude that foreign news reporting is governed by a national logic, meaning that news stories are adapted to fit the demands of predominantly nationally oriented news markets (Shoemaker, Cohen, Seo, & Johnson, 2012, p. 345; Strömbäck, Ørsten, & Aalberg, 2008). In a European context, Raeymaeckers, Cosijn, and Deprez (2007) have revealed that correspondents working in Brussels tend to connect a good EU story with 'domestic issues' or with issues that have 'relevance for national policy'. Against this background, the aim of this study is to map the broader field of foreign correspondents (FCs) operating in Sweden. The chapter will draw attention to the media organizations the FCs represent, the type of news they produce, and what implications the aforementioned political and economic changes have on newsgathering and working conditions.

When discussing the role of FCs in Sweden, it is necessary to reflect on some of the unique features of Sweden. Politically, Sweden has a long history of social democracy, which has had a profound impact on the social, political, and economic structures of the country (Möller, 2007). Like its Nordic neighbours, Sweden has one of the world's most extensive welfare systems, and historically the country has also been associated with a flourishing industry through companies such as IKEA, Volvo, SAAB, and H&M. After experiencing an economic crisis in the beginning of the 1990s, the welfare system began to erode as the government was forced to execute extensive cuts in public spending. In addition, the process of adapting to the increasingly globalized economy has been far from smooth.

Since 1991, Sweden has had seven governments, of which only three have been led by the Social Democrats. The Alliance, a centre-right constellation of four parties including the Moderate Party, the Liberals, the Center Party, and the Christian Democrats, has won the last two elections. Since 2006, The Alliance has continued the privatisation of the public sector, a process that was initiated already in the 1990s. However, Sweden still has a comparatively strong welfare state and has suffered relatively lightly from the present financial crisis. In the latest election, the political structure became increasingly complex as the right-wing Sweden Democrats entered the national political scene with a populist and anti-immigration agenda that gave them 6 per cent of the votes. When Sweden entered the European Union in 1995, many argued that it represented the end of Sweden's traditional policy concerning neutrality (Strandbrink, 2003). Sweden's cooperation with NATO in international military operations and training has increased significantly in recent years, but unlike Norway and Denmark, Sweden is still not a member of the organization. Sweden also chose to stay outside the euro cooperation in a national referendum in 2003.

The Nobel Prize is a Swedish annual event that receives global media attention. Sweden is also famous due to its successfulness in the international cultural economy; it has many prominent icons, such as the pop group ABBA and the authors Astrid Lindgren and Stieg Larsson. Sweden has also become well known for Spotify, a company that delivers an online music streaming service to millions of listeners internationally.

Sweden's policies on social responsibility are also reflected in the Swedish media system. Extensive press subsidies and a strong public service system make Sweden a typical example of the democratic corporatist model as defined by Hallin & Mancini (2004). However, it has also been defined as a mixed system inasmuch as newspapers still are commercially driven, and the public service broadcasters compete with a myriad of national and global channels (Nord, 2008).

WHO ARE THE FOREIGN CORRESPONDENTS?

A key institution for FCs working in Sweden is the Swedish ministry of foreign affairs. The ministry is responsible for the accreditation of foreign journalists—a precondition to get access to political institutions and authorities. Accreditation by the ministry is also a requirement for membership in the Foreign Press Association of Sweden, an organization that is located in the press centre at the Ministry of Foreign Affairs. Based on the official list of FCs provided by the Ministry, we have identified 228 journalists representing media organizations from a variety of nations and regions across the world. Gender data on these correspondents were unavailable.

Media organizations based in Germany (represented by 27 FCs), the United States (25 FCs), and Finland (23 FCs) are most frequent, followed by a variety of transnational media located in the Middle East (17 FCs). The fact that many news organizations are targeting groups located in transnational settings is also evident in the relatively high figures for China. Of the 16 people working for Chinese media, nine represent *New Tang Dynasty TV*, a news organization broadcasting news in Chinese to a global audience. Additionally, about 60 per cent of FCs work for organizations located in Europe.

If we instead take a closer look at the type of medium that the FCs work for, print appears the most common (with 103 FCs working for this medium: 84 for newspapers, 19 for magazines), followed by news agencies (55 FCs). Broadcast media (70 FCs) can be further broken down into those working for TV (43 FCs), radio (17 FCs), and mix (10 FCs). Regarding news agencies, it is important to emphasize the strong role held by corporations located in either the United States (35.2 per cent), Great Britain (14.8 per cent), or France (9.3 per cent). Many FCs are also working for agencies based in Turkey (9 per cent). Needless to say, these numbers do not indicate whether the FCs are fully employed or work part-time; nor do they reveal details about the working conditions for FCs in Sweden, questions that we address more specifically in the following analysis.

The study is based on a twofold research design, combining an online survey with semistructured qualitative interviews. As already noted, we identified 228 FCs, yet the online survey could be distributed to only the 185 individuals with registered email addresses. Sixty-one FCs (33 per cent) responded, which has to be taken into consideration when analyzing the data. Besides the survey, seven semistructured qualitative interviews were conducted with FCs working for newspapers or agencies in Russia, Germany, Spain, Poland, Bangladesh, France, and China. The interviewees were selected strategically in order to get a varied sample representing both European and non-European media organizations. Germany, Spain, Poland, and France are all members of the European Union and therefore highly relevant for this study. Russia and China were considered important because they have a huge political and economic impact on Europe. Bangladesh was included in order to address the working conditions for an FC from a developing country. In addition, we consulted the director of the press centre at the Swedish ministry for foreign affairs, who gave us important insights into the world of foreign correspondents in Sweden. Combined, the different methodological approaches helped us understand the current situation for foreign correspondents in Sweden.

The traditional image of the foreign correspondent has been that of a journalist sent out for a limited period of time to cover a region for a news outlet 'back home'. Yet, as several studies of FCs have shown, the working conditions are changing, which means that many of our understandings of the profession may no longer be valid (Hamilton & Jenner, 2004). For example, a majority of the respondents in this study, 62 per cent, stated that personal reasons motivated their present stay in Sweden. Only 27 per cent had professional reasons for coming to Sweden, most likely being sent by their employers. One of the interviewees came to Sweden due to a scholarship from the Swedish writers union, and even though professional reasons motivated the relocation, it was not linked to the person's profession as a journalist/correspondent. Eleven percent stated that they were born and raised in Sweden, which is a group of professionals who have great knowledge of the national setting in which they operate. In addition, they are financially viable to employ, being already positioned in Sweden (cf. Hamilton & Jenner, 2004). Although they are highly familiar with their home country, a drawback is that they might not be as familiar with the context where potential readers are located, which could be argued to be equally important. On the other hand, as natives, they have the advantage of language skills, which is crucial in order to be able to follow press conferences and other proceedings. The press officer at the Ministry for Foreign Affairs also emphasized language skills as very important, and he told us that most correspondents speak Swedish fluently. The journalist from China also said that she actually learned Swedish as a strategic choice because it made her unique and specialized in an increasingly competitive labour market.

It has been argued that in recent decades the working conditions for journalists in general and for FCs in particular have been altered in a direction often framed as negative for the profession. One aspect of this development is the type of contract that the journalist has with the employer. According to this study, 38 per cent of the FCs in Sweden are employed full–time, and 10 per cent have part-time contracts. As many as 52 per cent state that they work as freelancers or stringers. A German journalist emphasized the change within the profession: 'A few years ago I would recommend young people to become journalists. Today I don't. You just have to look at the working conditions of journalists today. You work as a freelancer, you have to cover all the costs and the risks are too high'.

Several correspondents told us how they have lost their full-time contracts and have been forced to become freelancers. One of them expressed it as 'being homeless'. However, some also expressed the new development in more positive terms: 'I left *Le Monde* in order to get more time to write. Currently, I am writing a book about the History of the Nobel Prize. As a freelancer you are freer. You don't have a boss and can therefore say 'no' to assignments. At the same time it is less financially stable'.

He also stressed that there are differences among newspapers, for example between his former employer *Le Monde* and *Le Croix*, which he represents today. When you work for an internationally renowned paper, it is much easier to get interviews, whereas you have to fight much harder when representing a smaller contender. Working for *Le Monde* also came with other benefits:

> The newspapers try to cut their costs. One has to be sensible financially; one cannot travel as much as before. If I were still working for

Le Monde I would not say the same. Then I would still be at a newspaper that still believes in sending their reporters out to the field and are still prepared to pay for it. Now I work for the newspaper *La Croix*, that has not got the same focus nor does it use its freelancers in the same way.

Differences among employers were also something that the correspondent from Bangladesh has had experience with: 'I can also work for Bengali newspapers, and I do it sometimes but I can't do it as seriously as I want to. If I invest time and energy here the payment is not good for me. The newspapers are not in the position to commission articles from here'.

For the majority of the journalists interviewed in this study, it is difficult to survive. According to the survey, the majority (55 per cent) stated that they write for newspapers. 37 per cent stated that they work for television, and as many as 35 per cent said that they work for news agencies. Thirty per cent of the respondents produce pieces for radio, and 23 per cent work for different online services. These figures suggest that many journalists work for several different media on a freelance basis. The survey shows that, on average, FCs work for three different media houses simultaneously. In addition, as much as 44 per cent are engaged in other work apart from journalism, most likely due to the fact that the amount of work they get as freelancers is not enough to sustain them financially. However, there are always exceptions to the rule. The correspondent from China told us that she used to cover Sweden, Denmark, Norway, and Iceland, yet new offices have been put up in both Denmark and Norway; thus the area of coverage has decreased. She has not experienced any financial cutback or that her working conditions have become harder, and she believes the explanation is that her employer is state owned and therefore gets the funds it needs.

REPORTING AGENDA: WHAT BECOMES NEWS AND WHEN?

Not surprisingly, politics appear to be the most common area of investigation for a correspondent working in Sweden. When asked what type of stories they mostly cover, 90 per cent answered politics, but economy, social questions, and culture were other themes that stood out as particularly prominent (see Figure 24.1).

The Polish journalist said that she often reports about Sweden as being a role model in some aspects because Sweden is 'ahead in terms of equality and ecology'. The French correspondent also underlined the strong focus on social issues: 'In France we are still convinced that there exists this social laboratory here in the North. To a certain degree it is true at least

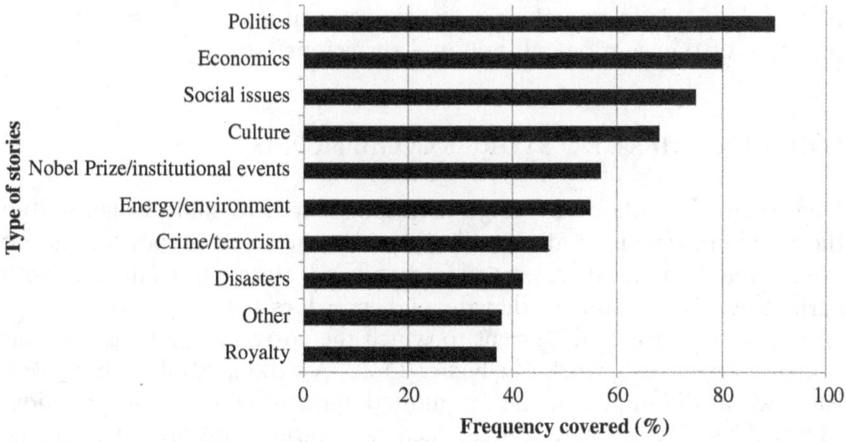

Figure 24.1 Stories covered in Sweden.

Question wording: 'What type of stories do you mostly cover?'

if you compare to France that is fairly conservative and where it takes a long time to change these things'.

Swedish culture is also one aspect that is popular to report about, at least about those celebrations that are considered unique (correct or not) for Sweden. The Chinese correspondents specifically pointed out Midsummer traditions and Christmas celebrations, which were seen as 'completely different compared to the Chinese culture'. The Swedish model, social issues, and culture are issues that the correspondents single out as particularly Swedish, and they are all part of the history of social democracy in Sweden. When asked to reflect about this, one of the journalists answered that certain stereotypes about Sweden also often tend to be reproduced: 'The Swedish welfare system is still a big icon. Since I read Spanish newspapers, I know how they look at the reality; I know how they work. They want to see ice bears on the streets and snow, but they don't want to see the real life in Sweden'.

The role of correspondents is to make something unknown familiar in order for the audience to be able to relate to it. One correspondent talks about it in terms of 'parallel subjects, if there is a similar discussion in Poland', and another one suggests that he has to 'give a context, a frame so we can understand what is happening from a French point of view'.

Another way to make Swedish news more relevant and thus easier to pitch to their home desk is to make them European issues. The increasing support in Sweden for the Sweden Democrats is one example; the financial crisis and terrorism are others. Sweden's ambiguous relationship to the EU is another interesting topic to cover: 'It still feels like Sweden is not fully part of the EU even though you are. However, it is also interesting to tell the story of this cautious, distant and suspicious attitude'.

SOURCES: WHERE DO STORIES COME FROM?

One traditional role of a foreign correspondent is to share insights from the field with a wider audience. The journalist acts as a witness of current events and is a 'local' expert who travels to places and interacts with various actors and sources that the audience does not have access to.

The survey reveals the extent to which the correspondents use various sources in their daily work (see Figure 24.2.). A striking result is that Swedish news media appear to be the most dominant source of information, followed by classical elite sources such as governmental officials, experts, and business leaders.

Paradoxically, the chart also shows that social networks and colleagues seem to have little influence. This indicates that interaction with journalistic texts is highly important, whereas interaction with people in the same profession is not. However, the widespread use of news media is not surprising. Journalism is a key institution in the public sphere, and thereby it reflects central discourses and power constellations in a given society. Nevertheless, using news media as a tool to understand a society is not the same as using media as the major source when conducting journalism. Recent research on the development of online news often emphasizes that news institutions become increasingly dependent on the content provided by their competitors and that journalists consequently spend most of their time in front of their desks searching for stories online rather than in the traditional journalistic field (Paterson & Domingo, 2008).

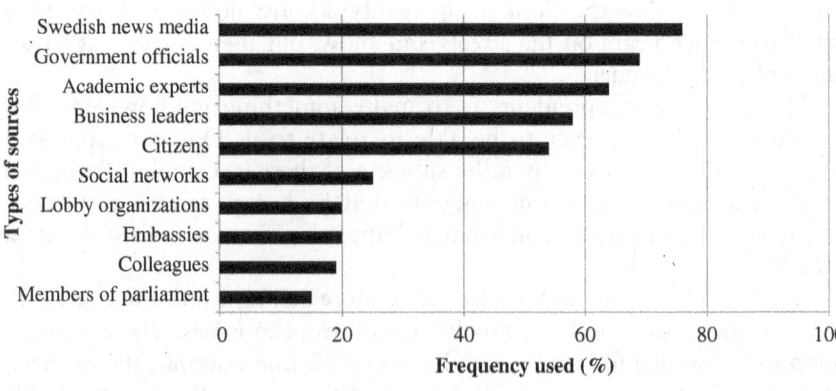

Figure 24.2 Important sources for FCs in Sweden.

Question wording: 'Which of the following sources would you regard as most important?'

The interviews underpin the notion that the Swedish news media are the most important source of information for a correspondent, but we also saw that adaptations and revisions are crucial elements in news work. A German correspondent, currently working for a business journal, explained it like this: 'The first source is the Swedish media. They play a very important role, but you need to find your angle, all aspects are not interesting for German readers. Sometimes you make an extra phone call and ask them [the cited actors in Swedish media] about issues of particular importance for Germany'.

The quote is also interesting in terms of how stories become foreign news because it indicates what previous research from a large array of countries has shown, namely how journalism is adapted through processes of domestication and that news reporting mainly follows a national logic (Riegert, 1998; Clausen, 2004; Shoemaker, Cohen, Seo, & Johnson, 2012). In this case, it is not only about selection of topics with relevance for a specific target group but also a way of adapting stories that originally were produced for another (national) audience. A correspondent from Poland explained that she always looks for ways to create a Polish 'niche', and the French reporter talked about 'context' and a 'French point of view'. These strategies are hardly surprising because every news media institution in the world needs to adapt content in ways that correspond to the demands of specific markets.

CONCLUDING REMARKS

Sweden is not a country that is prioritized by international news outlets, specifically not in a time characterized by financial crisis. This chapter has revealed that most FCs working in Sweden are hired as freelancers and that many of them also are engaged in other professional areas. Within such tough times, correspondents are increasingly pushed in a direction in which their role is 'doubled' because they need to be good journalists but also effective businesspeople, producing stories that are easy to sell. Drawing on our interviews, we have shown that Sweden's political history seems to impinge quite clearly on the news images of the country. The welfare system, environmental policies, and cultural news are examples that have been underlined as particularly central and saleable by the correspondents, potentially reinforcing rather stereotypical representations. The chapter has also showed that the FCs make use of various strategies of domestication, which makes their products more attractive and interesting for the media organizations they represent and in the end also for the audiences that consume the news. Domestication corresponds to national interest, expressed by one correspondent as 'parallel subjects'. These parallel subjects can either reinforce or contradict stereotypes about Sweden.

REFERENCES

CLAUSEN, L. (2004). Localizing the Global: 'Domestication' Processes in International News Production. *Media, Culture & Society.* 26 (1), pp. 25–44.
DE VREESE, C. (2003). *Framing Europe.* Somerset, NJ: Transaction.
HAFEZ, K. (2007). *The Myth of Media Globalization.* Cambridge: Polity.
HAMILTON, J., & JENNER, E. (2004). Redefining Foreign Correspondence. *Journalism.* 5 (3), pp. 301–321.
HALLIN, D., & MANCINI, P. (2004). *Comparing Media Systems: Three Models of Media and Politics.* New York: Cambridge University Press.
Merle, P. (2013). City of Lights? The Waning Elitism of US Correspondents in Paris between 1998 and 2010. *International Communication Gazette.* 75 (2), pp.157–173.
MÖLLER, T. (2007). *Svensk politisk historia: strid och samverkan under tvåhundra år.* Lund: Studentlitteratur.
NORD, L. (2008). Swedish Media System between Politics and Market. *Informacijos mokslai.* 47, pp. 10–21.
PATERSON, C., & DOMINGO, D. (EDS.), (2008). *Making Online News: The Ethnography of New Media Production.* New York: Peter Lang.
RAEYMAECKERS, K., COSIJN, L., & DEPREZ, A. (2007). Reporting the European Union: An Analysis of the Brussels Press Corps and the Mechanisms Influencing the News Flow. *Journalism Practice.* 1 (1), pp. 102–119.
RIEGERT, K. (1998). *'Nationalising' Foreign Conflict: Foreign Policy Orientation as a Factor in Television News Reporting.* DOctoral dissertation, Stockholm University.
SHOEMAKER, P., COHEN, A., SEO, H., & JOHNSON, P. (2012). Comparing News on Foreign and International Affairs. In ESSER, F., & HANITZSCH (EDS.), *The Handbook of Comparative Communication Research.* London: Routledge.
STRANDBRINK, P. (2003). Förnuftets entoniga röst: om EU-kampanjens demokratiska rum och medborgarskapets villkor. Huddinge: Södertörns högskola.
STRÖMBÄCK, J., ØRSTEN, M., & AALBERG, T. (EDS.). (2008). *Communicating Politics: Political Communication in the Nordic Countries.* Göteborg: Nordicom.

25 Foreign Correspondents in Switzerland

Hard News, No Chocolate

Michael Brüggemann, Guido Keel and Martina van Berkel

INTRODUCTION

Mapping the demographics and working practices of foreign correspondents is an important strand of research because correspondents are seen as important managers of meaning across national borders (Hannerz, 2004, p. 3). While there are a number of studies on foreign correspondents in the US (for an overview see Self, 2011, p. 30) and in some other European countries, and while some empirical research has been conducted on correspondents working for Swiss media titles (Gysin, 2000), there is no study focusing on foreign correspondents (FCs) in Switzerland. Filling this gap is of particular interest: Switzerland can on the one hand be seen as a country of great interest for a global media audience thanks to the presence of international business, international organizations and tourist attractions. On the other hand, it is also a very small, expensive country free of crisis, so one might also assume that not many foreign correspondents will be sent there.

Starting out with a theoretical reflection on the kind of news values that might apply to Switzerland, we will formulate hypotheses about the types of correspondents who work in Switzerland. This chapter will then map foreign correspondence in Switzerland. How many correspondents are there? Where are they from, which media outlets do they work for? And, finally, what topics do they work on? We would like to find out how topics like chocolate and mountains relate to stories about the UN institutions situated in Geneva or to the banking sector in Zurich.

SWITZERLAND—FROM THE PERSPECTIVE OF NEWS VALUE THEORY

News value theory assumes that journalists select events for publication depending on certain criteria of relevance (news factors) that journalists attribute to these events (Galtung & Ruge, 1965). This idea has been applied to explain why certain countries occur more frequently in foreign reporting than other countries; in research, this is sometimes referred to as 'news geography' (Rössler, 2004). The size, political and economic power of a country, its cultural and geographic proximity, and the presence of war and disaster, as well as structural factors like the presence of correspondents and news agencies, have been identified as important determinants of foreign coverage (Sreberny-Mohhamadi et al., 1985; Wu, 2000). As Galtung and Ruge (1965) had already predicted, the news factors work in a complementary as well as in an additive way: countries may get into the news because they are powerful or because they are a place of conflict and crisis. If both conditions are met, they will certainly get their place on the newsstand.

Applying this theory to Switzerland, we can say that the country is small, not particularly powerful, and there is neither war nor crisis—a country of low news value. Although Switzerland does have a tradition of being an international player both economically and politically, it does so behind the scenes. Its neutrality is an important part of its identity, and it stays away from open involvement in international conflicts. Even during World War II, with war raging all around the country, Switzerland remained an island of stability. Today, the economic, political, and social situation in Switzerland has brought a high level of economic welfare, leaving Switzerland virtually untouched by economic and financial crisis. This brings us to the more mundane reasons for expecting low levels of foreign correspondence from Switzerland: it is a very expensive country to live in and a difficult country to cover because a journalist needs to acquire at least a basic knowledge of three different languages (German, French, Italian).

Yet the very uniqueness of the country (often labelled 'Swissness'), with its diversity and the system of direct democracy as well as the beauty of the countryside, the tourist attractions, chocolate, and watches, could also attract journalistic interest. Although this might be the 'soft-news-reason' for sending journalists to Switzerland, other, harder factors enhance its newsworthiness. The reason why Switzerland is still an important location on the global map has to do with the stability, wealth, and absence of crisis: it has become a centre of international banking and trade. Besides being the home of various headquarters of multinational corporations, it is the seat of the headquarters of many international organizations, such as various United Nations organizations, the international football association FIFA, the International Olympic Committee (IOC), the International Red Cross, among others. All these factors result in a peculiar combination: a small and rather calm country with strong organizational ties to world politics and the global economy.

This leads us to expect more foreign correspondents being attracted to Switzerland than to other European countries of comparable size, such as Austria or Denmark. Also, we put forward the hypothesis that three different types of foreign correspondents can be expected in Switzerland One is traditional correspondent who covers Swiss politics and elections as well as chocolate, watches, and tourism. Following Hamilton and Jenner (2004), a second type might be labelled 'premium service foreign correspondent'. They are likely to specialize in economic coverage from the headquarters of banking and big business. Thirdly, a number of correspondents are likely to be tied to the international organizations situated in Switzerland. The empirical analysis will explore whether this scenario, derived from news value theory and an analysis of the country's general characteristics, is valid.

For the purpose of conducting a survey of foreign correspondents, however, it is first of all necessary to define the object of inquiry: a foreign correspondent (FC) can be defined as a journalist who works from and reports on a country different from the country where his employing media organization is located. This definition is meant to encompass the core of journalistic foreign correspondence. It excludes journalists working from the headquarters on international coverage (foreign editors) and journalists who come only for a short-term visit to a country (parachute journalists), as well as people who contribute to foreign correspondence in the widest sense but are not professional journalists (e.g., in-house correspondents—employees of big companies that report to their headquarters from their local office in Switzerland; see Hamilton & Jenner, 2004). Freelancers and part-time journalists, contrary to common practice in some journalist surveys, should by all means be included in our study because they are expected to form a significant proportion of contemporary foreign correspondents (Hamilton & Jenner, 2004). The traditional criterion of being employed full-time as a journalist with a fixed contract excludes a large group of people who do professionally contribute to foreign correspondence.

Although this definition is helpful in defining the object of interest, it is of limited help when it comes to the identification of individual correspondents for empirical research, as the following section will show.

METHOD

Different job titles, constant fluctuation, and a lack of motivation to be researched make it nearly impossible to survey all foreign correspondents in a given country. Because this is the first time a survey of foreign correspondents in Switzerland has been conducted, there are no existing data on the total number of FCs in Switzerland. Therefore, as a proxy for the unknown population, a sampling population comprising at least the 'core' population needed to be put together in several steps. For this purpose, the authors relied on existing registers of foreign correspondents in the country and added further research to fill in obvious gaps in existing lists of correspondents.

It was assumed that whoever worked as a foreign correspondent in Switzerland would either have to be registered as a foreign correspondent by the Swiss government if he or she was to report from the political capital of the country (Bern) or by the United Nations Media Centre if he or she was to report from the international organizations located in Geneva. Although the Swiss foreign office (EDA) disclosed only a list of registered foreign media titles without providing the names of individual foreign correspondents, the UN Media Centre provided the research team with a list of correspondents. In addition, this survey made use of the membership list of APES, the Foreign Press Association in Switzerland and Liechtenstein. Active members of the Association must be professional journalists working in Switzerland for one or more foreign press organizations headquartered abroad (APES, 2013). These lists were combined with correspondents' data obtained by contacting media houses that had correspondents registered with the Swiss foreign office but did not appear on the list of individuals provided by the UN and by APES and by conducting a general Internet search for foreign correspondents in Switzerland. Finally, the offices of the three leading news agencies *Reuters*, *AFP*, and *AP* were contacted and asked for a list of correspondents in Switzerland because we knew that they have offices in Zurich. With this combined search and after the elimination of correspondents appearing on several lists, a total of 202 foreign correspondents in Switzerland could be identified. During the process of conducting the survey, the list was further reduced by excluding people who did not work as foreign correspondents (anymore) to a sample of 189 foreign correspondents. This sample contains not all foreign correspondents but rather the core of people who produce foreign correspondence from Switzerland.

The actual survey was carried out using a standardized questionnaire developed for this volume. In Switzerland, the correspondents were contacted both in German and English, and they had a choice between these two languages when filling out the questionnaire online. Because Switzerland is a trilingual country, special emphasis was given to the correspondents' language skills.

After a pretest yielded some adjustments to the online questionnaire, the link to the survey was sent out in October 2012, and it turned out that 17 people were no longer working as correspondents in Switzerland and thus had to be eliminated from the sample. The final sample eventually consisted of 189 foreign correspondents. We were able to obtain the email addresses of 181 of them. Sixty filled out the questionnaire (response rate of 33 per cent).

WHO ARE THE FOREIGN CORRESPONDENTS IN SWITZERLAND AND WHOM DO THEY WORK FOR?

In our attempt to map foreign correspondents in Switzerland, we will therefore first look at the sampling population ($N = 189$) of the core foreign correspondents in Switzerland. Then we will compare it to the sample of survey responses (*N* = 60) in Table 25.1 in order to determine whether the sample of correspondents who have filled out the questionnaire is representative of foreign correspondents in Switzerland as far as very basic criteria, such as their local base and their gender, are concerned. Table 25.1 shows that the sample well represents the total population as far as the locations of correspondents are concerned (Zurich, Bern, Geneva). Yet with regard to gender, the sample has a bias: women are overrepresented among the 60 correspondents who filled out the questionnaire.

In order to respond to the question of mapping correspondents with regard to some very basic variables, we can draw on the target population (*N* = 189): Overall, roughly two-thirds (120) of all correspondents in Switzerland are male, one-third (69) are female (see Table 25.1). This is in line with the gender proportions among journalists in Switzerland in general (Keel, 2011, p. 160ff).

Identifying the 'home countries' of foreign correspondents, defined as the location of the headquarters of the media organization they work for and the audience they address, is less straightforward in Switzerland than expected. The reason is the prominence of a small number of transnational news agencies. Every fifth correspondent in Switzerland is affiliated with *Reuters*, *AP*, *Bloomberg*, *Dow Jones*, or *AFP*. They address audiences in different countries, and the location of their headquarters does not necessarily indicate a national affiliation: *Reuters*, traditionally being a British news agency, is situated in New York. Counting *Reuters* journalists as British leads to the impression that the UK is a country that is exceptionally interested in Switzerland. Placing the transnational news agencies in a separate category reveals a different picture: Among the top countries that send foreign correspondents to Switzerland are, unsurprisingly, the big neighbours: Germany (16 FCs), France (eight FCs), and Italy (eight FCs). The UK does not range among the top countries. Instead, Japan (16 FCs) and China (12 FCs) appear as major senders of foreign correspondents to Switzerland. They are important financial and economic players on the

Table 25.1 Population of foreign correspondents in Switzerland: sex and workplace.

Category	Characteristics	Population (*N* = 189) (%)	Survey Responses (*N* = 90) (%)
Sex	Male	(120)—64	52
	Female	(69)—36	48
Based in	Geneva and near Geneva	77	70
	Zurich and near Zurich	10	12
	Rest of Switzerland	2	2
	Outside of Switzerland	2	3
	No answer	9	13

global stage, and they send correspondents to Switzerland probably to report not about the country but about its banking sector and the transnational corporations situated there. Also, their print news outlets are less affected by the financial crisis than the newspapers of the United States and British newspapers and thus may have suffered from fewer cuts in the number of foreign correspondents. The United States has nine FCs in Switzerland, whereas Egypt and Brazil each have five FCs.

The nationality of the correspondents was covered by our questionnaire. The foreign correspondents are in fact less foreign than expected: one-fifth of the respondents in the survey say they have Swiss citizenship. The Swiss therefore represent the largest group in terms of citizenship, followed by the Germans, British, French and Japanese.

For reasons of limited space in this volume, only key results from the survey are summarized. First of all, it can be said that correspondents in Switzerland are well trained and experienced journalists. On average, they have been working as journalists for 20 years and as correspondents for 12 years, nine of them in Switzerland. Compared with the average Swiss journalist (see Keel, 2011), they have more professional experience. Also, a larger share of correspondents in Switzerland (92 per cent) have a university degree, compared to Swiss journalists (59 per cent).

When it comes to sociodemographics, the foreign correspondents surveyed are about the same age as their Swiss colleagues (47 years on average), and more than two-thirds say they live with a partner who also lives in Switzerland. Two-thirds also have children. With a little more than half earning €4,000 a month or less, the salaries of foreign correspondents are relatively small, considering the high costs of living in Switzerland.

Language skills are of particular interest in a small yet multilingual country like Switzerland. The survey shows that correspondents are not fully up to the challenge of the country's four official languages: their English is significantly better than their command of any of the official languages in Switzerland. Two-thirds of the correspondents say they speak French fluently; only half the correspondents say that they are fluent in German. This is a small share, taking into account that correspondents from Germany already form a very large group of all correspondents. English is the most important working language for 50 per cent of respondents, compared to 20 per cent for German and 20 per cent for French (and 10 per cent other). This can be seen as an indication that they gather their information from sources (international companies and organizations) that address an international rather than a Swiss audience in their PR activities. Foreign correspondents in Switzerland largely work for newspapers, news agencies, or public broadcasting organizations. Almost every second journalist works for either a newspaper or a news agency—sometimes among other employers. Private radio and TV play only a negligible role. No journalist works exclusively for an online outlet. This shows how foreign correspondence is very much dependent on a healthy press and public broadcasting. Having said that Switzerland has very a high cost of living, it is all the more surprising that two-thirds of the correspondents (and especially those from news agencies) work for only one media organization. Eighty-eight per cent work full–time, and almost 60 per cent are on a fixed contract. Almost one in two does not cover any other countries than Switzerland (and Liechtenstein). All this shows that the traditional foreign correspondent is alive and well in Switzerland. Hamilton and Jenner's (2004) assumption about the disappearance of the traditional elite correspondent does not seem to apply to Switzerland.

WHAT DO CORRESPONDENTS REPORT ON?

The correspondents say that they deal mostly with economic and political issues related to the UN, with economic stories being most important. Besides that, there are hardly any stories from the Swissness category (such as the mountainside, Swiss watches or chocolate, or the direct democratic system, to name just a few features typically associated with Switzerland), and domestic Swiss politics does not play an important role either. This can already be seen in the fact that the correspondents are either based in Zurich (the banking capital) or Geneva (the capital of international organizations) but not in Bern (the capital of Switzerland).

WHICH INFLUENCES AND WORKING CONDITIONS AFFECT FOREIGN CORRESPONDENTS?

The main sources for FCs' stories are the Swiss government, the UN and other official sources, the Swiss media, economic leaders, experts, and scientists. Two-fifths of the correspondents say that they monitor the Swiss media regularly. Other potential sources receive little attention, be it the average Swiss citizen, social media, or lobbies and associations. This reflects a strong elite orientation of correspondents in Switzerland. The view of ordinary Swiss people hardly plays a role in their reporting. Considering the fact that the knowledge of local languages is limited and that many correspondents are working in the world of international organizations in Geneva or in the corporate world in Zurich, it is all the more surprising that only little attention is paid to other foreign correspondents as well. A large majority of correspondents say that they hardly ever work with their colleagues. In spite of assumptions about journalistic collaboration, one-third say that they are not influenced in their work by their fellow correspondents.

Correspondents see their access to primary information from government agencies as good. More than half the correspondents say that access to government information is easy or very easy. In contrast, access to information

Table 25.2 Trends in foreign correspondence.

Trends	Mean	Total of Values 4 and 5 (%)
Decreasing availability of resources	3.5	51
Increasing work pressure	3.5	52
'The audience cares less about international news nowadays'	3.0	42
Parachute journalists are increasingly used as replacements	2.9	36
Afraid of job cut	2.8	29
Decreasing number of correspondents (job cuts)	2.7	31
Local journalists are increasingly used as replacements	2.7	32
Foreign coverage is increasingly done from headquarters	2.6	29
Amateur journalists/bloggers are increasingly used as replacements	2.0	14

Notes: 1 = not at all, 5 = to a great extent. Different letters mark significantly different means (CI of 95 per cent).

from corporations is significantly worse. One-third say that this information is hard or even very hard to obtain.

Finally, drawing on hypotheses that abound in the literature (e.g., Hamilton & Jenner, 2004), we have asked about the allegedly deteriorating working conditions of foreign correspondents (see Table 25.2). In our survey, correspondents could not agree on whether the situation has actually changed that much. Yet half of the correspondents say that their resources have been reduced and work pressure has increased. Many other trends that are sometimes taken as given in the academic debate about foreign correspondence apparently do not apply to Switzerland.

Journalists are divided over whether their audience has become less interested in foreign news. Even less relevant in the eyes of the correspondents are the alleged tendencies to replace correspondents with editors in their home countries, with works of native journalists in their guest country, or with contributions of citizen journalists, bloggers, and the like.

CONCLUSION: THREE TYPES OF FOREIGN CORRESPONDENCE RECONSIDERED

The results presented give a rough first impression of who the correspondents in Switzerland are and how they work, even though more in-depth studies are needed. In contrast to what is thought of as a universal trend in foreign correspondence, namely the decline of the elite correspondent who works full-time for traditional media outlets, we do find a relatively stable situation in Switzerland with journalists working for newspapers, news agencies, and public broadcasting with a regular contract and income, working full-time as correspondents. This finding sends an important message as to why it is important to study countries other than just the United States and correspondents other than US correspondents that are the focus of many of the international studies on foreign correspondence: in other countries with a vastly different context for foreign correspondence, we find different trends, and Switzerland might be an extreme example of this.

Coming back to the assumptions presented at the beginning of the chapter, we can conclude that, contrary to our expectations, two types of correspondents are important for Switzerland. Firstly, there is the 'premium-service' correspondent working on economic issues, trade, and banking for a global news agency and sometimes for a newspaper. Secondly, there is the correspondent in Geneva who caters to the UN institutions and other international organizations. Our third type, the Swissness correspondent who produces feel-good stories about Switzerland but also focuses on Swiss national politics, is almost nonexistent. This can possibly be explained with the higher news value of international organizations and stories on the financial industry compared to that of Swiss culture and politics. Even though international organizations and corporations constantly produce news through their ongoing activities, the traditional Swiss topics are rather static. Or to put it in other words: the Alps, the chocolate, the watches might be famous, but they have been so for many years. There is nothing new about them.

Hard news turns out to be much more important than chocolate for the relatively high number of foreign correspondents in Switzerland. Switzerland as a country is not the focus of foreign correspondents situated in Switzerland. The country is relevant mostly as the home of UN organizations and as a centre of international economic activity.

The correspondents surveyed in this study are key actors when it comes to news from and about Switzerland and the organizations and companies located in the country. However, if we are interested in how the image of Switzerland in the global news environment is forged, we would also need to study how the information provided by the correspondent eventually finds its way into the newspaper, TV station, or news Website. Furthermore, correspondents are by no means the sole source of news. Media rely on other sources, such as public relations information, parachute or travel correspondents, or social media, to report on what is happening in Switzerland. Our study shows that among the different sources of foreign correspondence, the traditional correspondent is alive and well in Switzerland. Deteriorating working conditions are felt by half of the correspondents. Yet this statement also means that they are not felt by the other half. Future research should go deeper into explaining why this is the case.

Sweeping statements about the demise of the traditional foreign correspondents may be wrong, but also the specific conditions of reporting from Switzerland should be kept in mind: global news agencies reporting financial information about the banking sector may not suffer to the same degree than the traditional correspondent reporting about a foreign country. Foreign correspondence thrives, at least where there is economic demand for it. And this demand does exist concerning not only the banks and corporations but also the international institutions situated in Switzerland.

REFERENCES

APES (2013). How to Join APES. www.apes-presse.org/en/members/how-to-join-apes/. Retrieved on July 30, 2014.

GALTUNG, J., & RUGE, M.H. (1965). The Structure of Foreign News. The Presentation of the Congo, Cuba and Cyprus Crisis in Four Norwegian Newspapers. *Journal of Peace Research*. 2, pp. 64–91.

GYSIN, N. (2000). *Der direkte Draht zur Welt? Eine Untersuchung über Auslandskorrespondentinnen und -korrespondenten Deutschschweizer Printmedien*. Bern: Institut für Medienwissenschaft, Universität Bern.

HAMILTON, J., & JENNER, E. (2004). Redefining Foreign Correspondence. *Journalism*. 5 (3), pp. 301–321.

HANNERZ, U. (2004). *Foreign News. Exploring the World of Foreign Correspondents*. Chicago/London: University of Chicago Press.

KEEL, G.(2011). *Journalisten in der Schweiz. Eine Berufsfeldstudie im Zeitverlauf*. Konstanz: UVK.

RÖSSLER, P. (2004). Political Communication Messages: Pictures of Our World on International Televison News. In ESSER, F., & PFETSCH, B. (eds.), *Comparing Political Communication. Theories, Cases, and Challenges*. Cambridge: Cambridge University Press, pp. 271–293.

SELF, C. (2011). Theoretical Perspectives and Research Methods in Studies of Foreign Correspondence. In Gross, P., & KOPPER, G. G. (eds.), *Understanding Foreign Correspondence. A Euro-American Perspective of Concepts, Methodologies, and Theories*. New York: Peter Lang, pp. 29–44.

SREBERNY-MOHAMMADI, A., NORDENSTRENG, K., STEVENSON, ROBERT, U., and OKWU, F. (1985). Foreign News in the Media: International Reporting in 29 Countries. *Reports and Papers on Mass Communication*. 93.

WU, D.H. (2000). Systemic Determinants of International News Coverage: A Comparison of 38 Countries. *Journal of Communication*. 50, pp. 110–130.

26 Foreign Correspondents in Turkey
Between the Home and Host Agendas

Eylem Yanardağoğlu and L. Doğan Tılıç

INTRODUCTION

The history of foreign press in Turkey can be traced back to the mid-19th century Ottoman Empire, the predecessor of modern Turkey. The Crimean War (1853–1856), which marked the emergence of a new type of journalist known as the 'foreign correspondent' and intensified the role of news agencies (Hess, 1996) in communication, also made Istanbul a centre of attraction for foreign media. Due to the city's strategic location, ships carrying soldiers and supplies back and forth docked at and sailed from Istanbul, making it also a place of refuge for the injured and casualties (Topuz, 2003). In the imperial capital, Istanbul, a considerable number of publications were also published in languages such as Armenian, Greek, and Arabic, which belonged to some of the ethnic and linguistic communities of the Ottoman Empire (Yanardağoğlu, 2009).

Despite the existence of a multilingual press system, Sultan Abdulhamid II (1842–1918), ruled with an extensive intelligence network and applied censorship. He considered foreign publications as '*evrak-i fesadiye*' (harmful documents) and banned their import into the Empire. Under his reign, only foreigners living in Istanbul could read the papers published abroad. The 'spies' of the Sultan took extreme measures to prevent them from reaching Turkish readers. Ironically, the Sultan himself was very much interested in foreign media coverage. The translation office in Yıldız Palace, regularly followed 154 foreign newspapers and journals and provided the monarch summaries and translations of important reports every day (Topuz, 2003, p. 80).

Despite Sultan Abdulhamid II's restrictive measures, *Havas News Agency* sent a reporter to Istanbul in 1854. A year later, the Vienna-Black Sea telegraph line was opened and connected to Istanbul. The *Havas* correspondent in Istanbul reported the development, noting, 'Istanbul is now connected to London via Paris' (Topuz, 2003, p. 81).

Istanbul was also *en route* to India. Several routes of the British Empire were indeed passing through the Ottoman Empire. *Reuters* news agency, which mainly operated in the realm of the British Empire, also realized the importance of Istanbul and sent a reporter there. In 1866, *Reuter*'s Istanbul-based correspondent received a privilege from the Ottoman government, which granted priority to *Reuters*' telegraphs (Storey, 1951).

Istanbul became an important centre for international news agencies, but reporting from abroad was an expensive business. On 17 January 1870, *Havas*, *Reuters*, and *Continental News Agencies* signed an agreement where they carved the world into regions of news coverage, within which the Ottoman Empire and Egypt comprised a 'common news region'. *Havas* and *Reuters* opened a joint bureau in Istanbul the same year, which became the first foreign news bureau in Istanbul (Topuz, 2003, p. 81).

During the Ottoman period, Istanbul was both an economic and political hub, making it a natural base for the national and foreign media. However, after the foundation of modern Turkey, Ankara became the new capital and political hub, and Istanbul remained as the commercial centre. According to this distinction, Istanbul hosted the headquarters for both Turkish and foreign media organizations. Ankara also held equal weight for national media.[1]

The Turkish Directorate General of Press and Information is the institution in Turkey where FCs should be registered for their accreditation and press cards. It was established in 1862 during the Ottoman period and continued its presence under different names during the Republican Era. It was rebranded as the Directorate General of Press and Information (*Basın Yayın ve Enformasyon Genel Müdürlüğü, BYEGM*) in 1984 and became affiliated with the Office of the Prime Minister.

Until the mid-1980s, many FCs preferred Athens over Istanbul and covered Turkey while being based in a 'European' city. They were living in Athens and flying to Istanbul and to other Turkish provinces when a news story developed in Turkey. Some then recruited Turkish 'stringers', who reported to the correspondent based in Athens. This situation eventually changed, and Turkey's appeal to international news organizations has risen dramatically in the last decade. In 1991, 85 accredited foreign reporters were based in Turkey; the number rose to 147 in 2000 and to 227 in 2005, according to the *BYEGM* Website.

BYEGM has kept the electronic records of accredited foreign media members since 1991, and its data demonstrate a steady increase in the number of correspondents in Turkey. The Directorate provided accreditation to 295 members of foreign media from 40 countries in 2011. In its 2013 report, the number of foreign media members was recorded as 327.[2] At the end of November 2013, the total number of foreign resident journalists accredited by BYEGM was 317.[3] Of this total number, 243 journalists are working for foreign media organizations, and 74 are working for Turkish media mostly in foreign languages.[4]

Officers working in the *BYEGM* attributed the increase in the numbers to be a positive result of better regulations and laws that governed the working conditions of FCs since the 1990s.[5] The shift took place in 1988 in the principles that apply to 'Foreigners Seeking to Do Scientific Research or Study or to Shoot Films and to Those Applying on Behalf of Foreigners and Foreign Members of the Media'.[6] The new principles aimed at providing FCs certain privileges for those journalists who get accredited in Turkey as resident journalists.[7]

The officers maintain that the new regulations were specifically aimed to attract FCs from Athens to Istanbul, by offering them a number of privileges provided that they make Istanbul their regional centre. The collapse of the Soviet Union in 1991 and the independence of Central Asian Turkic republics motivated FCs. It's clearly seen from the data of *BYEGM* that the number of FCs in Turkey more than doubled in the last 10 years.

It must be noted that FCs in Turkey always preferred Istanbul to Ankara. In addition to the historical reasons, choosing Istanbul as a base is also due to having access to better and more extensive direct international flight connections. There are also what we may call 'lifestyle' reasons for journalists to locate in Istanbul rather than Ankara because the city is considered to be a 'fascinating place' with a vibrant entertainment, music, and art scene.[8]

RESEARCH METHODOLOGY

The way foreign news outlets cover Turkey has been a matter of interest for the Turkish media. The national press usually dedicates space for the foreign media's comments on events in Turkish politics or social aspects. However, there was no empirical study of the ways in which international news regarding Turkey is produced on the ground. In this research, our aim is to focus on the issues/practices/challenges that influence the experiences and working routines of FCs based in Turkey.[9]

A total of 21 individuals responded to the online questionnaire that was developed with our colleagues for this book.[10] It was disseminated via a foreign correspondents' unofficial email group comprised of approximately 200 reporters at the time. The response rate to the online questionnaire was low, at around 10 per cent despite efforts to promote it three times in the email list. However, some correspondents were available for face-to-face interviews, which helped us to garner more in-depth data on their experiences.[11] Some of the reporters who gave face-to-face interviews between 2010 and 2013 are not based in Turkey any longer. Some of the interviewees have been in Turkey since the early 1980s and can be considered as 'local' journalists due to their various affiliations in the Turkish mainstream media. Similar to the Austrian chapter, we also adhere to a purely 'frequentist' approach to data evaluation due to low response rate to the online survey.[12]

WHO ARE THE FOREIGN CORRESPONDENTS?

Germany and Britain are the two European countries that have the largest number of correspondents in Turkey. Germany has the highest number of correspondents (37), represented by 32 different institutions (Germany's dominance in the field of FCs is reflected not in the online survey but in the in-depth interviews). The UK has 28 correspondents, represented by 28 different institutions. The United States has 34 correspondents and 45 different institutions. See Figure 26.1.

In the online questionnaire sample, there were 11 female and 10 male journalists. The ages of the FCs are divided. The majority of correspondents are younger than 50 years of age. More than half of the respondents (13) are between 30 and 49 years old, about a quarter are between 50 and 70, and only three respondents were younger than 30 years old. The nationality of respondents is spread out over a wide range of countries: two Spanish, four British, four American, three Turkish.[13] two Dutch, one Albanian, one Canadian, one Danish, one Finnish, one Greek, and one Moroccan.

More than half of the participants in the online questionnaire are single, one-third of them were married or in a relationship with a partner in Turkey, and only two had partners living outside Turkey. More than half of the respondents (13) did not have children. The correspondents have a high level of formal education: half of them hold bachelor's degrees, more than a third of them have master's degrees, and two participants hold doctoral degrees. Most FCs studied in the fields of humanities (journalism, languages, history) and social science (politics, sociology); two respondents studied arts subjects, such as photography, music, and theatre.

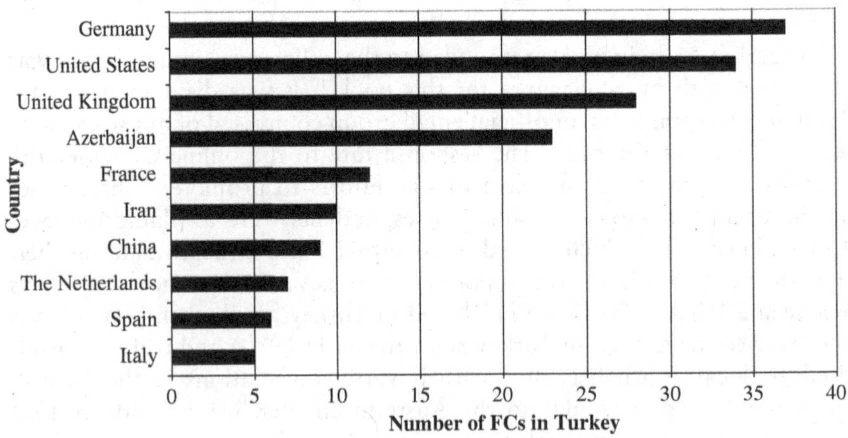

Figure 26.1 Top 10 countries with largest number of FCs in Turkey.

All correspondents in the online survey speak English fluently; about a third of them speak French on a fluent/native level and more than half of them on a basic level. Turkish language skills of the FCs are varied: about three-quarters of them had basic level competencies, one-fifth of them spoke Turkish at a native speaker level, and fewer than one-fifth stated that they spoke Turkish fluently.

PROFESSIONALISM

Almost all correspondents, (18 out of the 21) identified journalism as their main profession. When correspondents pursue other interests or part-time jobs, these include activities such as consultancy work on business and software; organizing lectures, research, or book projects; and translation or teaching languages (English). The correspondents in the online survey have spent a significant amount of time in journalism (average of 14 years). However, the number of years as an FC (average of 8.5 years) is considerably less. This would be due to the fact that the opportunity to work as an FC comes after some experience in the profession. Only a quarter of the respondents (6) indicated one media establishment as their prime employer. For the most part, correspondents work for more than one organization; four people work for two different organizations; two people work for three organizations; and the remaining respondents work for more than four organizations. In this light, about three-quarters of respondents work as freelancers, and they work for media organizations that have an international reach. Half of the FCs who responded to the question regarding their salary said they earn a net monthly income of between €1,000 and €4,000, three respondents said they earned more than €4,000, and seven said they earn less than €1,000 per month. During in-depth interviews, most journalists did not want to talk about their incomes.

The majority of respondents work for a print media organization. The distribution of public and private TV and radio are about the same (three or four correspondents each), but we must note that these outlets cross-cut each other, for instance, reporters working for an international news organization such as the BBC, will be expected to produce news for online, radio and TV platforms.

Participants of the online survey are actively using online platforms for journalistic purposes. More than half of the participants (14) use Facebook, a quarter use Twitter, and another quarter use personal Webpages, such as publishing platforms.

The average time frame our respondents have been reporting from Turkey is seven years. If we exclude the extremely long cases (36 and 29, respectively), the average number of years in Turkey drops to five. The reasons for choosing Turkey for a base as an FC brought mixed responses from respondents; more than a third of the respondents stated their main reason as 'personal interest to go abroad as a reporter', followed by another one-third of respondents who identified their main reasons as 'expertise/personal interest' in the country. We can see that in most cases, the reasons for choosing to be based in Turkey are personal, but another considerably significant reason for the respondents was the availability of posts/job offerings by the news organization they were working for. Three reporters stated a personal relationship and language skills.

REPORTING: HOW AND FOR WHOM?

Recent decades have seen a change in the way news is reported due to the concentration and conglomeration of Turkish media. This shift from traditional media ownership to concentrated forms of ownership begun in the 1980s and is characterized by media owners having investments in other economic areas, which can jeopardize their independence from the government in their businesses. This has led to a sensationalist and partisan (progovernment) reporting. Over the last 10 years, under the rule of the Justice and Development Party (AKP) of Prime Minister Recep Tayyip Erdoğan, self-censorship among Turkish journalists has risen considerably due to political, legal, and ownership-oriented pressures on journalists (Tılıç, 2009).

European journalists who are used to public authorities' accountability towards journalists and for sharing information with the public through the media, for example, could not imagine a PM asking media owners to sack a columnist, which happened in 2012 and 2013 at various occasions in Turkey. These FCs had to develop their own ways of obtaining reliable news over the years by creating their own networks and by developing the skill of 'reading between the lines' of Turkish newspaper reports and decoding the intricate relationship between newspaper owners and government.

For FCs, this has led to a weakening of their trust in the local media as a reliable source. Some correspondents pointed out that national news agency (*Anadolu Ajansı*) has become increasingly partisan in the last several years, and they use it as a source mostly to get exact quotes from the speeches of PM and ministers.

'Basic rules of reporting [are] often overstepped in Turkish papers. Sometimes I find very exciting news, which I myself wanted to work on and report, but I lose all my excitement after reading it all. They do not mention any source, or refer to an unknown source for very important news', said a German FC.

Almost all FCs underlined the problem of transparency in Turkey and the state's treatment of information.

> It was exactly the same in Greece before joining the EU and still it's a part of the culture of Greek bureaucracy. They treated the information they had as if it is their private property which they had to hide from others,

> from journalists. In other European countries bureaucrats and state officials consider the information as something they had to share with the public. They easily provide journalists the information they were asked for,

said a Greek journalist, stressing the difficulty of getting information from Turkish officials.

The survey and final interviews were conducted at a time (March and April 2013) when the Syrian conflict, the Kurdistan Workers Party (PKK) peace process, Kurdish cultural rights, and foreign policy made up the majority of the topics the correspondents dealt with.

Almost all foreign reporters consider themselves 'lucky' when compared to their colleagues in other countries where finding a 'story' can sometimes be difficult. The political agenda of Turkey has always been active, and this has turned the country and its surroundings into a 'paradise of news' for the reporters. 'Imagine being in Sweden or Norway. There you can find maybe in a year the exciting news stories you could find here in a few days', said an FC working for Spanish media.

FCs in Turkey consider themselves lucky for not having problems to find news, but on the other hand this means a higher workload for them. Half of the respondents reported that the interest of their editors in issues relating to Turkey has increased in the last five years.

When we consider the responses of the journalists, thematically, we can see that 'politics' and 'business' make the bulk of the typical stories correspondents in Turkey usually work on. But the nature of the media outlet usually dictates the theme or the style of the stories that are covered in relation to Turkey.

However, it was interesting to see how almost all the respondents were critical of the way their editors back in the 'home' country asked for what they considered 'cliché' news regarding Turkey. Ironically, this news, such as minority rights, freedom of expression, and Kurdish rights, also includes stories especially demanded by editors. During the in-depth interviews with correspondents, reporters made considerable effort to explain this dilemma and how they try to overcome it.

One of the respondents, a Dutch journalist, who studied Islamic history and culture, said he is fascinated by the modernization of Turkey as a Muslim country. In 2006, he quit his full-time job to become a freelancer for a major Dutch newspaper, only to be based in Turkey, which was his dream as a reporter since the early 1980s. He focuses mainly on news stories on economics, politics, and sports because he considers them interesting topics for the Dutch public. But he said he makes a conscious effort to go beyond hard news, which, he says, the editors sitting at the desk in Rotterdam can get from the wires. Instead, he focuses on stories that reflect 'under the surface developments and trends' in Turkey to allow his readers to form a more 'nuanced' opinion about Turkey. He believes this is necessary because, in his view, the public mainly has a negative perception of Turkey because of its negative preconceptions of the Turkish immigrant community living in Holland. To overcome such preconceived ideas, he says he focuses on Dutch entrepreneur investments in Turkey or on the Dutch footballers on Turkish teams as subjects of interest for Dutch readers.

Another respondent, a Spanish journalist working for a news agency, believes that the duty of the agency work is to

> summarize important daily news in the host country. This could be a speech by PM Erdoğan about [the] Kurdish peace process or an accidental shelling of Turkish territory at the Syrian frontier or an important soccer game. It can also include PKK conflict or peace process, too. Football, at the European level or Spanish teams involved, as well as visits by high-level foreign dignitaries.

According to a majority of interviewees, Turkey's experience as a predominantly Muslim secular country is also another major attraction for editors back 'home', but correspondents want to go beyond this and focus on other aspects, such as new trends; the impact of a globally interconnected Istanbul as a city that is a hub for the Balkans, Middle East, Central Asia, and Caucasus; the booming Turkish economy; and the 'trendy' art scene in Turkey.

A general trend that the in-depth interviews revealed is that the reporters consider themselves 'responsible for explaining the complexity of Turkey in Europe'.

CONCLUSION

FCs had no problem finding news stories in or around Turkey. The country's geopolitical position between the East and the West makes it attractive for international media institutions interested in covering European, Middle Eastern, and Central Asian politics and affairs. Depending on the political developments around Turkey's borders, as is recently the case with Syria, the interest of international media could shift into different issues in regional affairs. In the early 1980s, FCs were following the developments in Iran after the Khomaini-led Islamic revolution. In the 1990s and during the First Gulf War, they followed the massive Kurdish migration towards the Turkish border. They followed the Iraqi invasion, the fall of Saddam Hussain, and aftermath. These were international developments that had a bearing both on Turkey and on its neighbouring countries.

The main topics on Turkey that FCs have covered over the last three decades have similarly shifted according to the ways in which main political and social cleavages gained prominence in domestic politics in Turkey. Sometimes the focus has been the Kurdish question and the low-intensity war against the PKK; sometimes it was the question of political Islam. But freedom of expression and problems with further democratization have always been burning issues. For instance, in the 1980s and part of the 1990s, when reporting on 'the Kurdish question', FCs were given a hard time by Turkish authorities and security officials. Some even felt that they were followed by the police or considered spies. Turkey's acceptance as an accession country to the European Union in 2005 has been a catalyst that increased the number of correspondents covering Turkey. The developing relations with the EU and the reforms introduced as part of Turkey's increasing integration eased the restraints that FCs have experienced in gathering and writing news.

In the last five years, Turkey's economic well-being in the face of the global economic recession has attracted more media attention. In addition to the dynamics of domestic and foreign politics, its bourgeoning economy, reflected in a growing consumer culture as well as in an expanding art scene, has elevated Turkey, especially Istanbul, to a focal point for foreign media institutions. Due to a worsening economic situation in Western countries at this time, Turkey has begun to attract more freelance FCs who wish to escape the worsening economic and working conditions in their home countries. They had begun to feel less secure due to the job cuts in their countries and less comfortable in their reporting because their budget for newsgathering had been reduced. This trend was evident in our survey results, which showed that the majority (two-thirds) of the foreign correspondents based in Turkey have a 'freelance contract' with their media organizations. The FCs have expressed different reasons for becoming foreign correspondents in Turkey. Although some have followed their partners, others were truly fascinated by Turkey and deliberately chose to work there. The FCs are comprised of a diverse crowd whose personal needs especially determine freelancer role.

One of the most striking common features in the online survey and in-depth interviews is related to the FCs' efforts to strike a balance with the type of the news they want to cover about Turkey and the demands of the 'editors back home'. They expressed the opinion that Turkey's experience as a predominantly Muslim secular country is the main attraction for editors for the media organizations they work for. But the FCs want to go beyond this and focus on other aspects because they consider themselves 'responsible' for explaining the complexity of Turkey for Europe. This, perhaps, still constitutes the major challenge for the correspondents working in Turkey today.

NOTES

1. When Ankara became the capital of the new Turkish Republic, it was a small Anatolian town. The only newsworthy event was the Liberation War led by Mustafa Kemal Atatürk and the reforms he introduced afterwards. None of these necessitated foreign media to keep permanent correspondents.
2. See http://bit.ly/1fopuCb, pp. 7–13 According to an anonymous *BYEGM* officer, who gave an interview on 20 July 2013, the sudden increase in the last two years is considered to be due to the recruitment of Arab journalists for the Arabic service of the public broadcasting company *TRT.*

3. Numbers provided by officers in the Information Department of the *BYEGM* in email correspondence, 27 November 2013.
4. The list is according to media institutions and indicates 298 different organizations. Fourteen media organizations are based in Turkey and have 74 journalists working for them. These are *Cornucopia Magazine, Turkish Review Magazine, Hürriyet Daily News Newspaper, Sabah Newspaper, Olay Newspaper, Today's Zaman Newspaper, Ihlas News Agency, A Haber Television* and various parts of *Turkish Radio and Television (TRT)*, which usually use foreign languages. There are more organizations than journalists in this list because some FCs work for several media, and also the list does not include Turkish nationals working for foreign media.
5. Interview with an anonymous officer at the *BYEGM*, 16 May 2010.
6. Council of Ministers (Decision No. 88/12839), 4 April 1988. Published in *Official Gazette* (1988).
7. The privileges include duty-free importation of all sorts of technical equipments and spare parts, personal and household goods, and one personal and one service vehicle upon approval by the *BYEGM*; facilitation by *BYEGM* for interview and filming demands; opportunity to receive a residence permit until the expiry date of the press card. Accredited foreign media members get from *BYEGM* the same press card given to Turkish journalists, and upon their demand, they may also get a press traffic card that may be useful in executing their professional work.
8. Mentioned by all journalists with whom we conducted face-to-face interviews.
9. This research first began in 2010 as part of a smaller-scale research by Dr. Eylem Yanadağoğlu in Istanbul. Some of the data from the interviews mentioned here are based on interviews conducted for this initial project.
10. Cf. the contribution of Michael Brüggemann.
11. Three correspondents who filled in the online survey were also available for face-to-face interviews.
12. The online survey was sent to the 'foreign press club email list', via the moderator, three times over a period of two months in 2013.
13. We include Turkish nationals working for foreign media outlets in the sample for the survey and the interviews. One correspondent, who is half Turkish, preferred to be identified as a Turkish reporter working for foreign media.

REFERENCES

COUNCIL OF MINISTERS. (1988), Decision No. 88/12839. In *Official Gazette*, 19799 [Online]. 29 April 1988. Available from http://bit.ly/1fso9tN.

HESS, S. (1996). *International News & Foreign Correspondents.* Washington, DC: Brookings Institution.

MC PHAIL, T. L. (2005). *Global Communication: Theories, Stakeholders, and Trends.* Oxford: Wiley.

STOREY, G. (1951). *Reuter's Century 1851–1951.* London: Max Parrish [Online]. Available from http://bit.ly/1iAUWww.

TILIÇ, L. D. (2009). *Utanıyorum ama Gazeteciyim* [I Am Ashamed but I Am a Journalist]. Istanbul: İletişim.

TOPUZ, H. (2003). *Türk basın tarihi: II. Mahmut'tan holdinglere* [Turkish Press History: From Mahmut II to the Holdings]. Istanbul: Remiz Kitabevi.

YANARDAĞOĞLU, E. (2009). Maintaining Old Traditions of Media Diversity in Europe: The Non-Muslim Minority Media in Turkey. In CHARLES, A. (ed.), *Media in the Enlarged Europe: Politics, Policy and Industry.* Bristol: Intellect

27 Foreign Correspondents in the UK
London: A City 'Bathed in Light'

Michael Bromley, Howard Tumber and Julian Fritsch

INTRODUCTION

The birth of a child to the Duke and Duchess of Cambridge in July 2013 provided evidence of a continued global journalism focus on the United Kingdom as correspondents from around the world gathered outside the maternity hospital in London. Described variously as a 'show', a 'scrum', and a 'frenzy', the journalists themselves—a collection of about 200 reporters, camera operators, technicians, photographers, and producers—became the centre of some attention as they waited in the street for up to three weeks on eight- to ten-hour shifts for the royal birth. Symbolically, the first to set up outside St Mary's Hospital in Paddington was a cameraman from the *Associated Press Television News* (*APTN*), the American agency's video operation based in London. At the same time, *AP Global Media Services*, the agency's production arm, offered its television clients five stand-up locations from which to cover the event (AP, 2013). *CNN* broadcast from a webcam set up outside the hospital, and the US network *ABC* took a 'live' feed. While senior correspondents from the likes of the *Washington Post* and *New York Times* joined them (Mullin, 2013), the chief foreign correspondent of *People* magazine reported from the duchess's home village in Berkshire. The reason for all this journalistic interest was obvious: in one hour, 13 per cent of all media content consumed in the United States was about the birth, and the announcement previously that the duchess had gone into labour prompted almost half a million tweets, 29 per cent of them in the United States (Faull, 2013; Macleod, 2013).

After Washington, D.C., in 2013 London formally hosted the largest number of foreign correspondents in the world. About 2,000 were issued the official UK press card (see also Carter, 2005, p. 52)—1,700 of them through the Foreign Press Association (FPA). Not all were necessarily active, however. Furthermore, accreditation was granted to ancillary workers, including dispatch riders and drivers, as well as reporters, researchers, producers, photographers, and camera crews. In 2012, the FPA membership numbered 535, and in 2013, the Website of the Association of American Correspondents in London (AACL) listed 193 members, including 11 representing Canadian media (http://bit.ly/1is5FZn). Only 20 correspondents were members of both bodies. These numbers alone were 80 per cent greater than the 404 correspondents identified by Morrison and Tumber (1985, p. 447). In 2012, the British parliamentary press gallery had 220 overseas members representing media from 45 countries, and the parliamentary lobby about 200. However, many correspondents were members of no formal body; for example, none of *Agence France Presse*'s (*AFP*) 48 accredited correspondents were FPA members, and membership was not mandatory to receive accreditation. Furthermore, given that the press card scheme was itself voluntary, some correspondents may not have been cardholders at all. Notwithstanding the UK's relative decline as a world power, the shrinking away from investment in journalism by the traditional mass media, and the use of distributed communication systems, London remained a city 'bathed in light' (Franks, 2006, p. 91) as a major international journalism hub, pioneered by the Americans.

BACKGROUND

Starting in the first half of the 19th century, London was the first choice for stationing correspondents among American newspapers eager to supply their readers with European news (Hamilton, 2009, p. 57). This contributed to the Americans leading the way in the emergence of the foreign correspondent as a prominent figure in modern journalism (Hohenberg, 1995, p. 15; Williams, 2011, p. 46). London's advantages were considered to be the English language; a sympathetic wider general culture and narrower journalism culture (including a commitment to a 'free press' and a focus on 'hard' news) (Palmer, 1978, p. 210; Williams, 2011, pp. 52–53); a convenient time zone; the presence of *Reuters* as a major international news agency; economic dominance; control of the telegraph system inasmuch as journalists 'followed the cable'; comfortable surroundings; and good communications (for more discussion on these advantageous factors, see Hamilton, 2009, pp. 70–71; Hohenberg, 1995, pp. 6, 8–9; Kennedy, 1971, p. 729; Morus, 2000, p. 474; Williams, 2011, p. 51; Wu & Hamilton, 2004, p. 519). London was pivotal to two overlapping global spheres: one formed around the North Atlantic (Hannerz, 2004, pp. 51–52) and the other a 'British world' served by an 'imperial press system' (Potter, 2003). The city was the key node in a communications network based on the electric telegraph (Storey, 1951, p. 14), global commerce, and a growing popular demand for news (Morus, 2000, p. 457; Schudson, 2001, p. 181). London was at the epicentre of a 'global media system' that drew primarily on cooperation between the UK and the United States (Hamilton, 2009, p. 437; Williams, 2011, pp. 55–56; Winseck & Pike, 2008, pp. 10–11, 28–29).

By the 1890s, the *AP* London bureau was cabling 25,000 words a day (Hohenberg, 1995, pp. 11–12; Stanton, 1893, p. 747). The *Chicago Daily*

News expended US $122,000 (equivalent to almost €2.5 million at 2011 prices) on the first year of operation of its London-based service in 1899 (Hamilton, 2009, p. 165). As the transatlantic cable came into operation, correspondents set up in London, representing most of the newspapers published in New York, Chicago, and Boston (Della'Orto, 2002, p. 25; Hohenberg, 1995, p. 12). London was '*the* center of news-collecting for America' and 'a plum post[ing]' for US correspondents (Hamilton, 2009, pp. 70–71).

Correspondents from other countries also followed the cable (the first international connection having been established in 1850 between Dover and Calais). The FPA was founded in 1888 by Francophone correspondents sent to London to cover the Jack the Ripper case, by which time London was 'the centre of news collecting for all the leading continental papers' (Pollak, 1988, pp. 9–10). The AACL was only established more than 30 years later in 1919. By then the cable had connected London to the rest of the world, drawing correspondents from every continent.

The nature of foreign correspondence in London changed over time. Casual correspondents were succeeded by 'trained journalists', then high-quality professionals (Cole & Hamilton, 200, pp. 799–801) represented by the 'career correspondent, permanently based abroad' (Hamilton, 2009, p. 56): 'compleat correspondents' (Cole & Hamilton, 2008, pp. 802–804); 'top shelf' staffers (Brittain, 2002); 'a colorful lot' (Hamilton & Lawrence, 2010a, p. 631); glamorous heroes bringing news from 'obscure and alien environments' (Cozma & Hamilton, 2009, p. 489; Williams, 2011, p. 93). However, the fortunes of foreign correspondents waxed and waned—particularly among Americans. After reaching a 'new high' immediately following the World War II, the numbers fell dramatically (perhaps by as much as 90 per cent) in the 1950s, recovering somewhat by the mid-1960s, only to collapse again in the 1970s and 1980s. London's loss was Brussels' gain as the number of foreign correspondents posted there doubled between 1978 and 1987. But London was back in favour in the 1990s (Bromley, 2012, pp. 25–26; Bromley & Clarke, 2012, pp. 10–12; Terzis, 2008, p. 538). However, postings became more impermanent and were less tied to historically élite nations, such as the UK, and more to newly emerging powers and transient 'hot spots'. The élite status of foreign correspondents also diminished. The 'man in grey flannel' was already disappearing (Brittain, 2002: Bromley & Clarke, 2012, p. 3; Cohen, 1965, p. 17; Hamilton & Lawrence, 2010b, p. 692; Williams, 2011, p. 25).

In the 21st century, London was again a conduit into Europe and even further afield: among those using the city as a regional hub were *NBC*, *National Public Radio*, the *Boston Globe*, and *Forbes* magazine, as well as Australian (*ABC*), Canadian (*CBC*), and New Zealand (*3 News*) media. Its leading global role in financial services (Pickford, 2013), being second only to Los Angeles as a centre of celebrity culture (Baston & Henig, 2005, p. 117; Corner & Pels, 2003, p. 6; Furedi, 2010; Gibbons, 2005, p. 135), along with its status with New York as one of only two triple-A rated cities (Beaverstock, Smith, & Taylor, 2000, pp. 131–132; Immerfall, Conway, Crumley, & Jarausch, 1998, p. 184) and its transport and communications facilities—not least as jumping-off point for 'parachute journalism' (Hannerz, 2004, p. 52)—seemed to have contributed to ensuring London's continued pivotal role in the flow of world news. In addition, because foreign correspondence was more subject to the corporatized media's commercial concerns, London as a posting was relatively low risk—productive, safe, and accessible (Cole & Hamilton, 2008, pp. 805–806; Erikson & Hamilton, 2007, p. 135). These various factors offset the 'decline of Britain, its removal to the margins of international influence' (Morrison & Tumber, 1985, p. 448). Media outlets used London as their European or wider regional hub reaching as far as Africa and the Middle East, even though periodically other European cities—Paris in the 1920s (Hamilton, 2009, pp. 193–194) and later Brussels (as mentioned)—had temporarily challenged the dominance of London as a posting for foreign correspondents.

DATA COLLECTION

As Morrison and Tumber (1985, p. 447) noted, role ambiguity among such relatively large numbers of individuals—both British and foreign nationals—claiming the title 'foreign correspondent' confounded statistical sampling. However, partial quantitative data exist for the periods 1932–1954 (Kruglag, 1954) and the early 1980s (Morrison & Tumber, 1985). More recently, Archetti (2011b, pp. 3–4) conducted interviews with 25 London-based foreign correspondents and received completed surveys from a further 16.[1] The status of foreign correspondence has been canvassed, too, by practitioners and commentators (Brittain, 2002; Bundgaard, 2001; de Quetteville, 2008; Garton Ash, 2010; Greenslade, 2010; Halliburton, 2004), and relations with government have been the subject of official reports (Wilton, 2002; Carter, 2005).

The definition of 'foreign correspondent' utilized here was an amal gam firstly of the UK Press Card Authority's current classification of a 'journalist':

> [A]nyone working in the UK whose employment or self-employment is wholly or significantly concerned with the gathering, transport or processing of information or images for publication in broadcast electronic or written media including TV, radio, Internet-based services, newspapers and periodicals and who needs in the course of those duties to identify themselves in public or to official services.

And secondly of the restriction of the FPA's membership to "duly accredited and remunerated professional journalists stationed in the UK working for overseas media outlets'. Thus, both amateur correspondents and journalists whose work was primarily for UK media but available globally (Hamilton & Jenner, 2004, pp. 306–312) were excluded.

To provide an overall impression of 21st-century foreign correspondents in London—their demographics, experience, competence in using English, working conditions, uses of technology, and changing relationships with the UK government—we used a number of methods to gather data. These included consulting reports and scholarly and periodical literature. Quantitative and qualitative data were collected via the FPA and AACL; from information supplied by a number of media outlets; from embassy listings; by accessing (auto)biographical entries; and through both formal and informal interviews with 19 correspondents. The research was guided by a common 46-question survey instrument designed by colleagues for this book. However, the questionnaire was not used directly for reasons of time and expense, as well as the challenges of securing responses from a representative sample of the foreign correspondents based in London. The sampling was based on convenience, and the data were used heuristically. In all, we gathered information—not always complete and not always directly comparable—from 98 correspondents (approximately 5 per cent of the estimated total population).

FOREIGN CORRESPONDENTS AND THEIR MEDIA

The whole range of media—television, radio, newspapers, magazines, Websites, agencies—was represented. For many, these were their largest extraterritorial presences globally (*CNN*) or in Europe (*AFP*). Alongside a tendency to withdraw and downsize,[2] there was also expansion and recovery. In 2008, Canada's *Global TV* appointed two correspondents to London (and incidentally only one to Beijing). In 2013, the *Ghana News Agency* opened its first London operation. The Norwegian public service broadcaster, *NRK*, initially replaced its staff correspondent with a freelancer but subsequently reinstated a staff presence. The US agency, *UPI*, having relocated from London to Brussels, then returned to London in 2007. However, the closures continued too, perhaps the most surprising being that of the London bureau of the Irish public broadcaster, *Radio Telefis Eireann* (*RTE*), at the end of 2012. Traditional media have undoubtedly found it financially difficult to maintain their London presence at 20th-century levels (Archetti, 2012, p. 3). Print, especially newspapers and news magazines, have found it tough (Robinson, 2009), and television has become increasingly selective in what it aims to report (Robinson, 2005). This worked both against London as a posting for foreign correspondents (because of the relatively high costs) and for it (newsworthiness and comparative openness).

Australia might stand as an example. The country's only general interest national daily newspaper, *The Australian*, closed its London bureau and started taking syndicated content from *The Times* instead (both papers were owned by News Corp). Similarly, *Sky News Australia* relied on its London counterpart for content (both broadcasters were also News properties). The second largest Australian newspaper publisher, *Fairfax*, also withdrew the correspondents for the *Sydney Morning Herald* and *The* [Melbourne] *Age* (Knott, 2013). In 2013, the only full-time Australian newspaper correspondent in London was reporting for News's tabloid titles. On the other hand, the broadcaster *SBS* appointed its first ever foreign correspondent, based in London, in 2013 (Sinclair, 2013). While the global presence of the public service broadcaster, the *ABC*, shrank to just 12 bureaus, London remained the location of its coverage of Europe with two full-time correspondents. The *Nine* (television) *Network* closed its London bureau in 2008, reopened it in 2010, and by 2013 was using it to cover Europe, the Middle East, and Africa. The *Australian Associated Press* also maintained a London office. Others (*Channel 10*, the *Sydney Morning Herald*) employed freelancers.

DEMOGRAPHICS

Traditionally, London has likely been a posting for white male correspondents (Hess, 1996, p. 53). It was also a posting for senior correspondents (Hannerz, 2004, p. 84). This was logically tied to age and experience (as will be explained). Morrison and Tumber calculated that the average age of a foreign correspondent in London was 41 years and 85 per cent were men (1985, pp. 454–455). Almost 30 years later Archetti contended that a 'younger generation' was in place, but without suggesting an average age (2012, pp. 2–3). We found two dominant cohorts among contemporary correspondents, which had entered journalism in the 1990s and 2000s (more specifically between 2000 and 2004). There were exceptions, of course: our oldest subject was 73, and the youngest was still a student. This suggested that the bulk of correspondents was in their thirties (range *c*. 30–42 years). Correspondents working for national public service broadcasters tended to be slightly older than average (in their forties). There were certainly more women among the correspondents, but we could not determine how many, although they included some of the most prominent and long-standing. We calculated that women comprised about 40 per cent of North American correspondents in London, including three bureau chiefs. Of the Canadian Broadcasting Corporation's eight-person bureau, seven were women. Nevertheless, reflecting the status of women in journalism more generally, there was still an element of ongoing development in this area; for example, it was only in 2005 that the Taiwanese Central News Agency appointed its first female London bureau chief.

We noted a tendency for London correspondents to be, more than average, both unmarried and childless, which is likely to have been associated with work intensification (Sambrook, 2010, pp. 7–9) and performativity (Archetti, 2012, pp. 4–5; Hannerz, 2004, p. 40) (as will be discussed).

NATIONALITY

Of the 1,700 correspondents with press cards allocated through the FPA in 2012, about 1,000 were foreign nationals, the others being British. This was a huge increase on the 9 per cent who were identified as British 30 years ago (Morrison & Tumber, 1985, p. 450). However, since Morrison and Tumber surveyed only full-time staff correspondents, the discrepancy may be explained by the number of nonstaff correspondents with press cards (1985, p. 446). We certainly came across many examples of UK journalists working for foreign media, often as casual, contract, or freelance contributors. Some contributed simultaneously to media in different countries. Consequently, the term 'foreign correspondent' described both non-UK and UK nationals, a growing category (Hamilton & Jenner, 2004: Wu & Hamilton, 2004, p. 521). Measured purely by the media for which they worked, the Americans were the largest single group. Their relative presence may have fallen marginally—from 17 per cent (Morrison & Tumber, 1985, p. 447)[3] to 15 per cent of the total population—but the margin of error in the data was too great to be certain. This was in line with estimates that the US media had shed about 17 per cent of their foreign correspondents during the first decade of the century but perhaps less so in London than elsewhere (Carroll, 2006; Kumar, 2011). However, some believed as many as 500 journalists were working for US media, but we could not verify this. The next largest group holding official press cards were the Japanese corps (114, up from 31 in the 1980s).

In the numbers of correspondents representing media in the BRIC countries, there had been a significant increase to 128 from an estimated maximum of 53.[4] China, which did not appear separately in Morrison and Tumber's survey, by 2012 was represented by 72 correspondents. The Brazilian representation had more than doubled from 11 to 25. The situation was similar with regard to the Russian media. The Russian embassy listed seven television stations, four news agencies, and six newspapers with correspondents in London, some with multiperson bureaus, and in total at least 21 correspondents, whereas there had been nine from the USSR in the 1980s. After a decline in numbers, there appeared to be a resurgence among Indian correspondents back to 10. On the other hand, other former or current British imperial/Commonwealth countries had reduced their presence in London. The 19 South African correspondents noted by Morrison and Tumber had dwindled to just one member of the FPA. The Australian presence had fallen from 29 to a handful (as already pointed out).

The UK's evolving membership of the European Union appeared to have stimulated greater interest in posting correspondents to London. The number of German correspondents had risen from 42 (then representing media in West Germany; East Germans were counted separately) to 97, and there were 76 French correspondents. These alone were greater in number than all correspondents counted by Morrison and Tumber from Western (132) and Eastern (23) Europe together. Notwithstanding this, the European presence in London appeared to have declined significantly relative to the total population—from almost 40 per cent to perhaps less than 20 per cent. In 1985, the German presence was about 60 per cent of that of the Americans; by 2012, it was 50 per cent.

EDUCATION AND EXPERIENCE

A younger and more female cohort was likely to be associated with holding higher formal educational qualifications. There was considerable variation in this regard among our subjects. Nevertheless, foreign correspondence was a graduate occupation. Holding a postgraduate qualification correlated with having a higher-status position, such as a bureau chief, or a more established career as a correspondent. Not surprisingly, correspondents were multilingual—typically having two languages: English and another (French, Spanish, German), but many spoke three or more. There was a general consensus that competence in the use of English had improved noticeably. If London correspondents were now younger (as noted), were they less experienced?

The number of years they had spent in journalism ranged typically from 24 to nine, although a few had been journalists since the 1970s. One small group of Northern European public broadcast correspondents had between 16 and 28 years of experience. Years as a foreign correspondent were from zero to 22. Although some correspondents had been in London posts for 18, 15, or 13 years (the last all as a bureau chief), the average was six years and eight months. This was considerably longer than what we were told was the typical overseas posting of two to three years. We could not determine how common prior overseas postings were among the London cohort, but individuals reported having worked in Beijing, Hong Kong, Milan, Mexico City. Teheran, Afghanistan, Pakistan, Bahrain, Zimbabwe, Uganda, Seoul, Canberra, Bosnia, Iraq, Delhi, Moscow, Warsaw, Brussels, Vienna, and Paris. A number, mainly Americans, had served as correspondents in various US cities. These levels of experience—slightly above the average of 18 years reported by Morrison and Tumber (1985, p. 455)—were somewhat at odds with the youthfulness of the population. Apart from sampling error, they may be explained as a function of younger journalists working as foreign correspondents earlier in their careers (and sometimes at the outset of it). It remained the case, however, that London was a posting for both some veteran and novice correspondents (Archetti, 2012, p. 3).

WORK

Notwithstanding widespread anxieties over the survival of foreign correspondence, the numbers suggested that there had been no obvious overall decline in numbers in London between 2005 and 2013, and possibly a significant increase since the 1980s. Sambrook suggested that the fears were based in part on the demise of the large, static bureaus and in part on organizational decline (2010, p. 97). Morrison and Tumber found that in the 1980s only 16 per cent of correspondents worked in bureaus with five or more staff and about 40 per cent with two or three colleagues (1985, p. 458). Thirty per cent worked alone, and almost a quarter worked from home. These tendencies were noted later by Archetti (2012, p. 3). All the same, a number of larger bureaus continued to operate, particularly among the American broadcast media (*CNN*, *ABC*, *NBC*, *Bloomberg*), and new forms emerged. *Al Jazeera* established an English-language broadcast centre in London employing 160 people. As well as *Al Jazeera*, *Bloomberg TV*, and *CNN*, other 24/7 news channels (*Russia Today*, *CNBC*) had London-based broadcast operations. Many of the European national public service broadcasters had also maintained or even strengthened their presence in London.

Evidence of an increase in part-time, stringer, freelance, and casual employment existed, but it was difficult to quantify. Unfortunately, such journalists were especially hard to contact and were underrepresented in our sample. Kumar (2011) suggested that there was a trend among American media to 'franchising' and cited the example of the *Washington Post*, which had 35 foreign correspondents and 129 'franchise staff'. However, freelancing was nothing new to foreign correspondence in London. The Frontline Club (see the "Government" section) noted a marked increase globally in freelance foreign correspondence (see also Kuruvilla, 2012). We found freelancers working both in the media (*CNN*, *ABC* [Australia], *France 24*, *AJE*, *Xinhua*) and as self-employed contributors. Some freelanced while holding staff positions; for example, the London correspondent for one Eastern European television station also freelanced for a newspaper in her home country. The correspondent for the Dutch broadcaster *NOS* was a freelancer, and that was in line with the calculation of The Netherlands journalists' union that the majority of foreign correspondents from that country aged under 35 years were freelancers (Cnossen, 2013).

As suggested, one-person operations, reflecting the adoption of digital technology, were more commonplace than in the past (Garton Ash, 2010): *SBS*, which pioneered the practice in Australia, appointed a video journalist as its first London correspondent (Sinclair, 2013), although the idea that London's foreign correspondents were made up of 'armies of one' (Dorroh, 2008) seemed far-fetched. More substantiated was a rise in cross-platform working. Bureaus and individual correspondents—staff as well as freelancers—commonly served print, broadcast, and online media both within and across organizations. Not atypically, one Asian correspondent—a solo correspondent—worked for television and radio and blogged. Moreover, London appeared to be emerging as a hub (still with more than average numbers of staff correspondents) connected digitally to many spokes (in Europe, the Middle East, and Africa), commonly employing freelancers, stringers, and casuals (Dorroh, 2008). There were even cases where the 2010 soccer world cup in South Africa was being reported from London.[5] The groundwork for this had been laid in the 1990s when the numbers of large bureaus and roaming correspondents had been cut back as a cost-saving measure (Schauble, 1999, pp. 109–111).

These ways of working were facilitated by the adoption of digital technology. Local studios even offered the capacity to report without 'the need for foreign correspondents to travel to London'. However, the one technical development most mentioned by correspondents as impacting on their work was the 4G mobile smartphone and connected tablet.

Together, the correspondents felt, all these factors led to work intensification and performativity. Contributing correspondents reported being predominantly paid by the story (piecework), and staffers said they had to produce quickly to post to Websites and social media (speed-up). A majority said that they were being asked to do more, more quickly, and were being judged by immediate performance.

THE AGENDA

A news dichotomy appeared evident. On the one hand, the recognized 'big hitters'—the agencies, national broadcasters, major newspapers, and 24-hour channels—were seen as setting an agenda focused on politics. The FPA's briefings in the first half of 2013 featured the British prime minister, the leader of the UK Independence Party, a former European Union commissioner, a political analyst, the French ambassador for human rights, a former government minister, and the Scottish first minister. The other 'serious' topic routinely mentioned was the economy, business, and finance. These major media were also regarded as setting the agenda on special events, which led to temporary influxes of correspondents. More than 3,000 were in London for the 2011 royal wedding. About 25,000 personnel were accredited at the international broadcasting centre/main press centre for the 2012 Olympics. More than 300 journalists covered the 2013 deportation to Jordan of the terrorist suspect Abu Qatada (O'Carroll, 2013).

On the other hand, correspondents, especially those freelancing, told us that they sought to specialize in 'softer', more niche areas—for example, sport, particularly soccer, travel and tourism, culture and the arts, and fashion. Some reported a shift in the media's focus towards 'softer' stories. This was not novel. At the end of the 19th century, Victor Lawson at the

Chicago Daily News argued that 'serious' news was of less salience to many readers than human interest reporting (Hamilton, 2009, pp. 165–167).

GOVERNMENT

Some of the persistence of a large foreign correspondent presence in London may have been due to the UK government. The Labour government of 1997 had sidelined foreign correspondents in favour of domestic journalists on the basis that it saw advantage in influencing only British electors (what Morrison & Tumber [1985, p. 454] identified as the 'there are no votes abroad' approach). However, after 9/11, foreign correspondents in London experienced a 'dramatic shift in status' as the government's public diplomacy structures were 'comprehensively overhauled' (Miller, 2004, p. 80). Lobby briefings were relocated from Downing Street to the FPA (Bundgaard, 2001; Halliburton, 2004). The News Department at the Foreign and Commonwealth Office (FCO), which dated from 1916 and whose head had occupied 'a very special place' in the department with direct access to the top of the organization including ministers (Campbell, 2005, p. 171; Jamieson, 2003, p. 21), was discontinued in 2002. High-level briefings for foreign correspondents were introduced on the recommendation of the Wilton Review of public diplomacy. However, they had little effect (Carter, 2005, p. 11). The London Correspondents Unit, which was supposed to act as a kind of clearing house, was integrated into the FCO press office in 2004 following criticisms that it was too marginalized (Carter, 2005, p. 53). In 2005, a review recommended the provision of 'a better service for foreign correspondents', including full-time liaison officers in key government departments reporting to a manager in the FCO; a code identifying the information and contacts available (with a right of appeal); and improved access to parliament (Carter, 2005, p. 74). By 2006, the FPA had named the FCO Press Office the press office of the year for its help in supporting foreign media. These developments seemed to signal a return to a recognition that the UK's global standing through the exercise of soft power—defined as 'the ability to get what you want through . . . the attractiveness of a country's culture, political ideals, and policies'—and public diplomacy was dependent on reporting by foreign correspondents based in London; and that, in turn, what reporters sent back to their media was influenced by the access correspondents had to sources (Archetti, 2011b, pp. 4–5; Cohen, 1988, p. 124; Nye, 2004, p. ix).

The press office of the FCO provided what it described as 'a range of services' for foreign correspondents in the UK through its 'international media' team. These services included briefings, press conferences, and media tours on political, commercial, science, and cultural topics. There was also a mail service delivering press releases and operational notes. The FPA, membership of which increased by about two-thirds after 2008, offered a wide range of facilities for foreign journalists who were resident in or visiting Britain. Its committee members in 2012 represented media in Kuwait, Iran, Australia, France, Japan, Taiwan, Germany, India, Russia, and Greece. Its membership, however, included nonjournalists, such as public relations practitioners, as well as fully accredited correspondents. In addition, the Frontline Club, a private facility that opened in 2003, attracted many foreign correspondents (www.frontlineclub.com/). However, membership in and attendance at such clubs were not direct indicators of the overall numbers of foreign correspondents working in London (Morrison & Tumber, 1985, p. 449).

The UK Press Card Scheme came into existence in 1992 as a joint media-governmental initiative led by the Metropolitan Police. Seventeen bodies processed applications. An addition to the FPA, the other international gatekeeper was the International Visual Communication Association. Correspondents could also apply for the card through five trade unions, five peak media bodies, and, more unusually, five of the UK's media organizations (the *BBC*, *Sky News*, *Reuters*, *Independent Television News*, and *Independent Television*) (www.ukpresscardauthority.co.uk/).

WHERE TO?

Ryfe's research into US newsrooms indicated that journalists were limited to imagining their futures mostly as an extension of the past (2012, pp. 11ff; see also Brock, 2013, pp. 92ff). Foreign correspondents in London mainly believed that the trends and tendencies just outlined would continue, even intensify, in the foreseeable future. They expressed a kind of pragmatic empiricism tinged with more pessimism than optimism: what they considered to be the negative aspects of their work would get worse, and the positives would be under threat. Television correspondents in particular felt that the technical aspects of their work (camera operation, etc.) would assume greater importance. All the same, it looked unlikely that London would cease to be a major location for global foreign correspondence whatever its shape.

This might be explained more theoretically as a function of the interplay between external factors, such as the location and exercise of power (especially, 'soft' power [Archetti, 2011a]) and cultural affinities (Morrison & Tumber, 1985, p. 448), and internal factors, particularly the 'news investment' in foreign correspondence (Bromley & Clarke, 2012, p. 3). The benefits of access within a liberal media environment to diplomatic, economic, and cultural sources in a digitally networked world outweighed the costs of posting correspondents to London—but not to the extent always of investing in large, static bureaus or the historical idealized worldly-wise urbane specialist journalist (Garton Ash, 2010; Constable, 2007; Willmott, 2010). The picture that emerged from this study of foreign correspondents in London was one of a 'confederacy' of multiple actors blending the traditional with the new as a means of sustaining a significantly large, persistent presence (Cole & Hamilton, 2008, pp. 806–807; Hamilton, 2012, p. 220; Hamilton & Jenner, 2004, p. 303). Morrison and Tumber's (1985, pp. 449–450) proposition that this was based more on cultural habit than critical journalistic judgement suggested that the situation both arose from, and reinforced, historical Western dominance of international news flows (Kim & Barnett, 1996; Wu, 2000).

ACKNOWLEDGEMENTS

We would like to thank the correspondents and others who agreed to be interviewed for this chapter and Christopher Wyld, the director of the FPA, for his generous assistance.

NOTES

1. The bases of the surveys were not always the same.
2. For example, in 2008 *Time* magazine reduced its London staff from 28 to nine, and the US broadcaster *ABC* from 100 in the early 1990s to fewer than 20 in 2013 (Stelter, 2010).
3. All Morrison and Tumber's figures are at this reference.
4. Morrison and Tumber's figures include Pakistan as well as India.
5. Again, there was less novelty in this than might be expected. George Smalley, a path-breaking correspondent with the *New York Tribune*, insisted on reporting the 1870 Franco-Prussian war from his London office (Hamilton, 2009, pp. 60–61).

REFERENCES

AP. (2013). AP Announces Five Stand-Up Locations Available for Royal Baby Coverage [Online]. 8 July. Available from http://bit.ly/1gKoG8Y.

ARCHETTI, C. (2011a). Reporting the Nation: Understanding the Role of Foreign Correspondents in 21st Century Diplomacy. Paper presented to the International Studies Association, Montreal, 16–19 March.

———. (2011b). Which Future for Foreign Correspondence? London Foreign Correspondents in the Age of Global Media. Paper presented to the Future of Journalism conference, Cardiff, 8–9 September.

———. (2012). Which Future for Foreign Correspondence? London Foreign Correspondents in the Age of Global Media. *Journalism Studies*, 13 (5–6), pp. 1–10.

BASTON, L., & Henig, S. (2005). The Labour Party. In SELDON, A., & KAVANAGH, D. (eds.), *The Blair Effect, 2001–5*. Cambridge: Cambridge University Press, pp. 112–130.

BEAVERSTOCK, J. V., SMITH, R. G., & TAYLOR, P. J. (2000). World-city Network: A New Metageography? *Annals of the Association of American Geographers*. 90 (1), pp. 123–134.

BRITTAIN, V. (2002). The *NS* Profile—The Foreign Correspondent. *New Statesman*. 13 May [Online]. Available from www.newstatesman.com/.

BROCK, G. (2013). *Out of Print: Newspapers, Journalism and the Business of News in the Digital Age*. London: Kogan Page.

BROMLEY, M. (2012). From Spotlight to Echo Chamber? Citizen Journalism and International News. In BROMLEY, M., & CLARKE, J. (eds.), *International News in the Digital Age: East–West Perspectives of a New World Order.* New York: Routledge, pp. 23–40.

BROMLEY, M., & CLARKE, J. (2012). Continuity and Change in International News: An Introduction. In BROMLEY, M., & CLARKE, J. (eds.), *International News in the Digital Age: East–West Perspectives of a New World Order.* New York: Routledge, pp. 3–20.

BUNDGAARD, B. (2001). 'No Vote Media' with an Appetite for All Things British. *Focus* (Winter) [Online]. Available from http://bit.ly/Qr0Bda.

CAMPBELL, Sir A. (2005). From Carbon Paper to E-Mail: Changes in Methods in the Foreign Office, 1950–2000. In JOHNSON, G. (ed.), *The Foreign Office and British Diplomacy in the Twentieth Century.* New York: Routledge, pp. 168–176

CARROLL, J. (2006). Foreign News Coverage: The U.S. Media's Undervalued Asset. Working Paper Series. Cambridge, MA: Joan Shorenstein Center on the Press, Politics and Public Policy, Harvard University.

CARTER, Lord (2005). *Public Diplomacy Review*. London: Foreign and Commonwealth Office.

CNOSSEN, B. (2013). The Foreign Correspondent: Idealist and Entrepreneur. *Isle of Holland*. [Online]. 11 March. Available from http://bit.ly/1ns1oGc.

COHEN, B. (1965). *The Press and Foreign Policy* Princeton, NJ: Princeton University Press.

COHEN, Y. (1988). News Media and the News Department of the Foreign and Commonwealth Office. *Review of International Studies*. 14 (2), pp. 117–131.

COLE, J., & HAMILTON, J. M. (2008). The History of a Surviving Species: Defining Eras in the Evolution of Foreign Correspondence. *Journalism Studies*. 9 (5), pp. 798–812.

CONSTABLE, P. (2007). The Demise of the Foreign Correspondent. *Washington Post*. [Online]. 18 February. Available from http://wapo.st/Qr0COt.

CORNER, J., & PELS, D. (2003). Introduction: The Re-styling of Politics. In Corner, J., & Pels, D. (eds.), *Media and the Restyling of Politics*. London: Sage, pp. 1–18.

COZMA, R., & HAMILTON, J. M. (2009). Film Portrayal of Foreign Correspondents. *Journalism Studies*. 10 (4), pp. 489–505.

DELLA'ORTO, G. (2002). *Giving Meanings to the World: The First US Foreign Correspondents, 1838–1859*. Westport, CT: Greenwood.

DE QUETTEVILLE, H. (2008). Global London Meets the Global Press: *Die Zeit* and What the Germans Think of Us. *The Telegraph*. [Online]. 10 November. Available from http://bit.ly/1ns1spm.

DORROH, J. (2008). Armies of One. *American Journalism Review* [Online]. December/January. Available from http://bit.ly/1gKpavT.

ERIKSON, E., & HAMILTON, J.M. (2007). Happy Landings: A Defense of Parachute Journalism. In PERLMUTTER, D. D., & HAMILTON, J. M. (eds.), *From Pigeons to News Portals: Foreign Reporting and the Challenge of New Technology.* Baton Rouge: Louisiana State University Press, pp. 130–149.

FAULL, J. (2013). 13% of All Media Content Consumed in the US between 8–9 pm on Monday Was about the Royal Baby. *The Drum* [Online]. 25 July. Available from http://bit.ly/QfW3GP.

FRANKS, S. (2006). Lacking a Clear Narrative: Foreign Reporting after the Cold War. *Political Quarterly.* 76 (s1), pp. 91–101.

FUREDI, F. (2010). Celebrity Culture. *Society.* 47 (6), pp. 493–497.

GARTON ASH, T. (2010). The Foreign Correspondent Is Dead. Long Live the Foreign Correspondent. *The Guardian* [Online]. 8 December. Available from www.guardian.co.uk/commentisfree/.

GIBBONS, J. (2005). *Art & Advertising*. London: I. B. Taurus.

GREENSLADE, R. (2010). The Days of the Foreign Correspondent Have Quietly Passed. *London Evening Standard* [Online]. 8 December. Available from www.thisislondon.co.uk/.

HALLIBURTON, R. (2004). This Woman Can Have Blair Any Time. *London Evening Standard* [Online]. 8 January. Available from http://bit.ly/1qNI7kp.

HAMILTON, J. M. (2009). *Journalism's Roving Eye: A History of American Foreign Reporting*. Baton Rouge: Louisiana State University Press.

HAMILTON, J. M. (2012) Foreign Correspondence: One Age Ends, Another Begins. In J. CLARKE and M. BROMLEY (eds.) *International News in the Digital Age: East-West Perceptions of a New World Order*. New York: Routledge, pp. 211–222.

HAMILTON, J. M., & JENNER, E. (2004). Redefining Foreign Correspondence. *Journalism*. 5 (3), pp. 301–321.

HAMILTON, J. M., & LAWRENCE, R. G. (2010a). Foreign Correspondence. *Journalism Studies*. 11 (5), pp. 630–633.

———. (2010b). Bridging Past and Future. *Journalism Studies*. 11 (5), pp. 683–699.

HANNERZ, U. (2004). *Foreign News: Exploring the World of Foreign Correspondents*. Chicago: University of Chicago Press.

HESS, S. (1996). *International News & Foreign Correspondents*. Washington, DC: Brookings Institute Press.

HOHENBERG, J. (1995). *Foreign Correspondence: The Great Reporters and Their Times*, 2nd ed. New York: Columbia University Press.

IMMERFALL, S., CONWAY, P., CRUMLEY, C., & JARAUSCH, K. (1998). Disembeddeness and Localization: The Persistence of Territory. In IMMERFALL, S. (ed.), *Territoriality in the Globalizing Society: One Place or None?* Berlin: Springer, pp. 173–204

JAMIESON, J. (2003). Interview with Juliet Jeanne d'Auvergne [Online]. 3 March. Available from http://bit.ly/1eCstGr.

KENNEDY, P. M. (1971). Imperial Cable Communications and Strategy. *English Historical Review*. 86 (341), pp. 728–752.

KIM, K., & BARNETT, G.A. (1996). The Determinants of International News Flow: A Network Analysis. *Communication Research*. 23 (3), pp. 323–352.

KNOTT, M. (2013). Foreign Bureaux Get the Chop as News, Fairfax Cut Costs. *Crikey* [Online]. 9 January. Available from http://bit.ly/1j5fL0j.

KRUGLAK, T. E. (1954). Correspondents of US Media in the United Kingdom. *Journalism Quarterly*. 31 (3), pp. 324–330.

KUMAR, P. (2011). Foreign Correspondents: Who Covers What. *American Journalism Review* (December/January) [Online]. Available from http://bit.ly/1hOATv9.

KURUVILLA, C. (2012). Freelancing Can Be a Lifeline for Aspiring Foreign Correspondents. *Unity News* [Online]. Available from http://bit.ly/1l6nyR8.

MACLEOD, E. (2013). Almost 500,000 Tweets Sent in Hours Following Royal Baby Labour Announcement—with Less than Half from UK. *The Drum* [Online]. 22 July. Available from http://bit.ly/RqY4kC.

MILLER, D. (2004). The Propaganda Machine. In MILLER, D. (ed.), *Tell Me Lies: Propaganda and Media Distortion in the Attack on Iraq*. London: Pluto Press, pp. 80–99.

MORRISON, D., and TUMBER, H. (1985). The Foreign Correspondent: Date-line London. *Media, Culture & Society*. 7 (4), pp. 445–470.

MORUS, I. R. (2000). 'The Nervous System of Britain': Space, Time and the Electric Telegraph in the Victorian Age. *British Journal for the History of Science*. 33 (4), pp. 455–475.

MULLIN, C. (2013). Royal Baby: World's Media Focused on Duke and Duchess of Cambridge as Kate Goes into Labour. *WalesOnline* [Online]. 22 July. Available from http://bit.ly/1r1VLP7.

NYE, J.S. (2004). *Soft Power: The Means to Success in World Politics*. New York: Public Affairs.
O'CARROLL, L. (2013). Royal Baby: Media Corps Report on an 'Eight-step Event'. *The Guardian* [Online]. 23 July. Available from http://bit.ly/1hXARLA.
PALMER, M. (1978). The British Press and International News, 1851–99: Of Agencies and Newspapers. In BOYCE, G. CURRAN, J., & WINGATE, P. (eds.), *Newspaper History from the Seventeenth Century to the Present Day*, London: Constable, pp. 205–219.
PICKFORD, J, (2013). London Retains Financial Services Crown. *Financial Times* [Online]. 25 March. Available from http://on.ft.com/1kClQ7g.
POLLAK, H. (1988). The First Decade. In GOLDSMITH, S. (ed.), *Britain in the Eye of the World: The Foreign Press Association in London, 1888–1988*. London: Foreign Press Association, pp. 9–14.
POTTER, S. (2003). *News and the British World: The Emergence of an Imperial Press System*, 1876–1922. Oxford: Oxford University Press.
ROBINSON, J. (2005). American TV's Information Gap Creates a New World of Danger. *The Observer* [Online]. 10 April. Available from http://bit.ly/1mfZhoL.
———. (2009). A Timely Makeover for *Newsweek*—or Merely Going over Old Ground? *The Observer* [Online]. 1 March. Available from http://bit.ly/1pcrAsQ.
RYFE, D.M. (2012). *Can Journalism Survive? An Inside Look at American Newsrooms*. Cambridge: Polity.
SAMBROOK, R. (2010). *Are Foreign Correspondents Redundant? The Changing Face of International News*. Oxford: Reuters Institute for the Study of Journalism.
SCHAUBLE, J. (1999). Knighted in Their Profession: How Foreign Correspondents Are Selected by the Australian Pres. *Asia Pacific Media Educator*. 7, pp. 108–114.
SCHUDSON, M. (2001). The Emergence of the Objectivity Norm in American Journalism. In HECHTER, M., & HOPP, K-D. (eds.), *Social Norms*. New York: Russell Sage Foundation, pp. 165–185.
SINCLAIR, L. (2013). SBS Appoints First Foreign Correspondent. *The Australian* [Online]. 30 April. Available from www.theaustralian.com.au/media/.
STANTON, T. (1893). The Foreign Correspondent. *Lippicott's Monthly Magazine*. (June), pp. 746–751.
STELTER, B. (2010). Jobs Cuts at ABC Leave Workers Stunned and Downcast. *New York Times* [Online]. 30 April. Available from http://nyti.ms/QfWEIw.
STOREY, G. (1951). *Reuters' Century, 1851–1951*. London: Max Parrish.
TERZIS, G. (2008). The EU Correspondent. *Journalism*. 9 (4), pp. 537–550.
WILLIAMS, K. (2011). *International Journalism*. London: Sage.
WILLMOTT, O. (2010). The Decline of the Foreign Correspondent. *New Statesman* [Online]. 1 November. Available from http://bit.ly/1hN94lR.
WILTON, C. (2002). *Changing Perceptions: Review of Public Diplomacy*. London: Foreign and Commonwealth Office.
WINSECK, D.R., & Pike, R.M. (2008). Communication and Empire: Media Markets, Power and Globalization, 1860–1910. *Global Media and Communication*. 4 (1), pp. 7–36.
WU, H.D. (2000). Systemic Determinants of International News Coverage: A Comparison of 38 Countries. *Journal of Communication*. 50 (2), pp. 110–130.
WU, H.D., & HAMILTON, J.M. (2004). US Foreign Correspondents: Changes and Continuity at the Turn of the Century. *Gazette*. 66 (6), pp. 517–532.

Conclusions

The 'Professional Strangers' of Europe at the Dawn of the 21st Century

Georgios Terzis

WHY DO FOREIGN CORRESPONDENTS IN EUROPE MATTER?

According to the research in this book, in 2013 more than 6,600 foreign correspondents were working for 133 media outlets in the 27 European countries under investigation in this research. So why are these 'professional strangers' and their work important?

The media have historically been seen as a builders of nations, not only through unifying experiences by providing a platform for citizens to exchange opinions on common public matters (Habermas, 1962/1989; Siapera, 2004) but also through comparative experiences by providing a platform to discuss their differences or similarities with citizens and systems of other nations. Foreign news reporting allows people to be aware about events and issues around the world, and it can influence how people as well as institutions communicate and interact among themselves and with those of other nations (Obijiofor & Hanusch, 2011).

Scholars (Siapera, 2004) argue that foreign correspondents act as Europe's 'first public' because, first, the EU must spread its message through the media, and, second, FCs are the vehicles used by European governments to talk to other governments and to the public inside and outside Europe. European public sphere ideals and contemporary journalistic conventions, though, do not easily match up because the former promotes 'rational discussions of pan-European policy issues and promote(s) citizen participation', whereas the latter sells news that is personified, viewed from a nationalistic perspective, and focused on conflict (Salovaara-Morning, 2009). For example, journalists who work in Brussels have said that their job is not to educate the public, 'patch up' the EU or create a sense of European identity (De Bens, Paulussen, & Raeymaeckers, 2006, p. 16).

Despite these challenges, the results of this study confirm the increased importance of horizontal Europeanization. Brüggemann and Kleinen-von Königslöw define horizontal Europeanization as 'increasingly taking account of what happens in other member states of the EU' (2009, p. 29). They state this type of Europeanization will increase because nation states are increasingly interdependent inside the EU framework. It can be compared to vertical Europeanization, which is 'the process of paying closer attention to Brussels. . . . [and] enhanced coverage and debate about the EU' (Koopmans & Erbe, 2004).

The correspondents we interviewed and who responded to our survey remained relatively upbeat about their work. The feeling that Europe matters for foreign correspondents is also borne out by our analysis of the numbers of foreign correspondents based in the continent. There is little doubt that the economic crisis—as well as the existential crisis of the Eurozone—has helped keep the European correspondents numbers relatively buoyant while media organizations have been shedding foreign correspondents elsewhere. For the fact remains that as long as Brussels is the headquarters of the European Union and NATO and these organizations keep growing in size and importance, then correspondents will continue to flock to Europe.

WHO ARE EUROPE'S FCs, AND WHOM DO THEY WORK FOR?

The main trends observed by our study include:

- London hosts the biggest press corps in the world.
- FCs trend from working full-time to working as freelancers.
- FCs trend from being globetrotters to semipermanent residents.
- FCs trend from being expats to locals.
- FCs trend from working mainly for print media to working for all media platforms and multiple employers, sometimes from different countries.
- There's an increase of single-person bureaus.
- There's an increase of Chinese FCs.
- Foreign correspondence is still a mainly male occupation.

An FC is considered the primary person who must render confusing and foreign developments intelligible by bringing comprehendible nuances to these events and situations for their audiences in their respective home countries. However, the nature of their work often means that there's a conflict between their national identities, as well as their linguistic understanding and capabilities, and the peculiarities of the country at hand.

Most of our interviewees admit that English is serving as the lingua franca for FCs, and the inevitable consequences of this leads to information getting lost in translation, even misinterpreted or inaccurately delivered. Most of them agree that FCs need to be able to access the culture and to adequately speak and interact in the language of the country they are covering in order to be able to capture the pulse of the local society and provide the general public with an 'objective account' of the situation.

These constraints are 'alleviated' by another trend that this study found out. A foreign correspondent is often regarded as a globetrotter, with a cosmopolitan mind and a significant amount of cultural baggage. Yet the research conducted for this book has demonstrated that FCs often choose a location based on personal reasons, such as the presence of family and friends, thus often basing themselves in a country semi- or even completely permanently.

Again this is not the case for all the posts where FCs are based but mainly for the smaller ones. For example, according to Price (2010), UK journalists typically do not stay as correspondents in Brussels for more than four or five years, due to the fact that they are considered to 'go native' after a time. This idea, pejorative in the news world, was also confirmed by Terzis (2008, p. 537), though he argues it is misused because most Brussels correspondents live in an expatriate community that is 'almost untouched by the nation state of Belgium'. The term, argues a spokesperson for the European Commission interviewed by Price (2010), doesn't necessarily mean that the journalist becomes a great lover or fan of the EU but rather just comes to be too familiar with the EU project, and suddenly the stories are not as likely to be so critical and conflict prone.

The sizes and origins of news bureaus in Brussels and elsewhere in Europe also continue to change, with a dramatic increase in the number of correspondents for certain organizations such as those from China, while at the same time there are more and more single-person bureaus, a trend already identified 10 years ago (de Vreese, 2002; Preston, 2009; Mörä, 2009).

Additionally, it is important to note that the data collected in this book indicate that FCs are still predominantly male, but despite the fact that we do not currently have comparative data, interviewees indicated that the situation is slowly but steadily changing and that more and more women are entering the profession. This is not, however, consistent, and the trend is more obvious for correspondents from certain countries and for certain destinations.

The research conducted in this book indicates that there is also another observed inconsistency in the presence of expatriate correspondents in different countries, with certain countries such as Malta presenting none, and large metropolitan press hubs such as Brussels, Paris, or London boasting mostly expat FCs.

Our study also found that a disproportionate number of FCs in Europe are unmarried and childless, despite the fact that they were mainly older than 30 with more than five years of professional experience, a phenomenon that could be attributed to the intensification of their work and unstable working conditions.

Foreign correspondents based in Europe have several identities: gender, linguistic, political, professional, national, European or non-European—which they manage while reporting (Siapera, 2004). However, the nature of FCs' work often comes into conflict with their national and expected professional identities. A number of FCs interviewed for this study confessed that they have decided on several occasions to remain silent and to *surrender their professional identity to their national one* in order 'not to spoil the party' and/or run the risk of being labelled as 'traitors' by their official sources and even their peers.

Another observed trend from the research indicates the shift from full-time (formal) employment to freelance employment, and journalists who work for multiple employers, sometimes from different countries, at the same time. Reasons contributing to this trend are attributable to a variety of causes facilitated by the proliferation of new media and social media tools, increasing the information transmission rate even from the most distant of places, and by the efforts by some media organizations to reduce the costs of foreign correspondence.

Furthermore, the trend in the number of correspondents in the different countries observed varies among combinations of expats, locals, and parachute journalists. Such is the case of Greece, in which many FCs jumped in as a consequence of the financial crisis but will likewise get out when stability will return to the country.

However, this is not the case for the main press hubs of Europe. Priority is given on specific locations such as London (which is currently the biggest press hub in the world), Paris, Berlin, or Brussels because they are international hubs or influential cities where new political or financial developments occur constantly. Henceforth, foreign correspondents are needed to report the stories as they develop, especially because these are vital in covering the economic outlook across Europe and, consequently, the world.

Brussels in particular has, unlike recent research assumed, received a slight increase of FCs in the past years. Increasingly, editors have realized the importance of monitoring Europe's capital for the continent's financial and political outlook. Consequently, agencies have sent more FCs to the city in order to cover European and international affairs, a phenomenon that has been demonstrated through the largely informative impact FCs have had during the financial crisis, as well as spreading unnecessary cynicism at times.

Yet news- and opinion-making on European affairs can be a great challenge for Europe-based correspondents and their editors. Tension often arises between journalists and the central newsroom over which stories are 'newsworthy' (de Vreese, 2005). According to our survey, there is a considerable inconsistency as well, with more autonomy being given to FCs based in 'smaller' posts compared with those based on big press hubs of Europe.

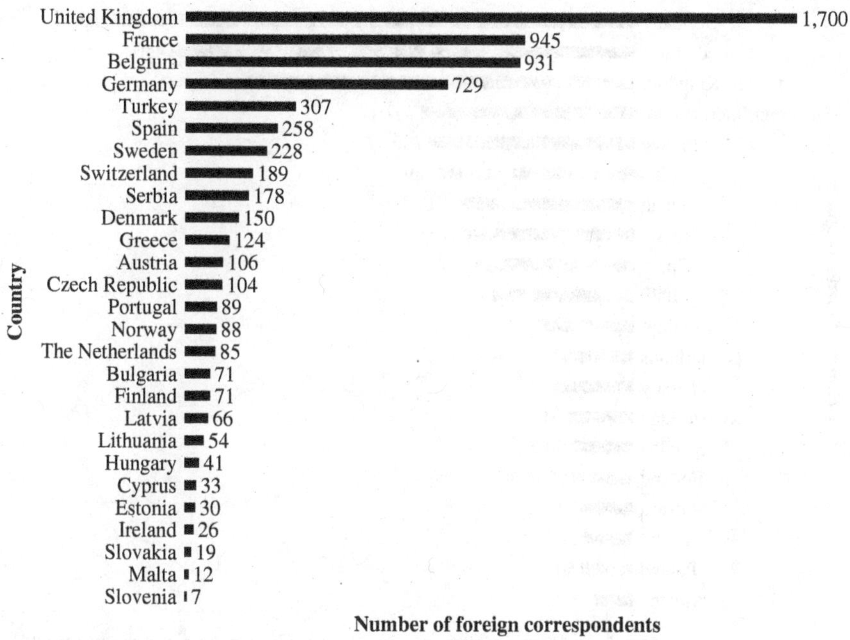

Figure 28.1 Total foreign correspondents per country.*

Please note the following for Figure 28.1:

- *France:* Estimate data from the French Ministry of Foreign Affairs (*Bureau de la Presse, de la Radio et de la Télévision Étrangère*). The actual number of FCs is likely higher.
- *Germany:* Based on information from the VAP and German government accreditation service (*Bundespresseamt*, BPA) and adjusted for possible overlap and the fact that some journalists are neither registered with the BPA nor members of the VAP. The actual number of FCs is likely higher.
- *Hungary:* Based on accreditation from the Hungarian International Press Association (HIPA) list.
- *Netherlands:* An estimated number; 75 per cent thought to be active.
- *UK:* Accreditation from the Foreign Press Association (FPA). The actual number of FCs is likely higher.

* These estimates are based on information made available to the authors on accredited journalists, often from official government or media agency sources. We acknowledge that not all foreign correspondents have official accreditation and that some journalists may be included in more than one list within the same country. An estimated 6,600 journalists work as foreign correspondents across the countries examined.

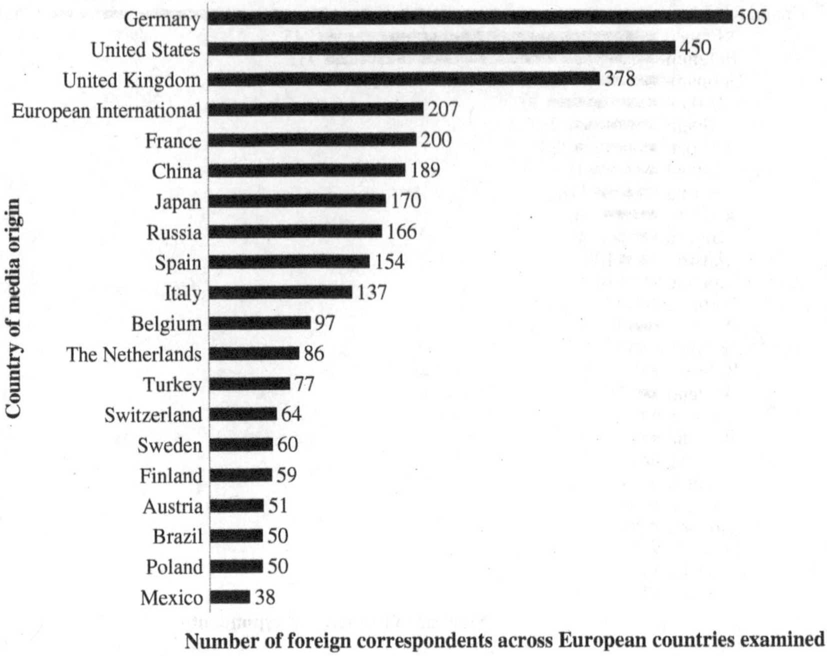

Figure 28.2 Top 20 countries of media origin.*

* These estimates are based on information made available to or determined by the authors for each country examined. We acknowledge that not all foreign correspondents have official accreditation and therefore may not be counted. Correspondents working for foreign-based media came from 113 different countries. Data were incomplete or unknown for the following European countries examined: Czech Republic (unknown), Estonia (unknown), Germany (incomplete), The Netherlands (unknown), Portugal (some FCs worked two or more foreign-based media), and the UK (unknown).

Table 28.1 Breakdown of main medium worked for by FCs (%).*

	Print	Online	Broadcast	News Agency	Mix (Cross-platform) or Unknown
Austria	35	0	21	25	19
Belgium	15	21	29	32	3
Bulgaria	17	14	21	48	0
Czech Republic	33	16	26	26	0
Denmark	31	6	19	14	30
Estonia	47	7	13	27	7
Finland	28	15	30	27	0
France	47	3	29	20	0
Greece	40	3	21	36	0
Hungary	17	0	24	59	0

	Print	Online	Broadcast	News Agency	Mix (Cross-platform) or Unknown
Ireland	35	4	12	50	0
Lithuania	17	0	52	28	4
Malta	17	0	25	58	0
Norway	36	0	19	25	19
Portugal	24	6	26	28	16
Serbia	30	1	46	24	0
Slovakia	53	0	26	21	0
Slovenia	14	14	0	71	0
Spain	44	0	22	34	0
Sweden	45	0	31	24	0
Switzerland	34	3	17	37	9
Turkey	45	4	33	18	0

* Data unavailable for Cyprus, Germany, Latvia, The Netherlands, and the UK. Data from the Czech Republic are based on the total number of foreign media worked for because individual FC data were unavailable. France's data are from the French Ministry of Foreign Affairs (*Bureau de la Presse, de la Radio et de la Télévision Étrangère*). Online medium data from Hungary were unavailable. In Portugal, some FCs were recorded as working for more than one medium when a 'main medium' could not be determined.

Figure 28.3 Total number of foreign correspondents working per medium.*

* Data unavailable for Cyprus, Germany, Latvia, Netherlands, and the UK. Data from the Czech Republic is based on the total number of foreign mediums worked for, as individual FC data was unavailable. France's data is from the French Ministry of Foreign Affairs (*Bureau de la Presse, de la Radio et de la Télévision Étrangère*). Online medium data from Hungary was unavailable. In Portugal, some FCs were recorded as working for more than one medium when a 'main medium' could not be determined.

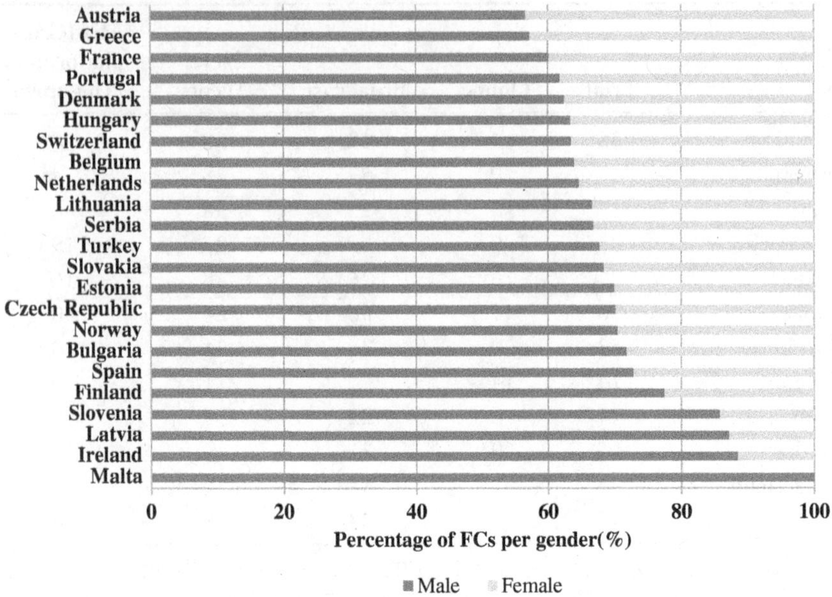

Figure 28.4 Gender breakdown of foreign correspondents.

Note: Data were unavailable for Cyprus, Germany, Sweden, and the UK.

WHAT MAKES IT ONTO THE REPORTING AGENDA?

The main trends observed by our study include:

- FCs remain influenced by their national journalistic cultures.
- An expanding number of FCs are assigned for regional (more-than-one-country) coverage.
- The expanding number of single-person bureaus and their function as 'generalists' had a significant impact on the reporting of the financial crisis.

Foreign news coverage (direction, flow, and patterns) has been studied on a global scale twice: once in 1979 and once in 1995. It was found that geographic proximity and national links with politics and economics dictated the majority of news coverage and that regionalism and politics are the major factors that influence international news reporting, no matter which region of the world is examined (Stevenson, 1997; Koponen, 2003; Obijiofor & Hanusch, 2011).

Therefore, it is unsurprising that literature identifies and our study confirms three similar principal factors or themes that influence an FC's reporting agenda in Europe. The first involves a process (which some authors call an 'obsession') of making foreign news nationally relevant (de Vreese,

2005; De Bens, Paulussen & Raeymaeckers, 2006; Mörä, 2009; Price, 2010; Obijiofor & Hanusch, 2011). The second factor is the assumed complexity of EU and foreign affairs, which many editors fear will not interest or be understood by the audience (de Vreese, 2005; Price, 2010). Linked to this are the shifts in tone that occur in the news over time and according to newsworthy circumstances. Finally, the subjects covered in the news are relatively limited, focusing on economics and politics and in some instances on culture or entertainment (Nosty, 1997; Kevin, 2003).

Furthermore, the commercialization of news requires that stories have a 'personal angle' or a hint of scandal or panic, especially when covering EU (political and cultural) news on TV (Kevin, 2003). Occasionally, entertainment coverage (for example, sport contests or music concerts) is EU-wide, but even this theme of coverage is inconsistent (Preston, 2009).

As mentioned already, journalists are already expected to be able to cover many fields, regions/countries, and events (Utley, 1997; Obijiofor & Hanusch, 2011). To improve cost efficiency, FCs are increasingly required to deliver regional coverage, such as the Balkan, Benelux, or Nordic regions. Unfortunately, this can lead to the loss of quality in what is reported through limiting linguistic and cultural factors, as well as an FC's lack of local connections.

Additionally, FCs can conversely be restricted to specific places such as the capitals (often due to budgetary restrictions), thus eliminating the delivery of country or contextual perspectives because the news is merely given from and about their prime location.

Finally, the trend for single-person bureaus has increased the problem of FCs as 'generalists' who in some places report during the same day politics, economics, environment, education, and security, as admitted by many interviewees. This has a detrimental impact on the quality of foreign correspondence and had a 'devastating' impact on the coverage of the Eurozone crisis, whereby most FCs had no training or experience in covering macroeconomic issues. As a result, most FCs based in Europe missed all the 'signs' of the impeding crises and when it unfolded, they either covered it in a very sensational way or just 'followed' the line given by the agencies and the *Financial Times*, as admitted by our interviewees and also documented by the literature (Engelen, 2010).

WHEN DOES A STORY BECOME A FOREIGN NEWS ITEM, AND WHERE DO THE STORIES COME FROM?

The main trends observed by our study include:

- A close and competitive relationship between news agencies and FCs for other media, who usually try to file more comprehensive versions of the stories covered by the agencies.

- Strong evidence of intermedia agenda setting by local media, news agencies, major foreign media, and other FCs based in the same country.
- An increasing use of press trips due to budget restrictions.
- An intensification of time pressures.
- An increasing reliance on official sources.
- Different levels of access to primary sources in different countries, especially regarding official sources.

A foreign correspondent writes an article for multiple reasons. According to Brüggemann (2012), the journalist usually has a 'difficult-to-explain' gut feeling. A study that 'reconstructed' the 'biographies' of news articles after their publication by interviewing the authors identified the following four explanations as generators of articles: 'occurrences' (institutional politics), 'trigger sources' (other media reports on the topic), 'evaluations' (buzzwords and news factors), and 'editorial context' (space for the news that day) (Brüggemann, 2012, p. 14). In addition, the study found that the triggers often grouped together into patterns: 'routine record-keeping', 'editorial agenda-setting', 'elite sound bites', and 'monitoring a mediated world' (Brüggemann, 2012, p. 15).

Our study results are also compatible with the above and with Mörä (2009), who found that correspondents often form coverage 'discussions' among themselves and that the correspondents follow one another's work. One commented:

> We communicate with other journalists and we try to read, not everything, but newspapers in other languages . . . So our point of view is not only our . . . point of view, and I think for this reason . . . it's so interesting to be a correspondent because you are between national and European . . . you are not really European but you are less national than your colleagues in [home country].
>
> (Mörä, 2009, pp. 90–91)

The *Financial Times*, for example, is considered the most dominant news source in Brussels due to high readership among politicians and journalists (Raeymaeckers, Cosijn, & Deprez, 2007; Terzis, 2008; Preston, 2009; de Vreese & Boomgaarden, 2009). At one time it was considered the 'house journal' of the European Commission (Price, 2010, p. 232). Yet in the 2000s, journalists started collaborating in a so-called Champions League to create an informal network that counterbalances the 'omnipotence of the *Financial Times* editorial staff' (Raeymaeckers, Cosijn, & Deprez, 2007, p. 116). *Le Monde*, *Frankfurter Allgemeine Zeitung*, and *El Pais* consistently have the best coverage among European newspapers and carry considerable more 'weight' among foreign correspondents based in Europe. *Liberation*, *Guardian*, *Le Figaro*, *Suddeutsche Zeitung*, *Gazeta Wyborca*, *Corrierre della Serra*, and *Le Soir* form a 'second tier'.

Our interviewees also admitted their heavy reliance on official sources. Due to the nature of the stories they mainly cover (politics and economics) and due to the necessary benchmark of 'source credibility', which could be much higher than the one for domestic news, our interviewees felt that official sources make for a 'safe' bet. They also feel much more inclined to report news coming from those sources because they are 'afraid' that their competitors and/or the agencies will report those stories and that they will be reprimanded by their editors back home for not covering it.

Foreign correspondents are also affected by the level of access to official sources that they are granted. Access differs greatly among countries, particularly between Nordic states such as Sweden and Denmark, which demonstrate full access, which contrasts with Mediterranean countries, such as Spain, where they face restrictive access. The main reason for this problem is, of course, attributable to societal and political circumstances, with free speech and transparency being more predominant in Nordic countries.

Our respondents agree that traditional news values relevant to the topic of the story such as clarity, proximity, entertainment, conflict, stories about death—but also rescues—apply in foreign news coverage. News values that are not relevant to the topic of the story also apply, such as the timing of the event, intermedia agenda-setting, financial and technical logistics for covering the story, regional subjectivities, and gatekeepers that take many forms, such as media editors and their different identities (ethnic, gender, social class, etc.), professional codes of conduct, company policies and institutional memories, legislation, and even computer algorithms.

But most of all the news values of foreign correspondence are about power and elite institutions, elite people, and elite nations, in the sense suggested by John Galtung earlier in this volume. When you have all three (the monarchy, a celebrity prince, and the UK), you get 8,500 journalists in London and more than 100 overseas broadcasting organizations covering the royal wedding that was the most televised event in history with an audience of 2 billion people.

HOW IS EUROPE FORMULATED IN DIFFERENT FRAMES?

The main trends observed by our study include:

- 'Us' vs. 'Them' is still prevalent, but the dichotomy takes different forms.
- Space and time of reporting are increasingly compressed, with short and simplified formats.
- Frames are based on domestic relevance and negative reporting.
- National professional cultures and the political orientation of the medium determine the frame.

- Frame variation is lessened, based on the funding base ('private' vs. 'public service broadcaster') or based on type of medium
- FCs rely heavily on official sources, who often 'kidnap' the framing of FCs' news.

A journalist's cultural sensitivity (including personal values and beliefs) impacts how he or she reports on and portrays the subject (Obijiofor & Hanusch, 2011). A lack of cultural sensitivity in foreign news reporting can result if, *inter alia*, a FC lacks contextual knowledge about issues, has inadequate time to cover the news, or his/her social status and gender bias coverage of the subject (d'Hænens, 2003; Obijiofor & Hanusch, 2011).

In addition to personal identities, several journalists interviewed by Preston (2009) felt that there is no common or shared journalism culture in Europe and that differences exist between journalism cultures and media systems, even throughout the EU member states that have similar political, cultural, and economic values/construction. For example, British journalists stated that less rigorous or 'boring' (reserved) journalism was common in France and Germany and therefore was markedly different from the UK media culture. Therefore, the framing of foreign affairs by FCs of different countries is different, and the response of official sources to FCs is very different across countries. Due to the heavy and most of the time disproportionate reliance of FCs on official sources, it is often the sources who are mainly responsible for the framing of the foreign correspondence in Europe.

News is often framed according to 'domestic relevance' (Hess, 1996; de Vreese, 2002, Kevin, 2003; Mörä, 2009; Obijiofor & Hanusch, 2011), specifically suggesting either that 'this is threatening to our security'. or implying conflict 'between countries, within political parties, and between EU institutions' (de Vreese, 2005, p. 117; Price, 2010). Context analysis for UK news sources, for example, identifies four subframes of conflict: domestic conflict, 'UK versus EU', 'EU versus EU', and 'EU versus external power'. National-based journalists are three times more likely to use a 'UK versus EU' frame for their reports than Brussels-based journalists, who most often use an 'EU versus external' power angle (Price, 2010).

The use also of short news frames, often accompanied with visual images, allows for the quick turnover of coverage (Kevin, 2003; Obijiofor & Hanusch, 2011). In an era in which news is available 24 hours a day, seven days a week, print and online newspapers, radio, and broadcast news is constantly updated, yet the borders defining those types of media are blurred. The challenge remains that journalists are involved in multimedia production modes (print, TV, radio, and online) and that crews are working constantly to produce news bulletins in different formats of the same story(ies) because deadlines are multiple and rolling. Even as correspondents are expected to act as mediators between their reported topic or location and their viewers, they are now more occupied with mediating between the quality of their work and their pending deadlines.

Furthermore, as indicated earlier by our research, there is a measureable decrease in FCs reporting exclusively for print media and an increase of ones who report mainly for online media and/or multiple platforms. Yet this causes increased pressure on the FCs. Whereas FCs used to have time to work on a story until printing time, they currently need to act fast in order to launch a story before other media outlets do so.

The ease and rapidity by which information is transmitted, in conjunction with the pressure on agencies and FCs to report a story instantly, are leading to the essential inability for stories to be developed into balanced reports through the assimilation of multiple or a variety of sources. This contributes to the distortion of current events or leads to the formation of misconceptions among viewers, therefore hindering improvements in foreign relations or, in extreme cases, hate.

Consequently, this necessity to rapidly deliver news is causing the contributions of foreign correspondence to diminish due to the potency of information technology that not only allows for first-hand information through citizen journalists who upload photos and videos directly to social media or news agencies but also cuts out the role of the foreign correspondent, who is meant to provide an objective account.

FINAL NOTE: WHERE TO?

The main future trends observed by our study include:

- FCs expect that they will report for all platforms 24/7.
- FCs currently use social media extensively to produce their work but also do not attach a great significance to social media to disseminate it.
- FCs are still part of public diplomacy.
- There is an increasing number of FCs from some of the BRICS countries.

Several trends in the future of foreign correspondence in Europe are connected mainly to global financial crises, globalization, and the rise of BRICS, technological developments, the emergence of citizen journalism, and media convergence.

The first relates to low resources for reporting on European affairs (Kevin, 2003; Mörä, 2009). Related to the slashing of budgets (Preston, 2009) while continuing the expectation of 24-hour news coverage is the transformation of the news bureau. Modern foreign reporting, according to Willnat and Martin (2012), has shifted to a world of one-person bureaus, where a single journalist with the latest digital equipment can record, edit, and send videos to report on events at a fraction of the cost of a full bureau. One step further and cheaper are 'virtual foreign correspondents', who assemble stories at the home office by using online sources and phone calls to compile their stories. The Internet thus has placed additional pressures on foreign correspondents to 'justify' their salary by producing more than is available online, by providing additional original content.

The second trend is the introduction of new information and communication technologies which 'have significantly transformed the way foreign news is reported' (Obijiofor & Hanusch, 2011, p. 128). Such changes include the quantity and diversity of international news, coverage frequency, and the speed and participation of 'citizen journalists', who produce and disseminate information. The Internet and globalization have opened up space for news and political discourse, with citizens joining in alongside professional foreign correspondents (Reese, Rutigliano, Hyun, & Jeong, 2006; Willnat & Martin, 2012). Bloggers and people with even the most basic technology are now able to contribute to news coverage and are gaining platforms online (Obijiofor & Hanusch, 2011). Some of our interviewees even suggested that a type of long-tail theory could be applied to foreign news coverage whereby certain mega stories become 'blockbusters' and dominate foreign news coverage around the world for a short period of time, and there is unlimited space for the limited coverage of events around the world.

Every day, 7,000 hours of news-related videos are uploaded on YouTube alone, the majority of which is created by amateurs (*The Economist*, 2013). This phenomenon, of course, raises concerns because citizen journalists often lack training and may not adhere to codes of ethics and other journalism conventions, and thus news organizations employ more and more social media 'editors' who search and verify those uploads. The abundance of unfiltered information can also overwhelm an average newsreader or even allow misinformation to be consumed along with everything else (Keller, 2013). Indeed, despite the social media editors of traditional media and companies like Storyful that are becoming very successful in the realm of verifying user-generated content for traditional media, as a journalist at the *New York Times* states, 'Social media isn't journalism. It's information. Journalism is what you do with it' (quoted in Keller, 2013). What the Wikileaks and the Snowden affairs proved, if nothing else, is that we need more journalism and foreign correspondence, not less. In both cases, the whistleblowers gave the material to traditional media, which are able to decipher the information out of the millions of email messages available because very few 'average' citizens have either the time or the necessary tools to 'translate' this information into anything remotely intelligible.

Scepticism of the professionalism of 'citizen journalists' is one of the main drawbacks of new technologies' influence over journalism, but many scholars (Wu & Hamilton, 2004; Obijiofor & Hanusch, 2011) argue that foreign news editors and journalists continue to be influenced mainly by traditional cultural practices and professional journalism values and use new media as 'supporting' instruments rather than as avenues for new audiences.

For example, Twitter has become popular among some journalists, but findings show that journalists typically do not 'break news' with Twitter. Rather, they use it as a platform for discussing current events and promoting their news outlet (Cozma & Chen, 2013). Our interviewees from almost all 27 countries agree.

There continue, of course, to be differences between broadcast and print journalists and their use of Twitter. For instance, broadcast journalists are more popular (with an average of 2,000 more followers) and are more likely to break news with Tweets, whereas print journalists generally share opinions and link to other outlets with their Tweets. Although more research needs to be done on Twitter's role in foreign correspondence, many of the 'Top 50 Trending Topics on Twitter of all time' include international topics such as the EU (Cozma & Chen, 2013).

Finally, as stated previously, foreign correspondents act more and more as Europe's 'first public' because, first, the European Union must spread its message through the media, and, second, FCs are the public diplomacy vehicles used by European governments to talk to other governments and publics inside and outside Europe (Siapera, 2004). As such, the current changes of power dynamics of foreign correspondents in Europe reflect the changes of global political dynamics with the rise of the BRICS. A growing example of this is the increasing presence of Chinese FCs in Europe, not only in strategic locations such as London and Brussels, but in countries such as Greece or even Bulgaria. This, for instance, is attributed not only to the interest of Chinese investment and opportunities in Greece following the financial crisis, but also for creating a gateway for Chinese public diplomacy and means of foreign policy.

As a closing statement, I would also like to offer a kind of disclaimer for this study. Mapping studies preclude ideologies of the seeking, evaluating, writing/presenting, and ways of distributing the information. We should be aware of biases related to issues, such as why we did the mapping in the first place, who did the mapping, what we mapped, and what we decided to include (and thus exclude, such as certain issues related to the ethics of foreign correspondents, for example), which countries we decided to include and thus our definition of Europe, what research tools we used, the time frame of the mapping exercise (which acts like a snapshot of a river that constantly changes), and finally that mapping studies themselves, like foreign correspondence, are reflections of power structures and dynamics.

REFERENCES

BRÜGGEMANN, M. (2005). How the EU Constructs the European Public Sphere: Seven Strategies of Information Policy. TranState Working Papers. (19).

———. (2010) Information Policy and the Public Sphere: EU Communications and the Promises of Dialogue and Transparency. Javnost- *The Public.* 17(1). pp. 5–22.

———. (2012). Transnational Trigger Constellations: Reconstructing the Story Behind the Story. *Journalism*. 1–18. Available from http://bit.ly/1hHnzat.

BRÜGGEMANN, M., & KLEINEN-VON KÖNIGSLÖW, K. (2009). 'Let's Talk about Europe': Why Europeanization Shows a Different Face in Different Newspapers. *European Journal of Communication*. 24, pp. 27–48.

COZMA, R., & CHEN, K.J. (2013). What's in a Tweet?: Foreign Correspondents' Use of Social Media. *Journalism Practice*. 7 (1), pp. 33–46.

DE BENS, E., PAULUSSEN, S., & RAEYMAECKERS, K. (2006). The Case of Belgium. In AIM Research Consortium (ed.), *Understanding the Logic of EU Reporting in Mass Media: Analysis of EU Media Coverage and Interviews in Editorial Offices in Europe*. Bochum/Freiberg: Projekt Verlag, pp. 11–20.

DE VREESE, C.H. (2002). *Framing Europe: Television News and European Integration*. Amsterdam: Het Spinhuis.

DE VREESE, C.H., & BOOMGAARDEN, H.G. (2009). A European Public Sphere: Media and Public Opinion. In Inka Salovaara-Moring (ed.), *Manufacturing Europe: Spaces of Democracy, Diversity and Communication*. Göteborg: Nordicom, pp. 117–128.

D'HAENENS, L. (2003). Editorial: Determinants of International News Production. *Gazette*. 65 (1), pp. 5–7.

ENGELEN, E. (2010). Financial Crisis and Story Telling by Distributive Coalition. *Covering the Crisis: The Role of Media in the Financial Crisis*. Maastricht: EJC Publications.

Correspondence: A Euro-American Perspective of Concepts, Methodologies, and Theories. New York: Peter Lang, pp. 1–28.

HABERMAS, J. (1962/1989). *The Structural Transformation of the Public Sphere: An Inquiry into a Category of Bourgeois Society*. Cambridge: Polity Press.

KELLER, B. (2013). It's the Golden Age of News. *The New York Times* [Online]. 3 November. Available from http://nyti.ms/1pnWxdN.

KEVIN, D. (2003). *Europe in the Media: A Comparison of Reporting, Representation, and Rhetoric in National media Systems in Europe*. London: Lawrence Erlbaum.

KOOPMANS, R., & ERBE, J. (2004). Towards a European Public Sphere? Vertical and Horizontal Dimensions of Europeanised Political Communications. *Innovation*. 17, pp. 97–118.

KOPONEN, J. (2003). The Structure of Foreign News Revisited. In MALMELIN, N. (ed.), *The Science of Mediation and Caring. Communicational Viewpoints of Society, Culture and Citizenship*. Helsinki: Helsingin yliopisto, pp. 144–166.

MÖRÄ, T. (2009). The European Union and Ideals of the Public Sphere. In SALOVAARA-MORING, I. (ed.), *Manufacturing Europe: Spaces of Democracy, Diversity and Communication*. Göteborg: Nordicom, pp. 81–96.

NOSTY, B.D. (1997). The European Union in the Press: Results of the Research. In ÁLVAREZ , C.L., & SCHWARTZ, P. (eds.), *The European Union in the Media: 1996*. Madrid: Fundesco, pp. 19–119.

OBIJIOFOR, L., & HANUSCH, F. (2011). *Journalism across Cultures: An Introduction*. London/New York: Palgrave Macmillan.

PRESTON, P. (2009). 'Where's Europe?' Emergent Post-national News Cultures. In PRESTON, P. (ed.), *Making the News: Journalism and News Cultures in Europe*. London/New York: Routledge, pp. 144–161.

PRICE, J. (2010). A Tale of Two Cultures: A Comparison of EU News Reporting by Brussels-Based and National-Based Journalists. In Valentini, C., & Nesti, G. (eds.), *Public Communication in the European Union: History, Perspectives and Challenges*. Newcastle upon Tyne: Cambridge Scholars Publishing, pp. 217–236.

RAEYMAECKERS, K., COSIJN, L., & DEPREZ, A. (2007). Reporting the European Union. *Journalism Practice*. 1 (1), pp. 102–119.

REESE, S.D., RUTIGLIANO, L., HYUN, K., & JEONG, J. (2006). Mapping the Blogsphere: Professional and Citizen-based Media in the Global News Arena [Online]. Available at http://bit.ly/1mUxaf9.

SALOVAARA-MORING, I. (2009). Manufacturing Europe, Restoring Communication? In Salovaara-Moring, I. (ed.), *Manufacturing Europe: Spaces of Democracy, Diversity and Communication*. Göteborg: Nordicom, pp. 9–16.

SIAPERA, E. (2004). EU Correspondents in Brussels: Between Europe and the Nation-state. In HERRMANN, R.K., RISSE, T., & BREWER, M.B. (eds.), *Transnational Identities: Becoming European in the EU*. Lanham, MD/Oxford: Rowman & Littlefield, pp. 129–157.

STEVENSON, R.L. (1997). Remapping the World [Online]. Available from http://bit.ly/1haEwtT.

TERZIS, G. (2008). The EU Correspondent. *Journalism*. 9, pp. 537–550.

THE ECONOMIST (2013), Citizen Journalism Foreign Correspondents. 1 June, pp. 57.

UTLEY, G. (1997). The Shrinking of Foreign News: From Broadcast to Narrowcast. *Foreign Affairs*. 76 (2), pp. 2–10.

VAN DE STEEG, M. (2002). Rethinking the Conditions for a Public Sphere in a European Union. *European Journal of Social Theory*. 5 (4), pp. 499–519.

WILLNAT, L., & MARTIN, J. (2012). Foreign Correspondents—An Endangered Species? In WEAVER, D.H., & WILLNAT, L. (eds.), *The Global Journalist in the 21st Century*. London/New York: Routledge, pp. 495–510.

Wolter, I. (2006). Determinants on International News Coverage. In CARPENTIER, N., PRUULMANN-VENGERFELDT, P., NORDENSTRENG, K., HARTMANN, M., VIHALEMM, P,, & CAMMAERTS, B. (eds.), *Researching Media, Democracy and Participation: The Intellectual Work of the 2006 European Media and Communication Doctoral Summer School*. Tartu, Estonia: Tartu University Press, pp. 59–71.

WU, H.D. (2007). A Brave New World for International News? Exploring the Determinants of the Coverage of Foreign Nations on US Websites. *The International Communication Gazette*. 69 (6), pp. 539–551.

WU, H.D., & Hamilton, J.M. (2004). US foreign correspondents: Changes and continuity at the turn of the century. *International Communication Gazette*. 66(6): 517–532.

YEMMA, J. (2007). Instant Connection: Foreign News Comes in from the Cold. In PERLMUTTER D.D., & HAMILTON, J.M. (eds.), *From Pigeons to News Portals: Foreign Reporting and the Challenge of New Technology*. Baton Rouge: Louisiana State University Press, pp. 110–129.

Epilogue

Cees J. Hamelink

What does one write in an epilogue? The reader has read already so many substantial, pertinent, and interesting contributions that I must ask, 'Who has energy left for a few last words?'

Should I summarize what the preceding studies have to offer? That would suggest that my academic colleagues cannot themselves read!

Should I interpret the meanings of the chapters? That would suggest that this group of scholarly authors needs assistance in explaining what they wanted to report and that the audience needs help in understanding what they read!

Should I write the mother of all concluding chapters? That would—mistakenly—suggest that science can offer definitive and authoritative statements!

The best I can do is to express the hopeful expectation that this useful collection finds its way to media students and media producers around Europe and—actually—to all those who understand the importance of media representations of the European realities that will affect their daily lives. The 21st-century reality is more than ever a mediated reality, and for everyone who wants to engage with the future of Europe (and he or she could also be a non-European or a non-European immigrant with hopes for a better life), it would seem essential to understand how this mediation works and who are its key operators. The interesting case in point is evidently that the studies suggest that Chinese news interest in the European region is on the increase.

Obviously, foreign correspondence, like all other news reporting, is affected by what Jaap van Ginneken calls 'selective articulation' (Van Ginneken, 1998, p. 16). Selective articulation is inherent in the 'media logic': that is, the specific way of operating that is common to most media. Media logic is characterized by the tendency to focus on incidents, to accentuate the sensational, to dramatize social reality, and to decontextualize developments. It is inherent to media logic that here is a strong pressure to answer the classical 5W questions in a news report. The five Ws (what, where, when, who, and why) were designed to improve objectivity in journalism. In real practice, they often stand in the way of this objectivity. The what, where, and when questions can often be answered without too much difficulty. The trouble arises with the who and why questions. They often require more time, more research, and more prudence. Mainstream journalism has serious problems with these requirements. There is a lot of editorial pressure on journalists to provide answers quickly and with certainty. Much journalism is haunted by an obsession with certainty that often in all honesty cannot be provided. However, the spin doctors that assist the political leaders in conflicts claim to have all the answers. As long as journalists do not find the courage to honestly say, 'I have no idea', they remain vulnerable to the perception management by spin doctors. However, with the massive shift to the use of freelance stringers, as the studies in this book indicate, this becomes even more difficult.

The words and images of foreign correspondents in Europe are essential to the construction of the European image in the minds of millions of people in media audiences. However, around the world, news media are primarily nationally oriented. News gatekeepers find 'us' more relevant than 'them', and due to the mechanisms of cultural proximity, most audiences may indeed find 'us' easier to understand and to relate to than 'them'.

As a Dutch media consumer, I would certainly wish to learn more about current affairs in other European countries (EU member states and beyond), but my daily newspapers serve me disappointingly sparsely.

In the UNESCO constitution (of 1945), we find the notion that if people were better informed about each other, they may be more inclined to understanding and peaceful coexistence. Although this may give too much credit to the role of information provision, it is also true that distortions of our knowledge about the European 'others' could promote dangerous animosities. As a European citizen, I am aware of our common destructive history. There are no atrocities that Europeans are not prepared to hand out to their fellow citizens. I am concerned about the possibility of recurrent collective political violence in this seemingly peaceful region. It could happen again. Despite the long peace after World War II, Europeans cannot sit back complacently. We need to mobilize all the tools at our disposal to remain alert to retain Europe's enlightenment, humanism, and artistic sophistication. Among those tools, foreign correspondence is a key instrument.

Having worked for a short time as a reporter in foreign countries myself, an intriguing question came up time and again: the insider vs. the outsider. Much of the debates about North-South news issues in the 1970s focused on the issue of non-Southern country nationals reporting about Southern issues. Could non-nationals deeply understand in-country events and developments, or would they inevitably be reported with the outsider bias? In this context, it is interesting to see the shift from expats to nationals in the studies. It is evident that both insiders and outsiders have their biases and limitations. The insider may have more in-depth knowledge and intimate understanding of local affairs but may miss the necessary critical distance from these affairs. The outsider may report more independently but may simply miss essential knowledge to interpret the local developments. In an ideal world, news reporting would combine both positions.

The notion of the ideal world brings me to a concluding observation about the future as would befit an epiloguist.

The beauty and the nuisance of the future is that it is unknown to us. Whatever clever techniques we may have developed for forecasting, most predictions (certainly on relations between communication and society) tend to be wrong. Therefore, there would seem to be no need to propose prospects on future foreign correspondence. It is possible, however, to propose a wish list, and on my list you find the following eight priorities.

1. Foreign correspondence should be a tandem exercise by teams of insiders and outsiders.
2. News organizations should put less pressure on the speed of news delivery and more on its journalistic quality.
3. Future generations of news audiences should be educated to understand how crucial foreign news reporting is in a globalizing world. That education should change the disequilibrium in most news reporting between the almost exclusive focus on national events and the interest for politics, economics, and culture in other countries.
4. Inasmuch as mainstream foreign correspondence tends to focus on political and economic matters, there should be more attention paid to news reports about cultural developments.
5. With all due respect for civil, participatory, and nonprofessional modalities of international reporting, news organizations and their audiences should demand that professional standards of news reporting are respected.
6. It should not be ignored that modern societies are highly complex and demand specialized experts to report about financial, technological, or military matters. News organizations should strike balances between the employment of generalists and specialists in matters relevant to foreign correspondence.
7. Because reporting about foreign countries is often guided by 'the needs of audiences', it would be good if these needs are analyzed more systematically than in the usual 'off the top of someone's commercial head' way.
8. There should be a digital platform on which foreign correspondents from all over Europe report about the events and developments they observe but that will not be published by their news media. The stories that are considered 'not fit to print' often provide the best insights about foreign countries.

Foreign correspondence is so important that the usual cliché ending of an academic article proclaiming that more research is needed should be stated here very forcefully! This research should take into account that the provision of foreign news is guided by the institutional environment within which correspondents work, whatever their professional ambitions or ideals may be, and we need to know more about how institutional structures affect the mediation of reality.

REFERENCE

VAN GINNEKEN, J. (1998). *Understanding Global News*. London: Sage.

Appendix

QUESTIONNAIRE

This questionnaire was developed by the editor together with Michael Brüggemann, who coordinated with all the members of the Swiss, the German and the Austrian teams who contributed to its finalization.

Welcome and thank you very much for participating in this survey on the changes in foreign correspondence in Europe. As a matter of course, your data will be anonymized prior to publication and not be passed on to third parties.

1. Please choose your language.

   ☐ English
   ☐ Other

2. What is your nationality / or your nationalities? Please insert your nationalities (no abbreviations). Example: Swiss, Japanese.

3. What is your mother tongue? Please insert the language (no abbreviations).

4. At which level do you speak [the language(s) of the country you cover]? Please indicate the respective level.

	(almost) Native speaker level	Fluent	Basic knowledge	No knowledge
Lang 1	☐	☐	☐	☐
Lang 2	☐	☐	☐	☐
Lang 3	☐	☐	☐	☐

In the remainder of the survey we will call the country where you are currently based your "host country," as opposed to your "home country" where your main audiences are located.

5. What is your primary working language in your host country when conducting interviews and doing research?

☐ English
☐ French
☐ German
☐ Other

6. Do you work full time as a journalist?

☐ Yes
☐ No

7. What job(s) do you pursue apart from working as a journalist?

8. What percentage of your working hours is journalistic work as opposed to work for another job / other jobs?
Please fill in the approximate percentage of journalistic work.

☐ %

9. How many years have you been working as a professional journalist?
Please fill in the number of years.

☐ years

10. How many years have you been working as a foreign correspondent?

☐ years

11. How many different media organizations / employers do you work for?

    ☐ media organizations / different employers

12. What types of media organizations do you work for at the moment? (Several may apply.)

    - ☐ Print Media Organization Private
    - ☐ TV
    - ☐ Public TV Private
    - ☐ Radio Public
    - ☐ Radio Online
    - ☐ News Agency
    - ☐ Other(s):

    ____.

13. Which social / Internet media do you use as publishing platforms? (Several may apply.)

    - ☐ Personal Website Blog
    - ☐ Twitter
    - ☐ YouTube
    - ☐ Facebook
    - ☐ Google+ None
    - ☐ Other(s):

    ____.

14. How long have you been reporting from your current host country? Please fill in the number of years.

    ☐ years

15. In which countries have you been based as a foreign correspondent? Please list the last three in chronological order, starting with the current country. Please insert the country's name (no abbreviations) and the number of years you have stayed in each country.

Country	Number of Years
1. ____________________	__________
2. ____________________	__________
3. ____________________	__________

The following questions concern your main journalistic employer, the media organization you primarily work for.

16. Does your main media organization have several correspondents in your current country of residence? If yes, please fill in the number.

☐ No

☐ Yes (number of other correspondents): ☐

☐ Don't know

17. What kind of contract do you have with your main media organization?

☐ Full-time

☐ Part-time

☐ Freelancer

☐ Local stringer (supporting the reporters / editors)

18. Where is your main media organization's headquarters located? Please insert the country (no abbreviations). Example: France

19. What is the reach of the main media organization you work for?

☐ International

☐ National

☐ Regional / Local

20. Are you a member of a journalist union(s) / journalist organization(s)?

☐ No

☐ Yes, of the following: ______________________________

21. For what reason are you working as a foreign correspondent in the country where you are situated (your host country)? Please indicate the two most relevant reasons / motives.

☐ Personal interest to go abroad as a foreign correspondent

☐ Personal ties / relationships to the country

☐ Offer by my media organization / post was available

☐ Expertise / personal interest in the country Language

☐ Skills

☐ Other(s):

____.

The following questions concern the kind of stories you typically write.

22. What topics do you cover mostly? (Several may apply.)

    ☐ Politics
    ☐ Economics
    ☐ Culture Sports
    ☐ Society
    ☐ Other(s):

    ____.

23. How important is it that you offer exclusive stories that no other media outlet covers?

    1 (not important at all) – 5 (very important)

    [ ]

24. How many countries do you currently cover?

    [ ] country / countries

25. Which countries are these? Please insert the country / countries (no abbreviations). Example: Japan, Italy

26. How many stories do you produce per week (on average)?

    [ ] stories

27. What percentage of those stories gets published?

    [ ] %

28. What are typical stories you work on? Briefly describe three typical story topics.

    1. ______________________________
    2. ______________________________
    3. ______________________________

29. All in all, how essential do you rate the relevance of information about your host country for your readers?

    1 (not important at all) – 5 (very important)

    ☐

30. Has interest (among your audience and the editorial office of your main employer) in news from your host country increased or decreased over the last five years?

    – 2 (drastic decrease of interest)   0 (about the same)   + 2 (drastic increase of interest)

    ☐

31. How many times were you invited to contribute to public debates / events in your host country (writing articles, being interviewed, attendance at public discussions, etc.) last year

    ☐ Never
    ☐ 1 – 3 times
    ☐ 4 – 10 times
    ☐ More than 10 times

The following questions concern the sources of foreign correspondents.

32. Which of the following sources are the main reasons to start investigating a story? Rank the three most important ones of the ten with numbers 1 (for the most important) to 3 by filling in the respective number in the answer box.

    Government officials ☐

    Members of the opposition ☐

    Lobbies ☐

    Other official national sources ☐

    Experts/academics ☐

    Other journalists ☐

Average citizens	☐
Social Media	☐
Blogs	☐
Coverage of national media in my host country	☐

33. Are there other important sources that trigger an investigation which aren't mentioned above?

34. As a foreign correspondent, how do you rate the accessibility of first-hand sources from government and big business in your host country, on a scale from 1 (very difficult) to 5 (very easy access)?

	Very difficult access				Very easy access	No answer
Government	☐	☐	☐	☐	☐	☐
Big business	☐	☐	☐	☐	☐	☐
Other sources	☐	☐	☐	☐	☐	☐

The following questions concern the sources which influence your work as a foreign correspondent.

35. Please indicate how much influence each of the following items has on your work, on a scale from 1 (no influence at all) to 5 (extremely influential):

	No influence at all				Extremely influential	No answer
Your personal values and beliefs	☐	☐	☐	☐	☐	☐
Your friends and family	☐	☐	☐	☐	☐	☐
Your personal network of sources	☐	☐	☐	☐	☐	☐
Other foreign correspondents in the country	☐	☐	☐	☐	☐	☐

Your peers in the newsroom and editorial supervisors	☐	☐	☐	☐	☐	☐
The managers and owners of your news organizations	☐	☐	☐	☐	☐	☐
Coverage from competing news organizations	☐	☐	☐	☐	☐	☐

36. Please indicate again how much influence each of the following items has on your work on a scale from 1 (no influence at all) to 5 (extremely influential).

	No influence at all				Extremely influential	No answer
Advertising considerations / profit expectations	☐	☐	☐	☐	☐	☐
Audience research / feedback from the audience	☐	☐	☐	☐	☐	☐
Resources limits (e.g. travel budget)	☐	☐	☐	☐	☐	☐
Time limits (your time available to cover a certain issue)	☐	☐	☐	☐	☐	☐
Space limits (in the newspaper, on the news broadcast, etc.)	☐	☐	☐	☐	☐	☐
Availability of press releases / PR material	☐	☐	☐	☐	☐	☐
Access to sources and information in your host country	☐	☐	☐	☐	☐	☐

37. Some other influential factors may come from your host country as well as from your home country. Please rate each item for your host country and your home country on a scale from 1 (no influence at all) to 5 (extremely influential).

	No influence at all				Extremely influential	No answer
Situation of media laws and regulation in your host country	☐	☐	☐	☐	☐	☐
Situation of media laws and regulation in your home country	☐	☐	☐	☐	☐	☐
Politicians / Governmental officials in your host country	☐	☐	☐	☐	☐	☐
Politicians / Governmental officials in your home country	☐	☐	☐	☐	☐	☐
Pressure groups (host country)						
Pressure groups (home country)	☐	☐	☐	☐	☐	☐
Business interests in the host country	☐	☐	☐	☐	☐	☐
Business interests in the home country	☐	☐	☐	☐	☐	☐

The following questions concern the most influential foreign correspondents and local media in your host country.

38. How often do you use the following sources? Please rate each item on a scale from 1 (on a daily basis) to 5 (never).

	On a daily basis	Several times a week	Once a week	Once a month	Never	No answer
Other foreign correspondents based in the same country	☐	☐	☐	☐	☐	☐
National / 'native' journalists working for media in my host country	☐	☐	☐	☐	☐	☐
National / local media from my 'host' country	☐	☐	☐	☐	☐	☐
Citizen journalists / blogs / social media	☐	☐	☐	☐	☐	☐

39. In some countries there is a hierarchy among the foreign media that have deployed correspondents in a host country. What are the most important foreign media organizations and correspondents situated in your host country? Please specify the media organization and / or the name of the correspondents.

	Media Organization	Correspondent
1.	________________	________________
2.	________________	________________
3.	________________	________________
4.	________________	________________
5.	________________	________________

40. Do you regularly cooperate with foreign correspondents from other media outlets?

☐ No

☐ Yes, with the following media outlets / persons: ______________

The following questions deal with recent trends in foreign correspondence and your opinion about these trends.

41. To what extent do the following trends apply to your job and media organization? Please rate the following items on a scale from 1 (not at all) to 5 (to a great extent).

	Not at all				To a great extent	No answer
I am afraid that my current post as foreign correspondent here may be cut in the near future.	☐	☐	☐	☐	☐	☐
The audience cares less about international news nowadays than in the past.	☐	☐	☐	☐	☐	☐
I feel increasing time pressure on my job.	☐	☐	☐	☐	☐	☐
The resources available to do my job have been cut down (e.g. budget for travelling).	☐	☐	☐	☐	☐	☐

42. The following questions concern your main employer/media organization. To what extent do the following statements apply, on a scale from 1 (not at all) to 5 (to a great extent)?

	Not at all				To a great extent	No answer
The number of correspondents has been substantially cut within the last five years.	☐	☐	☐	☐	☐	☐
Parachute journalists (journalists who fly into a place to report for a certain event only and leave again) have increasingly replaced traditional correspondents.	☐	☐	☐	☐	☐	☐
Local journalists are employed instead of traditional correspondents.	☐	☐	☐	☐	☐	☐
Foreign coverage is increasingly covered from headquarters.	☐	☐	☐	☐	☐	☐
Amateur journalists / bloggers / representatives of NGOs are increasingly used as replacements for traditional correspondents.	☐	☐	☐	☐	☐	☐

43. Overall, from your experience, how has the job of the foreign correspondent changed in recent years?

    –2 (to the worse) +2 (to the better)

    ☐

The following questions deal with socio-demographics.

44. What is your gender?

    ☐ male ☐ female

45. How old are you?

    ☐ years

46. What is your marital status?

    ☐ Single

    ☐ Married / in a partnership with a spouse / partner also living also in the host country

    ☐ Married / in a partnership with a spouse / partner NOT living in the host country

47. Do you have children?

    ☐ No

    ☐ Yes (Please indicate the number of children): ________________

48. What is the highest level of education you have completed?

    ☐ High school

    ☐ Bachelor's degree

    ☐ Master's degree

    ☐ Doctoral degree

49. If you graduated from a professional school or university: What was your field at the professional school or university?

50. In which category does your monthly average net income from journalistic work fall?

- ☐ Up to 1000 EUR 1001
- ☐ To 4000 EUR
- ☐ 4001 to 7000 EUR
- ☐ More than 7000 EUR

51. What media organization are you mainly working for? Please insert the name of the media organization. All data will be published in anonymous form only!

52. Do you wish to be informed about the results of this study by e-mail?

- ☐ No
- ☐ Yes (Please enter your e–mail address here): ____________________

53. If you have questions, praise, criticism or other helpful suggestions, please enter them here.

Contributors

Antonella Agostino is a journalist, PhD, and CIM Laboratory (Sorbonne nouvelle) researcher in media and communication sciences. Her research focuses on the relationship between the media and the European institutions, through a comparative analysis between the French and Italian correspondents based in Brussels, Rome, and Paris. She has worked in the field of corporate communication, including in the EU institutions, and currently works as an analyst on the question of the relations between the European Union and the media. She has participated in numerous conferences and publications, including four publications by the French publisher L'Harmattan, on European news media and EU accredited journalists and foreign correspondents.

Gintaras Aleknonis is professor at Mykolas Romeris University, Vilnius, Lithuania. His research interests include media and democracy, and the relationship between media and the state. The topics are discussed in his book *The New Censorship* (2011, in Lithuanian). For two decades, he worked as a radio journalist in Munich, Prague, and Vilnius.

Sigurd Allern, PhD (dr. polit.), is a professor of journalism studies at the Department of Communication, University of Oslo. He has been professor (II) at Volda University College (2007–2009), a Bonnier professor at the Department of Journalism, Media and Communication at Stockholm University (2008) and a visiting professor at Stockholm University 2009–2014. He was project leader for the Nordic Research Network in Journalism Studies, financed by NordForsk (2009–2013). His research interests include the political economy of the news media, journalists and their source relations, news values and news framing, and political communication and lobbying.

Carla Baptista, PhD, is a professor at the University Nova of Lisbon–Faculty of Social and Human Sciences. She teaches several undergraduate and master's courses at the Communication Sciences Department, namely journalistic genres (BA), journalism ethics (MA), and journalism history and theories (MA). Her PhD was about the history of Portuguese political journalism, and she is currently coordinating a research project funded by FCT (Portuguese Science Foundation) on journalism and culture. She is a founding member of CIMJ (Media and Journalism Research Center) and has published several books about journalism history in Portugal.

Joseph Borg, PhD, lectures in communication studies at the University of Malta. He occupied top executive positions in different media organizations in Malta. Borg was the editor of two radio stations, the editor of a weekly newspaper, and the first chairman of the editorial board of PBS Ltd., as well as the executive producer of several television series. He was a government consultant for audiovisual policies and the drafter of the National Broadcasting Policy. He occupied the post of head of the Media Education Research Section of IAMCR and was a member of the Media Literacy in Schools Expert Group, of the European Union. Borg is a member of the EU Kids Online Research Project. He published several papers and book chapters mainly about different aspects of the media in Malta and media education.

Inta Brikše is a professor in communication studies at the Department of Communication studies at the University of Latvia. Research interests are focused on media studies, especially public media, post-Soviet media, and national identity. She is the editor and author of two books, *Information Environment in Latvia: The Beginning of 21st Century* and *9th Saeima Election Campaign of the Republic of Latvia: The Public Space of Pre-elections* (both in Latvian). Three books are in preparatory stage: *Media in Latvia*, *Digital Latvia* (editor), and *Urban Communication: Identities of Riga* (with Uģis Bratuškins and Viktors Freibergs). Brikše is a board member of *Central European Journal of Communication*, *Media Transformations*, and *Journalism Research* and a member of Baltic Media Researchers Association (BAMR) and European Communication Research and Education Association (ECREA).

Isabelle Brodeßer is a research associate to the Chair of Journalism at the University of Passau/Germany. Her main areas of research include foreign correspondence, media in conflict areas, and public relations. Internet: http://www.uni-passau.de/hahn

Michael Bromley is professor of international journalism in the Graduate School of Journalism at City University London. A former journalist, he has taught in universities in Australia, the United States, and the UK. He was coeditor with Judith Clarke of *International News in the Digital Age* (Routledge, 2011) and is currently working on a study of British journalism in the 1960s.

Michael Brüggemann (PhD, University of Hamburg) is senior teaching and research associate at the Institute of Mass Communication and Media Research, University of Zurich. His research explores the transformations of journalism and of political and science communication from a comparative perspective. He is interested in understanding how and why journalistic practice is changing in a transnational and digital information environment. Current research projects deal with the role of journalists in framing climate change, typologies of media systems, and current changes in journalistic practice. For recent publications, see www.bruegge.net.

Johanna Dorer is an associate professor at the Department of Communication and member of the of Equal Opportunity Commission at the University of Vienna. Her research focus is feminist media studies, media theory, public relations, and noncommercial media. Her publications include Current Perspectives and Future Challenges in Feminist Media Studies (*Media and Cultural Politics*, 2014); Medien Journal: Internet und gender (editor, 2012); WikiLeaks and the construction of gender (*Media and Cultural Politics*, 2011); Medien—Politik—Geschlecht, Wiesbaden (coeditor,VS, 2008).

Vaia Doudaki is a lecturer in media and journalism studies at the Department of Communication and Internet Studies in Cyprus University of Technology and director of the master's programme in European journalism, offered by the same department. Her research interests and output focus on the study of media, conflict, and crisis; on the production of meaning in fictional and news content; on journalistic identities and journalistic practices in the Internet era; and on participatory media and audiences.

Julia Eder is a research assistant to the Chair of Journalism at the University of Passau/Germany. Her main fields of research are foreign correspondence, climate change journalism, and new media. Internet: www.julia-eder.de

Julian Fritsch is a freelance journalist and author, currently working in Munich. He has a master of arts degree in international journalism from City University London. He also holds a bachelor of arts degree in journalism and communication studies from the University of Vienna.

Johan Galtung, Prof. Dr., born 1930 in Oslo, Norway, is widely recognized as the founder of the academic discipline of peace studies. He has published over 1,500 articles and more than 150 books, with translations into 33 languages. Early in his career, he was an active journalist and now publishes a weekly column on the TRANSCEND Media Service (www.transcend.org/tms). He is one of the authors of an influential account of news values that are the factors determining what coverage is given to what stories in the news. Galtung also originated the concept of Peace Journalism, which is increasingly influential in communications and media studies. He has been a consultant to the United Nations and its family of organizations. His tireless commitment to peace has been recognized with 13 honorary doctorates and professorships and an alternative Nobel Prize.

Sarah Anne Ganter is research assistant and a PhD candidate in communication studies and media governance at the University of Vienna. Her dissertation focuses on global entanglements of audiovisual media governance in the digital era. Her research fields are media governance and policy change in South America, diffusion of communication policies, interpretative policy analysis, governance of cultural industries and democracy in times of crises (EU and Latin America), and international vommunication.

Iliana Giannouli is a journalist and a PhD candidate at the Faculty of Communication and Media Studies, National & Kapodistrian University of Athens.

Gerit Götzenbrucker, an associate professor at the Department of Communication, University of Vienna, searches in the fields of communication and media innovations, technology assessment, social networks, and organizational and intercultural communication. Recently, she works in the field of game studies and migration research within the research project, Serious Beats. Internet Use and Friendship Structures of Young Migrants in Vienna: The Question for Diversity within Social Networks and Online Social Games (forthcoming 2014 in *Games & Culture:* 'Gamedesign for Social Impact'.

Mirjam Goudswaard has her MA in media studies (Media & Journalism-programme at the Erasmus School of History, Culture & Communication) and has acted as research assistant to Dr. Bernadette Kester. Within the field of media studies, she is particularly interested in war journalism, photojournalism, and the framing of news.

Jessica Gustafsson, PhD, does research and teaches at the Department of Media Studies, Stockholm University, where she earned her PhD. Her research interests include journalism, democracy, and the relationship between media and social change.

Oliver Hahn, PhD, is a professor of journalism at the University of Passau/ Germany. His main research areas include, amongst others, foreign correspondents, international journalism cultures, EU journalism, crisis communication, and media in the Arab world. Internet: http://www.uni-passau.de/hahn

Cees J. Hamelink, PhD, is emeritus professor of international communication at the University of Amsterdam. He is currently professor for information management at the University of Aruba and professor of human rights and public health at the Vrije Universiteit of Amsterdam. He is also the editor-in-chief of the *International Communication Gazette* and honorary president of the International Association for Media and Communication Research. He is author of 17 monographs on communication, culture, and human rights. Professor Hamelink received lifetime achievement awards from various international organizations and has been consultant to many national governments and agencies in the UN system. In 2015, his textbook on global communication will be published by Sage.

Thomas Hanitzsch is professor of communication at the University of Munich, Germany. His main research areas include global journalism cultures, crisis and war communication, tabloid and celebrity news, as well as comparative methodology. Internet: http://www.thomas-hanitzsch.de

Gareth Harding is director of the Missouri School of Journalism's Brussels programme and a lecturer at IHECS communication school. Gareth reported on European affairs for 12 years for *European Voice*, *Time Magazine*, and from 2002 to 2006 as chief European correspondent for *United Press International*. He has also written for the *New York Times*, *International Herald Tribune*, *Washington Times*, *Wall Street Journal*, *The Guardian*, and *Independent* newspapers and *Foreign Policy Magazine*. Harding was educated at the London School of Economics and worked as a political advisor in the House of Commons and European Parliament before becoming a journalist.

Cláudia Henriques is a PhD student in communication sciences at the University Nova of Lisbon—Faculty of Social and Human Sciences and a researcher at CIMJ (Media and Journalism Research Center). She is currently working on a research project about censorship practices in cinema and theatre in Portugal and Brazil during dictatorship periods. Her main research interests are media and social conflict, community media, radio journalism, and the history of radio.

Marju Himma-Kadakas is a doctoral student of media and communication and works as an assistant of journalism at the University of Tartu. The topic of her doctoral thesis is related to the changing conventions of journalistic work in the light of changing technologies. She is engaged not only in the academic field but is a practitioner as well. She has extensive journalistic experiences in the biggest daily newspaper in Estonia, *Postimees*. She teaches courses on reporting, online journalism, and Web-based editing in the Institute of Journalism, Communication, and Information Studies at the University of Tartu.

Roman Hummel, Prof. Dr., holds the chair the Chair for Journalism at the Department for Communication, University of Salzburg. His focus lies on empirical research of conditions and structures of journalism, media politics, and media sociology. Recent research projects include Media Careers—Working Conditions and Expectations of Journalists (2010); Occupational Profiles of Journalists in Free Circulating Media (2012); How to Train Freelance Journalists (ongoing); Convergent Newspaper Production (ongoing); Best Practice: Analysis of Changing Publication Strategies of Media Enterprises (forthcoming).

Guido Keel is a lecturer for journalism studies at the Institute of Applied Media Studies of the Zurich University of Applied Sciences. He has published a comprehensive study on the journalists in Switzerland in 2011 ('Journalisten in der Schweiz', UVK). His teaching and research interests include journalism research, media quality management, media performance evaluation, both in Switzerland and in postconflict countries.

Bernadette C. M. Kester, PhD, is senior lecturer at the department of Media & Communication, Erasmus School of History, Culture & Media (Erasmus University Rotterdam). Her research focus is on journalism studies generally and more specifically on foreign correspondence, court journalism, press photography, and (historical) representation in media and film. She acted as coeditor (with Naomi Sakr) of a special issue of the *International Communication Gazette* titled 'Transparency in International News Reporting' (February 2010). Her latest publication is a chapter titled 'Sources, Transparency and Narrative. Foreign Correspondence in the People's Republic of China' (M. Broersma & C. Peters C. [2013]. *Retelling Journalism. Conveying Stories in a Digital Age*. Leuven: Peeters).

Ragne Kõuts is a lecturer in media studies and a manager of the journalism MA programme in the institute of Journalism and Communication at the University of Tartu in Estonia. She obtained her MA in sociology. Her doctoral studies in the field of media and communication involved research years at the Free University of Berlin and Humboldt-University. Her research interests cover topics of citizen journalism, audiences' changing media use patterns, and the role of the mass media in integration. She teaches theories of media and communication and courses about media use and media systems in Europe.

Stefan Kruschwitz is a Research Assistant to the Chair of Journalism at the University of Passau/Germany. His main fields of research are foreign correspondence, corporate communications and audience research. E-mail: stefan.kruschwitz@gmx.de.

Lulivera Krusteva, PhD, is associate professor at the School of Journalism and Mass Communication, St. Kliment Ohridski University of Sofia, the oldest university in Bulgaria. The topic of the first dissertation is 'Journalism and National Identity', and that for the habilitation for a university reader is 'Media and Social Conflicts'. In parallel with her lecturing at the university, she continues to work as a journalist for a newspaper and for an online. Her research fields include social conflicts and the media, state institutions and taboo topics, the value pyramid in the media, the new communication models, and media stereotypes. She has over 40 publications, some of which are in foreign scientific journals in Europe and America.

Filip Láb is a professor of photojournalism at the Faculty of Social Science, Charles University, Prague. He is an investigator of the Czech part of Worlds of Journalism Study project, a member of the Journalism Studies Section of ECREA and project leader of the Czech Website of European Journalism Observatory (EJO). He is interested in visual communication and the transformation of photojournalism practice. He is active as a journalist and photographer on field of fine art and commercial photography, collaborating with several cultural as well as commercial magazines. He is a coauthor of two monographs on photography—*Photography after Photography* (2009) and *The End of Photojournalism* (2009)—the article 'The Relationship between Journalism Studies and Media Professionals in the Czech Republic' (2011), and author of other articles and several book chapters.

Dimitra L. Milioni is assistant professor in media studies at the Department of Communication and Internet Studies, Cyprus University of Technology. She has published on the impact of new media on democracy and the public sphere, with particular emphasis on alternative media and oppositional publics. Her current research interests include alternative and participatory media, audience participation in Web 2.0 spaces, e-deliberation, citizenship, social movements, and new media. Her full research profile is available at http://cut.academia.edu/DimitraMilioni.

Marko Milosavljević, PhD, is an associate professor in the Department of Journalism at the Faculty of Social Sciences at the University of Ljubljana, Slovenia. He was the chair of the Expert Commission for Pluralisation of Media at Slovenian Ministry of Culture from 2009 to 2010. He was the chair of the Expert Commission for Radio and Television Programmes at Slovenian Ministry of Culture from 2002 to 2004. He is a member of National Committee for Information Society since 2010. He is also currently lecturing at the University of Novi Sad, Serbia, in the Faculty of Philosophy, Media Department.

Alice Němcová Tejkalová is an assistant professor of journalism at the Faculty of Social Science, Charles University, Prague. She is a principal investigator of the Czech part of Worlds of Journalism Study project, a member of the Journalism Studies Section of ECREA. She is interested in media stereotyping and framing of minor topics, such as paralympic sport. She has been working also as a freelance TV journalist since 2000. She has written a monograph titled *The Other Athletes* (2012), as well as a number of articles: 'Framing the National Indebtedness' (2013), 'The Relationship between Journalism Studies and Media Professionals in the Czech Republic' (2011), 'The Coverage of Paralympic Games in the Czech Media' (2010).Her writing also includes several book chapters: 'Sport Reportage Watched from a Slightly Different Point of View', 'Gains and Losses of the So-called New Media' (2009), 'DTV in the Czech Republic' (2008), among others.

Jérémie Nicey is associate professor at the Public School of Journalism of Tours (Université François-Rabelais de Tours) and belongs to the laboratory CIM (Communication Information Médias) at the University of Sorbonne Nouvelle, Paris 3. Before his study of foreign correspondents in France, he was a postdoctoral fellow in a research project on the archives of *Agence France-Presse* (*AFP*), where he had access to news flashes and could also investigate new procedures and new partners of the *AFP*. His research focuses on media practices (he was coauthor of *Lexique subjectif de l'homme informant*, Ed. Amandier, 2011), on the production of international news (he coedited *From NWICO to WSIS: 30 Years of Communication Geopolitics*, Ed. Intellect, 2012), and since then on participatory journalism.

John O'Sullivan is a lecturer at the School of Communications, Dublin City University, where he recently has been chair of the MA in Journalism Programme. With a background in national newspaper journalism, specializing in technology and communications as well as production journalism, he also has experience of magazines and of online publishing. He currently lectures in online journalism and new media, along with a wide range of other subjects, from feature writing to media and technology. His research interests have focused in particular on the interaction of journalism and the Internet, especially in relation to professional roles, media platforms, and interactivity. He is a founding vice chair of the Journalism Studies Section of the European Communication Research and Education Association (ECREA).

Stylianos Papathanassopoulos is Professor at the Faculty of Communication and Media Studies at the National and Kapodistrian University of Athens. He has written extensively on media developments in Europe and especially on television issues in various journals. He also edits the Greek communication journal *Zitimata Epikoinonias/Communication Issues*. He is the author or editor of 19 books about the media. Among his most recent books are *European Media, Structures, Policy & Identity* (with Ralph Negrine, Polity, 2011), *Media Perspectives* (editor, Routledge, 2011), *Television in the 21st century* (Kastaniotis, 2005 in Greek); *European Television in the Digital Age: Issues, Dynamics and Realties* (Polity Press, 2002).

Dimitri Prandner earned his master's degree in sociology, is research associate and is a PhD candidate at the Department of Communication at the University of Salzburg. His research concerns media and representations of past and foreign events, as well as methodology in the social sciences. Recently completed research projects are focused on the journalistic field in Austria and changes in the journalistic profession. He is member of the ECREA and Austrian representative for young scholars. Further he is involved with the Austrian communication (ÖGK) and sociology associations (ÖGS) and part of the working group for methodological questions in the ÖGS.

Jolán Róka is a professor and vice rector for international relations at BKF University of Applied Sciences, Budapest. She is the head of BA and MA in the communication and media studies programmes. She has participated in several international research projects on political communication and journalism for almost 20 years.

Verica Rupar, an associate professor, teaches journalism at AUT in Auckland, New Zealand. Her teaching and research interests are in the field of comparative journalism studies. Verica's publications include *Journalism and Meaning-Making* (Hampton Press, 2010), *Scooped: Politics and Power of Journalism in Aoteraoa New Zealand* (coedited with Sean Phelan and Martin Hirst, AUT Media 2012), and *Getting the Facts Right: Reporting Ethnicity and Religion in Europe* (IFJ, 2012). She serves as an academic consultant for the London-based Media Diversity Institute and has worked previously as a journalist and journalism educator in Serbia, Slovenia, Hungary, Australia, and UK.

Ramón Salaverría, PhD, is director of the Journalism Projects Department at the University of Navarra (Pamplona, Spain), where he has lectured on online journalism skills since 1990s. Salaverría has been chair of the Journalism Studies Section at the European Communication Research and Education Association (ECREA) during the term (2010–2012). His research focuses on media convergence, online storytelling, and new media trends. On these topics he has published many research papers, as well as the books *Integrated journalism* (2009), *Cibermedios* (2005), *Redacción periodística en internet* (2005), and *Manual de redacción ciberperiodística* (2003), among others. During the last few years, he has offered keynote speeches and courses in 28 countries. Thanks to all these activities, in 2012 the United Nations Alliance of Civilizations (UNAOC) appointed him to be member of Global Experts, a directory of 300 world-class specialists. Internet: www.salaverria.es

Raimo Salokangas has been professor in media and journalism at the University of Jyväskylä, Finland, since 1989. Before that, from 1982, he was assistant professor (Docent) in Finnish history, University of Turku. He has written a number of books (in Finnish) on press and broadcasting history in Finland, including a history of the Finnish Broadcasting Company (Yle). His most recent book (with Ohto Manninen) is a biography of the press baron Eljas Erkko.

Sonja Seizova is a PhD candidate at Belgrade University, Serbia. Her professional and research interests are in comparative media systems, media policy, and journalism studies. She has worked as a foreign correspondent, editor, and publisher based in Athens, Greece, where she acquired an MA degree in southeast European studies. Her recent professional engagement includes work with and consultancies for international development agencies in the fields of communications, media, and political monitoring and analysis.

Andrej Školkay is director of the School of Communication and Media, n.o., a research establishment based in Bratislava, Slovakia. He has finished most recently a study on 'Media Literacy in Informal Education' (together with Alberto Bitonti) and an article on 'International Approaches to Regulation of New Online Media Services'. The author is a member of the Association of European Journalists and Slovak Association for Scientific Literature, as well as a member of the Editorial Board of Central European Journal of Communication. His main interests include media policy, media education, and media regulation.

Morten Skovsgaard, PhD, is an Associate Professor at the Centre for Journalism/Department of Political Science at the University of Southern Denmark. He wrote his PhD dissertation on the professional norms, values, and autonomy of Danish journalists. His research interests are journalism and political communication, particularly on journalists' professional ideals, their practice, and the effects of their products on the audience. He has published in books such as *The Global Journalist in the 21th Century* (2012) and journals such as *Media, Culture & Society*, *Journalism*, *Journalism Studies* and *Information, Communication & Society.*

Georgios Terzis, PhD, is an associate professor and a senior associate researcher at Vrije Universiteit Brussel (Vesalius College & Institute for European Studies) and a senior expert at the Global Governance Institute.

His research focuses on media and security governance, European media governance, and the development of pan-European media. He is the founding chair of the Journalism Studies Section of the European Communication Research and Education Association. He worked as Brussels correspondent for Greek Media and as a course leader for the European Journalism Centre, training journalists from 25 countries on EU affairs.

L. Doğan Tılıç, associate professor, holds a PhD from the Sociology Department at the Middle East Technical University (METU). In 2002 he was promoted as associate professor. Tılıç has also been working as a journalist since 1986, covering conflicts in Afghanistan, Iraq, Azerbaijan, Yugoslavia, and Albania. He continues to serve as Turkey's representative of Spanish News Agency (EFE) and writes a column in the Turkish daily *BirGün*. He teaches postgraduate courses on media in the Media and Cultural Studies Master's Program of METU. Tılıç, who also served in national and international journalists' organizations, is at the moment Honorary Vice President of the Association of European Journalists (AEJ), founder and spokesperson of the G-9 Platform, which is an umbrella for 12 leading Turkish journalists associations. Tılıç has written numerous academic articles and five books. One of his books, *I'm Ashamed, but I Am a Journalist*, was translated into Greek and German.

Howard Tumber is professor of journalism and communications at City University London. He is director of research for the Department of Journalism and codirector of the Centre for Law, Justice & Journalism. He has published widely in the field of the sociology of news and journalism and is the author or coauthor/editor of eight books, including *Critical Concepts in Journalism* (2008), *Journalists under Fire* (2006), *Media at War: The Iraq Crisis* (2004), *Media Power, Policies and Professionals* (2000), *News: A Reader* (1999), *Reporting Crime—The Media Politics of Criminal Justice* (1994), *Journalists at War* (1988), *Television and Riots* (1982). He is a founder and coeditor of the academic journal *Journalism: Theory, Practice and Criticism*. His recent work concerns the role of journalists and the reporting of international conflict.

Martina van Berkel studied media and communication science, political science, and cultural anthropology at the University of Zurich. She contributed to the survey of foreign correspondents in Switzerland within the context of her master's thesis. Now she is working on her PhD, analyzing the interactions of sport, media, and economy in Switzerland.

Arjen van Dalen, PhD, is an assistant professor at the Centre for Journalism/Department of Political Science at the University of Southern Denmark. He wrote his PhD dissertation on political journalism in comparative perspective. His research interests are in comparative communication research, in particular the relations between journalists and politicians. He has published on these topics in *The Global Journalists in the 21st Century* (forthcoming 2012) and journals such as the *European Journal of Communication*, *Political Communication*, *International Journal of Press/Politics*, and *Journalism Studies*.

Andreas Widholm does research and teaches at the Department of Media Studies, Stockholm University. His research centers on media and identity, transnational news journalism, and social and cultural consequences of new media technologies. He has also conducted postdoctoral research at *Swedish Radio*, where he was researcher in residence 2011–2012.

Eylem Yanardağoğlu, PhD, is a lecturer in the New Media Department at Kadir Has University in Istanbul, where she teaches research methods and media theories on the undergraduate and postgraduate levels. She received her PhD at City University, Sociology Department, in London in 2008, where she studied the relationship between citizenship, minorities, and media in Turkey. Her research interests include the news production process in international news organizations, professional networks of foreign correspondents based in Turkey, and transnational media formats. In 2011, she was a visiting scholar at the Communication and Media Research Institute (CAMRI), University of Westminster, where she studied the news production and news culture of the BBC World Service and its Turkish section. Most recently, she published the results of one of the first empirical studies on the audience perceptions of Turkish TV series in Arab-speaking countries. She continues her research on television industry, transnational television, and international news.

Gašper Završnik graduated from the Faculty of Social Science (University of Ljubljana) in journalism. Currently he is doing master's degree in the sociology of everyday life at the same faculty. He also studied at the faculty of information science (Complutense University of Madrid) as a part of international Erasmus student exchange. He works as a journalist for the Slovenian daily newspaper *Žurnal24* and the weekly *Žurnal*, he mostly covers national and occasionally also international affairs.

Index